Defining America
Through Immigration Policy

In the series *Mapping Racisms*,
edited by Jo Carrillo, Darrell Y. Hamamoto,
Rodolfo D. Torres, and E. Frances White

Defining America Through Immigration Policy

Bill Ong Hing

Foreword by Anthony D. Romero,
Executive Director, American Civil Liberties Union

TEMPLE UNIVERSITY PRESS

PHILADELPHIA

Temple University Press, Philadelphia 19122
Copyright © 2004 by Temple University
All rights reserved
Published 2004
Printed in the United States of America

Library of Congress Cataloging-in-Publication Data

Hing, Bill Ong.
    Defining America through immigration policy / Bill Ong Hing.
        p. cm. — (Mapping racisms)
    Includes bibliographical references and index.
        ISBN 1-59213-232-4 (alk. paper) — ISBN 1-59213-233-2 (pbk. : alk. paper)
    1. United States—Emigration and immigration—Government policy—History.
    I. Title.   II. Series.
    JV6483.H56   2004
    325.73—dc21   2003053949

112007-6

ISBN 978-1-59213-233-1 (paper : alk. paper)

032210-P

In memory of my sister Lilly

Contents

Part IV: Deporting and Barring Non-Americans

Foreword

We call ourselves "a nation of immigrants." It is a point of pride. From across the world, immigrants have brought their hopes and dreams to our shores in search of freedom—the freedom to strive, to achieve, and above all to be judged on their merits, not the color of their skin, their religion, or their national origin.

America has never been free from prejudice; every immigrant group has faced tremendous hurdles to acceptance by the majority. But there has always been an understanding that tolerance would ultimately prevail, because the protection of the Constitution extends even to noncitizens.

The First Amendment, for example, guarantees the right of the *people* to assemble peacefully. The Fourth Amendment protects the right of the *people* against unreasonable searches and seizures. And the Fifth Amendment states that *no person* shall be deprived of life, liberty, or property without due process of law.

These were not accidents of language. The words were carefully chosen to imbue a sense of tolerance and respect for all. They make clear that the government, in particular, had to apply its policies in a fair and equal manner. But it has not done so since the tragic events of September 11, 2001.

Immigrants—especially Muslim, Arab American, and Asian immigrants—are bearing the brunt of the current war on terror. Soon after the attacks, the Department of Justice developed a list of 8,000 Middle Eastern men between the ages of eighteen and thirty-three for interviews. In sweeps across the country, the government eventually detained more than 1,100 under unprecedented secrecy. Less than a handful were ever charged with any connection to the attacks. The vast majority were arrested on immigration charges and effectively "disappeared"—as former Secretary of State Warren Christopher has described it. Their cases were not listed on any public docket and their hearings were closed to the public.

The USA Patriot Act, enacted within six weeks of 9/11 with little opposition, contained several provisions aimed at immigrants. The act authorizes the attorney general to detain noncitizens without a hearing; bars foreign citizens from entering the country solely on the basis of their language; and authorizes deportation based on any support to a disfavored group, without any requirement that the support be connected to a terrorist act. Had this law been in place in the 1980s, supporters of the African National Congress could have been prosecuted. It would have empowered the attorney general to detain and deport anyone who contributed to Nelson Mandela's antiapartheid political activities, because until the ANC defeated apartheid in South Africa, our State Department designated it as a terrorist organization.

The government also ramped up its efforts to locate more than 300,000 foreign nationals, known as "absconders," who it said had failed to comply with court orders to leave the country. The Department of Justice said it was focusing first on about 6,000 immigrants from countries identified as al Qaeda strongholds, though the vast majority turned out to be Latinos. But by December 2002, it had embarked on a much larger fishing expedition. Immigration officials required every male with a temporary visa from Iran, Iraq, Libya, Syria, and Sudan to register. Citizens of fifteen other countries, including North Korea, Saudi Arabia, Indonesia, Pakistan, and North African nations, had to register by April 2003, and nationals of other Arab and Middle Eastern countries were added to the list. By late spring, according to the new Department of Homeland Security, nearly 77,000 noncitizen Arab men over the age of 16 had been questioned, photographed and fingerprinted. Some 56,000 others were interviewed at ports of entry; and 2,400 were detained. More than 13,000 of those who came forward voluntarily now face deportation.

Advocates warned that the war on terror had turned into a war on immigrants, but it took more than eighteen months for any part of the federal government to admit to any wrongdoing. In the spring of 2003, the Department of Justice's own inspector general, who functions as an internal watchdog, finally criticized the "hold until cleared" policies under which immigrants had been detained. According to his report, many with no connection to the 9/11 terrorist attacks had languished in federal lockup for months at a time under an official "no bond policy" that actively opposed their release. Attorneys within the INS itself complained that the FBI had given them no evidence to justify continued detention, yet some immigrants spent up to eight months waiting for release. The report went on to document in extensive detail that many immigrants had been denied access to their lawyers and family members, while others were subjected to abusive conditions in government custody.

Immigration restrictions and enforcement have become the government's primary tools in the war on terrorism. But as the Migration Policy Institute has argued, their use would not prevent many of the September 11 terrorists from being admitted to the United States today "since most had no previous criminal, terrorist or immigration records." So the persecution of immigrants has not made us safer. Moreover, as one federal judge warned, "A government operating in the shadow of secrecy stands in complete opposition to the society envisioned by the framers of our Constitution."

The American Civil Liberties Union has stepped up to the plate at this important juncture, along with other organizations, to warn that "when the rights of any are sacrificed, the rights of none are safe." Scholars, jurists, policymakers, and advocates will find important ballast for that argument in this volume.

Anti-immigrant hysteria based on race or political views is nothing new in America, as we are reminded by Bill Hing, an activist scholar and a voice of reason in the debate over immigration policy since the mid-1970s. He has worked with immigrants on a day-to-day basis, counseling their community-based representatives, lobbying their congressional leaders for fairer laws, influencing funding streams to their causes, and writing to give voice to their issues. He persuaded Congress to resist challenges to sibling immigration and family visas in the 1980s and 1990s, and his arguments regarding the 1980 Refugee Act before the Ninth Circuit Court of Appeals in *McMullen v. INS* and then before the Supreme Court in *INS v. Cardoza-Fonseca* helped to convince the courts to interpret the asylum laws more generously. He also represented dozens of Iranian students in the U.S. crackdown following the 1979 takeover of our embassy in Tehran, served on a panel monitoring United States—Mexico border patrol abuses in the Clinton administration, and worked with advocates from the California Rural Legal Assistance Foundation and American Friends Services Committee on Operation Gatekeeper and the deaths that ensued.

I had the good fortune to study immigration policy with Bill Hing at Stanford Law School and was greatly influenced by his views on human and civil rights and public interest lawyering. His understanding of history, drawn from personal experience and participation, is piercing and helps to put the recent hysteria in perspective.

In this book, he applies the lessons of his decades-long research and experience to fundamental issues at a critical time in our nation's history. "A nation of immigrants" we are. Whether we will continue to offer freedom, tolerance, and equal opportunity to all who seek them is the challenge this generation of Americans must now confront. Bill Hing points us in the right direction.

Anthony D. Romero
Executive Director
American Civil Liberties Union

Introduction

On a different September 11—the one in 1998—the body of a man was found floating in the All-American Canal in the Imperial Valley of southern California. The next day, Saturday, September 12, another man, who had been in a coma since August, when he was found in the valley's desert with a core body temperature of 108 degrees, died. On Sunday, the Border Patrol discovered the body of Asuncion Hernandez Uriel in the same desert. Some of her group stayed with her, but she died of heat stress. The same day, the decomposed body of Oscar Cardoso Varon was pulled out of the canal. In all, the bodies of four migrants attempting to cross to the United States from Mexico were found that weekend. That Monday, a headline in the *San Diego Union-Tribune* read, "Woman 113th border crosser to die."[1]

Unlike the reaction of the American public to the horrors of September 11, 2001, no outrage or sympathy was expressed after the weekend border deaths beginning September 11, 1998. One could point to a difference in scale—some 3,000 deaths on September 11, 2001—but try 2,000 in the border situation; 2,000 deaths that were avoidable.

Six months earlier, at the end of March 1998, four migrants died after a foot of snow had fallen and the temperature dropped to 22 degrees in the mountains they tried to cross.[2] Two years later the *San Francisco Examiner* reported that the bodies of three men had been pulled from the mountains of the Cleveland National Forest, a corridor for illegal immigration from Mexico. Asked to identify one body, a young man held in a Border Patrol truck nodded "yes" to acknowledge that the victim had been part of his group of border-crossers. Sick and cold illegal immigrants continued to stumble out of the Laguna Mountains all day after a weekend storm dumped 6 to 8 inches of snow. Temperatures plummeted to lows of between 20 and 34 degrees. "Eight people who were rescued by fire workers near Mount Laguna on Monday could barely move, said assistant chief Dave Strohte. They had been caught in the wet snow wearing only tennis shoes, cotton pants and light jackets, he said. 'They were completely unprepared for this.' Strohte said."[3]

No mainstream public outcry has been heard on behalf of these border victims. No massive protests have been held. Why? The American public has come to devalue the lives of undocumented Mexican border-crossers, having been conditioned to view these people as something other than potential Americans. And sadly, because of that conditioning, Americans are willing to put up with the deaths of these migrants without wanting to learn even a little about what brought them to the point of death.

A year after President Bill Clinton took office in January 1993, the Border Patrol embarked upon a strategy of "control through deterrence" that resulted in more than 2,000 Mexican migrant deaths over a ten-year period. The deaths resulted from heat stroke, hypothermia, and drowning, as the victims were pushed to cross the desert or hazardous mountains because the Border Patrol had cut off the safest points of entry. In other words, spending over a billion dollars on more officers, fencing, and high-tech equipment did not deter migrants from entering; rather, they simply moved on to different corridors to attempt entry even though the danger of death from searing heat or freezing cold increased.

When deaths resulting from these strategies—with names like Operation Gatekeeper, Operation Safeguard, Operation Blockade—started being reported, the Border Patrol was not surprised. Its 1994 strategic plan recognized that pushing migrants to cross through remote, uninhabited expanses would place them in "mortal danger." When the strategy to move the undocumented foot traffic to the east of San Diego as part of Operation Gatekeeper got underway, a Border Patrol supervisor said, "Eventually we'd like to see them all out in the desert."[4]

What is it about our nation that condones this strategy and resulting deaths? Why is it that reports of this nature are not part of the public consciousness? Because the majority of policy makers and most Americans do not view the Mexican migrant as "one of us," or even *potentially* one of us. America, and therefore who a *real* American is, has been defined in a manner that excludes the Mexican migrant. And this is not simply a function of the fact that these victims are undocumented or attempting surreptitious entries; if their faces and language were accepted in the conventional image of *an American,* the reaction would be far different.

The racialization of who is a *true* or *real* American has affected U.S. enforcement policies directed at only certain undocumented aliens. While strict enforcement policies are in force against undocumented Mexicans, the large numbers of undocumented Irish nationals in the United States in the 1980s were rewarded with special visa allocations. Chinese from China's Fujian Province smuggled in by boat in the early 1990s were rounded up and eventually deported, whereas the largest number of undocumented in Chicago in the 1980s—Polish nationals—were not arrested, as Lech Walensa's struggle for human rights was waged.

Immigration policies are not simply reflections of whom we regard as potential Americans, they are vehicles for keeping out those who do not fit the image and welcoming those who do. Consider the battle over immigration reform in 1952. By an overwhelming margin on June 25, Congress passed legislation overhauling the nation's immigration laws that included broad provisions relating to the exclusion and deportation of subversives and Communists. President Harry S. Truman was a strong supporter of those provisions. After all, he had established the Loyalty Review Board in 1947 to scrutinize government employees in order to dispel charges that he was soft on communism, and his "Truman Doctrine" symbolized the country's support for "free peoples" of other lands who were resisting communist domination. Yet the immigration reform was incomplete in Truman's view; he was deeply disappointed in Congress's refusal to repeal the nation's immigration selection system: the national origins quota system enacted in the 1920s to favor western Europeans. So he vetoed the legislation, explaining,

> The idea behind this discriminatory policy was, to put it baldly, that Americans with English or Irish names were better people and better citizens than Americans with Italian or Greek or Polish names. It was thought that people of West European origin made better citizens than Rumanians or Yugoslavs or Ukrainians or Hungarians or Balts or Austrians. Such a concept is utterly unworthy of our traditions and our ideals. It violates the great political doctrine of the Declaration of Independence that "all men are created equal." It denies the humanitarian creed inscribed beneath the Statue of Liberty proclaiming to all nations, "Give me your tired, your poor, your huddled masses yearning to breathe free."

We are a nation of immigrants. However, the simplicity of that statement conceals the nation's consistent history of tension over whom we collectively regard as "real Americans" and, therefore, whom we would allow into our community. As Truman's debate with Congress over the perpetuation of the national origins quota system demonstrates, we are not, and never have been, of one mind on that issue. Thus, while we are a nation of immigrants, we are a nation that debates immigration policy, and that debate reflects the battle over how we define who is an American.

Although immigration laws did not become a permanent fixture in federal statutes until the mid-1800s, debate over newcomers was a part of the political and social discourse even before the Declaration of Independence. As early as 1751, no less an icon of the New World than Benjamin Franklin opposed the influx of German immigrants, warning that "Pennsylvania will in a few years become a German colony; instead of their learning our language, we must learn theirs, or live as in a foreign country." He later expanded his thoughts:

> Those who came hither are generally the most stupid of their own nation, and as ignorance is often attended with great credulity, when knavery would mislead it, and with suspicion when honesty would set it right; and few of the English understand the German language, and so cannot address them either from the press or pulpit, it is almost impossible to remove any prejudices they may entertain. . . . Not being used to liberty, they know not how to make modest use of it.[5]

These critical statements by one of the framers of our Constitution should be contrasted with the sentiments of George Washington, who in 1783 proclaimed, "The bosom of American is open to receive not only the opulent and respectable stranger, but the oppressed and persecuted of all nations and religions."[6] His words are strikingly reminiscent of the famous lines of the Jewish American poet Emma Lazarus engraved at the base of the Statue of Liberty in 1886:

> *Give me your tired, your poor,*
> *Your huddled masses yearning to breathe free,*
> *The wretched refuse of your teeming shore,*
> *Send these, the homeless, tempest-tost to me.*
> *I lift my lamp beside the golden door!*

Immigration prior to restrictions set the stage for debate. Those "original" people who populated the country in its initial years formed the basis for what many would regard as "real Americans." This wave was primarily an eighteenth-century undertaking that lasted until 1803 and brought with it white, predominantly English-speaking, mainly Protestant Europeans. By contrast, the next wave, which began in the 1820s and lasted until the immigration restriction laws of the 1920s, was a more diverse and controversial phenomenon. That current brought more Catholics and Jews, more southern Europeans and non-English speakers. The restrictions of the 1920s succeeded in drastically reducing that diversity through 1965. The latest wave after 1965 has fueled a new diversity from Asia and Latin America that makes one wonder if the Statue of Liberty might be facing the wrong direction.

Thus, immigration data from 1820 to 2000 tell much of the story about how immigration policies have affected the makeup of the country. (See Appendix.) From 1820 to 1850, about 2.5 million immigrants came to the United States. Almost 90 percent were European (87 percent alone from France, Germany, Ireland, and Great Britain). Only 132 Asians entered at the time, and 14,688 (less than one percent) were Mexican during that thirty-one-year period (of course, much of what we know as the southwestern part of the United States was actually Mexico during that time). The discovery of gold in California in 1848 contributed to an influx of Chinese immigrants until 1882, when the Chinese Exclusion Act was passed. From 1851 to 1880, 228,899 Chinese entered, but this still represented less than 3 percent of the total (7.7 million) number of immigrants during that period, which remained dominated by Europeans (88 percent). Obviously, after Chinese laborers were excluded in 1882, the number of Chinese entering declined; from 1891 to 1900, less than 15,000 entered out of a total of 3.7 million immigrants for the decade.

During the first two decades of the twentieth century, southern and eastern Europeans entered in large numbers. (See Figure I-1.) Of the 14.5 million immigrants who entered, 60 percent were from Italy, Austria, Hungary, and the area that became the Soviet Union. A literacy law was enacted in 1917 specifically targeting southern and eastern Europeans, and from 1921 to 1930, immigrants from those areas declined to about 14 percent of all immigrants. The national origins quota system of 1924 that restricted the same groups had even greater impact. For example, from 1951 to 1960, those groups made up only 6 percent of all immigrants. (See Figure I-2.)

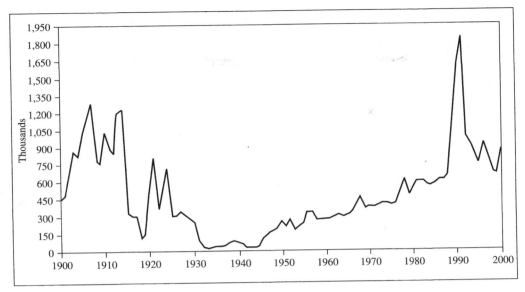

FIGURE I-I   Immigrants Admitted, Fiscal Years 1900–2000
Source: 2000 INS Statistical Yearbook, 3.

Since 1965, when the national origins quota was finally repealed, the face of immigration has become even more diverse. For example, of all immigrants in fiscal year 2000, 65 percent were from Asia and Latin America. The 2000 census found that one-third of the foreign-born population in the United States was from Mexico or another Central American country, and a quarter was from Asia. Fifteen percent were from Europe. As a result of the immigration policies since 1965, including new refugee laws in 1980 and a legalization (or amnesty) program for undocumented immigrants in 1986, the ethnic makeup of the country is changing. While 75 percent of the nation claimed European heritage in the year 2000, the proportion had dropped from 80 percent in 1990. In contrast, the Latino proportion increased from 9 percent to 12.5 percent during the decade, and that of Asian Americans increased from 2.8 percent to 3.6 percent.

There have always been two Americas. Both begin with the understanding that America is a land of immigrants. One America has embraced the notion of welcoming newcomers from different parts of the world, although depending on the era, even this more welcoming perspective may not have been open to people from certain parts of the world or of different persuasions. This America has understood that Americans are not necessarily of the same background or tongue. The other America has remained largely mired in a Eurocentric (originally *western* Eurocentric) vision of America that idealized the *true* American as white, Anglo-Saxon, English-speaking, and Christian. For the most part, this America has opposed more immigration, especially immigration from regions of the world that are not white or supportive of our brand of democracy.

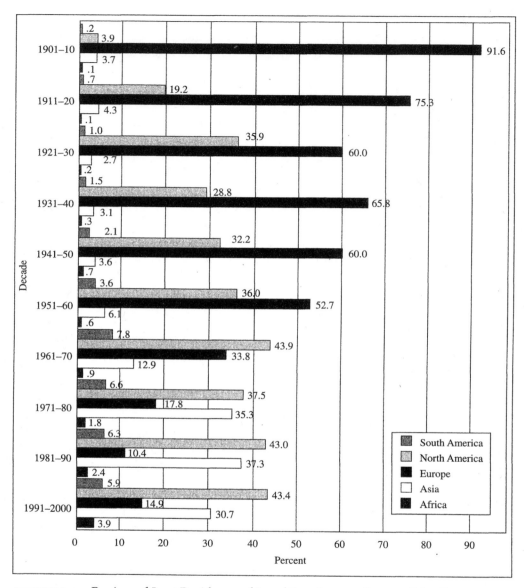

FIGURE 1-2 Region of Last Residence of Legal Immigrants, Percent Distribution by Decade

Source: 2000 INS Statistical Yearbook, 4.

Note: Oceania and unspecified region represent no more than one percent of legal immigration each decade.

The history of U.S. immigration policy reflects the tension of the two Americas that has been a part of the national debate since the founding of the country. As some colonists frowned upon German speakers, others attacked Catholics and Quakers. By the time the nation's second president, John Adams, took office, the debate was on between the two visions of America—one nativistic and xenophobic, the other embracing of immigrants. The tug-of-war between the two visions has been constant ever since. As such the country has generally moved forward with policies that fall somewhere in the middle. The battle is constant because the country knows, just as Truman's veto message implied, that our immigration policy defines our character. As such, major changes to our immigration and refugee laws and decisions on enforcement policies represent defining moments in our history.

Thus, "who is an American" has been defined and redefined throughout our history. When restrictionists—the standard-bearers of the Eurocentric *real American* concept—have had their way, exclusionist rationales have been codified reflecting negative views toward particular races or nationalities, political views (e.g., Communists or anarchists), religions (e.g., Catholics, Jews, Muslims), or social groups (e.g., illiterates, homosexuals). Those grounds for exclusion are every bit about membership in a Eurocentric American standard that requires that undesirables are kept out. Other times, broader visions of America have prevailed, as restrictions are beaten back and more egalitarian language is made part of the law, as in the case of the 1965 amendments and the Refugee Act of 1980. So in spite of its billing as a "nation of immigrants," the United States has constantly struggled with the "impact" of immigrants socially and economically. Influxes of immigrants at different times have provided fodder for anti-immigrant sentiment within national and local communities and for the anti-immigrant cottage industry. The last third of the twentieth century was a particularly heated time. As diversity among immigrants increased, the sheer number of immigrants and refugees admitted suggested a generous system. In truth, exclusionary enforcement mechanisms were often extreme.

This book discusses major immigration policy reforms and enforcement strategies in U.S. history that exemplify the constant battle to define America.[7] The discussion will take us from the earlier years of the nation, when ideas from a rebellious France were feared, to discussions of interning Muslims and Arab Americans after the attacks of September 11, 2001; from the era of Asian exclusion laws to the distaste for Jews and Italians; from the Red Scare and McCarthy era to the final push for a more egalitarian regime in the 1960s; from the debates over how to control the southern border to the institutional scheming to deprive Haitians and Central Americans of their right to asylum. In all of these instances, the struggle over immigration policy is clear even though different groups may be involved. The conflict is over whether another group will be welcomed into our society of Americans.

This volume does not attempt to cover every aspect of the history of U.S. immigration policies. The classics on European immigration by such writers as John Higham and Oscar Handlin certainly lend credence to my argument that even early on certain southern and eastern Europeans were defined as outside the convention of who an

American could be. Similarly, specialized works on Mexicans such as by Gerald López and various Asian immigration restrictions, including my own, are consistent and need not be duplicated here. And while I have to discuss the basic provisions of the Asian exclusion laws, the 1917 literacy act, the 1924 national origins quota system, the 1952 overhaul, the 1965 amendments, and restrictions of the 1990s for a foundational understanding of immigration policies, I have refrained from adding too much detail when it would be unnecessary to my argument. On the other hand, I have included descriptions (at times lengthy) of many aspects of immigration policy that have received little if any review in the extant works: the exclusion of homosexuals, border and workplace enforcement against Mexicans, how the anticommunism provisions were implemented, the attack on dissidents like the Beatle John Lennon, asylum discrimination against Haitians and Salvadorans, Nazi war criminals, the troubled implementation of amnesty in 1986, the hypocrisy of diversity visas, and the dark side of border deaths. While the first six chapters are in chronological order, the rest are not. I have grouped several chapters together that address Mexican migration issues that have dominated much of the debate on immigration and diversity for the past several decades. Separate chapters on the development of deportation provisions and asylum also seemed appropriate.

So which sentiment would guide America: Franklin's disgust for the "most stupid of their own nation," or the open arms of Washington and Lazarus to the poor and oppressed? The contrast is emblematic of the debate on immigration and immigrants that has been a constant part of the American psyche since the nascent stages of the country. Refugees, immigrants, and their advocates have come to rely on the rhetorical examples of Washington and Lazarus. But this sentimental language is not part of the Constitution. Its force may be moral, but its sentiment remains absent from the language of our laws.

Part I

Defining America

CHAPTER 1

The Western European New World and the New Americans

Prior to Columbus's arrival at the islands off our southeastern shores, perhaps 18 million Native Americans resided in what is now the United States and Canada. Although the first people to colonize the New World were the Spanish and French, the European explorers who followed Christopher Columbus to North America in the sixteenth century had no notion of founding a new nation. Neither did the first European settlers who peopled the thirteen colonies on the eastern shores of the continent in the seventeenth and eighteenth centuries. They regarded America as but the western rim of a transatlantic European world. By 1640, the population of the colonies had reached about 25,000. These original colonists may have fled poverty or religious persecution in the Old World, but they continued to view themselves as Europeans and as subjects of the English king.

Yet life in the New World made the colonists different from their European cousins, and eventually, during the American Revolution, these new Americans came to embrace a vision of their country as an independent nation. They had much in common to begin with. The colonies had been *British* colonies. Most people came determined to create an agricultural society modeled on English customs. Conditions in the New World deepened their common bonds. Most learned to live lives unfettered by the tyrannies of royal authority, official religion, and social hierarchies that they had left behind. They grew to cherish ideals that became synonymous with American life— reverence for individual liberty, self-government, religious tolerance, and economic opportunity. The original colonists and their progeny became the "founders" of a new nation, and as such they are regarded as the original Americans. By accepting this notion, we have come to view an "American" as someone attached to the United States of America. Almost immediately, the original Americans displayed a willingness to exclude certain others from the concept of a true American, to subjugate outsiders—first Indians, who were nearly annihilated through war and disease, and then Africans, who were brought in chains to serve as slave labor, especially on the tobacco, rice, and indigo plantations of the southern colonies.

But if the settlement experience gave people a common stock of values, both good and bad, it also divided them. The thirteen colonies were quite different from one another. Puritans carved right, pious, and relatively democratic communities of small family farms out of rocky-soiled New England. Theirs was a homogeneous world in comparison to most of the southern colonies, where large landholders, mostly Anglicans, built plantations along the coast from which they lorded over a labor force of black slaves and looked down upon the poor white farmers who settled the backcountry. Different still were the middle colonies stretching from New York to Delaware. There, diversity reigned. Well-to-do merchants put their stamp on New York City, as Quakers did on Pennsylvania, while out in the countryside sprawling estates were interspersed with modest homesteads. Within individual colonies, conflicts festered over economic interests, ethnic rivalries, and religious practices. All these clashes made it difficult for colonists to imagine that they were a single people with a common identity, much less that they ought to break free from Britain.[1] British tyranny unified the colonies, and a new nation was born, peopled by those who were openly welcomed, those who withstood discouraging sentiment, and slaves.

During the early colonial period, some individual colonies attempted to regulate immigration, but essentially there was no integrated immigration policy. The first settlers were French and Spanish. Prior to 1680, most newcomers were English Protestants. A combination of religious, political, and economic motives brought these settlers to the New World. However, when English emigration began to decline in the 1680s, colonies—particularly Pennsylvania and North Carolina—began to promote the immigration of certain other nationalities and ethnic groups while attempting to exclude undesirables. This produced an influx of French Huguenots, Irish Quakers, and German Pietists. Newcomers from Scotland, Portugal, Spain, Switzerland, the Netherlands, and the Rhineland followed. About 450,000 immigrants, representing a dozen nationalities, arrived during the eighteenth century.

These new immigrants came for myriad reasons. German Pietist sects, including the Mennonites and Moravians, fled persecution in search of religious freedom, many in response to the sympathetic Quaker teachings of William Penn. A later German group, the Hessians, came to fight as mercenaries with the British in the American Revolution, and 5,000 stayed to become immigrants. Dutch and Swedes came for political freedom and economic opportunity, and the Scotch-Irish came throughout the eighteenth century for economic, religious, and political reasons. European migration was not limited to the original thirteen colonies. Spain wanted to expand the Spanish Empire and sent immigrants to California, Florida, and Mexico to search for gold, to trade with Native Americans, and to convert them to Christianity. French settlers came to Louisiana and Canada to seek land and business opportunities, convert the Native Americans, and protect French trading interests. The French Huguenots immigrated to flee religious persecution after the revocation of the Edict of Nantes in 1685.

Even during this "open" era of immigration, the original colonies attempted to define their new America by promoting immigration only to select groups. When the first census was taken in 1790, the total population was recorded at 3,227,000. English, Scots, and Scotch-Irish accounted for 75 percent; Germans made up 8 percent; and other nationalities with substantial numbers included the Dutch, French, Swedes, and Spanish. In addition, the 1790 census recorded a population of 750,000 blacks, a result of the involuntary migration of 350,000 African slaves into the colonies. By the census of 1810, the white population had increased to approximately 6 million, and the black population to approximately 1,378,000.[2]

State Immigration Control

As the new nation emerged, "immigration policies" continued to be handled by individual states with little federal intervention. As in the colonial period, these policies were aimed at the exclusion of certain undesirables, as individual states begin to delineate who should become part of their community. Yet beyond those who were not wanted, the doors were open to unlimited numbers of able-bodied souls who made the trek to the new nation. In fact, one of the complaints the authors of the Declaration of Independence made against King George III was that his policies sharply restricted immigration. King George saw a burgeoning population as a threat to his hold on the colonies and tried to strangle further influx.[3] Thus, in the Declaration of Independence, King George was castigated as having "endeavored to prevent the population of these States; for that purpose obstructing the laws for naturalization of foreigners, refusing to pass others to encourage their migrations hither, and raising the conditions of new appropriations of lands."[4]

Prior to 1875, state immigration provisions, which often applied to interstate as well as foreign migrants, regulated at least four groups: criminals, paupers, slaves or free blacks, and adherents of certain religions. A fifth category involved those espousing unorthodox or unpopular views, although state colonial screening on the basis of political belief was implemented on only a limited basis. This early sentiment—seeking only those who would become patriotic loyalists—represents an early version of a viewpoint (manifested in anticommunist, antianarchist, and antiterrorist screening) that has remained an important part of the immigration policy debate throughout the nation's history. While the migration of a sixth group of individuals—those suspected of carrying contagious diseases—raised concerns among the colonists, regulation through quarantine was not immigrant-specific.[5]

Criminals

The early colonies opposed the immigration of persons convicted of crimes. Under modern immigration laws, individuals with certain criminal backgrounds are barred from entering the country. Thus, for example, an individual who might fall into an immigration category reserved for relatives of U.S. citizens or for those with special job skills can still be excluded if Immigration and Naturalization Service (INS) officials discover that the applicant has been convicted of a narcotics offense or a crime involving moral turpitude. In the seventeenth and eighteenth centuries, however, British attempts to transport criminals to the United States concerned the colonists. English judges could sentence felons to the colonies as punishment, and felons could also be shipped to the colonies as indentured servants. Several colonies enacted restrictions on the entry of such individuals, only to be overruled by the British government.[6] The British lost this veto authority after the War of Independence, but even after 1783, they continued to send convicts as indentured servants. In 1788, the Congress of the Confederation adopted a resolution recommending that states "pass proper laws for preventing the transportation of convicted malefactors from foreign countries into the U.S."[7] Within a year, several states responded. Massachusetts, Pennsylvania, South Carolina, and Virginia prohibited the importation of persons who had been previously convicted of a crime. In later years, after the federal Constitution had taken effect, other states enacted similar legislation: Maine, Maryland, New Jersey, New York, and Rhode Island.[8]

Paupers

The Statue of Liberty's "give us your tired, your poor" refrain written by political dissenter Emma Lazarus in 1883 was definitely not the philosophy of the colonies, nor is it today's philosophy, as modern laws exclude those immigrants who are "likely to become a public charge."[9] The colonists were comfortable with the notion of members of the lower class fleeing the overcrowded, rigid social structure of Europe, as long as they were hardworking and honest. But the colonists feared that Europe was using the New World as a dumping ground for the lazy and disabled. After all, English judges could banish vagrants along with felons to the colonies. Thus, after independence, a number of states instituted legislation aimed at the poor from abroad as well as those from other states. In Massachusetts, the 1794 poor laws imposed a penalty on any person who knowingly brought a pauper or indigent person into any town in the Commonwealth and left him there. This applied to intrastate, interstate, and international transporting of the poor. Beginning in 1820, Massachusetts returned to the colonial system of demanding security from masters of vessels when their passengers seemed likely to become paupers. In New York, a 1788 statute authorized the justice of the peace to order a newcomer removed if it was determined that the person would likely become a public charge within the first year of residence. Until 1813, paupers who returned after removal were subject to severe corporal punishment as well as retransportation. The 1788 poor law required masters of vessels arriving in the New York City harbor to report within twenty-four hours the names and occupations of all passengers; if any passenger appeared likely to become a charge, the vessel was required to either return the passenger or post a bond.[10]

Blacks

Prior to the Civil War, Southern slave states adopted legislation prohibiting the migration of free blacks and urged free Northern states to do the same. Since many white inhabitants of the North were prejudiced against blacks, several free states obliged. They did so by either blocking the movement of blacks into the state or requiring good behavior and assurances that blacks would not become public charges. Slave states also subjected their free black residents to more stringent regulations and criminal laws than whites. The sentiment behind some of these laws was related to immigration from abroad. Many states did not welcome fleeing French slaveowners who brought slaves that may have been influenced by the ideals of freedom. These fears were not entirely unfounded. A successful slave revolt in Saint Dominique ultimately produced the nation of Haiti. In 1803, Southern states succeeded in pushing for federal legislation prohibiting the importation of foreign blacks into states whose laws prohibited their entry. Relatedly, in the early 1800s, Southern states regulated free black sailors aboard vessels arriving in Southern ports. States such as South Carolina did not want black sailors wandering its streets, even temporarily. Because of this, South Carolina and other states required black seamen to be held in jail or quarantine on the ship, barring communication with local blacks.[11]

In addition to legislation adopted by the states, blacks were also attacked through early federal immigration policy. In the First Congress, on March 26, 1790, a provision was made, pursuant to constitutional power (Art. 1, § 8, clause 4), to establish a uniform rule of naturalization for aliens who were "free white males" and who had two years' residence.[12] This provision excluded indentured servants, slaves, and most women, all of whom were considered dependents and thus incapable of casting an independent vote. The person had to be of good moral character, a requirement that remains today.[13]

Religious Views

Religious belief often limited one's choice of domicile in the New World. In the spirit of the time, colonial charters frequently denied admission to Catholics. Virginia is an example of one such state that denied admission on the basis of religious belief. The first settlers in Virginia were emigrants from England who belonged to the English church, at a point in time when the church was flush with complete victory over the religious of all other persuasions. Yet the settlers were intolerant of their Presbyterian brethren, who had emigrated to the northern colonies. Furthermore, Virginia passed several laws aimed at Quakers, who had fled from persecution in England and cast their eyes on the New World as an asylum of civil and religious freedom. Sadly, the Quakers found the New World free only from the reigning sect. Several acts of the Virginia assembly of 1659, 1662, and 1693 aimed at Quakers espoused Virginia's strong religious beliefs. These laws made it a crime for parents to refuse to have their children baptized, prohibited the unlawful assembling of Quakers, and penalized any master of a vessel who brought a Quaker into the state. The laws further ordered Quakers already present in Virginia and Quakers who attempted to enter the state to be imprisoned until they left the country, providing a mild punishment for their first and second returns, and death for the third. In addition, the laws prohibited all persons from holding Quaker meetings in or near their homes, entertaining Quakers individually, or circulating books that supported Quaker tenets.[14] Statutory oppressions of religion were wiped away in 1776.

In contrast to Virginia's stringent anti-Quaker laws, Pennsylvania espoused a broader religious philosophy. King Charles II granted the charter for Pennsylvania to William Penn in 1681. Penn, a Quaker, was driven by two principal motives in founding the colony: "the desire to found a free commonwealth on liberal and humane principles, and the desire to provide a safe home for persecuted Friends." English Quakers were the dominant element, although many English settlers were Anglican.

Penn was far in advance of his time in his views of mankind's capacity for democratic government, and equally so in his broad-minded tolerance of different religious beliefs. He crafted the Charter of Privileges in 1701 that began the first Constitution of Pennsylvania, assuring that no citizen would be "molested or prejudiced" because of their faith, nor "compelled to frequent or [maintain] any Religious Worship or place . . . contrary to [their] mind." The character gave religious liberty to Protestants, Catholics, Unitarians, Christians, Jews, Muslims, and Quakers, and is regarded by some to be the American *Magna Charta* of religious liberty.

Penn's toleration of other forms of religious belief was in no way halfhearted and imbued the Society of Friends with feelings of kindness toward Catholics, or at least accentuated those feelings in them. In the 1720s, a Catholic chapel was erected in Pennsylvania, which was thought to be contrary to the laws of Parliament. The chapel was not suppressed pending a decision of the British government on the question of whether immunity granted by the Pennsylvania law did not protect Catholics. When, after Braddock's defeat during the French War, hostility to France led to an attack upon the Pennsylvania Catholics by a mob, the Quakers protected them. No other American colony had "such a mixture of languages, nationalities and religions. Dutch, Swedes, English, Germans, Scotch-Irish and Welsh; Quakers, Presbyterians, Episcopalians, Lutherans, Reformed, Mennonites, Tunkers and Moravians all had a share in creating it." Although the constitution of Pennsylvania protected religious freedom, it held that Christianity was part of the common law of Pennsylvania—not Christianity founded on any particular tenets, but Christianity with liberty of conscience to all men.[15]

Another example of religious tolerance was New York, a colony that accommodated Quakers in its constitutional convention. In its provision related to requirements of voters, the convention provided "that every elector, before he is admitted to vote, shall, if required by the returning-officer or either of the inspectors, take an oath, or, if of the people called Quakers, an affirmation, of allegiance to the State."[16] In fact, although the convention affirmed that the "common law of England" would continue to be the law of the state, any "such parts of the said common law . . . as may be construed to establish or maintain any particular denomination of Christians or their ministers . . . are abrogated and rejected."[17]

Anti-Catholicism persisted in some quarters after the American Revolution. Several states enacted legislation against the Catholic religion. The Carolinas had a law preventing a Catholic from holding office, and New Hampshire had a similar provision in its constitution. Anti-Catholic violence occurred in 1834, when the Ursuline Convent in Charleston was burned. In Philadelphia in 1844, anti-Catholicism led to riots that lasted three days.[18]

Unorthodox Views

Some colonies attempted to exclude or screen would-be immigrants on the basis of political belief or affiliation. For example, a 1727 Pennsylvania act required immigrants "to take an oath of allegiance to the king and fidelity to the proprietors and the provincial constitution." Banishment—the probable antecedent of deportation as an instrument of immigration policy—was sometimes used during the colonial era to punish persons espousing unorthodox or unpopular views.

Several of the nation's most prominent people spoke out about foreign influence during this time period. Benjamin Franklin's 1755 expression against further German migration to Pennsylvania is not simply about language:

> Why should the Palatine [German] boors be suffered to swarm in our settlements and, by herding together, establish their language and *manners* to the exclusion of ours? Why should Pennsylvania, founded by the English, become a colony of *aliens,* who will shortly be so numerous as to **germanize** us instead of our anglifying them?[19] (Emphasis added)

Franklin continued these expressions during the Continental Congress, warning of the increasing German influence in American society. Similarly, in 1788 John Jay (a year later appointed to be the first chief justice of the Supreme Court by George Washington) noted in *The Federalist* No. 2:

> Providence has been pleased to give this one connected country to one united people—a people descended from the same ancestors, speaking the same language, professing the same religion, *attached to the same principles of government, very similar in their manners and customs,* and who, by their joint counsels, arms, and efforts, fighting side by side throughout a long and bloody war, have nobly established general liberty and independence.[20] (Emphasis added)

In the same vein, Thomas Jefferson stated:

> It is impossible not to look forward to distant times, when our rapid multiplication will expand itself . . . [and] cover the whole northern, if not the southern continent, with a people speaking the same language, governed in similar forms, [and] by similar laws; nor can we contemplate with satisfaction either *blot or mixture on that surface.*[21] (Emphasis added)

In addition to Franklin and Jefferson, John Adams, a Federalist and the nation's second president, was also wary of foreign influence. In his inaugural address, March 4, 1797, he warned that the nation should never "lose sight of the danger to our liberties if anything partial or extraneous should infect the purity of our free, fair, virtuous, and independent elections. . . . If that solitary suffrage can be obtained by foreign nations by flattery or menaces, by fraud or violence, by terror, intrigue, or venality, the Government may not be the choice of the American people, but of foreign nations. . . .

[It is] the pestilence of foreign influence, which is the angel of destruction to elective governments."[22]

Federal Immigration Control

Fears of foreign influence led to an early attempt at federal immigration control. The 1798 Alien and Sedition Laws, a series of four laws passed by the Federalist-controlled U.S. Congress and signed by President Adams, purportedly were enacted not only to respond to hostile actions of the French Revolutionary government on the seas, but also to quell political opposition from the Democratic-Republican Party, led by Jefferson and James Madison. The first of the laws was the Naturalization Act, passed by Congress on June 18. This act required that aliens be residents for fourteen years instead of five before they became eligible for U.S. citizenship. This adversely affected Jefferson's party, which depended on recent arrivals from Europe for much of its voting strength. Congress then passed the Alien Friends Act on June 25, authorizing the president to deport aliens "dangerous to the peace and safety of the United States" during peacetime. The naturalization and alien acts were aimed largely at Irish immigrants and French refugees who had participated in political activities critical of the Adams administration. The third law, the Alien Enemies Act, was enacted by Congress on July 6. This act allowed the wartime arrest, imprisonment, and deportation of any alien subject to an enemy power. President Adams made no use of the alien acts. The last of the laws, the Sedition Act, passed on July 14, declared that any treasonable activity, including the publication of "any false, scandalous and malicious writing," was a high misdemeanor, punishable by fine and imprisonment. Under this legislation, twenty-five men, most of them editors of Democractic-Republican newspapers, were arrested and the newspapers were forced to shut down. One of the men arrested was Benjamin Franklin's grandson, Benjamin Franklin Bache, editor of the Philadelphia Democrat-Republican *Aurora,* charged with libeling President Adams. Bache's arrest evoked a public outcry against the Alien and Sedition Acts. Resolutions against them became part of the Democratic-Republican platform in the 1800 presidential election, and were partly responsible for the election of Jefferson to the presidency. Once in office, Jefferson pardoned all those convicted under the Sedition Act, and Congress restored all fines paid with interest. The Alien Friends Act and the Sedition Act expired by 1801; Congress repealed the Naturalization Act in 1802 (restoring the residency requirement to five years), and the Alien Enemies Act was amended.

The impetus behind the Alien and Sedition Acts was fear of foreign influence. For example, in the Sedition Act, the U.S. government was in effect declaring war on the ideas of the French Revolution. To protect the American way—as interpreted by the Federalists—the people were to be safeguarded against the dangerous opinions spreading over the world. According to this theory, the only way to preserve the health of the body politic was to impose a "quarantine upon ideas."[23] Federalists believed that many Republicans, being more French than American at heart, would join a French army of invasion should it land on American shores. The Federalists craved security from the threat of Bonaparte's army, revolutions, and subversive ideas. As upholders of the implied and inherent powers of the national government, the Federalists found support for the Alien Act in the right of Congress to defend the country against foreign aggression. To them, self-preservation was the higher law—a power with which every government was endowed. Every morning Secretary of State Timothy Pickering methodically pored over the Republican newspapers in search of seditious material. He demanded all U.S. district attorneys to closely scrutinize Republican newspapers published in their districts, insisting on prosecution of both author and publisher.[24]

Tale of the Tubs. One celebrated incident initially appeared to vindicate the Federalists, only to end in their embarrassment. Early in 1799, Pickering received word that a former deputy to the French National Convention, a mulatto named Matthew Salmon, was aboard the *Minerva*, a Danish ship bound for Charleston, South Carolina. The allegation was that Salmon was carrying, concealed in tubs with false bottoms, dispatches establishing a French-engineered plot to overthrow the United States. Pickering also imagined that as a mulatto, Salmon was probably also intent on stirring up an insurrection among black slaves in the South. When the *Minerva* dropped anchor in Charleston, armed officials boarded and found Salmon with four other French citizens, and several others, including a woman, all traveling with Swiss passports. Indeed, documents in French were found in tubs with false bottoms. The individuals were arrested and the papers sent to a General Pinckney, who, along with the governor of South Carolina, were for the moment acclaimed saviors of the Republic. One Federalist newspaper exhorted, "look on Frenchmen with the eye of suspicion, and prepare to meet them as enemies, with the sword: and BEWARE OF FRENCH EMIGRANTS."[25] After investigation, however, the facts revealed that the travelers were actually hostile to the ruling party of France. Indeed, they planned to proceed from Charleston to Saint Dominique to help with the struggle against the French.

In spite of these early colonial, state, and federal expressions of exclusion, until Chinese were excluded in 1882, no limits on the numbers of immigrants or refugees to what has become the United States existed. Immigration was limited or discouraged principally by the cost of travel, diseases, conflict with indigenous inhabitants, or racial, religious, or political discrimination by prior immigrant groups.

An 1853 map shows the boundaries of what would become the contiguous forty-eight states. This included the 1846 Oregon Territory, 1848 Mexican Territory, 1845 Republic of Texas, 1803 Louisiana Purchase, and Florida cessation in 1819.

Of course, the presence of Native American tribes did not stand in the way of the country's expansion. In 1892, Supreme Court Chief Justice John Marshall explained the power of conquest:

America, separated from Europe by a wide ocean, was inhabited by a distinct people, divided into separate nations, independent of each other and of the rest of the world, having institutions of their own, and governing themselves by their own laws. It is difficult to comprehend the proposition, that the inhabitants of either quarter of the globe could have rightful original claims of dominion over the inhabitants of the other, or over the lands they

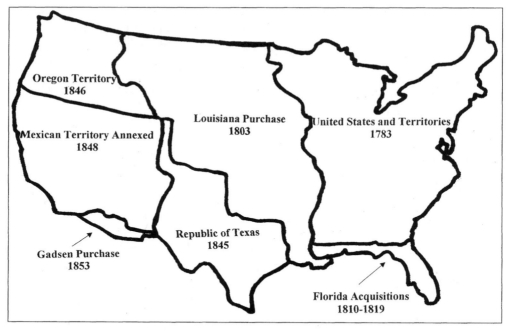

FIGURE 1-1   U.S. Expansion to 1853

occupied; or that the discovery of either by the other should give the discoverer rights in the country discovered, which annulled the pre-existing rights of its ancient possessors.

After lying concealed for a series of ages, the enterprise of Europe, guided by nautical science, conducted some of her adventurous sons into this western world. They found it in possession of a people who had made small progress in agriculture or manufactures, and whose general employment was war, hunting, and fishing.

Did these adventurers, by sailing along the coast, and occasionally landing on it, acquire for the several governments to whom they belonged, or by whom they were commissioned, a rightful property in the soil, from the Atlantic to the Pacific; or rightful dominion over the numerous people who occupied it? Or has nature, or the great Creator of all things, conferred these rights over hunters and fishermen, on agriculturalists and manufacturers? But power, war, conquest, give rights, which after possession, are conceded by the world; and which can never be controverted by those on whom they descend.[26]

As long as they were the *right kind* of immigrants, the new nation wanted them. In 1791, Alexander Hamilton warned Congress that if the United States were to develop into an industrial power, immigration would have to be encouraged so as to offset the "scarcity of hands" and the "dearness of labor."[27] The nineteenth century witnessed recruitment efforts by the U.S. government and the states, as well as private employers, who saturated Europe with promotional campaigns to stir up emigration to the United

States. Substantial European immigration, especially from Germany, occurred in the two decades prior to the Civil War. As Andrew Carnegie explained it, "the value to the country of the annual foreign influx is very great indeed. . . . These adults are surely worth $1500 each—for in former days an efficient slave sold for that sum." To Carnegie, immigration was a "golden stream which flows into the country each year."[28] Policy makers throughout the nineteenth century extolled the economic benefits of abundant immigration and fashioned U.S. immigration policies to maximize the flow. The Republican Party platform of 1864, which Abraham Lincoln helped to draft, fostered the same philosophy: "Foreign immigration which in the past has added so much to the wealth, resources, and increase of power to this nation—the asylum of the oppressed of all nations—should be fostered and encouraged by a liberal and just policy."[29]

Months earlier, on December 8, 1863, President Lincoln strongly recommended legislation to the Thirty-seventh Congress that would encourage immigration:

> I again submit to your consideration the expediency of establishing a system for the encouragement of immigration. Although this source of national wealth and strength is again flowing with greater freedom than for several years before the insurrection occurred, there is still a great deficiency of laborers in every field of industry, especially in agriculture and in our mines, as well of iron and coal as of the precious metals. While the demand for labor is thus increased here, tens of thousands of persons destitute of remunerative occupation are thronging our foreign consulates and offering to emigrate to the United States if essential but very cheap assistance can be afforded them. It is very easy to see that under the sharp discipline of civil war the Nation is beginning a new life. This noble effort demands the aid and ought to receive the attention and support of the Government.[30]

Not surprisingly, the first comprehensive federal immigration law, passed in 1864, was an Act to Encourage Immigration. This law established the first U.S. Immigration Bureau, whose primary function was to increase immigration so that American industries would have an adequate supply of workers to meet production needs during the Civil War. In addition, in an effort to reduce the number of immigrants who left industry for homesteading or army enlistment, the law made pre-emigration contracts binding. Although the law was repealed in 1868, it spawned the host of private labor recruitment agencies that for many years continued to be a significant force behind European emigration.[31]

Of course, immigration was not without its critics. During the decades preceding the Civil War, when the massive wave of immigrants, mostly from Ireland and Germany, came to America, prejudice or nativism reached new heights. The Irish were Catholic, a fact that fed Protestant fears that the papacy intended to take over the U.S. government. Even though the immigrants were vital to the industrial and economic expansion of the nation, many natives attacked them as foes of the Republic. Some joined nativist groups to combat the "alien menace." Others pressured the Whigs and Democrats to pass anti-immigrant legislation, such as laws lengthening the time it took to become a citizen. Several such groups combined to form the Order of the Star-Spangled Banner, which adopted a pledge of secrecy; if people asked them about their program, they responded "I know nothing." The organization became the most powerful nativist organization of the era. The basic tenets that defined the order's ideology included a belief that Protestantism sustained and preserved the Republic because it emphasized individualism, democracy, and equality, while Roman Catholicism threatened the Republic because it stressed authoritarianism, opposed freedom of thought, dictated how Catholics should vote, and insisted that priests act as intercessors between God and the faithful. This culminated in the birth of the American or Know-Nothing Party in the 1850s. In 1856, the American Party nominated ex-President Millard Fillmore as their presidential candidate, and he garnered almost 900,000 votes. The American Party platform included the following planks:

III. *Americans must rule America;* and to this end, *native*-born citizens should be selected for all state, federal, or municipal offices of government employment, in preference to naturalized citizens. . . .

IX. A change in the laws of naturalization, making continued residence of twenty-one years, of all not heretofore provided for, an indispensable requisite for citizenship hereafter.

Yet, mostly pro-immigration sentiment prevailed through the 1800s. That sentiment is reflected in "True Americanism," an 1859 patriotic sermon by Carl Schurz, a German-born immigrant and a leader of the newly formed Republican Party. He was part of the wave of German immigrants prior to the Civil War and campaigned for Lincoln. He was a U.S. senator from Missouri from 1869 to 1875, and in 1877 became secretary of the interior. The immediate purpose of his words was in opposing a proposal before the Massachusetts state legislature restricting the rights of the foreign-born, in particular. Ironically, Schurz shared some of the native-born's prejudices toward Irish Catholics, although, as becomes clear in his sermon, ultimately he felt that democracy rested on the principle of inclusion and tolerance, not exclusion and self-righteousness.

The dignity of the Roman citizen consisted in his exclusive privileges; the dignity of the American citizen consists in his holding the natural rights of his neighbor just as sacred as his own. . . . The Roman Republic perished by the sword; the American Republic will stand as long as the equality of human rights remains inviolate. Which of the two republics is the greater—the republic of the Roman or the republic of man?

Sir, I wish the words of the Declaration of Independence, "that all men are created free and equal, and are endowed with certain inalienable rights," were inscribed upon every gatepost within the limits of this republic. . . .

True, there are difficulties connected with an organization of society founded upon the basis of equal rights. Nobody denies it. A large number of those who come to you from foreign lands are not as capable of taking part in the administration of government as the man who was fortunate enough to drink the milk of liberty in his cradle. And certain religious denominations do, perhaps, nourish principles which are hardly in accordance with the doctrines of true democracy. There is a conglomeration on this continent of heterogeneous elements; there is a warfare of clashing interest and unruly aspirations; and, with all this, our democratic system gives rights to the ignorant and power to the inexperienced. And the

ILLUSTRATION I-I   The undesirable Irish is illustrated in a cartoon depicting the Irish as unmixable in the National Pot.
Source: Puck, June 26, 1889 [in Bernard A. Weisberger, *The American Heritage History of the American People,* 1971, 175].

ILLUSTRATION I-2   "The Great Fear of the Period—That Uncle Sam may be swallowed by foreigners," reflects the anti-Irish and anti-Chinese sentiment of the time. *Source:* Library of Congress, 1865 cartoon.

billows of passion will lash the sides of the ship, and the storm of party warfare will bend its masts, and the pusillanimous will cry out—"Master, master, we perish!" But the genius of true democracy will arise from his slumber and rebuke the winds and the raging of the water, and say unto them—"Where is your faith?" Aye, where is the faith that led the fathers of this republic to invite the weary and burdened of all nations to the enjoyment of equal rights? Where is that broad and generous confidence in the efficiency of true democratic institutions? Has the present generation forgotten that true democracy bears in itself the remedy for all the difficulties that may grow out of it?

It is an old dodge of the advocates of despotism throughout the world that the people who are not experienced in self-government are not fit for the exercise of self-government and must first be educated under the rule of a superior authority. But at the same time the advocates of despotism will never offer them an opportunity to acquire experience in self-government lest they suddenly become fit for its independent exercise. To this treacherous sophistry the fathers of this republic opposed the noble doctrine that liberty is the best school for liberty, and that self-government cannot be learned but by practicing it. This, sir, is a truly American idea; this is true Americanism; and to this I pay tribute of my devotion.[32]

Schurz's views predominated, as the restrictive piece of legislation before the Massachusetts legislature failed and, more important, the Know-Nothing Party disappeared and the more inclusive Republican Party flourished.

The mass migration of the nineteenth century was the result of a near perfect match between the needs of a new country and overcrowded Europe. Europe at the time was undergoing drastic social change and economic reorganization, severely compounded by overpopulation. An extraordinary increase in population coincided with the breakup of the old agricultural order that had been in place since medieval times throughout much of Europe. Commonly held lands were broken up into individually owned farms, resulting in landless status for peasants from Ireland to Russia. At approximately the same time, the industrial revolution was underway, moving from Great Britain to western Europe, and then to southern and eastern Europe. For Germany, Sweden, Russia, and Japan, the highest points of emigration coincided with the beginnings of industrialization and the ensuing general disruption of employment patterns. The artisans joined the peasants evicted from their land as immigrants to the United States. Population pressure and related economic problems, sometimes in the extreme form of famine, were the major causes of the mass migration of this long period, followed by religious persecution and the desire for political freedom.[33]

America, on the other hand, had a boundless need for people to push back the frontier, to build the railways, to defend unstable boundaries, and to populate new states. The belief in America as a land of asylum for the oppressed was reinforced by the commitment to the philosophy of manifest destiny. Immigration was required for settlement, defense, and economic well-being.[34]

Early Numbers

The number of immigrants entering the United States between the end of the Revolutionary War and 1819 was 250,000. In 1820, 8,385 entries were recorded; by 1840 annual immigration had increased tenfold, to 84,066. Germany, the United Kingdom, and Ireland accounted for 70 percent of the 750,949 entries between 1820 and 1840. (See Appendix.) Emigration from Ireland and England was primarily in response to economic problems. In Germany, economic problems were aggravated by liberal discontent with political developments following the Napoleonic Wars.[35]

Immigration increased almost 600 percent, to 4,211,465, during the subsequent twenty-year period, 1841–60. Ireland, Germany, and Great Britain accounted for 87.5 percent of the total. This was the period of the potato famine, which hit hardest in Ireland but affected other parts of Europe as well.[36] When the entire potato crop was wiped out in 1846 and 1847, half a million people died, 3 million lived on charity, and hundreds of thousands fled to America. Just under 1.7 million came from Ireland between 1841 and 1860. Emigration from Ireland reduced rather than simply slowed population growth, and in the second half of the century significant amounts of money flowed back into the country in the form of remittances from America.[37]

On the West Coast, where Asians first arrived, Chinese were the first to enter in significant numbers. Driven by the rice shortage and the devastation of the Taiping Rebellion, and drawn by the lure of gold, Chinese peasants and laborers began making the long journey in the 1840s. By 1882, when the Chinese Exclusion Act was passed, more than 100,000 Chinese resided in the United States.[38]

Germany sent almost 1.4 million immigrants to America during the 1841–60 period. Germany suffered a severe economic crisis during the 1840s, as well as political unrest culminating in the revolution of 1848. The "forty-eighters" joined those fleeing to America from the potato famine, high prices, and widespread unemployment. An additional 700,000 came from Great Britain.[39]

By 1860, the population of the United States had increased to 31 million, from 7 million in 1810. More than 5 million immigrants had added to this increase. About half of them were from Great Britain and Ireland, followed by more than 1.5 million Germans and 50,000 Scandinavians.[40]

Immigration to the United States was widely, although not universally, encouraged during the mid-nineteenth century; pull factors were operative in addition to the push factors mentioned. Of major importance was the so-called American letter. These were letters to relatives at home encouraging others to follow, and sometimes including one-way steamship tickets. Another important factor was the active recruitment of passengers by steamship companies and railroad workers by the railroads.

Following the Civil War, the development of the Union Pacific and other railways required the western movement of European immigrants. Western states encouraged the migration of immigrants by brochures and agents sent to New York and abroad, and by reducing the residence period required to vote. The Homestead Act of 1862 made western lands available to immigrants as well as to the native-born. The Contract Labor Law passed in 1864 was intended to encourage immigration by advancing money for passage. However, it was repealed in 1868, under pressure from U.S. labor groups.[41]

Immigration increased to 5,127,015 during the 1861–80 period, a figure approximately equal to total previous immigration since the country had gained its independence. Germany, Great Britain, and Ireland continued to account for the largest numbers. Additionally, there were significant numbers from Sweden, Norway, and China. The high level of immigration during this period reflected the growing improvements in international communication and transportation, which resulted in widespread circulation of stories about new land, as well as a less arduous sea voyage.

In Sweden, the winter of 1867–68 brought a monetary crisis, followed by a crop failure and local famine. These developments, in combination with precarious agricultural conditions, the displacement of artisans by industrial development, and ideological and religious differences, resulted in mass Swedish emigration in the late 1860s. A similar pattern was repeated in Norway and throughout other countries as agrarian difficulties beset Europe during the 1880s.[42]

Immigration reached a high of 5,246,613 in 1881–90, followed by 3,687,564 in the final decade of the nineteenth century. Germany, the United Kingdom, and Ireland accounted for almost half of the immigration during this period, although their numbers all declined significantly in the 1890s. Immigration from these countries continued a steady and sharp decline into the first two decades of the twentieth century. This was due largely to improved economic conditions in those countries, resulting from the leveling off of population growth and the increase in industrialization that absorbed increasing numbers of workers.

In contrast, immigration from Italy and Austria-Hungary increased rapidly in the 1880s and 1890s, as it did from other countries in southern and eastern Europe. More than 2 million entered during the first decade of the twentieth century from both Italy and Austria-Hungary, and more than 1.5 million came from Russia.[43]

Conclusion

Although the first European settlers to the New World did not arrive contemplating the establishment of a new nation, their immediate descendants came to embrace a vision of America as an independent nation. In spite of this "independence" and the promotion of immigration from France, Ireland, Germany, Scotland, Portugal, Spain, Switzerland, the Netherlands, and a half dozen other nationalities beginning in the late 1600s, a sense of an "American" was developing, grounded in English or Anglo-conformity tradition. Certainly some of the early state efforts to "control" immigration, such as the exclusion of criminals, may not contradict the idea of America as a "land of immigrants," accepting of those from different racial, ethnic, or political backgrounds. But from the colonial period through the Civil War, examples of powerful forces attempting to define America in specific racial, ethnic, social, and political ways abound.

Colonial and state efforts to bar certain immigrants are revealing. Prior to the Civil War, Southern slave states adopted legislation prohibiting the migration of free blacks; since whites in the North were also prejudiced against blacks, several Northern states did the same. Colonial charters frequently denied admission to Catholics. And although Quakers fled from persecution in England, sadly Virginia passed laws against Quakers in the late 1600s, including death to any Quaker who had entered the state a third time.

An early federal effort to define America is embodied in the President Adams-backed Alien and Sedition Laws of 1798, enacted out of fears of foreign influence. While the influence of French revolutionaries was the target of those laws, at the Continental Congress years earlier, Benjamin Franklin warned of the increasing German influence in American society.

The influx of Germans and Irish Catholics in the mid-1800s gave rise to a number of nativist societies disturbed by the "alien menace." The Know-Nothing Party became prominent, and its presidential candidate in 1856, ex-President Millard Fillmore, received almost 900,000 votes in the election.

In spite of powerful forces against full inclusion during these eras, voices of inclusion often prevailed. In the early days of the union, Pennsylvania and New York were more tolerant of different religions, and some Northern states resisted efforts to exclude free blacks. Jefferson fought against the Alien and Sedition Laws. And in the 1850s and 1860s, Lincoln and Schurz strongly supported immigration. Thus, at least through the mid-1850s, federal immigration policies remained open.

CHAPTER 2

The Undesirable Asian

The discovery of gold, a rice shortage, and the recruitment of Asian labor led to noticeable Asian migration in the nineteenth century, which in turn triggered a backlash against that migration. Examining the impetus and development of exclusion laws directed first at Chinese and eventually at all Asian immigrants reveals a sordid tale of racism and xenophobia that demonstrates the extremes to which the nation would go to keep out groups that simply did not fit into the prevailing image of community and *true Americans*. The antipathy demonstrated toward Asians paralleled the repugnance that America showed to African slaves. The attack on Asians would later serve as the model for exclusion of eastern and southern Europeans.

For 350 years after Columbus, Asian immigration to America was virtually nonexistent. The United States imposed no restrictions, but beginning in the seventeenth century Japan, Korea, and China executed émigrés upon their return. In other Asian countries, there appears to have been less desire, need, and ability to resettle in the United States. Few Asians did so before the mid-1800s, even though the era was one of free and open immigration from the U.S. federal perspective.

Indispensable Yet Undesirable

Chinese were the first to enter the United States in numbers. Driven by the rice shortage and devastation of the Taiping Rebellion and drawn by the lure of gold, Chinese peasants and laborers began making the long journey in the 1840s. As the population of China increased dramatically from 275 million in 1779 to 430 million in 1850, rice became scarce, particularly in the populous Guangdong and Fujian provinces. The declining Qing dynasty government, severely weakened by the 1839–42 Opium War with Britain and the 1850–64 Taiping Rebellion, was unable to control its own borders, let alone enforce its emigration law. With the cession of Hong Kong to Britain at the conclusion of the war in 1842, southeastern China was for the first time open to travelers and trade with the West.

Early on, the Chinese were officially welcomed in the United States. The simultaneous opening of both China and the American West, along with the discovery of gold in 1848, led to a growing demand for and a ready supply of Chinese labor. Chinese were actively recruited to fill needs in railroad construction, laundries, and domestic service. In 1852, the governor of California even recommended a system of land grants to induce the immigration and settlement of Chinese. A decade later, a select committee of the California legislature advocated continued support of Chinese immigration. It reported that the 50,000 Chinese in the state paid almost $14 million annually in taxes, licenses, duties, freights, and other charges, that their cheap labor would be of great value in developing the new industries of the state, and that trade with China should be fostered. After the Civil War, some Southern plantation owners seriously considered replacing their former slaves with Chinese laborers.

Drawing praise for their industriousness and abilities and for their willingness to accept lower wages, Chinese were considered almost indispensable. Chinese immigrants were regarded as less demanding and more dependable than other laborers. After all, they were escaping a rice shortage and the devastation of war, so they desperately needed work. Even the skeptical had their reasons for coming to see the usefulness of the Chinese. The Central Pacific Railroad, doubtful about Chinese ability to handle heavy construction but frustrated over the dependability of the native workforce, decided nonetheless to hire them. They were available, placer mining was giving out, and they could be purchased for two-thirds the price of white workers. Eventually, it was widely acknowledged that without the Chinese, it would have been impossible to complete the western portion of the transcontinental railroad in the time required by Congress.[1] By 1882, about 300,000 Chinese had entered the country and about 100,000 remained working on the West Coast.

Favorable sentiment was certainly not universal. In 1857 at the Oregon constitutional convention, a nativist amendment was introduced to exclude Chinese. It failed principally because most in attendance felt that Chinese made "good washers, good cooks, and good servants."[2] Despite official encouragement of importing Chinese labor by some, the Chinese who arrived encountered fierce racial animosity by the 1840s, as did miners from Mexico, South America, Hawaii, and even France. Irish Roman Catholics in California, replicating the prejudice they had suffered on the East Coast, rallied against the brown, black, and yellow foreigners in the mines. This racial prejudice, exacerbated by fear of competition from aliens, prompted calls for restrictive federal immigration laws.

In the meantime, control was also asserted over aliens by state and local laws. Responding to the demands of the Irish and German miners, California enacted a foreign miners' tax in 1850. The law, primarily directed at forcing Latinos out of the mines, required all persons who were not native-born (California Native Americans excepted) or who had not become citizens under the Treaty of Guadalupe Hidalgo (see Chapter 7) to take out a license to mine at $20 per month. The law accomplished its aim of forcing out Latino miners, who refused to pay the exorbitant tax.

With the expulsion of many Latinos, the Chinese stood out as the largest body of foreigners in California, and in the West the full weight of prejudice fell upon them. A new foreign miners' tax, this time directed at the Chinese, was enacted in 1852. "Anticoolie" clubs surfaced in the early 1850s, and sporadic boycotts of Chinese-made goods soon followed. By 1853, anti-Chinese editorials were common in San Francisco newspapers. State statutes and local ordinances like the 1858 Oregon law that required Chinese miners and merchants to obtain monthly, four-dollar licenses were not unusual.

For a time this sentiment gained powerful political backing from the newly formed Know-Nothing Party. (See Chapter 1.) On the East Coast it fought against Irish Catholic immigration, while on the West Coast the target was usually the Chinese. Members fostered the attitude that these immigrants were subversive influences, and induced the federal government to pass restrictive regulations governing the entry of foreign workers. A division within the party over the question of slavery, and the voluntary enlistment of thousands of immigrants (principally on the East Coast) into the Union armies during the Civil War, led to the demise of the Know-Nothings in the 1860s.

The demise of the Know-Nothing Party notwithstanding, by the late 1860s, the Chinese question had become a major issue in California and Oregon politics. Many white workers felt threatened by the competition they perceived from the Chinese, while many employers continued to seek them as inexpensive laborers and subservient domestics. Employment of Chinese by the Central Pacific Railroad was by this time at its peak. Anticoolie clubs increased in number, and mob attacks against Chinese became frequent. Seldom outdone in such matters, many newly organized labor unions were by then demanding legislation against Chinese immigration. Chinese were at once admired and resented for their resourcefulness in turning a profit on abandoned mines and for their reputed frugality. Much of this resentment was transformed into or sustained by a need to preserve "racial purity" and "Western civilization."[3]

Organized Resistance to Chinese Labor

An anticoolie labor meeting on March 6, 1867, shows that none of the trades were in direct competition with Chinese, but nonetheless, they targeted the Chinese as a cause of their hardship.[4] Perhaps this was largely due to the transitory status of Chinese immigrants, who predominantly intended to raise cash that they would later take back home.[5] Due to difficult economic trends in California in the 1870s (largely caused by the creation of new enterprises able to mass-produce and distribute in areas once served only by local companies), smaller businesses were facing potential elimination.[6] In part, anti-Chinese agitation grew out of the frustration of losing the ability to compete: "unable to fight economic forces, small manufacturers and laborers in California chose to wage their battle against the Chinese."[7] Hostility toward the Chinese in the late nineteenth century has also been identified as a symptom of deep racism.[8] Given the dynamic changes in the American economy, especially in California, it seems that the Chinese were laborers caught in the middle of a strong depression in which labor and management disagreed on the best escape route. This situation certainly did nothing to dispel the mystique of the Chinese immigrants perceived by Euro-Americans at the time.

The purpose of the early anticoolie clubs may be found in their activities, rather than just in the name.[9] Primarily, these were groups of people who succeeded in systematically placing Chinese laborers under threat: evicting miners from their production areas, confronting railroad workers, forcing workers from their jobs on a railway by rolling rocks on the workers at the job site.[10]

After twelve Chinese laborers were injured, barracks destroyed, and shanties burned by the attack at one railway site, the leaders of the riot were arrested and ten eventually were convicted.[11] The conviction came with jail sentences, which invoked resentment and increased organization among "workingmen."[12] These "workingmen" convened to establish a committee that would evolve into a permanent organization. The beginning of this organization was quickly followed by the review of the earlier convictions and finally the finding of error in all ten of the convicted rioters' sentences. Throughout the proceedings, violence against the Chinese continued in the form of stonings, beatings, and fires in factories employing Chinese. The operation of the anticoolie clubs reenacted previous acts of discrimination formerly inflicted upon immigrants in the slums and suburbs of various East Coast and European cities.[13] The anticoolie clubs created both the front and energy for subterranean terrorist activity. Through consumer boycotts of Chinese-made products and extensive community organizing, the clubs fostered public acceptance of their actions, as well as interrelated violent acts.

To many workers, the depression of the 1870s was due entirely to the competition of the Chinese. Exclusion of Chinese became the supposed remedy for economic injustice and imbalances. The issue of race overshadowed reform as encapsulated by one of the slogans of an early Workingmen's Party leader: "Chinese must go."[14] But there was no agreement about the appropriate legislation to exclude Chinese. So long as their availability to the labor force existed, the opportunity for Euro-American workers was in jeopardy.[15] Though employers argued laissez-faire economics, politics refined their situation and required them to overlook the "material advancement of the state under Chinese labor, and to consider the moral and political welfare" of the country.[16] Employers were not arguing racial equality, but equality in terms of labor, skill, and wages. During the depression, however, these laissez-faire arguments would not suffice to calm a public more interested in securing employment that they thought had been taken from them by Chinese laborers.[17] The white workers argued the supremacy of their human rights over economic considerations. The debate became mired in moral rhetoric suggesting that the nation had a responsibility to provide first for its own citizens and its own race.[18] The Chinese clearly were regarded as the outsiders—not Americans—by this stance. The workers argued for the substitution of Chinese workers with white workers because their consumption and spending was only limited by wage, whereas they asserted the Chinese ways of life were not likely to change.[19] The reduction of the white workers' spending power was also argued as a contributing cause of the depression.

At the time, Chinese were charged with "monopolizing" certain industries to the exclusion of white workers, but their exclusive involvement in industries like clothing, shoe, and cigar manufacturing was partially a by-product of the anti-Chinese movement itself. After being discharged from factories and sweatshops, the Chinese often set up shop for themselves. It is precisely capitalism that kept white workers out; the wages were low as were the profit margins.[20]

While the battle was over economic enterprises, the war was about who was rightfully doing business in America. The consumer boycotts prompted the use of identifying labels by cigar manufacturers and shoemakers. On the lids of cigar boxes, a stamp would read, "The cigars herein contained are made by WHITE MEN."[21] Activity of the unemployed as the 1870s continued started to become more threatening to Chinese laborers in San Francisco. After the drafting of a new California constitution, the Workingmen's Party traveled the state in support of its ratification. Though the courts removed many of the substantive changes, the hatred for Chinese in California was confirmed by a 1879 referendum of California voters questioned about whether Chinese were wanted in the state. By a margin of 150,000 to 900, the voters favored total exclusion.[22]

The Workingmen's Party was committed to solving the Chinese "problem" by using the law to achieve exclusion and to finding relief for the unemployed.[23] By 1879, the Workingmen's Party held San Francisco's elected positions of mayor, sheriff, auditor, tax collector, district attorney, and public administrator.[24] The party did not, however, have any seats on the board of supervisors or the police force, which were controlled by the bipartisan establishment.[25] Because of the riff between the executive and legislative arms of the city government, many of the Workingmen's platforms were not implemented. Though the mayor determined that Chinatown constituted a menace to health that required abatement, the police would not cooperate with the unspecified orders.[26]

Meanwhile, the unemployed began to develop their own leadership during the long depression.[27] They gathered daily to march along Mission and Market streets, and to call upon factories using Chinese employees to demand their immediate dismissal.[28] When the constitutional provision and enforcing statute requiring the exclusion of Chinese from enterprise were both invalidated by the courts in March 1880, the anti-Chinese movements no longer had recourse to the law to implement their interests.[29] The threat of a massacre of the Chinese immigrants in San Francisco was great. But the sheriff called on the workingmen to clear out of Chinatown and the city police provided protection.[30]

While officially sanctioned physical violence against the Chinese may have been thwarted for the moment, the San Francisco board of supervisors soon bowed to anti-Chinese pressures. On May 26, 1880, the board passed an ordinance making it unlawful to operate a laundry without the consent of the board of supervisors, except in a brick or stone building. The clear intent of the ordinance was to put Chinese laundrymen out of business since most Chinese operated laundries in buildings made of wood. Some 320 laundries were operating in the city, 240 of which were owned by Chinese. Of the 320, 310 were constructed of wood. More than 150 Chinese were arrested for

ILLUSTRATION 2-1   Anti-Chinese advertisement for cleaning fluid showing Uncle Sam giving the boot to a Chinese man, implying that America can get along without recourse to cheap Chinese labor.

Source: 1886 [in Mary Cable and the Eds. of American Heritage, *American Manners and Morals*, 1969, 243].

violating the ordinance, while non-Chinese who operated about 80 such wood-building laundries were not harassed at all. It took 6 long years before the ordinance was challenged successfully before the U.S. Supreme Court. The challenge was led by Yick Wo, a Chinese alien who had operated a laundry for 22 years. He had certificates from the health and fire authorities, but was refused permission to operate by the board. For violating the ordinance, he was fined $10 and jailed for nonpayment. The Supreme Court's decision in *Yick Wo v. Hopkins* (1886) would not condone the blatant racial discrimination directed at the Chinese:

> The facts shown establish an administration directed so exclusively against a particular class of persons as to warrant and require the conclusion, that, whatever may have been the intent of the ordinances as adopted, they are applied by the public authorities charged with their administration, and thus representing the State itself, with a mind so unequal and oppressive as to amount to a practical denial by the State of that equal protection of the laws which is secured to the petitioners, as to all other persons, by the broad and benign provisions of the Fourteenth Amendment to the Constitution of the United States. Though the law itself be fair on its face and impartial in appearance, yet, if it is applied and administered by public authority with an evil eye and an unequal hand, so as practically to make unjust and illegal discriminations between persons in similar circumstances, material to their rights, the denial of equal justice is still within the prohibition of the Constitution. . . .
>
> The present cases, as shown by the facts disclosed in the record, are within this class. It appears that both petitioners have complied with every requisite, deemed by the law or by the public officers charged with its administration, necessary for the protection of neighboring property from fire, or as a precaution against injury to the public health. No reason whatever, except the will of the supervisors, is assigned why they should not be permitted to carry on, in the accustomed manner, their harmless and useful occupation, on which they depend for a livelihood. And while this consent of the supervisors is withheld from them and from two hundred others who have also petitioned, all of whom happen to be Chinese subjects, eighty others, not Chinese subjects, are permitted to carry on the same business under similar conditions. The fact of this discrimination is admitted. No reason for it is shown, and the conclusion cannot be resisted, that no reason for it exists except hostility to the race and nationality to which the petitioners belong, and which in the eye of the law is not justified. The discrimination is, therefore, illegal, and the public administration which enforces it is a denial of the equal protection of the laws and a violation of the Fourteenth Amendment of the Constitution.[31]

The Reluctant and Exclusive Development of Trade Unions

Perhaps because of the difficult financial times facing the United States after the Civil War, or maybe because of an interest in laissez-faire economics, the nascent growth of trade unionism was hindered by the hostile perceptions of many workers who viewed trade unions with skepticism. Indeed, opponents described unions as having a "vindictive, arbitrary spirit."[32] The sentiment related to the same hostility toward Chinese laborers; at a time of incipient depression, working men distrusted any limitation on access to employment. In California at the time, Chinese were the "target in lieu of impersonal forces of depression."[33] Due to the circumstances of Chinese labor contracts, in which several hundred or more Chinese would often be hired at once, it could appear to many workers as though these laborers were organized uniquely as a metaphorical union. In addition, Chinese laborers throughout the United States consistently resisted unfair labor practices imposed upon them.

In 1867, the National Labor Union drafted a manifesto that stated the "true character" of trade unions, in hopes of changing the skepticism many workers had about unions.[34] Attempting to reconcile the conflict between craft orientation and working-class consciousness or loyalty, the manifesto explained that the interest in craft would always be outweighed by a broader "producer ethic"; therefore, skilled workers should join appropriate unions for the benefit of the producers.[35] Crafting the ideology was difficult, but incorporating "all mankind" to the producer ethic proved even harder.[36] When the question arose about admitting "respectable colored mechanics," young men from trade locals demanded that they receive the power to determine local membership.[37] Black delegates were admitted to national meetings of the labor union, but "nothing was done about admission to local meetings."[38]

This history informed the discrimination that would taint the California labor force entering into the 1870s. The unifying aspect between the initial reluctance of union formation, and then the refusal to allow all people to join, and the exclusion and hostility toward Chinese labor was based on an "intense shared conviction of displacement and deprivation."[39] Just as the blacks were excluded from their trades, so were the Chinese excluded from participating in the labor force.

The Burlingame Treaty

The tension between a desire for Chinese labor and nativist/racist resentment of Chinese immigrants is best captured by the commotion surrounding the 1868 Burlingame Treaty. This treaty between the U.S. and Chinese governments represents the high-water mark of official Chinese acceptance. China agreed to end its strict control over emigration and recognized the "inherent and inalienable right of man to change his home and allegiance, and also the mutual advantage of the free migration and emigration of their citizens."

The treaty was greeted with fanfare and delight. Enjoying the international prestige and eager for trade after the Civil War, Congress readily approved it. According to Secretary of State William Seward, the treaty would greatly benefit the United States: "The free emigration of the Chinese to the American [continent] is the essential element of trade and commerce [and] will tend to increase the wealth and strength of all Western nations; while at the same time, the removal of the surplus population of China will tend much to take away the obstructions which now impede the introduction into China of art, science [and] religion."[40]

In discussing the treaty many writers lauded the cultural greatness of China. Some wrote of the "special destiny" connecting the United States, the youngest nation, with China, the most ancient one. Others stressed the cultural rewards that intermingling with the Middle Kingdom would bring, noting that at a time when our forebears were "digging for roots in swamps and forests . . . , the Chinese were rich, civilized, fertile in poets, philosophers, economists, moralists, and statesmen."[41]

Anti-Chinese Sentiment Prevails

The salutary view toward China and its people reflected in the Burlingame Treaty, however, soon clashed head on with rising anti-Chinese sentiment in California and other parts of the West. Eventually, the Sinophobic sentiment prevailed, and the treaty's provisions for free emigration were overrun by a series of laws that first limited and then entirely excluded Chinese from the United States. Only two years after the passage of the treaty and just months after the enactment of civil rights legislation responding in part to Chinese grievances, Chinese immigrants were judged unworthy of citizenship and, as such, unworthy of entrance into the community of true Americans. In amending the Nationality Act of 1790, which had limited citizenship through naturalization to "free white persons" (specifically excluding African Americans and Native Americans), Congress in 1870 extended the right to naturalize to aliens of African descent. But it deliberately denied Chinese that right because of their "undesirable qualities."[42] Chinese did have their supporters. One senator (Senator Sumner) who argued for their inclusion illustrated a broader view of America: "If the Chinese come here they will come for citizenship, or merely for labor. If they come for citizenship then in this desire do they give a pledge of loyalty to our institutions, and where is the peril in such vows? They are peaceful and industrious; how can their citizenship be the occasion of solicitude." Another senator (Senator Morton) on the prevailing side demonstrated the narrow view:

> This amendment involves the whole Chinese problem. . . . The country has just awakened to the question and to the enormous magnitude of the question, involving a possible immigration of many millions, involving another civilization; involving labor problems that no intellect can solve without study and time. Are you now prepared to settle the Chinese problem, thus in advance inviting that immigration?[43]

Histories of Asian exclusion policies generally begin with the Chinese Exclusion Act of 1882, to the neglect of earlier federal laws (as well as the effect of local efforts) that discouraged immigration. The 1870 denial of the opportunity to naturalize was the first congressional step toward excluding Chinese and the first such limitation based on national origin beyond the subordination of African Americans. Another far less publicized statute enacted five years later proved to be equally pivotal.

Responding to law enforcement claims that Chinese women were being imported for prostitution, Congress in 1875 passed legislation prohibiting their importation for immoral purposes. In one case twenty-one Chinese women were disallowed entry on the ground that they were "lewd," although this action was overturned by the Supreme Court.[44] But the overzealous enforcement of the statute, commonly referred to as the Page Law, effectively barred Chinese women and further worsened an already imbalanced sex ratio among Chinese.

The exclusion of prostitutes marked the beginning of direct federal regulation of immigration, though it did little to stem nationwide pressure for further significant curbs on Chinese immigration. During the 1881 session of Congress, twenty-five anti-Chinese petitions were presented by a number of civic groups, like the Methodist Church and the New York Union League Corps, and from many states, including Alabama, Ohio, West Virginia, and Wisconsin. The California legislature declared a legal holiday to facilitate anti-Chinese public rallies that attracted thousands of demonstrators.

By 1882, the Republican-controlled Congress pushed for exclusion of Chinese. While most public sentiment now favored exclusion, *Harper's Weekly* editorialized against passage of the Chinese bill:

THE CHINESE BILL

Mr. Taylor, the successor in the House of General Garfield, made an admirable speech against the Chinese bill during the late debate, in which he exposed the singular inconsistency of the arguments advanced to sustain it. The Chinese are represented in one breath as a rotten race; the victims of hideous immorality, and in the next as a people who are going to drive intelligent and sturdy American laborers out of the field. At one moment every man, woman, and child on the Pacific coast loathes and detests the leprous interlopers, and the next the same protesting people neglect the honest American and intrust the care of their homes and of their children to the leprous pariahs because they can be hired more cheaply. They are alleged to be a class of persons who will never assimilate with us like other foreigners. But those who assert this forget to state that our laws prevent assimilation by making the Chinese incapable of naturalization. Moreover, if they are so disreputable and dangerous and degrading, and if the Pacific population is so unanimously opposed to their coming, that population has an obvious and easy remedy in its own hands. It has only to refuse to hire the lepers, and they will come no longer. Part of the complaint is that they do not wish to stay longer than will enable them to pick up a little money. The hope of wages alone unwillingly brings them. If they can get no wages, they will be only too glad to stay at home.

The only ground upon which the bill prohibiting the voluntary immigration of free laborers into this country can be sustained is self-defense. Every nation may justly decide for itself what foreigners it will tolerate, and upon what terms. But the honor and character of the nation will be tested by the motives of exclusion. Thus in 1803 a bill passed Congress which prohibited bringing to the country certain negro and mulatto immigrants. But it was a bill which sprang from the fears of slave-holders, and which was intended to protect slavery. In the same year South Carolina repealed her State law prohibiting the slave-trade. The objection was to black freemen, not to black slaves; and it is not legislation to which an American can recur with pride, because it was an inhuman abuse of an undoubted national right. We may, unquestionably, determine who shall come, and upon what conditions, as we may decide upon what terms the new-comers shall be naturalized. Against a palpable peril arising from the advent of foreigners, we may justly defend ourselves. Now during the last twenty-five years the Chinese immigration—and a large part of it was cooly traffic—amounted to 228,000 persons, of which more than a hundred thousand have returned, so that by the census of 1880 the Chinese population in the country was 105,000. "All the Chinese in California," says Mr. Hoar, "hardly surpass the number which is easily governed in Shanghai by a police of a hundred men."

Considering the traditional declaration of our pride and patriotism that America is the home for the oppressed of every clime and race, considering the spirit of our constitutional provision that neither race, color, nor previous condition of servitude shall bar a citizen from voting, is it not both monstrous and ludicrous to decree that American civilization is endangered by the "Mongolian invasion"?

For the Republican party, which is responsible for national legislation, the simple question is, whether a free laborer who wishes to come to this country for a time and work honestly for honest wages shall be prohibited from coming, lest China should be precipitated upon Western America and overwhelm the New World. Can any such peril or the chance of it be inferred from the facts? Mr. Jones, of Nevada, speaks of the colored race. But that race was brought here by force and fraud. It is not a migratory race. So the Mongolians are not migratory. The coming of 230,000 or 240,000 Chinese in a quarter of a century, and the presence of 100,000 in the country at the end of that time, are not the precursor of an overwhelming invasion. The bill is founded on race hatred and panic. These are both familiar facts even in this country. It is not a very long time since one of the most familiar objections to the antislavery movement was that the fanatics wanted to free the "naygurs," who would immediately overrun the North and supplant the Irish. It was mere panic. We have always invited everybody to come and settle among us, because the chance of bettering his condition was fairer here than anywhere else in the world. If we now exercise our right to select new-comers, not upon great public considerations the truth of which is demonstrated, but because of race hatred, or of honest labor competition, or fear of local disorder, the movement will not stop there. The native American crusade of twenty-five years ago was another form of the same spirit. Senator George was logical in his implication that if a whole race may be excluded from the national domain because of a local desire, a whole enfranchised class may be excluded from the suffrage for the same reason. Mr. Taylor said of the Chinese bill: "It revolutionizes our traditions. I would deem the new country we will have after this bill becomes law as changed from the old country we have to-day as our country would have been changed if the rebellion of 1861 had succeeded." The exclusion bill has passed Congress by a large majority. Public opinion seems to favor it, as it has often favored unwise legislation. Even the amendment to try the experiment of exclusion for ten years failed. It is not probable that there will be a veto, and the only benefit to be anticipated is that, as we have now decided to regulate immigration, we shall exclude every class whose coming can not be considered to be advantageous to the national welfare.[45]

Responding to the xenophobic national clamor, the Forty-seventh Congress enacted the Chinese Exclusion Act on May 6, 1882. The law excluded laborers for ten years, and effectively slammed the door on all Chinese immigration. It did permit the entry of teachers, students, and merchants, but their quota was quite small.

The act arrested the development of the Chinese American community because Chinese women were defined as laborers. Chinese laborers who had already immigrated therefore had no way to bring wives and families left behind. Chinese pleas for a different statutory interpretation were to no avail. Initially men could leave and return, but they could not bring their spouses with them. As a result, the only women permitted to enter were the wives of American-born Chinese and of a few merchants. The ban on laborers' spouses effectively halted the immigration of Chinese women, thereby exacerbating the restraints imposed by the exclusion of women through expanded enforcement of the Page Law and preventing family formation for Chinese immigrants.

While anti-Chinese sentiment in the West pervaded the halls of Congress from 1875 to 1882, European immigration was encouraged. By then, the Know-Nothing Party had fallen apart; except for the anti-Chinese legislation, exclusion laws at the time focused on nonracial characteristics such as criminality, poverty, and mental disorders. In spite of a depression from 1873 to 1877, Americans were confident in the country's ability to revive itself economically, and the majority saw little reason to fear the influence of European foreigners.

Leaders of the anti-Chinese movement, however, were not satisfied. They pressed for something beyond the ten-year exclusion period, using undisguisedly Sinophobic sentiment to protect white labor. They succeeded, over the next dozen years, through a series of treaties and new laws that led to an indefinite ban on Chinese immigration in 1904. Most notable among them for their increasingly clever techniques and rationales for control were the Scott Act of 1888 and the Geary Act of 1892.

Under the Scott Act, Chinese laborers who left the United States could not return. The Geary Act was based on the claim that Chinese names and faces were all alike, and that a registration requirement was necessary to distinguish those legally in the United States prior to exclusion from those who might have been smuggled in afterward. In the Geary Act, Congress readily acceded to the unprecedented demand for registration of all Chinese laborers with immigration officials, and the exclusion laws were extended another ten years. The Geary Act also denied bail to Chinese in habeas corpus proceedings and provided that, prior to deportation, any Chinese not lawfully entitled to be or remain in the United States would be imprisoned at hard labor for up to a year.

According to the Geary Act, those failing to register within a year were deportable. Many Chinese resisted registration, arguing that it was unconstitutionally selective. But in *Fong Yue Ting v. United States* (1892), the Supreme Court concluded that registration was a necessary extension of the power to exclude and expel aliens. Lawful residents who violated the act's provisions might be deported, the Court observed, since as aliens they were permitted to remain only by the grace of the federal government. After the Court upheld the law, the registration period was extended for six months, and a majority of Chinese did register. If the extension had not been granted, a mass deportation of Chinese could have resulted—something that California agriculture wanted to avert because Chinese labor remained necessary for the expanding fruit industry. The upholding of these federal exclusion laws by the Supreme Court, in contrast to its striking down of state and local laws and ordinances aimed at exclusion, demonstrated the vast power to control aliens that the high court was willing to accord the federal Congress.

Two years after the passage of the Geary Act, the United States concluded an 1894 treaty with the crumbling Qing government in which China agreed to accept the act's provisions. In exchange, the United States revised the Scott Act to permit the return of any lawful resident laborer who had left temporarily, and who had a wife, child, or parent who had property valued at $1,000 in the United States. But in 1904, when China declined to renew the treaty, Congress reenacted the Chinese exclusion laws indefinitely.

The extension of the exclusion laws coincided with a shift in the national mood against immigrants. After another depression from 1883 to 1886 threatened the livelihood of the working class, many workers became convinced that immigration was a major problem, and they successfully lobbied state legislatures to exclude immigrants from certain types of jobs. By the late 1880s, Congress had enacted labor laws and deportation provisions aimed at curtailing the practice of importing cheap foreign labor under contracts that were believed to depress the labor market. Continued industrial depression in the 1890s fueled nativist movements almost until the end of the century.

The 1904 legislation extending Chinese exclusion indefinitely marked the culmination of a thirty-five-year series of laws that, beginning with the 1870 naturalization act specifically barring Chinese, limited and then excluded Chinese immigrants. Not until the alliance with China during World War II would Congress reconsider any aspect of these barriers to membership; Chinese simply were not viewed as worthy of being American. And not until 1965 would Congress substantially alter nearly a century of laws aimed at keeping the Chinese marginalized.

The Gentlemen's Agreement with Japan

The early history of Japanese immigration differs considerably from that of the Chinese mainly because of the strength of the restored Meiji government. Unlike the decaying Qing dynasty (that fell in 1911), the Japanese government was able to negotiate mutually beneficial emigration treaties with the United States and to enforce its own emigration laws. That kind of stature left its imprint on the lives of Japanese immigrants who, at least for a while, won some battles for inclusion into the American image.

The Japanese opening to the West commenced with the arrival of Commodore Matthew Perry and four U.S. naval ships in Tokyo Bay in 1854. Perry forced the Japanese to sign the Treaty of Peace and Amity, in which Japan agreed to open its doors to foreign trade, and which helped to bring about the Meiji Restoration of 1868. In the decades that followed, Japan rapidly emerged from centuries of feudalism and isolation into modern industrialization and international commerce. Yet, for a decade and a half the Meiji government, which was very protective of its citizens' interests abroad, continued to strictly regulate travel by students, bureaucrats, and statesmen.

Between 1860 and 1880, when almost 200,000 Chinese laborers came to the United States, the Japanese permitted only 335 emigrants.

Not coincidentally, the first appreciable numbers entered at the height of the Chinese exclusion movement. Agricultural labor demands, particularly in Hawaii and California, led to increased efforts to attract Japanese workers after the exclusion of the Chinese. In 1884, two years after the Chinese Exclusion Act, the Japanese government yielded to internal pressures to permit laborers to emigrate to work on Hawaiian sugar plantations. The next year, in the midst of Meiji Japan's newfound interest in foreign lands, the Japanese Diet passed the country's first modern emigration law, allowing government-sponsored contract laborers to travel to Hawaii.

Like the initial wave of Chinese immigrants, Japanese laborers were at first warmly received by employers. These young and healthy men were needed to perform the strenuous work on Hawaiian sugar plantations. So many of them came that the Japanese became the largest group of foreigners on the islands. Few came to the mainland, so little effective political pressure was incited to exclude them. In San Francisco in 1869, the new immigrants were described as "gentlemen of refinement and culture . . . [who] have brought their wives, children, and . . . new industries among us."[46] By 1894, the same year China was forced to accept the exclusionary provisions of the Geary Act, Japan and the United States reaffirmed their commitment to open travel, each promising the other's citizens liberty to enter, travel, and reside in the receiving country.

This treaty applied only to Japanese citizens until Korea became a Japanese protectorate in 1905. The United States and Korea had entered into a Treaty of Amity and Trade in 1882, ending Korea's self-imposed isolation as the Hermit Kingdom. Nonetheless, for twenty years there was no recorded Korean emigration. The earliest Korean immigrants were 7,500 laborers who came to Hawaii between 1902 and 1905; only a few hundred of these went on to the Pacific coast of the mainland. But after Korea's protectorate status was formalized in 1905, Japan severely limited Korean emigration.

By the turn of the century, unfavorable sentiment toward the Japanese laborers grew as they began to migrate to the western United States. After Hawaii was annexed in 1898, the Japanese were able to use it as a stepping stone to the mainland, where the majority engaged in agricultural work. Economic competition with white farm workers soon erupted.

Japanese agricultural workers were more financially independent than the Chinese. They were not fleeing abject poverty as much as deliberately pursuing alternative economic opportunities and higher wages. They had survived a screening process in Japan required of prospective immigrants, which was aimed at ensuring that they were healthy and literate. They were determined not to submit to the constraints imposed by agricultural employers. Many intended to become independent farmers, and menial work was regarded simply as a step toward something far better. They considered themselves the competent equals of white workers, with a right to make the most of their opportunities for success.

The determination of the Japanese to secure their place in American society was greatly resented by a rising chorus of white workers. By the 1890s, when economic xenophobia was gaining greater acceptance on the East Coast, nativists—many motivated by racial dislike for Asians—with the backing of organized labor in California formed the Japanese and Korean Exclusion League (later renamed the Asiatic Exclusion League). The league joined forces (and membership often overlapped) with smaller organizations such as the Anti-Jap Laundry League and the Anti-Japanese League of Alameda County. In those California cities and agricultural communities where competition was most intense and conspicuous, immigrants encountered violence from whites who claimed that California would be overrun by Japanese. Exclusion once again became a major political issue, only this time the Japanese were the target.

After Japan's crushing victories over China in 1895 and Russia in 1905, policy makers viewed exclusion as a means of controlling a potential enemy. Many Americans had regarded Japan as an eager student at the feet of the United States. But when the Japanese Navy defeated its Russian counterpart, American observers realized how much Japan had advanced since Commodore Perry's visit a half-century before and how powerful the "yellow" nation had become, signaling a turning point in relations between the United States and Japan. America was so concerned about geo-political change that President Theodore Roosevelt helped negotiate the 1905 Treaty of Portsmouth that ended the Russo-Japanese War and ceded Korea to Japan as a protectorate. In 1910, Japan would possess Korea outright.

In the wake of the 1906 San Francisco earthquake, fierce anti-Japanese rioting resulted in countless incidents of physical violence. Japanese students in San Francisco were ordered to attend segregated schools—an act that incensed Japan and later proved a major stumbling block in negotiations over restrictions on Japanese laborers. Demands for limits on Japanese immigration resonated.

Japanese laborers were eventually restricted but not in conventional legislative fashion. Japan's emergence as a major world power meant that the United States could not restrict Japanese immigration in the heavy-handed, self-serving fashion with which it had curtailed Chinese immigration. To do so would have offended an increasingly assertive Japan when the United States was concerned about keeping an open door to Japanese markets. To minimize potential disharmony between the two nations while retaining the initiative to control immigration, President Roosevelt negotiated an informal agreement with Japan. Under the terms of the so-called Gentlemen's Agreement reached in 1907 and 1908, the Japanese government refrained from issuing travel documents to laborers destined for the United States. In exchange for this severe but voluntary limitation, Japanese wives and children could be reunited with their husbands and fathers in the United States, and the San Francisco school board would be pressured into rescinding its segregation order. Because Japanese immigrants could have and form families a community of natural growth could evolve, in distinction from the more bachelor-oriented Chinese immigrant community, whose population began to decline after the Chinese exclusion laws.

Yet the reduction in Japanese immigration contrasted sharply with general immigration policies at the time. The first decade of the century actually witnessed expanded tolerance toward other immigrants because of the national economic recovery. This resulted in the largest influx ever, particularly of (mostly southern and eastern) European immigrants. Exclusionists, of course, were not muzzled and the decade's record-setting influx was sufficient impetus for the convening of the Dillingham Commission in 1907 to investigate the entire immigration system. (See Chapter 3.)

Japan's growing military power in the Pacific tempered any congressional inclination to give in to calls for the total exclusion of Japanese immigrants. Concerned about its citizens abroad and now capable of demanding respect, Japan proved effective in countering the most zealous exclusionists' demands through vigorous efforts on behalf of Japanese Americans. Japan challenged school segregation in San Francisco and later complained formally to the federal government over the passage of alien land laws in state legislatures that prohibited ownership and leasing of property. Since the Japanese believed that their nation had made much progress in its relations with Westerners, they were appalled that their emigrants were viewed as "undesirable Asiatics."[47] Though there is little evidence that mainstream social and racial attitudes were any more tolerant of the Japanese than the Chinese, Congress remained unable to enact a set of Japanese exclusion laws that paralleled those for the Chinese.

Alien Land Laws

Unlike the Chinese, the Japanese were able to have families in the United States. Since the wives and children of Japanese men in the United States could continue to enter, Japanese immigrants could marry and form families. Japan bitterly resented the restrictions and fought to keep the few family reunification channels that the agreement provided.

But exclusionists continued their attacks and found alternative means of discouraging newcomers. In addition to continued racial animosity, a sense of economic competition persisted. By the 1910s, Japanese immigrants using intensive farming techniques produced more than 10 percent of California produce while owning only one percent of its farmland. So in 1913, the California legislature passed the Alien Land Law (later mimicked by other states), which provided that "all aliens eligible to citizenship may acquire, possess, enjoy, transmit and inherit property or any interest therein."[48] Since the Naturalization Act of 1870 denied Asians the right to become citizens, the Land Law precluded Japanese from owning property. If they could not halt all immigrants at the border, exclusionists at least hoped to make life in the United States so difficult that many would depart and prospective immigrants would refrain from entering.

Japanese immigrants attempted to attack their preclusion from citizenship without success. In *Takao Ozawa v. United States* (1922), one Japanese immigrant took his claim to the Supreme Court, arguing that he should be regarded a "free white person" under the naturalization laws. The Court disagreed, simply concluding,

To adopt the color test alone would result in a confused overlapping of races and a gradual merging of one into the other, without any practical line of separation. . . . The federal and state courts, in an almost unbroken line, have held that the words "white person" were meant to indicate only a person of what is *popularly known* as the Caucasian race. . . . With the conclusion reached in these several decisions we see no reason to differ. (Emphasis added)

So until the Alien Land Law was ruled unconstitutional by the California Supreme Court in 1952, Japanese and all other Asian immigrants were barred from owning land in many states because they were not eligible for citizenship. The message was clear: Japanese were not wanted.

The Entry of Filipinos and Asian Indians

At the turn of the century, the United States was beginning its relationship with the Philippines as it was changing its view toward Japan. After the U.S. victory over Spain in the 1898 Spanish-American War, President McKinley concluded that the people of the Philippines, then a Spanish colony, were "unfit for self-government" and that "there was nothing left for [the United States] to do but to take them all, and to educate the Filipinos, and uplift and civilize and Christianize them."[49] The U.S. takeover met with violent resistance from many Filipinos who had struggled for independence from colonial domination.

The words of the president suggest that a people "unfit for self-government" and in need of uplifting and Christianizing certainly did not have much potential for becoming Americans. Ironically, the fact that the Philippines became a U.S. colony meant that Filipinos automatically became noncitizen nationals of the United States. They could travel in and out of the United States without regard to immigration laws, they were not subject to exclusion or deportation, and requirements for obtaining full citizenship were relaxed. Yet fewer than 3,000 Filipinos, most of them farm workers in Hawaii, had immigrated by 1910. Not until appreciable numbers came in after World War I (when Chinese and Japanese workers could no longer be recruited) did exclusionary efforts against them begin.

The advent of the twentieth century witnessed the entry of other Asians, such as Asian Indians, but in small numbers. Even though those seeking trade were among some of the earliest migrants to the United States, Indians had insignificant contacts with this country during the nineteenth century. The poorer workers among them found labor opportunities in British colonies. Furthermore, the voyage to America from India was longer, more complicated, and more expensive. The few thousand who did come, most of them men, settled primarily in California, and most of them found agricultural jobs.[50] Their families remained in India while husbands and fathers worked to earn money to send for them or to return. A small number of more educated Indians also entered, bringing the total number of arrivals from 1881 to 1917 to only about 7,000.

Even small numbers of Asian Indians managed to agitate the Asiatic Exclusion League, which had sprung up in response to Japanese and Korean immigration. Racial and economic nativism was again at the core of the agitation. Asian Indians competed for agricultural jobs and were willing to work for lower wages in other jobs, so nativists used violence to force them out of local jobs. Not satisfied with making life in the United States miserable and even dangerous, exclusionists also persuaded federal immigration authorities to block their entry. Asian Indians, too, did not fit the concept of a true American by those with influence. The California commissioner of state labor statistics concluded that the "Hindu is the most undesirable immigrant in the state. His lack of personal cleanliness, his low morals and his blind adherence to theories and teachings, so entirely repugnant to American principles, make him unfit for association with American people."[51] Although about 2,000 Asian Indians immigrated from 1911 to 1917, more than 1,700 were denied entry during the same period, mostly on the grounds that they would need public assistance.

Like the Chinese and Japanese before them, many Asian Indians fought for acceptance. Some sought to have laws discriminating against them overturned by the courts. Lower federal courts had granted them the right to naturalize on the grounds that they were Caucasians and thus eligible "white persons" under the citizenship laws of 1790 and 1870. But in *United States v. Bhagat Singh Thind* (1923), the Supreme Court reversed this racial stance, deciding that Indians, like Japanese, would no longer be considered white persons, and were therefore ineligible to become naturalized citizens. Naturalization certificates previously granted were subject to cancellation, also making the "undesirable" Asian Indian ineligible to own or lease land under the Alien Land Law. Thind's attorneys had introduced strong scientific evidence that as a high-caste Hindu, he fell in a line of descent from Caucasian ancestors and was well within the meaning of "free white persons." Ethnological evidence demonstrated that high-class Hindus belong to the Aryan race, and that the Aryans came to India around 2000 B.C. But the Court revealed the real problem that Thind faced: he simply was not within the group that was acceptable to be an American:

> It is a matter of familiar observation and knowledge that the physical group characteristics of the Hindus render them readily distinguishable from the various groups of persons in this country commonly recognized as white. The children of English, French, German, Italian, Scandinavian, and other European parentage, quickly merge into the mass of our population and lose the distinctive hallmarks of their European origin. On the other hand, it cannot be doubted that the children born in this country of Hindu parents would retain indefinitely the clear evidence of their ancestry. It is very far from our thought to suggest the slightest question of racial superiority or inferiority. What we suggest is merely racial difference, and it is of such character and extent that the great body of our people instinctively recognize it and reject the thought of assimilation.

In short, "our people," or *real* Americans, "reject the thought" that Asian Indians could be part of us. The high court's interpretation of the laws made sure that Asian Indians would be kept out—at least from the ranks of full citizenship.

But preventing Asian Indian and other Asian immigrants from being naturalized was not enough to keep them from being defined as Americans; immigration bars had to be erected. Strict control of Chinese and Japanese immigration had done little to satisfy the demands of American nativists, who maintained a closed view of the American society. They insisted that *all* Asians were racially inferior to whites and should be completely barred. One California legislator called for amending immigration laws so that instead of merely excluding all those "ineligible to citizenship," they would exclude "Hindus and all persons of the Mongolian or yellow race, the brown race or the African race." The U.S. Immigration (Dillingham) Commission defined any native of India as Hindu, and the term was often misused to describe all Indians.

Congress responded to this anti-Asian clamor and a renewed xenophobia aroused by the influx of southern and eastern Europeans by passing a new law on February 5, 1917. The constant flow of Italians, Russians, and Hungarians, which peaked in the first decade of the century, fueled racial nativism and anti-Catholicism, culminating in a controversial requirement that excluded aliens "who cannot read and understand some language or dialect." (See Chapter 3.) But the act also created the "Asiatic barred zone" by extending the Chinese exclusion laws to all other Asians. The zone covered South Asia from Arabia to Indochina, as well as the adjacent islands. It included India, Burma, Thailand, the Malay States, the East Indian Islands, Asiatic Russia, the Polynesian Islands, and parts of Arabia and Afghanistan. China and Japan did not have to be included because of the Chinese exclusion laws and the Gentlemen's Agreement. But together these provisions declared inadmissible all Asians except teachers, merchants, and students. Only Filipinos and Guamanians, under U.S. jurisdiction at the time, were not included.

The 1924 Exclusion of Asians Ineligible for Citizenship

The reactionary, isolationist political climate that followed World War I, manifested in the Red Scare of 1919–20, led to even greater exclusionist demands. The landmark Immigration Act of 1924, opposed by only six senators, once again took direct aim at southern and eastern Europeans, whom the Protestant majority in the United States viewed with dogmatic disapproval. (See Chapter 4.) The arguments advanced in support of the bill stressed recurring themes: the racial superiority of Anglo-Saxons, the fact that immigrants would cause the lowering of wages, and the unassimilability of foreigners, while citing the usual threats to the nation's social unity and order posed by immigration.

The act restructured criteria for admission to respond to nativist demands and represented a general selection policy that remained in place until 1952. The scheme provided that immigrants of any particular country be limited to 2 percent of their nationality in 1890. The law struck most deeply at Jews, Italians, Slavs, and Greeks, who had immigrated in great numbers after 1890 and who would be most disfavored by such a quota system.

Though sponsors of the act were primarily concerned with limiting immigration from southern and eastern Europe, they simultaneously eliminated the few remaining categories for Asians. The act provided for the permanent exclusion of any "alien ineligible to citizenship." Since Asians were barred from naturalization under the 1790 and 1870 laws, the possibility of their entry was cut off indefinitely. The prohibition even included previously exempted merchants, teachers, and students. Asians were not allowed even under the 2 percent quota rule. The primary target were the Japanese, who, while subject to the Gentlemen's Agreement, had never been totally barred by federal immigration law until then. Now the message of exclusion to Japanese immigrants was reinforced in no uncertain terms.

Barring Filipino "Savages" and Interracial Marriages

The only Asians not affected by the 1924 act were Filipinos, who remained exempt as nationals and who by then had settled into a familiar pattern of immigration. Before 1920, a few resided mostly in Hawaii; their presence on the islands helped establish conditions later conducive to a more substantial labor migration. They became a convenient source of cheap labor after Japanese immigration was restricted in 1908. Just as the Chinese exclusion law had encouraged employers to look to Japan, so the limitations on Japanese immigrants led to an intense recruitment, especially by the Hawaiian Sugar Planters' Association, of Filipino laborers because of their open travel status as noncitizen nationals.

Growers thought Filipinos (like Mexicans on the mainland; see Chapter 7) were well-suited to stoop labor and were not as aggressive as the Japanese or as enterprising as the Chinese. They were praised as especially hardworking, submissive, and reliable—praise that ironically rooted itself in well-entrenched racist sentiment. Despite the arduousness of the work in the sugar and pineapple industries, the steady pay lured many Filipino laborers (most of whom came from the Ilocos region and other economically underdeveloped areas of the Philippines populated by poor peasants and farm workers) who could not earn comparable wages in their home country.

By the late 1920s, Filipino laborers began to look beyond Hawaii, where the demand for their labor was shrinking, to the mainland where the need for cheap labor, especially in agriculture, was growing. Many left Hawaii partly in response to employers' recruitment efforts. Most Filipinos who had come to the mainland previously had been students. But in the late 1920s, laborers came to California predominantly to work on citrus and vegetable farms.

Filipino laborers differed significantly from those from Japan, China, and India. They were Catholics and had been exposed to American culture in their schooling. They entered as wards of the United States and were free to come and go. Because of their special immigration status, they often considered themselves American in important respects. Still, on their arrival familiar cycles of rejection quickly surfaced, much to their consternation. They were met with acceptance by eager employers and then, almost immediately, resentment from white workers, particularly as their numbers increased on the mainland in the late 1920s.

One strain of American thought regarded Filipinos as "savages."[52] The 1904 St. Louis Exposition had featured certain Philippine tribes that practiced head-hunting. Returning American missionaries described "shocking" practices.[53] The paternalistic view was that Filipinos depended on the United States to help them develop socially and culturally; after all, they were regarded as never having "produced a great teacher, priest, businessman, or statesman."[54] Nevertheless, most white racism directed at Filipino laborers sprang, perhaps paradoxically, not so much from tabloid impressions but more from the immigrants' success at acculturation. They were resented largely for their ability to get jobs and even for their contact with white women. In many respects they were perceived as a greater threat to white laborers than their Chinese and Japanese predecessors had been.

The fact that Filipino men fraternized with white women in dance halls and in some cases lived with and even married white women caused considerable consternation in some circles. California had enacted an antimiscegenation law (prohibiting marriages between "white persons" and "negroes") at the first session of the California legislature in 1850. In 1905, the law was amended to prohibit marriages between white persons and "Mongolians." But in 1933 the law was extended to bar marriages between white persons and members of the "Malay" races, after a court of appeals decided that the prior law did not prohibit the marriage of a white woman and a Filipino man—a member of the Malay race.[55] The new law provided that "all marriages of white persons with negroes, Mongolians, members of the Malay race, or mulattos are illegal and void." Not until 1948 was the statute struck down by the California Supreme Court in *Perez v. Sharp*.[56] The court held that the statute was an unenforceable regulation of a fundamental right, and also violated equal protection by impairing the rights of individuals to marry on the basis of race, and by arbitrarily and unreasonably discriminating against certain racial groups. In the process, however, the language of a dissenting California Supreme Court justice revealed that people of influence continued to hold strong views against welcoming Filipinos:

> On the biological phase there is authority for the conclusion that the crossing of the primary races leads gradually to retrogression and to eventual extinction of the resultant type unless it is fortified by reunion with the parent stock [citing fifty-year-old scientific journal articles]. In September, 1927, in an article entitled, "Race Mixture," which appeared in "Science," volume 66, page X, Dr. Charles B. Davenport of the Carnegie Foundation of Washington, Department of Experimental Evolution, said: "In the absence of any uniform rule as to consequences of race crosses, it is well to discourage it except in those cases where, as in the Hawaiian-Chinese crosses, it clearly produces superior progeny," and that the Negro-white and Filipino-European crosses do not seem to fall within the exception.[57]

To white workers in California, the privileged immigration status of Filipinos did not change the fact that they were an economic threat who had the physical characteristics of Asiatics. They were just another undesirable Asian race who had a disturbing attitude, because they knew something of American culture, could speak English, and in some cases lived with white women. They also seemed to be taking over white jobs and lowering standards for white wages and working conditions. As it had toward Chinese and Japanese, white resentment of Filipinos soon boiled over into violence, and numerous anti-Filipino outbursts erupted in California between 1929 and 1934. Filipinos' strong concentration in agriculture made them visible and competitive (of the 45,000 reported on the mainland in 1930, about 82 percent were farm laborers), especially during the severe unemployment of the Great Depression. Since Filipinos were often on the bottom of the economic ladder, the Depression struck them particularly hard. Exclusionists suggested that the United States ought to repatriate unemployed Filipino workers, for their own benefit as well as for that of the United States.

Calls for the exclusion of Filipino workers were warmly received in Congress, which welcomed any seemingly uncomplicated proposal that promised relief for the Depression's high unemployment. For policy makers, however, dealing with anti-Filipino agitation was not as simple as responding to earlier anti-Chinese, anti-Asian Indian, and even anti-Japanese campaigns. Filipinos could travel in and out of the country without constraint because they were not aliens, so until the Philippines was granted independence, Congress could not exclude Filipinos.

An unlikely coalition of exclusionists, anticolonialists, and Filipino nationalists managed to band together to promote the passage of the Tydings–McDuffie Act in 1934. Many of the exclusionists had initially wished to keep the Philippines, but they soon realized that to exclude Filipino laborers they had to support Filipino nationalists and anticolonialists and grant the nation its freedom. Independence and exclusion became so intertwined that the former was often used as a motive for the latter.

Tydings–McDuffie was everything exclusionists could hope for. When their nation would become independent on July 4, 1946, Filipinos would lose their status as nationals of the United States, regardless of where they lived. Those in the United States would be deported unless they became immigrants. Between 1934 and 1946, however, any Filipino who desired to immigrate became subject to the immigration acts of 1917 and 1924, and the Philippines was considered a separate country with an annual quota of only fifty visas! This was an especially bitter pill for Filipinos to swallow. After first being stripped of their noncitizen national status, they now were given half the minimum quota that the 1924 act had established for all other non-Asian nationalities. And the Supreme Court had made it clear in 1925 that, like Japanese and Asian Indians, Filipinos were not "free white persons" eligible for naturalization.

The passage of Tydings–McDuffie, the last congressional act excluding immigration from Asia, signaled the formal end of an era. The refusal to extend to Asians the right to naturalize, the laws against the Chinese, the Gentlemen's Agreement with Japan, the 1917 and 1924 immigration acts, and Tydings–McDuffie were the legacy of the schizophrenic attempt by Congress to satisfy economic ambitions, some egalitarian views of the world, and nativist prejudice. These exclusion laws remained in full force throughout the 1930s and much of the 1940s, symbolizing a peak in anti-immigrant power.

World War II finally inspired policy makers to extend citizenship to some Asian immigrants. Limited immigration numbers and naturalization rights were granted to Chinese in 1943 and to Filipinos and Asian Indians because their countries were wartime allies.[58] Remaining vestiges of the Asian exclusion laws were not addressed until 1965 (see Chapter 6).

Conclusion

The seriatim exclusion of immigrants from China, Japan, India, the Philippines, and the rest of Asia from the 1870s through the 1930s is one of the most stark examples of the use of immigration policies to define America. Asians simply did not fall within that definition. Although economic competition between white workers and their Asian counterparts on the West Coast fomented much of the resentment, time and again the resulting cry for exclusion from the mouths of white Americans was about doing something to protect "our citizens." And certainly the concept of "our citizens" did not include Asian immigrants. In fact, from the time of the first naturalization law of 1790 that restricted those rights to "free white persons" and the vivid reminder of 1870 changes that explicitly rejected including Chinese, even those Asians who could make it to U.S. shores were confined to second-class status. Although tension over recruitment and rejection of low-wage Asian workers was constant throughout the era, even the employers who sought a flow of Asian workers did not call for full citizenship rights for Asians; the workers were commodities, certainly not individuals to be fully welcomed into U.S. society.

CHAPTER 3

"Translate This": The 1917 Literacy Law

Upon her arrival in New York on March 17, 1923, Ms. Friedman, a twenty-three-year-old Yiddish-speaking native of Ratno, province of Vohlyn, in the Pinsk region of Poland, was asked by the immigration inspector, "Do you read any other language than Yiddish?" "No," she replied. As part of Ms. Friedman's entry examination, her literacy was then tested using a printed slip in Yiddish, the English translation of which was, "Blessed is the man that walketh not in the counsel of the ungodly, nor standeth in the way of sinners, nor sitteth in the seat of the scornful." Although she was able to read a large majority of the words, she could not explain the meaning of them. Ms. Friedman was denied admission.[1]

The Immigration Act of 1917 required all aliens over sixteen years old, who were physically capable of reading, to be able to read English or some other language or dialect. The history of the immigration literacy requirement finds its origins in the nativism that was directed at southern and eastern Europeans who dominated the numbers of immigrants to the United States around the turn of the century, and particularly in the first decade of the twentieth century. At the time, southern and eastern Europeans did not fit the image of *true Americans*.

The literacy requirement is an important example of the "who-is-a-real-American" enactments that have pervaded immigration policy throughout the country's history. The enactment of the legislation also demonstrates the nation's persistent tension over the issues of immigration and who ought to be welcomed into the community. Three separate presidents resisted the exclusionary message of the literacy proposal and vetoed the legislation over a twenty-year period. But ultimately the literacy act of 1917 passed with a two-thirds majority vote in the House and the Senate over President Wilson's second veto.

The Early Peak of Immigration, Eugenics, and Hyphenated Americans

During the middle of the nineteenth century a new wave of public concern swept the nation as the total number of immigrants coming to the United States sharply increased. More Catholics from Ireland and Jews from Germany fled the famines, depressions, stifling social systems, and authoritative governments of Europe. It was during this period that the Know-Nothing Party, officially known as the "Native American Party," flourished in the United States. The Know-Nothings advocated such measures as increasing the naturalization period from five to twenty-one years and prohibiting Catholics and immigrants from holding office.[2]

During this time, eastern European Jews had fled Russian and eastern European pogroms and systemic persecution. Though poorer than their German relations, eastern European Jews were also oriented toward urban life, education, and market capitalism. Jews prospered in American cities, becoming the subject of jealous stereotypes aimed at their new wealth and success. Jews were targeted as tailors, peddlers, pawnbrokers, bankers, and greedy industrialists. Italians arrived in American cities in great numbers around the same time.

Until the 1990s, the decade from 1900 to 1910 witnessed the largest influx of immigrants to the United States. (See charts in Introduction and Appendix.) The new immigration from southern and eastern Europe thoroughly overshadowed the dwindling stream from Germany, Scandinavia, the Low Countries, and the British Isles.

Xenophobia was on the rise at the time. Antiforeign feelings steadily gathered strength at a time when the dominant force of progressivism was also surging upward in potency and enthusiasm. Among the score or more of nationalities now funneling through Ellis Island, only Italians and Jews were commonly distinguishable in American eyes; thus, they suffered the most resentment. Newspaper headlines trumpeted the tale of Italian blood lust incessantly: "Caro Stabs Piro . . . Cantania Murdered . . . Ear-Biting Crime . . . Rinaldo Kills Malvino . . . Gascani Assaulted . . . Vendetta near Oak Street."

Criticism of the Jews included the well-worn claim that they were wrecking the American economy and conspiring to rule the world. But it also involved the older Shylock tradition: the notion of the Jews as an immoral, unmannerly people, given to greed and vulgarity. They met the most economic discrimination.

At the time, organized business, wanting more immigrants, launched a massive attack on labor, and the American Federation of Labor (AFL) turned to immigration restriction with determination. A literacy test became one of its primary legislative objectives, to serve as a tool for exclusion. An alliance developed between patricians and union labor (represented in the activity of Samuel Gompers and Henry Cabot Lodge). But not all labor supported restrictions. In fact, by 1909, new immigrants constituted the majority of the industrial working class; that year 60 percent of men and 47 percent of women wageworkers in the twenty largest mining and manufacturing industries in the United States were recent immigrants. Because immigrants almost invariably occupied the least desirable and most unstable positions in each industry,

ILLUSTRATION 3-1   "Parting with the wedding ring." Caricatures of Jews, such as this 1872 drawing of a pawnbroker and his apprehensive customer, often ran in newspapers of the time.
Source: 1872 [in Wayne Moquin, ed., *Makers of America*, vol. 4, William Benton, Publisher, 1972, 67].

wage reductions and layoffs inevitably hit them first and hardest. It should not be surprising, then, that these newcomers, driven to desperation, began to fight back.[3]

With the support of the Industrial Workers of the World (IWW) and a variety of small, independent unions, many spontaneous uprisings led by immigrant workers early in the twentieth century stunned both their employers and, increasingly, their American co-workers. Foreign workers on streetcars, in the clothing trades, textiles, packinghouses, and steel mills launched some of the most crippling strikes of the period. The Lawrence Textile Strike of 1912 is a good example of the new role that southern and eastern European immigrants played in the labor movement. Watching tens of thousands of immigrant mill workers fill the streets of Lawrence, Massachusetts, in 1912 to protest wage reductions and line speedups, an observer noted that "the capacity of this great host of recent immigrants . . . for continuous effective solidarity is one of the revelations of the present strike." Immigrants continued to strengthen the labor movement by joining labor unions (those from which they were not excluded). For example, the International Ladies Garment Workers and the Amalgamated Clothing Workers of America—each claiming 175,000 members, overwhelmingly Jews, Italians, and Poles—were "two of the strongest labor unions in America by 1920."[4]

As World War I erupted in 1914, an ideological movement swept across the United States. Racial and ethnic stereotyping and eugenics were popularly discussed as an exact science. The president of the New York Zoological Society, Madison Grant, published *Passing of the Great Race*, which called for "Nordic supremacy." In his work, Grant compared old immigration from northern and western Europe to the strong species of the animal kingdom and new immigration from southern and eastern Europe to the weakest species. During the same period, Majority Whip Harold Knutson complained about the "mongrelizing" effect the new immigration had on American society. In addition, the eugenicist for the Congressional Committee on Immigration, Harry Laughlin, theorized that the recent immigration possessed a high percentage of inborn socially deviant qualities based on empirical data.[5]

With anti-Asian immigration sentiment in full swing, however, southern congressmen picked up the nativist ferment on other fronts. An advocate of the literacy test was Senator Simmons of North Carolina, who appealed fervently for the preservation of Anglo-Saxon civilization against immigrants who "are nothing more than the degenerate progeny of the Asiatic hoards [*sic*] which, long centuries ago, overran the shores of the Mediterranean . . . the spawn of the Phoenician curse." The sentiment of Congressman Martin Dies of Texas illustrates how the southern assault on the new immigration blended race-feelings with the ideas of Anglo-Saxon nationalism: "I would quarantine this Nation against people of any government in Europe incapable of self-government for any reason, as I would against the bubonic plague. . . . I will admit the old immigration of the English, Irish, Germans, Scandinavians, and Swedes, the light-haired, blue-eyed Anglo-Saxons, or Celts." In other words, he would admit only pure Caucasians.

So by 1914, nativism displayed renewed symptoms of hysteria and violence. Racism and anxieties over the war beginning in Europe were major forces. The depression preyed heavily on the workingmen who coveted inferior jobs held by immigrants. In Arizona, the State Federation of Labor, supported by the miners, secured as an initiative measure a law requiring all employers of more than five workers to recruit at least 80 percent of their labor force from American citizens.

As the United States was drawn into World War I, the anti-immigrant mood was marked by sentiment opposing the "hyphenated American." Theodore Roosevelt pushed a "100 percent American" movement and Woodrow Wilson surrendered to it. "New Nationalism" and "America for Americans" were the slogans of the day. The *Literary Digest* of October 1915 asserted that the hyphenated issue was the most vital one of the day.

> Since the war has been in progress certain organs and organizations, claiming to speak for large sections of our citizenry of foreign extraction, have at times used language and advocated action provocative of the suspicion that their Americanism was outweighed in the balance by their European sympathies and affiliations. In denouncing this "menace of the hyphen" President Wilson and ex-President [Theodore] Roosevelt find themselves on common ground, and Americans of recent foreign origin have themselves launched a nationwide movement in behalf of an undivided Americanism. This movement was started by a

widely published appeal signed by twenty-four New York business and professional men of foreign derivation, most of the names being German. The appeal calls upon American citizens of foreign birth or parentage to come forward and declare themselves for the United States, first, last, and for all time. . . .

The President . . . [expressed] himself in favor of a "line-up" to "let the men who are thinking first of other countries stand on one side—biblically, it should be the left—and all those that are for America first, last, and all the time, on the other." . . . Speaking . . . to the Daughters of the American Revolution, President Wilson went on to say: "Now we have come to a time of special stress and test. There never was a time when we needed more clearly to conserve the principles of our own patriotism than this present time. The rest of the world from which our politics was drawn seems for the time in the crucible, and no man can predict what will come out of that crucible. We stand apart unembroiled, conscious of our own principles, conscious of what we hope and purpose so far as our powers permit for the world at large, and it is necessary that we should consolidate the American principle. . . .

"We are not trying to keep out of trouble; we are trying to preserve the foundations upon which peace can be rebuilt. Peace can be rebuilt only upon the ancient and accepted principles of international law, only upon those things which remind nations of their duties to each other, and deeper than that, of their duties to mankind and to humanity. . . .

"I look forward to the necessity in every political agitation in the years which are immediately at hand of calling upon every man to declare himself, where he stands. Is it America first or is it not? We ought to be very careful about some of the impressions that we are forming just now. There is too general an impression, I fear, that very large numbers of our fellow-citizens born in other lands have not entertained with sufficient intensity and affection the American ideal; but their numbers are not large. Those who would seek to represent them are very vocal but they are not very influential. . . .

"I am not deceived as to the balance of opinion among the foreign-born citizens of the United States, but I am in a hurry to have an opportunity to have a line-up."[6]

The next day, Roosevelt, addressing a gathering of the Knights of Columbus, an organization composed mainly of Irish Americans, was loudly cheered when he declared: "For an American citizen to vote as a German-American, an Irish-American, or an English-American is to be a traitor to American institutions, and those hyphenated Americans who terrorize American politicians by threats of the foreign vote are engaged in treason to the American Republic."[7] The *Washington Post* also declared: "Now is the time for pseudo-Americans to search their hearts and choose their flags, for if war should come they might be too late."[8] The 100 percent American campaign helped pave the way to the enactment of the 1917 immigration act that contained the literacy test.

Anti-Catholic Sentiment in the United States as Impetus for the Literacy Law

The United States has long been characterized by a unique blend of "nativism."[9] European settlers to North America brought traditions of cultural, ethnic, and racial prejudice with them from their home countries. The supremacy of the English after the wars of the mid-seventeenth century, and more important, 1763, would ensure the dominance of British biases in English-language media in America. Early-nineteenth-century American publications would feature anti-Catholic, anti-Spanish, and anti-Irish depictions, despite two rather desperate wars with Great Britain.

Anti-Catholic sentiment among the majority of people in England remained strong for decades, even centuries. "No Popery" was a rallying cry even as late as the 1780 Gordon Riots when a mob controlled London for four days. The November 5, 1780 execution of the "Gunpowder Conspirator" demonstrates an anti-Catholic sentiment that the United States has struggled with since its inception. Until 1797, English law mandated that no Catholic male could vote in local elections, and until 1829, the same restriction applied to parliamentary elections. Repression of this kind over such a long time led to an impoverishment of the whole kingdom. (See also Chapter 1.)

Fear of immigrants was a significant issue in the 1800s. As John Higham points out, however, both antiradical and anti-Catholic strains of nativism "aimed from the outset to define the nation's enemies rather than its essence. The essence of nativism developed later. The belief that the United States belongs in some special sense to the Anglo-Saxon race offered an interpretation of the source of national greatness."[10]

Screeds against the Spanish, and later Mexico, during the 1820s and 1840s seemed reminiscent of the era of the Spanish Armada. As late as the mid-1800s, American images of Catholic monks and nuns seemed to have been drawn from the time of Henry VIII. Between 1890 and 1920, anti-immigrant sentiment peaked among Protestant Anglo-Americans. Competing periodicals and newspapers at the time regularly featured familiar ethnic and racial images.[11]

One example of anti-Italian sentiment around the turn of the century was the "Crescent City Lynchings" scandal that rocked New Orleans. New Orleans was one of the first cities in the United States to see large numbers of Italian immigrants, who began arriving in the late nineteenth century. Primarily from Sicily, they tended to live isolated from everybody else and usually endeavored to corner a particular market or trade. In this case, the thriving docks of New Orleans primarily employed the Italians in the import and export of fruit. While most Sicilians went about it honestly under the rules of the free market, some preferred to do it another way—through the Mafia. The bungled 1890 attempt to find and convict alleged Italian killers of the New Orleans police chief disintegrated into the worst mass lynching in American history and the most famous international incident of "The Gilded Age."[12]

An hour before midnight on October 15, 1890, Chief David Hennessy was fatally wounded as he walked home from New Orleans police headquarters. As he lay dying, he murmured that "Dagos" had shot him. Because the popular young police chief had intended to testify in a trial involving two rival families of Italian fruit stevedores later that week, he was taken at his word. Mass arrests shook New Orleans' Italian immigrant community. After four months of police and municipal bungling, nineteen Italians and Italian Americans were indicted for the murder. Nine men were tried in what has been called "the greatest legal event in New Orleans history." When the jury acquitted six of the defendants and announced mistrials for the remaining three, a mob of 8,000 people led by the city's political and social elite smashed their way into the Parish Prison. Nine of the prisoners were shot. One was hanged from a lamppost, another from a tree. The mob's leaders argued that their actions returned the rule of law to New Orleans. The incident made the term *Mafia* a household word in America for the first time and gave rise to an international incident that led the United States to the brink of war with Italy.[13]

Though the New Orleans lynchings were among the worst in American history, many Italians were killed in other parts of the country as well. Most of the murders and lynchings occurred in the South, where the Ku Klux Klan began a campaign of terror against Italians. Academics and social scientists also set out to "prove" that Italians were violent, corrupt, lazy, and untrustworthy by nature. These stereotypes stimulated the spread of nativism.

In some respects Italians inherited the animosity previously aimed at the Irish (as Catholics). Most Italian immigrants were preindustrial peasants, unfamiliar with the industrial cities in which they sought to work. Early stereotypes of Italians featured organ grinders with bandannas, earrings, slouch hats, and large mustaches. Following the sensational Mafia/Black Hand trial in New Orleans at the turn of the century, Italians became inextricably linked with urban organized crime in the minds of the Protestant middle class. The Anglo-Protestant contempt for the Irish was reshaped and redirected at Italians.

The ideological preferences associated with Italians did nothing to mitigate the discrimination aimed at them. On July 29, 1900, Gaetano Bresci, an anarchist from Paterson, New Jersey, assassinated King Umberto I of Italy after the Italian government killed hundreds of workers gathered for peaceful demonstrations in Milan. From about 1880 until World War I, anarchism was a popular political force in Italy. Many Italian communities in America became centers for anarchist groups. Although Italian anarchists did not advocate the use of indiscriminate violence, in the American popular consciousness, the Italian immigrant came to be seen as a dangerous political subversive, with a bomb in one hand and a dagger in the other.

Italians had become an important part of labor and the working class by the turn of the century. In 1910, a Chicago strike led by Italian workers resulted in the formation of the Amalgamated Clothing Workers of America. A fire on March 25, 1911, at the Triangle Shirtwaist Factory in New York City claimed the lives of 145 female garment workers, trapped by locked exit doors; 75 of the women were Italian American. The tragedy forced the country to pass legislation to improve working conditions. By then, the Italian American population was noticeable in major U.S. cities: New York: 340,765; San Francisco: 16,918; New Orleans: 8,066; Chicago: 45,169; Philadelphia: 45,308; Boston: 31,308.

When the United States entered World War I in 1917—the same year the literacy requirement was enacted in an attempt to stem the flow of immigrants from southern and eastern Europe—12 percent of the U.S. Army was composed of Italian Americans.

The Storied Path toward the Literacy Law

In 1887, economist Edward W. Bemis, one of the first intellectuals to perceive a shift in the sources of immigration, proposed in a series of lectures that the United States should exclude all male adults unable to read and write in their own language. This, he contended, would help American wage earners by reducing by 50 percent the influx of nationalities with a low standard of living—the Italians, Poles, and Hungarians.

The literacy proposal erupted with political force, under the aegis of the American Protective Association (APA), during the economic troubles of the 1880s and 1890s. The APA, an anti-Catholic organization, reached its peak of influence in the state and congressional elections of 1894.

As the federal government began building the Ellis Island facility in New York Harbor, the Immigration Act of 1891 was enacted, which included the first provision for deporting aliens. (See Chapter 11.) But restrictionists were unsatisfied and continued to lobby, without success, for a law to require literacy tests of immigrants.

Bemis's proposal made no headway until Henry Cabot Lodge (by then a member of the U.S. House of Representatives, later a leader of the conservative wing of the Republican Party as a U.S. senator) took it up in early 1891. For Bemis, as well as for most subsequent advocates, the literacy requirement was chiefly a means of discriminating against "alien races" rather than of elevating American workingmen. And the increasing concerns of the American workingmen were a real issue when Ellis Island in New York harbor became the nation's primary immigration station on January 1, 1892. In 1902 the station became the focal point of the first of a long line of corruption and brutality scandals that would sweep over the United States's efforts to regulate immigration. President Theodore Roosevelt was shocked and appointed a respected Wall Street lawyer to clean up the problems.[14] The literacy proponents realized that consular inspection would not discriminate between nationalities and that a large head tax would establish a blatantly undemocratic property qualification.

The literacy test, on the other hand, provided a highly "respectable" cultural determinant that would also minister to Anglo-Saxon sensibilities. Riding on the wave of anti-immigrant feeling that was supported by the progressive labor movement, a still festering anti-Catholic sentiment, and prominent New England figures like Henry Cabot Lodge, additional legislation was approved establishing a permanent superintendent of immigration and extending the list of inadmissible aliens to polygamists and those suffering from "loathsome and contagious diseases." "No one," said Senator Chandler in 1892, "has suggested a race distinction. We are confronted with the fact, however, that the poorest immigrants do come from certain races."

As the Republican Congress assembled in December 1895, Senator Lodge introduced and took charge of the literacy bill drawn up by the Immigration Restriction League. Congressman McCall of Massachusetts submitted the same bill to the House of Representatives.[15] A sudden revival of Italian immigration in the spring of 1896 added impetus to the restriction movement.[16]

In April 1846, after two days of fierce debate, the bill passed in the House by 195 to 26. However, Senator Lodge was unable to secure the same result in the Senate. The best he could do was secure an agreement that left the bill as unfinished business to be called up when Congress reconvened after the elections.[17]

After the new session opened in December 1896, the Republican Senate caucus pressed for action on the immigration bill. With the help of most of the Democratic senators the literacy test passed by a top-heavy margin. In fact, confident of support, restrictionists secured a conference committee that "harmonized" the House and Senate versions by writing a *more drastic* measure than either House alone had adopted.[18]

The final conference report came before the Senate in February 1897; however, due to a number of factors, the tide had changed again and the report went through by a bare majority. President Grover Cleveland vetoed the bill, and the Senate lacked the votes to override the presidential veto (although the House of Representatives speedily overrode the veto).[19]

A year later, in 1898, Senator Lodge reintroduced the Immigration Restriction League's literacy bill. Now, with additional support from the American Federation of Labor, the Senate passed the bill largely on party lines; only one Republican opposed it, few Democrats favored it. But the House now was less enthusiastic, apparently because of the foreign vote's increasing strength and a new social complacency born of reviving prosperity.[20]

Although anti-immigrant (especially anti-Catholic) sentiment increased during the Spanish-American War in 1898, a literacy test proposal was defeated again in 1902. But by 1906, increased support for the restrictionist perspective was bolstered when labor began to organize efforts in support of an immigrant literacy test (forced largely by employers' demands for immigrant labor). The support was primarily generated in the South and the Far West by nativist labor leaders like Underwood, Gompers, and Lodge.[21]

Though immigration legislation was enacted in 1907, a compromise was reached by those opposing the literacy test. The European immigrant head tax was doubled, and the Bureau of Immigration's Department of Information established a commission charged with making an "exhaustive investigation of the impact of immigration on the nation." The empanelment of a commission was a substitute for the literacy test, meant to pacify nativists until immigrant opposition to the literacy test was better organized.[22]

On the heels of the largest immigration decade in U.S. history to that point, in 1911, the Immigration (Dillingham) Commission revealed its much-anticipated report in forty-two volumes. Its recommendations were largely technical, but it took a moderately restrictionist position. The commission endorsed the old device of a literacy test; it favored on economic grounds a reduction in the supply of unskilled immigrant labor; and it cast its mountainous social and economic data in the form of an invidious contrast between the northwestern and southeastern Europeans in the United States at the time. Instantly the struggle reopened in Congress; for a year the commission's recommendations were bottled up in committees. Restrictionists finally pushed a general bill out of the Senate committee in 1912 and attached the literacy test. But a presidential campaign was imminent; this was no time to antagonize the foreign vote. Southern Democrats raged at their party for cowering before foreign flags, but the Rules Committee refused to release an immigration bill before November.[23]

During this same period, the West Coast also began to react to the immigrant "problem" with severely restrictionist measures. As immigration from Japan increased, anti-Japanese sentiment burst forth in 1905. Alive with hysteria, the California legislature unanimously called for Japanese exclusion, boycotts of Japanese business began, and the San Francisco School Board ordered the segregation of Asian pupils. (See Chapter 2.) By 1912 not a single member of Congress from the eight westernmost states voted against the literacy proviso.[24]

By 1912 southern senators voted 16 to 1 for the literacy test; southern representatives voted 68 to 5.[25] Yet, concurrently, both political parties made unprecedented efforts to curry favor among immigrants in the election year of 1912.[26]

In 1913, Congress returned after the "love feast" of 1912; both Houses hastily completed action on a general immigration bill by recodifying all previous legislation and limiting admission to those able to read some language, except for the immediate family of a qualified immigrant. Ultimately, President Taft vetoed the bill. The Senate overrode the veto, but the House failed to do so by a margin of only five votes.[27]

As Woodrow Wilson took office in 1914, he focused his efforts on economic reform, showing little interest in the literacy law debate. By January 1915, both Houses pressed for action, easily passing the legislation. The legislation was sent to President Wilson for his signature, but he too vetoed the bill, making it the third time in American history that a president had rejected the proposal.[28] On February 4, the House of Representatives failed by four votes to pass the bill over the president's veto.

On the same day, Imperial Germany announced a policy of unrestricted submarine warfare in all the waters surrounding the British Isles.[29] The next outburst of nativism accompanied World War I: now German Americans were subjected "to the plain and simple accusation in which every type of xenophobia culminated: the charge of disloyalty, the gravest sin in the morality of nationalism." The crusade against "hyphenated Americans" widened and enveloped President Wilson and former president Theodore Roosevelt. Roosevelt denounced divided loyalties as "moral treason" and demanded allegiance to his maxim, "the simple and loyal motto, *America for Americans*."[30]

That kind of sentiment, coupled with wartime hysteria, led, in February 1917, to an omnibus measure containing very broad antiradical provisions introduced before the outbreak of the European war. An anarchist provision from 1903 was expanded in two ways: first, to exclude from the United States not only individual advocates of violent revolution but also those who supported sabotage or belonged to revolutionary organizations; second, to deport any alien who at any time after entry was found preaching such doctrines. Thus organizational membership ("guilt by association") became a test of exclusion, and, in contrast to the original three-year time limit on deportation, an alien revolutionist might be sent back to his homeland even for beliefs acquired after long residence in America.[31]

Before the measure became law, the lure of the immigrant vote in a national election once more forced a delay. The Democrats posed in 1916 as the party of pure Americanism, but a Democratic senatorial caucus agreed not to take up the immigration bill until after the election. A group of southern Democrats revolted against the caucus decision but were brought to heel.

As soon as Wilson was safely reelected, the Senate passed the bill with only seven negative votes. In the final tally the bill met virtually no opposition outside of industrial centers. Wilson, still keeping faith with the immigrants, put aside his support for the 100 percent American movement and vetoed it for a second time. But on February 5, 1917, his veto was overridden. The provision excluding from the United States adult immigrants unable to read a simple passage in some language became part of the nation's immigration laws.[32]

Conclusion

The history of the efforts that led to the enactment of the 1917 literacy law makes it clear that southern and eastern Europeans, particularly Jews and Italians, were not welcomed as Americans by much of the polity. The eugenics movement was in full swing, and racial distinctions were now placed on a scientific hierarchy with those of Nordic descent (i.e., western Europeans) at the zenith. Now, barring certain races from intermingling was not only socially desirable but also scientifically appropriate.

On the eve of World War I, the hyphenated American became suspect: to be part American was no longer enough; the "100 percent American" movement was underway. The literacy test had many roots. Anti-Catholic sentiment had been strong since the early European settlement of the United States. Being from western Europe was not enough; one had to be a *Protestant* from western Europe. Moreover, the influx of Italian Americans into certain trades (just one more example of a "hyphenated group") brought about the widespread "Mafioso" stereotype, along with fear of the proliferation of anarchy and violence in heavily populated Italian immigrant communities. Anti-German sentiment was also on the rise as part of the campaign against the hyphenated American. Although the length of time that it took for a literacy requirement to be enacted epitomizes the debate between narrow and broad visions of who could become an American, by 1917, the prevailing sentiment excluded southern and eastern Europeans and those who could not be trusted to cast off their ethnic background.

CHAPTER 4

The Xenophobic 1920s

Manifested in the Red Scare of 1919–20, the reactionary, isolationist political climate that followed World War I led to even greater exclusionist demands. To many Americans, the ghost of Bolshevism seemed to haunt the land in the specter of immigrant radicals, especially after the 1919 wave of industrial unrest in immigrant-dominated workforces of the coal, steel, meatpacking, and transportation industries. In 1919, an anarchist placed a bomb on the doorstep of Attorney General A. Mitchell Palmer, and while the blast's only victim was the would-be terrorist, it sparked Palmer and his young assistant, J. Edgar Hoover, to launch a crusade to deport all alien "Reds." (See Chapter 11.) In reaction to the isolationist political climate, Congress passed a variety of laws placing numerical restrictions on immigration.

The reactionary, exclusionist sentiment of the time was combined with the ethnic. The 1917 literacy law (see Chapter 3) was inadequate for restrictionists, who remained concerned about the continuing entry of southern and eastern Europeans. Southern and eastern European immigrants numbered 4.5 million in 1910; by 1920 the figure surged to 5.67 million. The 100 percent American campaign was alarmed that one-fifth of the California population was Italian American by then.

Shortly after the 1917 act, the Anarchist Act of 1918 expanded the provisions for exclusion and deportation of subversive aliens and authorized their expulsion without time limitations. Until that time, the law had dealt only with the quality of the aliens who sought to enter from Europe through the literacy requirement. The number of Chinese, Japanese, and most other Asians was under control by then. No attempt had been made to limit the number of eastern and southern European entrants. At the conclusion of World War I, immigration again began to increase. Widespread fear of inundation by a flood of immigrants from the war-devastated countries of Europe developed. The isolationist mood of the period and a severe postwar depression augmented the already strong sentiment for further restrictions.[1]

In addition to the menace of leftist political influence emanating from parts of Europe, public and congressional arguments in support of more restrictive legislation stressed recurring themes: the racial superiority of Anglo-Saxons, the fact that immigrants would cause the lowering of wages, the unassimilability of foreigners, and the usual threats to the nation's social unity and order posed by immigration. Popular biological theories of the period alleging the superiority of certain races were influential. The theories of Dr. Harry N. Laughlin, a eugenics consultant to the House Judiciary Committee on Immigration and Naturalization in the 1920s, were influential:

> We in this country have been so imbued with the idea of democracy, or the equality of all men, that we have left out of consideration the matter of blood or natural born hereditary mental and moral differences. No man who breeds pedigreed plants and animals can afford to neglect this thing. . . .
>
> The National Origins provisions of the immigration control law of 1924 marked the actual turning point from immigration control based on the asylum idea . . . definitely in favor of the biological basis.[2]

The immigration laws of the 1920s were the culmination of strong political and social arguments that eastern and southern Europeans were not the right stock from which true Americans were bred.

Understanding the Sacco and Vanzetti Case in the Context of America in the 1920s

The confluence of negative social and political images of certain unwanted immigrants in the 1920s is epitomized by the Sacco and Vanzetti case. Negative sentiment toward Italian immigrants was exacerbated by the arrest of two immigrants, Nicola Sacco and Bartolomeo Vanzetti, for armed robbery and murder. Sacco and Vanzetti were poor, atheists, and draft dodgers. They were exactly the kind of people Americans felt might be guilty of anything. In addition, they were anarchists who believed, as many anarchists did, that violence could remedy the injustices of society.[3]

At 3:00 P.M. on April 15, 1920, a paymaster and his guard were carrying a factory payroll of $15,776 through the main street of South Braintree, Massachusetts, a small industrial town south of Boston. Two men standing by a fence suddenly pulled out guns and fired on them. The gunmen snatched up the cash boxes dropped by the mortally wounded pair and jumped into a waiting automobile. The bandit gang, numbering four or five in all, sped away, eluding their pursuers. At first this brutal murder and robbery, not uncommon in post–World War I America, aroused only local interest.

Three weeks later, on the evening of May 5, 1920, Sacco and Vanzetti fell into a police trap that had been set for a suspect in the Braintree crime. Both men were carrying guns at the time of their arrest and their behavior aroused suspicion. As a result they were held and eventually indicted for the Braintree crimes. Vanzetti was also charged with an earlier holdup attempt that had taken place on December 24, 1919, in the nearby town of Bridgewater. This marked the beginning of one of twentieth-century America's most notorious political trials.

Contrary to the usual practice of Massachusetts's courts, Vanzetti was tried first in the summer of 1920 on the lesser of the two charges, the failed Bridgewater robbery. Despite a strong alibi supported by many witnesses, Vanzetti was found guilty. Most of Vanzetti's witnesses were Italians who spoke English poorly, and their trial testimony, given largely in translation, failed to convince the jury. Vanzetti's case had also been seriously damaged when he, for fear of revealing his radical activities, did not take the stand in his own defense.

For a first criminal offense in which no one was harmed, Vanzetti received a prison sentence that was much harsher than usual—ten to fifteen years. This signaled to the two men and their supporters a hostile bias on the part of the authorities that was political in nature and pointed to the need for a new defense strategy in the Braintree trial. The arrest of Sacco and Vanzetti coincided with the intensive, politically repressive Red Scare era of 1919 to 1920. The police trap they had fallen into had been set for a comrade of theirs, suspected primarily because he was a foreign-born radical.

While neither Sacco nor Vanzetti had any previous criminal record, they were long recognized by the authorities and by their communities as anarchist militants who had been extensively involved in labor strikes, political agitation, and antiwar propaganda. They were also known to be dedicated supporters of Luigi Galleani's Italian-language journal *Cronaca Sovversiva*, the most influential anarchist journal in America, feared by the authorities for its militancy and its acceptance of revolutionary violence.

Cronaca, because of its uncompromising antiwar stance, had been forced to halt publication immediately upon the entry of the U.S. government into World War I in 1917. Several of its editors were arrested and at war's end deported to Italy in 1919. The repression of the journal involved a bitter social struggle between the U.S. government and the journal's supporters. It was a former editor of *Cronaca* who was suspected of blowing himself up during a bombing attempt at Attorney General Palmer's home in Washington, D.C., on June 2, 1919; that act led Congress to vote funds for antiradical investigations and launched the career of J. Edgar Hoover as the director of the General Intelligence Division in the Department of Justice. The Sacco–Vanzetti case would become one of Hoover's first major responsibilities.

In 1920, as the Italian anarchist movement was trying to regroup, Andrea Salsedo, a comrade of Sacco and Vanzetti, was detained and, while in custody of the Department of Justice, hurled to his death. On the night of Sacco's and Vanzetti's arrests, authorities found in Sacco's pocket a draft of a handbill for an anarchist meeting that featured Vanzetti as the main speaker. In this treacherous atmosphere, when initial questioning by the police focused on their radical activities and not on the specifics of the Braintree crime, the two men lied about their political views.

The Trial and Its Aftermath

These falsehoods created a "consciousness of guilt" in the minds of the authorities, but the implications of that phrase soon became a central issue in the Sacco–Vanzetti case.

Did the lies of the two men signify criminal involvement in the Braintree murder and robbery, as the authorities claimed, or an understandable attempt to conceal their radicalism and protect their friends during a time of national hysteria concerning foreign-born radicals, as their supporters were to claim? On the advice of the anarchist militant and editor Carlo Tresca, a new legal counsel was brought in—Fred H. Moore, a well-known socialist lawyer from the West. He had collaborated in many labor and IWW trials and was especially noted for his important role in the celebrated Ettor–Giovannitti case, which came out of a 1912 textile strike in Lawrence, Massachusetts.

Moore completely changed the nature of the legal strategy. He decided it was no longer possible to defend Sacco and Vanzetti solely against the criminal charges of murder and robbery. Instead, he would have them frankly acknowledge their anarchism in court, try to establish that their arrest and prosecution stemmed from their radical activities, and dispute the prosecution's insistence that only hard, nonpolitical evidence had implicated the two men in common crimes. Moore would try to expose the prosecution's hidden motive: its desire to aid the federal and military authorities in suppressing the Italian anarchist movement to which Sacco and Vanzetti belonged.

Moore's defense of the two men soon became so openly and energetically political that its scope quickly transcended its local roots. He organized public meetings, solicited the support of labor unions, contacted international organizations, initiated new investigations, and distributed tens of thousands of defense pamphlets throughout the United States and the world. Much to the chagrin of some anarchist comrades, Moore would even enlist the aid of the Italian government in the defense of Sacco and Vanzetti, who were still, nominally at least, Italian citizens. Moore's aggressive strategy transformed a little known case into an international cause célèbre.

On July 14, 1921, after a hard-fought, six-week trial, during which the themes of patriotism and radicalism were often sharply debated by the prosecution and the defense, the jury found Sacco and Vanzetti guilty of robbery and murder. However, the verdict marked only the beginning of a lengthy legal struggle to save the two men. It extended until 1927, during which time the defense made many separate motions, appeals, and petitions to both state and federal courts in an attempt to gain a new trial.

The petitions and motions contained evidence of perjury by prosecution witnesses, indications of illegal activities by the police and the federal authorities, a confession to the Braintree crimes by convicted bank robber Celestino Madeiros, and powerful evidence that identified the actual gang involved in the Braintree affair as the notorious Morelli Gang. All of the requests were rejected by Judge Webster Thayer, the same judge who earlier had so severely sentenced Vanzetti. Judge Thayer even ruled on a motion accusing him of judicial prejudice. His conduct—or misconduct—during the trials and the appeals was another of the controversial issues surrounding the case, but it too would prove insufficient to bring about a new trial.

From the beginning, Moore's strategy of politicizing the trial in tradition-bound Massachusetts had been controversial and confrontational. His manner of utilizing the mass media was quite modern and effective in terms of publicizing the case, but it required enormous sums of money, which he spent too freely in the eyes of many of the anarchist comrades of Sacco and Vanzetti, who had to raise most of it painstakingly from workingpeople, twenty-five and fifty cents at a time. Moore's efforts were called into question even by the defendants, when he, contrary to anarchist ideals, offered a large reward to find the real criminals. As a result, in 1924 a respected Boston lawyer, William Thompson, replaced Moore and assumed control of the legal defense. Thompson, a Brahmin who wanted to defend the reputation of Massachusetts law as well as the two men, had no particular sympathy for the ideas of the two men, but he later came to admire them deeply as individuals.

Thompson's defense focus no longer emphasized the political, but these aspects of the case, once they had been set in motion, could not be stopped and continued to gain momentum. Throughout America, liberals and well-meaning people of every sort, troubled and outraged by the injustice of the legal process, joined the more politically radical anarchists, Socialists, and Communists in protesting the verdict against Sacco and Vanzetti. Harvard law professor Felix Frankfurter, the future Supreme Court justice, who did more than any individual to rally "respectable" opinion behind the two men, saw the case as a test of the rule of law itself. His own research revealed that members of the "Joe Morelli gang" and "Celestino Madeiros" were the culprits at South Braintree, not Sacco and Vanzetti. Standing against the defenders of Sacco and Vanzetti were conservatives and patriots who wanted to defend the honor of American justice and to uphold law and order. The defendants' detractors came to see these protests as an attack upon the "American way of life" on behalf of two common criminals.

On April 9, 1927, after all recourse in the Massachusetts courts had failed, Sacco and Vanzetti were sentenced to death. By then the dignity and the words of the two men had turned them into powerful symbols of social justice for many throughout the world. Public agitation on their behalf by radicals, workers, immigrants, and Italians had become international in scope, and many demonstrations in the world's great cities—Paris, London, Mexico City, and Buenos Aires—protested the unfairness of their trial. Prominent individuals like Albert Einstein, Anatole France, Dorothy Parker, Thomas Mann, John Dos Passos, and Edna St. Vincent Millay spoke in favor of the defendants. Letters of protest flooded American consulates and embassies in Europe and South America. Judge Webster Thayer's house was placed under protection. The *Communist International* urged all Communists, Socialists, anarchists, and trade unionists to organize efforts to rescue Sacco and Vanzetti.

This great public pressure, combined with influential behind-the-scenes interventions, finally persuaded the governor of Massachusetts, Alvan T. Fuller, to consider the question of executive clemency for the two men. It was at this penultimate moment that Fuller asked Harvard President Lawrence Lowell to head a special commission—one of the century's notorious "blue-ribbon panels" designed to legitimate state authority—to review the Sacco and Vanzetti case. The Lowell Commission began with an assumption of guilt and, while it criticized certain aspects of Judge Thayer's conduct, the panel upheld the verdict and sentence. An appeal to President Calvin Coolidge was refused. Sacco and Vanzetti were electrocuted on August 21, 1927.[4]

After their execution, the fight to clear Sacco's and Vanzetti's names continued for the next fifty years. In 1977, then-Massachusetts Governor Michael Dukakis issued a proclamation declaring August 23 a memorial day for Sacco and Vanzetti, as well as all the Italian immigrants who had been denied a fair trial. This proclamation, which was based on the review of the case by Dukakis's legal counsel, recognized for the first time that the prosecutors and Judge Webster Thayer had committed a variety of abuses during the trial. It sought to vindicate the names of Sacco and Vanzetti and their families, and called for vigilance "against our susceptibility to prejudice, our intolerance of unorthodox ideas and our failure to defend the rights of persons who are looked upon as strangers in our midst."

Massachusetts's attempts to clear Sacco and Vanzetti—and its own reputation—continued as recently as 1997. On the seventieth anniversary of their execution, Thomas Menino, the first Italian American mayor of Boston, formally accepted and dedicated a memorial to Sacco and Vanzetti that had been previously rejected three times. The bronze sculpture, made in 1927 by Gutzon Borglum, who is best known for carving the presidential faces in Mt. Rushmore, shows Sacco and Vanzetti facing tilted scales of justices. Borglum carved it when President Calvin Coolidge refused to grant them a stay of execution. Merino said that accepting the memorial was Boston's acknowledgment that Sacco and Vanzetti did not receive a fair trial.[5]

The 1927 outcome of the Sacco and Vanzetti case effectively killed the anarchist movement in the Italian American community. Italian anarchists created a sort of "alternative society" within American capitalism. They formed in their communities small enclaves, close networks of family and friends. Their strong ethical imperative was part of their culture as much as the belief in the necessity of violence in political activity. It informed not only the urge to political action as a means to obtain freedom and justice, but their social norms and personal code of behavior as well. Their networks were bound by deeply felt solidarity, by a sense of belonging to a community with a mission, and by a commitment to the betterment of humanity. The vivid vignettes of militant anarchists support, albeit with romantic overtones, such a contention.[6]

The revolutionary anarchists believed that social revolution was not just a remote possibility. They may have been mistaken, but their view was far from irrational. Before 1914 the world—at least the world of Europe and the cultures derived from it—was still full of hope.[7]

When the United States entered the war in 1917, a great wave of repression was mobilized against all radical movements in the country. The war meant the triumph of American finance-capitalism and the American state, and it brought down the curtain on the radical movements of the time.[8]

By the time that Sacco and Vanzetti were arrested, the work of repression had been done. The Italian-immigrant anarchist movement did not disappear but it gradually ceased to be a significant force, and with the cut off of immigration its years were numbered.[9]

Italian immigrants did, of course, come from a country where traditions of anti-authoritarianism—antistate, anticlerical, antipadrone—were strong and the same kind of battles as in the United States were in fact fought out in Italy during the same era. More than immigrants from some other countries, Italian immigrants may have brought with them a certain intolerance toward authoritarian systems. But only a few came with radical ideas; they sought a better life and found a world that was not very different from the old. If in Italy they had been despised as peasants, here they were despised as Italians. Their life-situations and job-situations in the United States, and the political and economic developments here, were the reasons why many Italian immigrants, like immigrants from other cultures, were responsive to radical ideas, including anarchism. The Italian immigrants heard these anarchist ideas mainly from intellectuals who escaped persecution at home by going off to the New World, where they helped create new circles of anarchism. Unintentionally, the Italian government contributed to the dissemination of anarchism around the world: the anarchist ideas of the exiles found resonance in the lives immigrants were living.[10]

National Origins Quotas

On the immigration policy front, the result of the continued assault on southern and eastern European immigrants was the Quota Law of 1921, enacted as a temporary measure. This legislation introduced for the first time numerical limitations on immigration. With certain exceptions, the law allocated quotas to each nationality totaling 3 percent of the foreign-born persons of that nationality residing in the United States in 1910, for an annual total of approximately 350,000. Since most of those living in the United States in 1910 were northern or western European, the quota for southern and eastern Europeans was smaller (about 45,000 less). The latter groups filled their quotas easily, but northern and western European countries did not fill their quotas under this law.[11] This law was scheduled to expire in 1922, but was extended to June 30, 1924.

In the meantime, a permanent policy of numerical restrictions was under consideration and was enacted in 1924. One problem with the 1910 model for the 1921 law was that that was the end of the decade that had witnessed a large influx of southern and eastern Europeans. So a 1910 population model would include a higher proportion of southern and eastern Europeans than earlier years. Thus, the landmark Immigration Act of 1924, opposed by only six senators, took an even greater malicious aim at southern and eastern Europeans, whom the Protestant majority in the United States viewed with dogmatic disapproval.

The 1924 legislation adopted a national origins formula that eventually based the quota for each nationality on the number of foreign-born persons of that national origin in the United States in 1890—prior to the major wave of southern and eastern Europeans. The law provided that immigrants of any particular country be reduced from 3 percent under the 1921 law to 2 percent of the group's population under the new law. And instead of 1910 as the population model year for determining how many could enter, the 2 percent was based on a particular nationality's population in 1890, when even fewer immigrants from southern and eastern Europe lived in the United States. The message could not have been clearer: the racial and ethnic makeup of the country in 1890 should be perpetuated, prior to the influx of southern and eastern Europeans (and, for that matter, Asians). The quota formula was hailed as the "most far reaching change that occurred in America during the course of this quarter century," enabling a halt to "the tendency toward a change in the fundamental composition of the American stock." The *fundamental American stock* was western European, and the quota laws were designed to keep it that way.

This formula resulted in a sharp curtailment of immigrants from southern and eastern Europe, and struck most deeply at Jews, Italians, Slavs, and Greeks, who had immigrated in great numbers after, and who would be most disfavored by such a quota system. Quota immigrants were limited to approximately 165,000 per year, with the proportion and number even smaller for southern and eastern Europeans than before. However, natives of the Western Hemisphere countries could enter without numerical restriction. Other nonquota groups included wives and children of U.S. citizens and returning lawful residents. Those who entered in violation of visa and quota requirements were deportable without time limitation. Another provision, aimed at Asians, barred all aliens ineligible to citizenship, thus completely barring Japanese (as well as all other Asians), some of whom had continued to enter under the 1907 Gentlemen's Agreement. (See Chapter 2.)

The 1924 law provided that in 1929 a new quota would take effect. The national origins formula used the ethnic background of the entire U.S. population, rather than the first-generation immigration population, as its base for calculating national quotas. Because the U.S. population was still predominantly Anglo-Saxon, the national origins quota restricted the newer immigrant groups more severely than the foreign-born formula of the previous quota laws. The national origins quota allotted 85 percent of the total 150,000 to countries from northern and western Europe, while southern and eastern countries received only 15 percent of the total.

The national origins formula was complicated by economic times. Soon after it took effect, the U.S. economy collapsed. The Great Depression limited immigration; only about half a million immigrants arrived during the 1930s. (See Appendix.) In 1932, at the height of the Great Depression, emigration far exceeded immigration, as 35,576 entered while over 100,000 departed. The potential for immigration increased during those years, however, with the growth of highways and increased airplane traffic. By 1938, there were 186 ports of entry into the country. On June 14, 1940, the INS was transferred from the Department of Labor to the Department of Justice.[12]

The impact of the national origins quota system on the southern and eastern European population in the United States is evident from census information on the foreign-born population of the country. They numbered about 1.67 million in 1900. After the big immigrant wave of the first decade of the twentieth century, the figure almost tripled to 4.5 million in 1910. The population surged again in the next decade to 5.67 million in 1920. However, after the quota systems of 1921 and 1924 took effect, the number of immigrants from those regions of Europe declined. (See charts in the Introduction.) The population increased to only 5.92 million by 1930. The figures for immigrants from specific countries are also telling. The population of Italian immigrants increased only 11.18 percent between 1920 and 1930, after experiencing a 176 percent jump in the first decade of the century. The number of Polish immigrants in the United States increased only 11.4 percent during the 1920s, and the number of Hungarians in the country actually declined from 397,283 to 274,450.

Conclusion

The national origins quota laws of the 1920s resulted from the continued sense of ethnic and racial superiority of Anglo or western European stock for the foundation of who could become a true American. The 1917 literacy law alone was insufficient to stem the flow of Jews, Catholics, and Italians seeking to immigrate. By reverting to the 1890 population as the model from which to gauge the "right" proportion of immigrants to enter, southern and eastern Europeans were blatantly targeted, since their U.S. populations were relatively small in that census. The 1920s also witnessed increasing hysteria aimed at Socialists and anarchists, many of whom were believed to be developing in southern and eastern Europe. Sacco and Vanzetti and their supporters came to epitomize all that was potentially wrong with Italian immigrants: they were poor, not particularly educated, non-English-speaking, Catholic, and filled with radical anarchist ideals on behalf of the working class.

The Immigration Acts of 1917 and 1924 thus became the twin elements of immigration policy, one proclaiming qualitative restrictions and the other numerical limitations. These provisions remained pillars of immigration policy for decades.

Part II

Redefining America

CHAPTER 5

The 1952 Act: Excluding Communists, Homosexuals, and Other Undesirables

Influenced by the cold war atmosphere and anticommunist fervor of the post–World War II era and the onset of the Korean War, the McCarran–Walter Act of 1952 was enacted, overhauling the country's immigration laws in major ways. While the quota system of the 1920s was influenced by the Red Scare of 1919–20, the limitation on southern and eastern Europeans was not an explicit restraint on the entry of Communists and subversives. The 1952 law was more direct and reminiscent of the Alien and Sedition Laws of early America: individuals who held certain political viewpoints were not welcome; those viewpoints were deemed un-American. Moreover, the 1952 law lay the groundwork to exclude another social group that was un-American: homosexuals.

The fear of communism and other "nondemocratic" ideas was an important part of the national psyche since the 1920s. The Smith Act of 1940, which made it illegal to advocate the overthrow of the government by force or to belong to an organized group advocating such a position, was used by the Truman administration to jail leaders of the American Communist Party. In response to criticism, particularly from the House Committee on Un-American Activities, that his administration was "soft on communism," Truman established the Loyalty Review Board in 1947 to review government employees. In 1950, Senator Pat McCarran of Nevada (the co-author of the 1952 legislation) sponsored the Internal Security Act, which required communist-front organizations to register with the attorney general and barred their members from defense work and travel abroad. The same year, Alger Hiss, a former State Department official who had become president of the Carnegie Endowment for International Peace, was convicted of perjury, following allegations that he was a Communist who had supplied classified documents to the Soviet Union. Also, in 1950, Julius and Ethel Rosenberg, as well as Harry Gold, were charged with and convicted of giving atomic secrets to the Soviet Union; eventually, the Rosenbergs were executed. Earlier in 1950, Senator Joseph R. McCarthy embarked on his notorious hunt for subversives, stating that he had a list of known Communists who were working in the State Department; later his attacks expanded to include diplomats, scholars, and moviemakers. It was not until 1954 that he was censured and discredited by the state after making charges against the army.

With this backdrop, little wonder that the 1952 act contained several provisions relating to the exclusion and deportation of subversives and Communists. For example, the law provided these exclusion provisions that, in large part, have endured:

Aliens who are, or at any time have been, members of any of the following classes:

(A) Aliens who are anarchists;
(B) Aliens who advocate or teach, or who are members of or affiliated with any organization that advocates or teaches, opposition to all organized government;
(C) Aliens who are members or affiliated with (i) the Communist Party of the United States, (ii) any other totalitarian party of the United States, (iii) the Communist Political Association, (iv) the Communist or any other totalitarian party of any State of the United States, of any foreign state, or of any political or geographical subdivision of any foreign state . . . *Provided,* that nothing in this paragraph, or in any other provision of this Act, shall be construed as declaring that the Communist Party does not advocate the overthrow of the Government of the United States by force, violence, or other unconstitutional means;
(D) Aliens . . . who advocate the economic, international, and governmental doctrines of world communism or the establishment in the United States of a totalitarian dictatorship, or who are members of or affiliated with any organization that advocates the economic, or international, and governmental doctrines of world communism . . .
(E) Aliens who write or publish, or cause to be written or published, or who knowingly circulate, distribute, print, or display . . . any written or printed matter, advocating or teaching opposition to all organized government, or advocating or teaching . . . the overthrow by force, violence, or other unconstitutional means of the Government of the United States or of all forms of law.[1]

The act also called for grounds for exclusion, and contained detailed provisions relating to health, criminal, moral, economic, and subversive criteria. Thus, even today when an alien receives a visa he or she still must establish admissibility to an immigration officer at a port of entry in the United States. Every alien seeking to enter the United States must first procure an immigrant visa or a nonimmigrant visa from an American consul overseas. The consul cannot issue the visa unless he or she is convinced that the alien is admissible to the United States. A consul's decision denying a visa cannot be appealed.

In addition to these already harsh standards, expulsion was authorized without time limitation of aliens who enter unlawfully, nonimmigrants who overstay their allotted time, and those who are guilty of certain misconduct such as criminals, narcotics violators, prostitutes, and, of course, subversives.

Truman's Veto Message

In spite of his sensitivity to being called "soft on communism," President Truman opposed the enactment of the 1952 act. His veto, which was easily overridden by Congress, was not based on opposition to the subversion and anticommunism provisions nor the new entry or deportation sections. In fact, he was certainly not averse to jailing or throwing Communists out of the country. But the 1952 act was not simply about subversion and anticommunism when it came to defining America. The act continued the national origins quota selection system of the 1920s, perpetuating the policy that defined immigrants from one part of the world as better than others. This continuation of the racialized quota system triggered Truman's adamant opposition to the legislation, clearly evident in his veto message:

I have long urged that racial or national barriers to naturalization be abolished. This was one of the recommendations in my civil rights message to the Congress on February 2, 1948. On February 19, 1951, the House of Representatives unanimously passed a bill to carry it out.

But now this most desirable provision comes before me embedded in a mass of legislation which would perpetuate injustices of long standing against many other nations of the world, hamper the efforts we are making to rally the men of East and West alike to the cause of freedom, and intensify the repressive and inhumane aspects of our immigration procedures. The price is too high, and in good conscience I cannot agree to pay it. . . .

The bill would continue, practically without change, the national origins quota system, which was enacted into law in 1924. . . . This quota system—always based upon assumptions at variance with our American ideals—is long since out of date and more than ever unrealistic in the face of present world conditions. . . .

The overall quota limitation, under the law of 1924, restricted annual immigration to approximately 150,000. This was about one-seventh of one percent of our total population in 1920. Taking into account the growth in population since 1920, the law does not allow us but one-tenth of one percent of our total population. And since the largest national quotas are only partly used, the number actually coming in has been in the neighborhood of one-fifteenth of one percent. This is far less than we must have in the years ahead to keep up with the growing needs of the Nation for manpower to maintain the strength and vigor of our economy.

The greatest vice of the present quota system, however, is that it discriminates, deliberately and intentionally, against many of the peoples of the world. The purpose behind it was to cut down and virtually eliminate immigration to this country from Southern and Eastern Europe. A theory was invented to rationalize this objective. The theory was that in order to be readily assimilable, European immigrants should be admitted in proportion to the numbers of persons of their respective national stocks already here as shown by the census of 1920. Since Americans of English, Irish, and German descent were most numerous, immigrants of those three nationalities got the lion's share—more than two-thirds—of the total quota. The remaining third was divided up among all the other nations given quotas.

The desired effect was obtained. Immigration from the newer sources of Southern and Eastern Europe was reduced to a trickle. The quotas allotted to England and Ireland remained largely unused, as was intended. Total quota immigration fell to a half or a third—and sometimes even less—of the annual limit of 154,000. People from such countries as Greece, or Spain, or Latvia were virtually deprived of any opportunity to come here at all, simply because Greeks or Spaniards or Latvians had not come here before 1920 in any substantial numbers.

The idea behind this discriminatory policy was, to put it baldly, that Americans with English or Irish names were better people and better citizens than Americans with Italian or Greek or Polish names. It was thought that people of West European origin made better citizens than Rumanians or Yugoslavs or Ukrainians or Hungarians or Balts or Austrians. Such a concept is utterly unworthy of our traditions and our ideals. It violates the great political doctrine of the Declaration of Independence that "all men are created equal." It denies the humanitarian creed inscribed beneath the Statue of Liberty proclaiming to all nations. "Give me your tired, your huddled masses yearning to breathe free."

It repudiates our basic religious concepts, our belief in the brotherhood of man, and in the words of St. Paul that "there is neither Jew nor Greek, there neither bond nor free . . . for ye are all one in Christ Jesus." . . .

In no other realm of our national life are we so hampered and stultified by the dead hand of the past, as we are in this field of immigration. We do not limit our cities to their 1920 boundaries—we do not hold our corporations to their 1920 capitalizations—we welcome progress and change to meet changing conditions in every sphere of life, except in the field of immigration. . . .

The only consequential change in the 1924 quota system which the bill would make is to extend a small quota to each of the countries of Asia. But most of the beneficial effects of this gesture are offset by other provisions of the bill. . . .

Some of the new grounds of deportation which the bill would provide are unnecessarily severe. Defects and mistakes in admission would serve to deport at any time because of the bill's elimination, retroactively as well as prospectively, of the present humane provision barring deportations on such grounds five years after entry. Narcotic drug addicts would be deportable at any time, whether or not the addiction was curable, and whether or not cured. The threat of deportation would drive the addict into hiding beyond the reach of cure, and the danger to the country from drug addiction would be increased. . . .

These provisions are worse than the infamous Alien Act of 1798, passed in a time of national fear and distrust of foreigners, which gave the President power to deport any alien deemed "dangerous to the peace and safety of the United States." Alien residents were thoroughly frightened and citizens much disturbed by that threat to liberty.

Such powers are inconsistent with our democratic ideals. Conferring powers like that upon the Attorney General is unfair to him as well as to our alien residents. Once fully informed of such vast discretionary powers vested in the Attorney General, Americans now would and should be just as alarmed as Americans were in 1798 over less drastic powers vested in the President.[2]

Truman's veto was clear evidence of the tension over defining America at the time. His call for racial and ethnic fairness in the country's immigration laws was consistent with his position on civil rights, as noted in his reference to a 1948 civil rights message. In 1946, he had appointed the President's Committee on Civil Rights, which later produced a report that called for the elimination of all aspects of segregation. In 1947, he banned racial discrimination in federal hiring practices and ordered desegregation of the armed forces.

But on June 27, 1952, Congress passed the bill over Truman's veto.[3] By now, the case being made for the continuation of the national origins quota system in the 1950s attempted to be different from that in the 1920s. In the 1920s, claims of racial superiority were blatant; in the 1950s, sociological theories relating to cultural assimilation were substituted.[4] As noted in a report of the Senate Judiciary Committee, "Without giving credence to any theory of Nordic superiority, the subcommittee believes that the adoption of the national origins quota formula was a rational and logical method of numerically restricting immigration in such a manner as to best preserve the sociological and cultural balance of the United States."[5]

Whatever the language, the basis for perpetuating the national origins quota system in 1952 remained the majority's sense of who could be a *true American*. "Preserv[ing] the sociological and cultural balance" of the country through immigration restrictions was a clear message that the number of immigrants from southern and eastern Europe and Asia had to be minimized because more would spoil the pot.

In addition to continuing the national origins quota system for the Eastern Hemisphere, the 1952 act also established a four-category selection system. Fifty percent of each national quota was allocated for first preference distribution to aliens with high education or exceptional abilities, and the remaining three preferences were divided among specified relatives of U.S. citizens and lawful permanent resident aliens. This selection system was the antecedent of the current preference system that places higher priority on family reunification than on needed skills. However, under the 1952 law national origins remained the determining factor in immigrant admissions, and northern and western Europe were heavily favored. As in the past, the Western Hemisphere was not subject to numerical limitations. Although the Asian exclusion laws were finally deleted, in its place a new "Asia-Pacific Triangle" was established with a trivial annual quota of 2,000 continuing the blatant form of racial and ethnic discrimination that epitomized the retained quota laws.

Immigration between 1951 and 1960 totaled 2.5 million, the highest since the 1920s. (See Appendix.) This was not surprising, since the two intervening decades included the Depression of the 1930s and World War II. The gap between Eastern and Western Hemispheres immigration narrowed: of the 2.5 million entries, almost a million entered from the Western Hemisphere.

Subversives and Communists: Case Examples

Provisions of the 1952 act relating to subversives and Communists continue to remain an important part of the law. These provisions also have been put into use much more than those relating to the removal of "radicals" or "dissidents" from our shores under the Alien and Sedition Laws of the early nation. (See Chapter 1.) The following two cases illustrate how the 1952 provisions were used.

Berenyi v. District Director

Berenyi v. District Director[6] is an example of how the anticommunist provisions of the 1952 act were used to deny citizenship to a naturalization applicant who had been a member of the Hungarian Communist Party. The Supreme Court upheld the decision of the lower courts to deny citizenship to Berenyi on the grounds that he had "given false testimony" in support of his application, and therefore was not a person "of good moral character," one of the basic requirements for naturalization.

During the preparation of his application for naturalization, Berenyi was asked the following question: "Have you ever, in the United States or in any other place . . . been a member of, or in any other way connected with, or associated with the Communist Party either directly, or indirectly through another organization, group, or person?" Under oath he answered, "No." On two subsequent occasions during the preliminary proceedings on his petition for naturalization, Berenyi again swore that he had never been a member of the Communist Party.

At the final hearing before the district judge, the government produced two witnesses whose testimony indicated that Berenyi had been a member of the Communist Party in Hungary. Dr. Pal Halasz stated that he had known Berenyi when they were both students at the University of Budapest Medical School and had seen him attend Communist Party meetings there on one or more occasions. While such meetings were sometimes open to persons who were not Party members, and Dr. Halasz was not sure that Berenyi was a Party member, his attendance at Party meetings gave Dr. Halasz the impression that Berenyi was. Dr. Gyorgy Kury related that he had attended a study group at the university in September 1948. These groups met to discuss Marxist-Leninist ideology, and students were required to attend regardless of Party membership. One student in each group was responsible for leading this discussion. Dr. Kury testified that, at the meeting in question, Berenyi introduced himself as a member of the Communist Party and the student leader responsible for the group's ideological education. Dr. Kury further testified that Berenyi had told the group that he had become a member of the Communist Party after Soviet troops had occupied Hungary in 1945.

Berenyi testified that he had never been a Party member or the ideological leader of any student discussion group. He related the heavy pressures on students at the university to attend Party functions and become members, conceding that these pressures had led him to attend some open Party meetings as a nonmember. But he added that he had not been an active participant at these meetings. He also emphasized his religious upbringing and other factors in his personal life that, he contended, made it unlikely that he would become a Party member. Berenyi's wife testified that he had never been a Party member, and four other witnesses stated that, while in Hungary and after his arrival in the United States, Berenyi had expressed his strong opposition to the Communist Party and the communist regime in Hungary.

Basing his decision solely on his own evaluation of the testimony adduced at this hearing, the district judge concluded that Berenyi had become a Party member in 1945 and had remained a member for an indefinite number of years, that he had attended meetings of the Party, and that he had instructed student study groups in communist ideology. Accordingly, the court concluded that Berenyi had testified falsely in the preliminary naturalization proceedings, and denied his application for citizenship on the ground that he was, therefore, "not a person of good moral character within the meaning of the Immigration and Nationality Act."

On appeal, although the Supreme Court noted that Berenyi may have merely joined the Party as a nominal member in deference to the strong pressures that the Party exerted on students to become members, pressures that several witnesses, including Berenyi himself, recited in detail, the Court would not overturn the decision of the lower courts. There was no "very obvious and exceptional" error in the conclusion of the lower courts that Berenyi had been a member of the Communist Party. The testimony of Dr. Kury gave a concrete basis for this conclusion, and that of Dr. Halasz lent further evidentiary support.

Bong Youn Choy v. Barber

Another illustration of the aggressive tactics that the government used in pursuing alleged Communist Party members is contained in *Bong Youn Choy v. Barber*.[7] Bong Youn Choy and his wife Tung Suck Choy, who were both born in Korea, came to the United States from Japan as students, he in 1938 and she in 1941. They married in California in 1942 and had three children, all American citizens. During World War II, Mr. Choy continued his studies, earning a master's degree in political science from the University of California at Berkeley. He also translated Japanese documents for the government and taught the language to members of the armed forces. During that time, immigration officials extended his visa from time to time.

In 1946, Mr. Choy was employed by the War Department for work with the American Military Government in Korea. His wife and children subsequently joined him there. The family was brought back to the United States by the government in 1948, Mr. and Mrs. Choy entering under visitors' visas. Soon after their return to this country, the Choys moved to Seattle, Washington, the primary scene of their ensuing troubles.

In May 1950, the Immigration Service issued deportation warrants charging the Choys with overstaying their visas. Mr. Choy was brought before a hearing officer in Seattle in July 1951, his wife apparently forgotten by the authorities for the time being. The charges then lodged against Mr. Choy were that in 1948 he had entered the United States as an immigrant without an immigrant visa in violation of the law, and that he had become a member of the Communist Party of the United States subsequent to his entry. At his hearing Choy testified that he had joined the Communist Party of the

United States late in 1948 and that for a period of about five months he had attended monthly Party meetings comprised of himself and three Korean friends. He admitted that at one of these meetings he had filled out an application for membership in the Party. The purpose of the meetings, said Choy, was to discuss communism and its various ramifications. Furthermore, Choy conceded that he had paid Party dues through one of his Korean friends in amounts ranging from fifty cents to a dollar each month. A statement taken from Choy on April 17, 1951, describing his communist activities in similar terms was also admitted into evidence at the hearing.

Choy further testified that when he arrived in the United States in 1948, he intended a temporary visit of sufficient duration to enable him to complete his studies for a doctorate degree. He also planned to arrange to remain in this country long enough to afford his children an American high school education.

As a result of this hearing Mr. Choy was ordered deported on the charges lodged against him. However, the deportation order was subsequently withdrawn, and the hearing was reopened in San Francisco in 1953.

This time Choy testified that he had never joined the Communist Party of the United States, that during the months of his alleged communist activity he and his three Korean friends had held monthly meetings simply to discuss the political situation in their native land, and that they had discussed communism in its relation to Korea's divided condition. Choy did not think that these gatherings were Communist Party meetings, and although he did sign a card of some sort, he could not remember what it was. He admitted paying fifty cents to a dollar each month to one of his friends. However, he claimed that the payments were not designated on his part as Communist Party membership dues but were given rather for friendship's sake.

Mr. Choy also testified to events that led to the statement taken from him in April 1951 regarding his communist activities. According to Choy, whose testimony was unchallenged by the government, he was asked to come to Immigration offices on the evening of April 16, 1951, soon after supper. He waited in a room there for about fifteen minutes before the arrival of a Mr. Garvey. Garvey greeted Choy harshly. He had Choy draw a pencil line on a piece of paper and write above the line "South Korean Police and American M.P." Below the line Choy was asked to write "I have a wife and three American-born children." Following this exercise, Garvey asked Choy if he knew what would happen to him if he were deported. Choy replied that he would be persecuted. Garvey agreed and again upbraided Choy. Garvey then left the room, returning with a Mr. Stevens and a stenographer. Stevens proceeded to interview Choy, who continually denied that he was involved with the Communists. Stevens confronted Choy with a statement by Mr. Namkung, one of the Koreans with whom Choy met at several monthly meetings. The statement disclosed that these monthly meetings were Communist Party gatherings. Garvey emphasized the significance of this statement by calling Choy a liar. Namkung was brought in to identify Choy, who still denied Communist Party membership. The interview ended at midnight and Garvey took Choy home. On the drive home, Garvey noted to Choy that Namkung was cooperative whereas Choy was not. Choy agreed to talk further and returned with Garvey to Immigration offices. A second interview took place, terminating at 3:00 A.M. Choy still denied Party affiliation.

Upon parting, Garvey told Choy that if he did not agree with Namkung's statement, he would either be deported within three weeks or charged with perjury. Choy was upset by these happenings and could not sleep. He contacted Namkung, who acknowledged accusing Choy of Party membership. The next day at 8:30 in the morning, Choy made the statement that was admitted in evidence against him.

Charges against Mrs. Choy were also lodged at the San Francisco hearing. She was accused of being an excludable alien at the time of entry in that she had entered in 1948, as an immigrant without an immigrant's visa. She testified that she did not intend to stay in this country permanently at the time she entered, but intended only to attempt to arrange to stay if such an arrangement was possible. Following this hearing, the Choys were both ordered deported.

The Court of Appeals was not sympathetic to the government's charge of illegal entry. The record showed that Mr. Choy wished to do three things on his return to the United States: to continue his graduate education, to support his family, by working, if necessary, and to provide his three children, if possible, with an American high school education. None of these purposes were inconsistent with the statements made by Mr. Choy when he obtained a visitor's visa from the American consul in Seoul, Korea. The consul was apparently well aware that Choy would remain in the United States if it were legally possible for him to do so. None of Mr. Choy's actions indicated fraud or misrepresentation.

The Court of Appeals also did not approve of the government's Communist Party allegation. The court was sympathetic to Mr. Choy's contention that the admissions contained in the statement taken from him on April 17, 1951, were obtained through coercion by agents of the Immigration Service in violation of the due process clause of the Fifth Amendment. The court concluded that the conduct of the Immigration officers on the night of April 16, including seven hours of interrogation and heavy-handed threats, rendered the statement made by Mr. Choy on the following day inadmissible at his hearing. In the court's view, deportation proceedings had to conform "to traditional standards of fairness encompassed in due process of law."

The court stated:

We think the undisputed evidence demonstrates that the admissions obtained from Choy on the morning of April 17 were the product of the abusive interrogation which was followed by the threat of imminent deportation or prosecution for perjury. A statement which was followed by the threat of imminent deportation or prosecution for perjury. A statement obtained by the government by inducing fear through official threats of prosecution is not voluntarily given. . . . It can no more be used as a basis for deportation than for conviction of a crime. In the instant case, the record leaves no room for doubt that the improper conduct of the Immigration agents induced the admissions made by Choy on the following day. . . . It requires a stretch of the imagination to appreciate the mental terror the government officials' treatment caused Choy. Consequently, the inclusion into evidence of Choy's April 17 statement transgressed due process of law.

Therefore, the Choys' deportation order was reversed.

The subversive and Communist provisions of the 1952 act provided the framework for similar actions in the 1960s and 1970s whenever concern was raised over aliens whose admission might adversely affect national security. In 1966, the Immigration and Naturalization Service (INS) implemented the Anti-Subversive Program to get rid of foreign-born subversives and to develop evidence used to exclude and expel. Concern with organizations and individuals involved in antiwar demonstrations was also raised, and security was heightened at the Canadian and Mexican borders. Under the Anti-Subversive Program, a citizen of Italy was denied lawful permanent residence status because he had been a member of the Italian Communist Party; a citizen of Yugoslavia was apprehended because he was involved in bombings of Yugoslav consulates in the United States and Canada; a citizen of Orange Free State, United Kingdom, was admitted as a student and became active in demonstrations. All three were forced to leave.[8]

In 1977, as the Anti-Subversive Program continued, the INS participated in a program called the Cabinet Committee to Combat Terrorism. At the same time, progress was made investigating Nazi war criminals residing in the United States, with 242 allegations made, leading to 162 full investigations. Four such individuals were placed under deportation proceedings, and seven were in denaturalization proceedings.[9] (See Chapter II.) These provisions all laid the foundation for much of the antiterrorism legislation and enforcement strategies after September 11, 2001, as well as earlier in the 1990s. (See Epilogue.)

Exclusion of Gays and Lesbians

The ostracism that gays and lesbians endure in American life also has immigration-related underpinnings partially rooted in the 1952 law. The immigration laws of the nation, especially provisions related to who can enter, who cannot enter, and who can be removed, represent the judgment of our elected leaders as to whom we would allow or not allow to become an American. For decades, the immigration laws contained provisions that were intended to keep immigrant homosexuals out of the country, thereby institutionalizing the sentiment that homosexuals should not be Americans. Homosexuals were first statutorily excluded from entry by the Immigration Act of 1917, which prohibited the admission of "persons of constitutional psychopathic inferiority" certified by a physician to be "mentally . . . defective."[10] In 1950, the Senate subcommittee that eventually recommended the overhaul of the Immigration and Nationality Act reported that the "purpose of [an existing] provision against 'persons with constitutional psychopathic inferiority' will be more adequately served by changing that term to 'persons afflicted with psychopathic personality,' and that the classes of mentally defectives should be enlarged to include homosexuals and other sex perverts."[11] Thus, among the major changes to the immigration laws that resulted in 1952, Congress included in the list of individuals to be excluded those "afflicted with psychopathic personality."[12]

In 1962, the federal Ninth Circuit Court of Appeals, in *Fleuti v. Rosenberg*,[13] allowed a homosexual man to reenter the country, ruling that the term *psychopathic personality* was too vague to encompass homosexuals under certain circumstances. In response, in 1965 Congress amended the law to include the words "sexual deviation" in order to "serve the purpose of resolving any doubt on this point."[14] Now the law excluded "aliens afflicted with psychopathic personality, sexual deviation, or a mental defect."[15]

The constitutionality of the exclusion of homosexuals was resolved by the Supreme Court a few years later in *Boutlier v. INS* (1967),[16] a deportation case. Clive Boutilier, a Canadian national, was first admitted to the United States as a lawful permanent resident on June 22, 1955, at the age of twenty-one. His mother, stepfather, and three of his siblings also lived in the United States. In 1963 he applied for citizenship through naturalization and submitted an affidavit to the examiner in which he admitted that he was arrested in New York in October 1959, on a charge of sodomy, which was later reduced to simple assault and thereafter dismissed. In 1964, Boutilier, at the request of the government, submitted another affidavit that revealed the full history of his sexual behavior. It stated that his first homosexual experience occurred when he was fourteen years of age, some seven years before his entry into the United States. Boutilier was evidently a passive participant in this encounter. His next episode was at age sixteen and occurred in a public park in Halifax, Nova Scotia. Boutilier was an active participant in this affair. During the next five years immediately preceding his first entry into the United States, Boutilier had homosexual relations on an average of three or four times a year. He stated that prior to his entry he also had engaged in heterosexual relations on three or four occasions. During the eight and one-half years immediately subsequent to his entry, and up to the time of his second statement, Boutilier continued to have homosexual relations on an average of three or four times a year. Since 1959, he had shared an apartment with a man with whom he had had homosexual relations.

The 1964 affidavit was submitted to the Public Health Service (PHS) for its opinion as to whether Boutilier was excludable for any reason at the time of his entry. The PHS issued a certificate in 1964 stating that in the opinion of the staff physicians, Boutilier "was afflicted with a class A condition, namely, psychopathic personality, sexual deviate," at the time of his admission. Deportation proceedings were then instituted.

The Supreme Court held that the legislative history of the provision indicated "beyond a shadow of a doubt" that Congress intended to exclude immigrants who were homosexuals via the "psychopathic personality" provision. As a result, the Court upheld Boutilier's deportation, because prior to his entry in the United States when he was twenty-one years old, he had engaged in homosexual activity on a regular basis. Since he was excludable at the time of his immigration, he could now be deported.

The intended exclusion of gays from the conventional vision of a real American through immigration policies also comes through clearly in the interpretation of the term *spouse* for purposes of immigration. An alien spouse of a U.S. citizen can immigrate to the United States and become a lawful permanent resident alien. However, the term *spouse* has been limited to marriages involving heterosexual relationships. In *Adams v. Howerton* (1981),[17] the Ninth Circuit Court of Appeals endorsed that position, stating that Congress had a rational basis for that limitation because "homosexual marriages never produce offspring, because they are *not recognized in most, if in any, states,* or because they *violate traditional and often prevailing societal mores"* (emphasis added). Similarly, it was not unusual for the naturalization applications of gay lawful permanent resident aliens to be challenged on the grounds that they were not of "good moral character."[18]

In spite of Congress's clear intent to exclude homosexuals and the Supreme Court's finding of the constitutionality of doing so, the ability of the INS to enforce the homosexual exclusion provision continued to be tested. Ultimately, the reliance on the PHS procedure to effectuate the deportation of Clive Boutilier proved to be critical. Apparently the administrative practice had been to exclude for homosexuality only those persons for whom a PHS certificate was issued.[19] General Counsel for the INS, David Crosland, stated in a memorandum dated February 15, 1979, to INS Commissioner Leonel Castillo.

> Moreover it appears to us that every alien who is suspected of being a homosexual, and certainly this would include an individual who makes such a declaration [admission of being a homosexual] to an immigration officer, must be referred to a medical officer of the Public Health Service for examination before he may be excluded on that ground.

Prior to the 1952 act, the PHS, in a report to the House of Representatives on the medical aspects of the House bill that later became the 1952 act, suggested grouping together excludable "conditions related to the field of mental disorders and subject to medical determination."[20] For a number of years thereafter, PHS medical officers issued certificates declaring that aliens were excludable for homosexuality as well as for the other conditions listed in the part of the statute dealing with medical conditions.

Up until 1979, the INS processed applicants suspected of being homosexuals in the same manner as it processed those suspected of being afflicted with any other mental or physical defect. The INS referred individuals seeking entry into the United States, whom INS officials suspected were suffering from mental or physical defect, such as homosexuality, to a PHS officer for a medical examination. If the result of the examination was a diagnosis by the PHS official that such a mental or physical defect existed, the officer certified these findings in a "Class A certificate" (as was done in the Boutilier case) to the INS officer. This certificate constituted the evidentiary basis for exclusion at the hearing.

In June 1979, Carl Hill, a British photographer for the *London Gay News,* flew into San Francisco International Airport, sporting a "Gay Pride" button on his lapel, intending to attend and report on San Francisco's Lesbian/Gay Freedom Day Parade. Spotting the button, INS inspectors referred Hill to the PHS for an examination and medical certificate. But before the PHS could act, Hill retained an attorney and went to court to stop the PHS from conducting the evaluation.[21]

The basis for Hill's argument was the fact that in 1973, the board of trustees of the American Psychiatric Association voted to remove homosexuality from its list of mental disorders.[22] Homosexuality had previously been listed under "sexual deviation." Although the trustees recognized that some homosexual persons might suffer from mental disorder or sexual deviation due to disturbance or conflict with their sexual orientation, the trustees made it clear that homosexuality per se does not constitute a mental disorder or sexual deviation, and that homosexuality per se implies no impairment in judgment, stability, reliability, or vocational capabilities. The full membership of the American Psychiatric Association approved the action of the trustees, and numerous other medical organizations endorsed the American Psychiatric Association's position. The federal court ordered the PHS to refrain from evaluating Hill for purposes of determining whether he was excludable for being a homosexual. (In fact, U.S. Surgeon General Julius Richmond agreed with Hill's attorneys and had notified the INS that his Public Health Service doctors would no longer provide the medical certification required to expel gays.)

Based on these events, and especially the 1973 position of the American Psychiatric Association, on August 2, 1979, the surgeon general of the United States revised the policy of the Public Health Service and instructed PHS officers not to accept immigration referrals for medical examinations when the sole basis was to establish homosexuality as a grounds for exclusion. The surgeon general concluded that "homosexuality per se will no longer be considered a 'mental disease or defect.'"[23]

Clearly, the decision to revise PHS policy had been based on changes in medical thinking. In making the policy change, the surgeon general stated that "the change will reflect current and generally accepted canons of medical practice with respect to homosexuality" since the American Psychiatric Association omitted homosexuality from the mental disorders listed in its Diagnostic and Statistical Manual.[24] The surgeon general especially noted that this manual was "one of the most authoritative diagnostic manuals for the conduct of psychiatric examinations in the United States, and constitute[d] the complete listing of currently recognized psychiatric diagnoses." Also, the PHS relied on the American Psychiatric Association for advice and information.[25]

Left without its PHS medical certificate tool for excluding homosexual aliens from entry, the INS initially allowed all suspected homosexuals to enter the United States conditionally under parole status while it sought advice from the Office of Legal Counsel (U.S. Department of Justice) to determine whether it still had an obligation to enforce the law to exclude homosexuals. The Office of Legal Counsel informed the INS that enforcement was still required even though PHS examinations and certifications were no longer available.[26]

The INS then adopted a new policy for the exclusion of homosexual aliens entitled "Guidelines and Procedures for the Inspection of Aliens Who Are Suspected of Being Homosexual."[27] The policy provided that an arriving alien would not be asked any questions regarding his or her sexual preference. However, if an alien made "an unambiguous oral or written admission of homosexuality" (which was not to include buttons, literature, or other similar material), or if a third person who was also presenting himself or herself for inspection "voluntarily state[d], without prompting or prior questioning, that an alien who arrived in the United States at the same time . . . [was] a homosexual," the alien could be examined privately by an immigration official, and would be asked to sign a statement to the effect that he or she was a homosexual.[28] On the basis of such a self-admission, the person could be excluded.

Subsequent controversy over the adoption of this new policy in light of the surgeon general's new position on homosexuality demonstrated the tension over whether gays and lesbians should be accepted into the world of *real* Americans. Consider two cases— the second Carl Hill case and the naturalization attempt by Richard John Longstaff.

The Carl Hill Challenge

The "unambiguous admission" exclusion policy was challenged immediately after its adoption. Once again, Carl Hill was the litigant. A year after his first encounter with the INS, Hill returned on November 5, 1980, seeking entry into the United States as a tourist. His attorneys knew he was coming, and the local INS authorities were notified that he would be testing the new policy.[29] On arrival, Hill made an unsolicited statement to the immigration inspector that he was a homosexual. The inspector then issued to Hill Form I-122, entitled "Notice to Applicant for Admission Detained for Hearing Before Immigration Judge," notifying Hill that he appeared to be excludable pursuant to the law.

At the exclusion hearing held on November 7, 1980, Hill acknowledged that he made the statement that he was a homosexual to the INS officer, and testified that he was a homosexual. However, federal immigration judge Bernard Hornbach determined that Hill could not be found excludable based on this self-admission. The judge felt compelled to rule in this manner because no medical certification was issued by a PHS officer that Hill was afflicted with a sexual deviation or mental defect. The judge ruled that such certification was statutorily required. In his decision, Judge Hornback stated: "The stand which the Surgeon General has taken leaves the Justice Department and the Immigration Service in the unenviable position of being charged with the enforcement of a law whose tools of enforcement have been withdrawn. Without the Class 'A' Certificate of the Surgeon General, I am powerless to exclude this man."[30] The "stand" of the surgeon general that the immigration judge referred to related to the surgeon general's amended position on homosexuality, refusing to recognize homosexuality as a medical problem.

However, a few months later, the Board of Immigration Appeals overruled Judge Hornbach's decision, ruling that an individual seeking entry who made an unsolicited, unambiguous statement admitting homosexuality failed to meet the burden of establishing admissibility to the United States. Under those circumstances, the board ruled that the INS was not required to obtain a PHS medical certificate that the homosexual alien was afflicted with a sexual deviation or mental disorder.

Hill appealed the ruling of the Board of Immigration Appeals to the federal district court in San Francisco. The issue for the federal court was clear: whether the INS could exclude a homosexual applicant from entry into the United States in the absence of a Class A medical certificate by the PHS where the applicant had made an unambiguous statement that he or she was a homosexual.

The federal district court and ultimately the federal Ninth Circuit Court of Appeals again ruled in Hill's favor.[31] The courts felt that a reading of the applicable portions of the Immigration and Nationality Act, and corresponding legislative history, indicated the intent of Congress that homosexuality be a medical exclusion, and therefore a medical certificate was required to exclude a homosexual from entry into the United States. The excludable aliens statute placed persons afflicted with a psychopathic personality, a sexual deviation, or a mental defect among six other classes of aliens excludable for medical reasons.[32] The statutes governing the detention, observation, and examination of arriving aliens also affirmed the medical basis for the exclusion of homosexuals, and pointed out the requirement of obtaining a medical certificate to exclude. True, the act did not explicitly state that a medical certificate was required for exclusion under the law. But to the federal courts, the language and structure of the act made it clear that such was the intent of Congress.

The first relevant section provided:

For the purpose of determining whether aliens (including alien crewmen) arriving at ports of the United States belong to any of the classes excluded by this chapter, by reason of being afflicted with any of the diseases or mental or physical defects or disabilities set forth in section 1182(a) of this title . . . , such aliens *shall be detained* . . . , for a sufficient time to enable the immigration officers and medical officers to subject such aliens to observation and an examination sufficient to determine whether or not they belong to the excluded classes.[33]

Congress's proviso that aliens suspected of affliction with mental disability "shall be detained" before entering the country to allow for observation and examination was convincing evidence that Congress intended for such examinations to take place and to be a prerequisite to exclusion on such grounds.

The next relevant section provided:

The physical and mental examination of arriving aliens (including alien crewmen) *shall* be made by medical officers of the United States Public Health Service, who *shall* conduct *all* medical examinations and *shall certify,* for the information of the immigration officers and the special inquiry officers, any physical and mental defect or disease observed by such medical officers in any such alien. . . . Medical officers of the United States Public Health Service who have had *special training in the diagnosis of insanity and mental defects* shall be detailed for duty or employed at such ports of entry as the Attorney General may designate, and such medical officers shall be provided with suitable facilities for the detention and examination of all arriving aliens who it is suspected may be excludable under paragraphs (1) to (4) or (5) of section 1182(a) of this title.[34]

The section thus contemplated that aliens sought to be excluded would be given a medical examination. Moreover, the section required that medical officers conduct all medical examinations. It would thus violate Congress's direction to allow INS officers who were not medically trained to determine psychopathic personality, sexual deviation, or mental defect by trained physicians was borne out by the last sentence of section 1224, which allowed for an appeal of a medical determination of excludability under 8 U.S.C. § 1182(a)(4) to a board of medical officers of the PHS to be convened by the surgeon general.

Congress made its intent to require a medical examination even clearer in another section, which provided:

> If a medical officer or civil surgeon or board of medical officers has certified under section 1224 of this title that an alien is afflicted with a disease specified in section 1182(a)(6) of this title, or with any mental disease, defect, or disability which would bring such alien within any of the classes excluded from admission to the United States under paragraphs (1) to (4) or (5) of section 1182(a) of this title, the decision of the special inquiry officer shall be based *solely* upon such certification.[35]

The provision that a decision to exclude be based *solely* on the medical certificate had to be considered with the prior sections mandating physical and mental examinations by public health doctors, and the omission of any other means of determining this type of excludability. A strong implication arose that the certificate was a prerequisite to exclusion. The sections imply that other evidence, such as admissions made to an immigration officer, should not be considered.

The final relevant section stated:

> The inspection, *other than the physical and mental examination,* of aliens (including alien crewmen) seeking admission or readmission to or the privilege of passing through the United States shall be conducted by immigration officers, except as otherwise provided in regard to special inquiry officers.[36]

The import of this section was that immigration officers were not to perform physical and mental examinations by obtaining admissions; doctors were to perform the mental and physical examinations.

The legislative history of the 1952 act reinforced the opinion that a medical certificate was required for a person to be excluded as a psychopathic personality or sexual deviate. The House report on the act referred to exclusion under 8 U.S.C.§ 1182(a)(4) as one of "the medical grounds for exclusion."[37] Similarly, in the report of the PHS on the pending legislation, the recommendations referred to the exclusion under section 1182(a)(4) as one of "the classes subject to *determination* on medical grounds."[38] The PHS recommendation that "conditions related to the field of mental disorders and subject to medical determination, be grouped together, and that item 5 of [8 U.S.C. § 1182(a)], relating to paupers, etc., be placed in the group not subject to medical determination," was adopted.[39] This made clear the organization of section 1182 into two categories: medically determined exclusions and nonmedically determined exclusions.

The PHS report further elaborated on the point that homosexuality was to be medically determined. The report referred to "the diagnosis of homosexuality," and mentioned the utility of "psychological tests [that] may be helpful in uncovering homosexuality of which the individual, himself, may be unaware." These comments were important for two reasons. First, they show that Congress and the PHS thought, at the time of the adoption of the act, that homosexuality was diagnosable, and that a medical determination would be made. Accordingly, there was no indication in the legislative history that Congress or the PHS believed that homosexuality should be determined by admissions any more than schizophrenia could be self-diagnosed. Second, the latter comment demonstrated the PHS's and Congress's understanding that homosexuals who were unaware themselves of their homosexuality would be excluded. This understanding conflicted with a procedure that depended on homosexuals' admission of homosexuality rather than medical observation and determination.

The PHS report concluded by discussing the procedure for exclusion for physical defect, disease, or disability that affected the ability of the alien to earn a living. Such determination was a two-part process. The medical officer determined "the extent to which a person is incapacitated or handicapped, leaving it to [the consular or immigration officer] to determine whether or not the person would be able to earn a living." This was the only mention of a joint medical-nonmedical determination of excludability, and was impliedly contrasted with other determinations that would be made either by medical officers on medical grounds or by nonmedical officers on nonmedical grounds. "The medical officer does not make this [nonmedical] determination [of ability to earn a living], because of the socio-economic factors involved."

The House report further discussed the procedures for exclusion.

> Every alien arriving at a port of entry must be examined by an immigration officer before he may enter, and such officers are empowered to detain the aliens on board the arriving vessel or at the airport of arrival for observation if suspected of being afflicted with mental or physical defects and may order the temporary removal of the alien for examination and inspection. Medical examinations are to be made by at least one qualified medical officer of the United States Public Health Service or by a qualified civil surgeon.[40]

The procedure was explicit. If the immigration officer suspected an alien of having an excludable mental or physical affliction, the officer was empowered to detain the alien and order an examination and inspection. The officer was not empowered to take admissions or conduct inquiries concerning the affliction. Rather, the medical examination was to be made by "at least one qualified medical officer." Finally, both the House and Senate reports stated in terms similar to 8 U.S.C. § 1226(d), that when a medical officer certified that an alien was afflicted with an excludable mental or physical affliction, the special inquiry officer "must base his decision *solely* upon such certification and there is no right of appeal from the excluding decision."[41]

Richard John Longstaff's Naturalization Case

The philosophy of the federal court opinions in the Hill case, originating in San Francisco, were not, however, followed throughout the country. For example, Richard John Longstaff was denied naturalization because he admitted to being a homosexual.

Longstaff, a native and citizen of the United Kingdom of Great Britain and Northern Ireland, immigrated to the United States on November 14, 1965, at the age of twenty-five. Before he arrived in the United States, Longstaff filled out a form entitled "Application for Immigrant Visa and Alien Registration." To the question "3(b) Are you now or have you ever been afflicted with psychopathic personality, epilepsy, mental defect, fits, fainting spells, convulsions or a nervous breakdown?" Longstaff answered, "No." Of course, based on legislative history, since Congress intended the term *psychopathic personality* to designate homosexuals as well as persons having psychopathic disorders, the question was meant to address Longstaff's sexual preference. However, no evidence suggested that Longstaff knew or had reason to know that "psychopathic personality" was a term that included homosexuals.

Fifteen years later, Longstaff sought citizenship through naturalization but his request was denied by the federal district court, which ruled that Longstaff had violated the Texas Penal Code by engaging in homosexual activity, that he exhibited a lack of candor in answering questions about his sexual activities, and that he failed to carry his burden of establishing good moral character, a naturalization requirement. After Longstaff was given the opportunity to produce more evidence of his moral character, an INS examiner interrogated Longstaff. The examiner concluded that Longstaff had met his burden of establishing good moral character; nevertheless, he recommended denial of the petition on a different basis: since Longstaff had engaged in homosexual activity before entering the United States in 1965, he concluded that Longstaff (1) had been excludable under the law at the time of entry (as in the *Boutilier* case); (2) had not been "lawfully admitted," as the law requires for naturalization; and (3) could not be naturalized.

On appeal to the federal Fifth Circuit Court of Appeals, Longstaff essentially made the same argument as Carl Hill did in the Ninth Circuit—that he could not be deemed excludable as a person of psychopathic personality without the determination of a physician. But by a 2–1 decision, the Fifth Circuit Court disagreed with the Ninth Circuit that decided the Carl Hill case.

The Fifth Circuit Court in Texas used the following reasoning. Congress unmistakably declared its intention to exclude homosexuals by amending the statute to bar "sexual deviates." If only certification of homosexuality by a medical officer could warrant exclusion of homosexuals, then the surgeon general would have effectively checkmated congressional policy by refusing to conduct examinations. To this court, the term *homosexual* was not a scientific designation, and studies indicated that many males have homosexual experiences; there could be no doubt that Longstaff both knew what the term meant and was not uncertain about his sexual preferences. He stated that he had been a homosexual "as far back as [he could] remember in [his] life." He testified that he had engaged in "homosexual activities" before his entry into the United States. He considered himself "now a known homosexual in the community."

The Fifth Circuit felt that congressional intent should not be thwarted by PHS's lack of cooperation. There was no reason why an informed applicant's admission that he fell within an excludable class was not competent evidence on which to base an exclusion decision.[42]

In the court's view, requesting a medical determination of homosexuality in this case would be asking for a certification of the obvious. Sexual preference could not be determined by a blood test or physical examination; even doctors had to reach a decision by interrogation of the person involved or of others professing knowledge about that person. To require the INS to disregard the most reliable source of information, the statements of the person involved, would have substituted secondary evidence for primary.

What about the fact that homosexuality was no longer considered a psychopathic condition in the opinion of the government's highest medical officer, the surgeon general? The Fifth Circuit felt bound by the Supreme Court's *Boutilier* ruling that the term *psychopathic personality* was a term not dependent on medical definition, and by the congressional bar against persons "afflicted with . . . sexual deviation." Under the INS guidelines, homosexuality could now be demonstrated in INS proceedings by an alien's unambiguous admission or by the voluntary statement of a third person, made without either prompting or questioning. Longstaff was thus barred from naturalization by his own truthful statements that he was excludable as a homosexual at the time of his entry, and, therefore, was not lawfully admitted for permanent residence. In the eighteen years of his residence, he had led a constructive life. The court felt bound, however, to decide according to a law made in the exercise of a federal plenary power. If Congress's policy was misguided, Congress would have to revise that policy—not the surgeon general. If the result achieved by the policy was unfair to a deserving person who desired to become a citizen, the injustice must be corrected by lawmakers.

A year later, the PHS was directed to resume Class A certificates on homosexuals.[43]

After years of intense debate over the exclusion of homosexuals, the Immigration Act of 1990 removed the psychopathic personality and sexual deviation language from the exclusion provisions along with all language referring to mental retardation, insanity, and mental defects. One of the immediate effects was apparent in an INS determination that a visitor's visa would be available for a nonspouse, same-sex life partner of a nonimmigrant intracompany transferee coming to work in the United States for a multinational company for a number of years.[44] But immigrant visas for spouses of U.S. citizens or lawful permanent residents continue to be limited to spouses of the opposite sex.

Conclusion

In spite of criticisms by President Truman, the 1952 act perpetuated the ideals embodied in the 1917 literacy act and the national origins quota system of the 1920s that southern and eastern Europeans were not as welcome to be Americans as were western Europeans. And although World War II had chipped away at the wall of exclusion erected in the way of Asian immigrants, the 1952 act did little to remedy those laws, as a small, Asia-Pacific Triangle annual quota of 2,000 visas was established.

But the 1952 law was not just about perpetuating old exclusion regimes directed at Asians, Jews, Catholics, and southern and eastern Europeans. The fear of others who would not fit into a conventional vision of Americans was deeply influenced by the vestiges of the Red Scare and the advent of the cold war. Policy makers utilized the well-honed racial/ethnic immigration exclusion tool against Communists and other "subversives." While this effort may have reflected the sign of the times, the effects have remained part of the immigration laws ever since and, in fact, served as a model for exclusionary political and terrorism efforts in the 1990s and post-September 11 era.

Similarly, the 1952 act reinforced the vision that gays and lesbians were not welcome as Americans. The language of exclusion directed at homosexuals was expanded, although the tension over its implementation and procedural requirements is another example of the duel between those attempting to define America broadly and the more narrow-minded.

CHAPTER 6

1965 to 1990: From Discriminatory Quotas to Discriminatory Diversity Visas

Since the 1952 act changed little in the immigration selection system, the policy makers continued to battle over which immigrants to admit to the United States. Some voiced concern about the class background and skills that would-be immigrants might bring, but often the struggle largely focused on matters of ethnicity and race. Most proposals were couched in nonracial terms, but their effects usually disadvantaged nationals of certain countries. Determining who fit the image of potential Americans was still a contentious process.

The 1965 Framework for Selection

The survival of the national origins quota system of the 1920s through the 1952 act illustrates the western European dominance over the accepted image of "an American" in the minds of policy makers and the public. Critics including President Truman felt the system perpetuated the philosophy that some people are more equal than others and cited the law as an embarrassment that was inconsistent with our stature as leader of the free world.

Truman and others did not relent. Soon after the enactment of the 1952 law, he appointed a special Commission on Immigration and Naturalization to study the system. A 319-page report issued in 1953 strongly urged the abolition of the national origins system and recommended quotas without regard to national origin, race, creed, or color. Although Truman's successor, President Eisenhower, embraced the findings, his push for corrective legislation failed, as did repeated attempts at new legislation over the next decade.

Entering office in January 1961, President Kennedy submitted a comprehensive program that reflected his long-standing interest in immigration reform and provided the impetus for ultimate reform. Kennedy called for the repeal of the discriminatory national origins quota system and the racial exclusion from the Asia-Pacific Triangle, while assailing the nativism that led to the infamous Chinese exclusion laws. He envisioned a system governed by the skills of the immigrant and family reunification. For him, these proposed changes meant both an increase in fairness to applicants and in benefits to the United States. His approach recognized the interdependence among nations, making the old system appear anachronistic.

Although Kennedy's global vision had its detractors, it remained the driving theme for the proponents of reform for whom repeal of the national origins system was only one aspect of the more open movement across international borders, in which the United States would stand both as a leader and as an example. Their rhetoric was meant to evoke a romantic allegiance to the highest sort of aspirations. People were supposed to feel as if they could transcend the world in which they were living.

The vision was mesmerizing. In fact, much of the critical support for the legislation came from those who perceived it as aiding the national economy because of the skills and training brought by immigrants as well as those who sought the elimination of the racial discrimination that had burdened nonwhite immigrants for a century. After Kennedy's assassination in November 1963, President Johnson took up the cause of reform, emphasizing the need for corrective measures on behalf of southern and eastern European immigrants and criticizing the existing selection system in his 1964 State of the Union address:

> We must also lift by legislation the bars of discrimination against those who seek entry into our country, particularly those who have much needed skills and those joining their families.
>
> In establishing preferences, a nation that was built by the immigrants of all lands can ask those who now seek admission: "What can you do for our country?" But we should not be asking: "In what country were you born?"

Nevertheless, the national origins quota system still had supporters, like southern Senators Sam Ervin, Strom Thurmond, and James Eastland, who remained loyal to what they perceived as the idea underlying the national origins system. They branded the new proposals discriminatory against prospective English-speaking immigrants, and condemned the legislation as an assault on immigration laws by those who "appeal to organized minority blocs in the great urban areas," charging that the purpose of the bill was to increase immigration and change its composition.[1] Echoing the words of his predecessors in the 1920s, Senator Ervin argued that the quota law "recognized the obvious and natural fact that those [English-speaking] immigrants can best be assimilated into our society who have relatives, friends or others of similar background already here."[2]

In fact, while the supporters of the legislation may have had egalitarian motives, they were not predicting (or perhaps hoping for) wholesale changes in the racial and ethnic makeup of the country. For example, Senator Robert Kennedy of New York (who served as attorney general until 1964) supported the 1965 legislation, stating:

> In fact, the distribution of limited quota immigration can have no significant effect on the ethnic balance of the United States . . . Total quota immigration is now 156,782; under the proposed bill, it would rise to 164,482 . . . Immigration from any single country would be limited to 10 percent of the total—16,500—with the possible exception of the two countries now sending more than that number, Great Britain and Germany. But the extreme case should set to rest any fears that this bill will change the ethnic, political, or economic makeup of the United States.[3]

Senator Ted Kennedy of Massachusetts made similar assurances:

> Out of deference to the critics, I want to comment on . . . what the bill will not do. First, our cities will not be flooded with a million immigrants annually. Under the proposed bill, the present level of immigration remains substantially the same . . . Secondly, the ethnic mix of this country will not be upset . . . Contrary to the charges in some quarters, S.500 (Senate Bill 500) will not inundate America with immigrants from any one country or area, or the most populated and economically deprived nations of Africa and Asia . . . In the final analysis, the ethnic pattern of immigration under the proposed measure is not expected to change as sharply as critics seem to think. . . .The charges I have mentioned are highly emotional, irrational, and with little foundation in fact. They are out of line with the obligations of responsible citizenship. They breed hate of our heritage.[4]

Even President Johnson noted, "This is not a revolutionary bill. It does not affect the lives of millions. It will not reshape the structure of our daily lives."[5]

So, for the time being, nativism was quieted and a broader vision of America emerged, as the legislation was debated at the height of congressional sensitivity over civil rights.

President Kennedy's hopes for abolishing the quota system were realized when the 1965 amendments were enacted. The Asia-Pacific Triangle geographic restrictions were also eliminated (although the ceiling of 2,000 visas for that area had already been deleted in 1961). But his egalitarian vision of visas on a first-come, first-served basis gave way to a narrower and more historically parochial framework that provided few, if any, obvious advantages for prospective Asian immigrants. The new law allowed 20,000 immigrant visas annually for every country not in the Western Hemisphere. The allotment was made regardless of the size of a country, so that mainland China had the same quota as Tunisia. Of the 170,000 visas set aside for the Eastern Hemisphere, 75 percent were for specified "preference" relatives of citizens and lawful permanent residents, and an unlimited number was available to immediate relatives (parents of adults, minor unmarried children, and spouses) of U.S. citizens. First preference was for the adult, unmarried sons and daughters of U.S. citizens; second preference for the spouses and unmarried children of lawful permanent resident aliens; fourth preference for married sons and daughters of U.S. citizens; and fifth preference for the siblings of U.S. citizens.

Two occupational categories (third and sixth preferences) and a nonpreference category were also established. The occupational categories helped professionals and other aliens who filled jobs for which qualified U.S. workers were not available, although, for the first time, aliens seeking entry as skilled and unskilled labor were required to have approval of the secretary of labor. Under the nonpreference category, an alien who invested $40,000 in a business could qualify for immigration to the United States. A seventh preference was a refugee-like category for conditional entrants who were fleeing communist-dominated countries or the Middle East.

While not exactly what President Kennedy wanted, a more global vision of international relations did prevail. At least for a while, xenophobic impulses were softened as the pernicious national origins quota system that had tarnished the country's image in the eyes of the world was repealed. Public support for the repeal of the national origins system reflected change in public attitudes toward race and national origins—and the possibility that the image of an *American* was expanding.. Arguably, the 1965 legislation was as much a product of the mid-1960s and the heavily Democratic Eighty-ninth Congress that also produced major civil rights legislation, as the 1952 act had been a product of the cold war period of the early 1950s.[6]

These policy reforms did not moderate the strong prejudice against people of color. After World War II, the proportion of Spanish-speaking immigrants increased, and much prejudice was directed toward these newcomers from Mexico as well as Central and South America.[7] Although the 1952 act did not place a numerical limit on immigration from these areas, Congress included the Western Hemisphere quota of 120,000 in the 1965 amendments as a compromise for abolishing the national origins system. As a result, a steadily growing backlog of Latin American applicants were forced to wait several years for visas.

Changes Limiting Foreign Doctors

While the basic structure of the immigration selection system has remained the same since 1965, examples of some of the subsequent changes reveal interesting policy choices made by Congress in deciding who is welcomed into American society.

An example of a choice that reflects a negative attitude toward welcoming professionals of color relates to foreign medical graduates (FMGs). On October 12, 1976, Congress enacted the Health Professions Educational Assistance Act of 1976, declaring that there was no longer a shortage of physicians and surgeons in the United States and that no further need existed for the admission of aliens to fill those positions. The statute made FMGs coming to the United States principally to perform as members of the medical profession an excludable class, unless they had passed Parts I and II of the National Board of Medical Examiners' Examination and were competent in oral and written English.

The main group that advocated the exclusion of FMGs was the Coordinating Council on Medical Education (CCME). CCME was comprised of the American Medical

Association, the American Hospital Association, the Association of American Medical Colleges, the American Board of Medical Specialties, and the Council of Medical Specialty Societies.[8] While some members of CCME sought a waiver of these requirements for rural areas where FMGs would be hard to replace,[9] the basic position of the CCME leadership was total exclusion of FMGs from the ability to engage in patient care in the United States.[10] CCME was also troubled by the incongruity that many state psychiatric institutions had 100 percent FMG staff. The irony, it was argued, was the fact that psychiatry was an area of medicine based on communication between doctor and patient, and many of the alien physicians had great difficulty with English.[11]

While CCME relied on the argument that FMGs were providing substandard medical care, others, like the National Association of Counties, opposed the dependence on FMGs from a different angle. They argued that accepting FMGs would create a "brain drain" in other countries.[12] Although the National Association of Counties recognized the maldistribution of physicians in the United States, in its view increased immigration of FMGs was not the solution. Instead, it questioned why the United States should hoard FMGs when Third World countries needed the talent more than the United States.[13] One spokesperson for the Department of Social Security noted that there were more Thai physicians in New York than in the whole country of Thailand.[14]

When the new restrictions were enacted in 1976, about 20 percent of the active physicians practicing in the United States were FMGs.[15] It was clear that FMGs were providing a critical service throughout the United States, particularly in rural areas and state-run facilities. Yet, reminiscent of the competition felt by white workers when Chinese, Japanese, and Asian Indian immigrant workers arrived in the United States from 1850 to 1917 and the white efforts to exclude them, CCME and the American Medical Association were able to strike fear in the minds of policy makers in 1976. Prior to the changes, thousands of FMGs from the Philippines and South Korea entered to fill important gaps in the medical profession. But after the changes, their numbers declined dramatically.

Restraints on Mexican Immigration in the 1970s

The national origins quota system and statutory vestiges of Asian exclusion laws were abolished in the 1965 amendments to the immigration laws. But by that time, increased immigration from countries of the Western Hemisphere, particularly from Mexico, raised concern. Although the rest of the world enjoyed an expansion of numerical limitations and a definite preference system after 1965, Mexico and the Western Hemisphere were suddenly faced with numerical restrictions for the first time. The Western Hemisphere was allotted a total of 120,000 immigrant visas each year, and while the first-come, first-served basis for immigration sounded fair, applicants had to meet strict labor certification requirements and demonstrate that they would not be displacing U.S. workers. Waivers of the labor certification requirement were available, however, for certain applicants, such as parents of U.S. citizen children. As one might expect given the new numerical limitations, by 1976 the procedure resulted in a severe backlog of approximately three years and a waiting list with nearly 300,000 names.[16]

During the 1965–76 experience, several noteworthy things happened. First, Mexicans used about 40,000 of the Western Hemisphere's allocation of 120,000 visas annually. Second, during this eleven-year period, the State Department wrongfully subtracted about 150,000 visas from the Western Hemisphere quota and gave them to Cuban refugees, who were supposed to be admitted without regard to quotas.[17] Additionally, during this period undocumented Mexicans became the target of INS sweeps and enforcement activities, even though Mexicans did not make up the majority of the undocumented aliens in the country. Exclusionists argued that Mexican workers were taking jobs from U.S. citizens, and Congress considered an employer sanction law that was referred to as the Rodino Bill. (See Chapter 9.) Exclusionists constantly complained about undocumented workers coming across the United States–Mexico border, and the commissioner of the INS routinely alleged that 12 million undocumented aliens were in the United States.

As the immigration of Mexicans became the focus of more debate, Congress enacted legislation in 1976 curtailing Mexican migration even more. The law imposed the preference system on Mexico and the Western Hemisphere along with a 20,000 visa per country numerical limitation. Thus, Mexico's annual visa usage rate (which had been about 40,000) was virtually cut in half overnight, and thousands were left stranded on the old system's waiting list.[18] In 1978, the 120,000 Western Hemisphere and 170,000 Eastern Hemisphere quotas were merged into a single 290,000 worldwide numerical limit on immigration.

The eleven-year misallocation of visas to Cuba eventually led to a permanent injunction and a "recapturing" of the wrongfully issued visas in *Silva v. Bell*.[19] Finally, people who would have been able to immigrate years earlier, but for the mistake in taking away visas from the Western Hemisphere allocation, were now able to immigrate lawfully. However, Mexicans again received the short end of the stick when the State Department's formula for reallocation, which failed to provide sufficient visas for thousands of Mexicans on the *Silva* waiting list, was upheld. As a result, in February 1982, INS authorities began to round up those *Silva* class members who had not been accorded immigrant visas, advising them that they were now deportable and that work permission was terminated. The recipients were further informed that unless provisions of the existing immigration law qualified them to remain in the United States, they would have thirty days for voluntary departure. Although the INS delayed enforcement for awhile, by February 1, 1983, the Enforcement Branch of the INS resumed the roundup of *Silva* class members.[20]

To make matters worse, in the first year of the new Western Hemisphere preference system and 20,000 limit on countries in the region, Mexico lost 14,000 visas due to a congressional mistake. The enactment date of the new law was January 1, 1977. However, since the government's fiscal year runs from October 1 to September 30, the amendments did not become effective until after one full quarter of fiscal year 1977 had expired. During that first quarter, 14,203 visas were issued to Mexicans pursuant to the immigration system that prevailed in the Western Hemisphere before the new law became effective. The State Department nevertheless charged those visas against the newly imposed national quota of 20,000, leaving only 5,797 visas available for Mexican immigrants between January 1 and September 30, 1977. In *De Avila v. Civiletti*,[21] the Seventh Circuit Court of Appeals sustained the State Department's approach even though it was "obvious that Congress . . . through inadvertence failed to inform the State Department how to administer during a fraction of the fiscal year a statute designed to apply on a full fiscal year basis."

The effect on Mexican immigration following the 1977 imposition of the preference system and 20,000 visa limitation (modified in 1990) is not surprising. Mexico and Asian countries have the largest backlogs in family reunification categories.[22] For example, the category for married sons and daughters of U.S. citizens (third preference) for Mexico is backlogged more than ten years. Brothers and sisters of U.S. citizens (fourth preference) must wait at least twelve years if they are from Mexico and twenty years if they are from the Philippines.

Mexicans continued to be victims of highly publicized INS raids. Dubbed Operation Jobs or Operation Cooperation, these raids recall Operation Wetback and raids directed at Asian immigrants in the past. In what the INS labeled Operation Jobs in April 1982, 5,000 people of primarily Latin appearance were arrested in nine metropolitan areas across the country.[23] Critics of the raids charged that the operation was directed at Mexicans, whipped up antialien hysteria, and caused much fear in the Latino community, while providing no jobs for native-born citizens.[24] Curiously, Operation Jobs was timed during the same week that restrictive legislation (the Simpson–Mazzoli Bill) was being marked up in the Senate subcommittee on immigration. The raids also coincided with Congress's consideration of additional funds for the INS.

Operation Jobs merely highlighted what had been going on for many years. (See Chapter 8.) A review of litigation initiated long before the 1982 operation indicates that the INS has long focused its sweeps on persons of Latino descent.[25] In fiscal year 1977, for example, of the deportable aliens arrested, more than 90 percent were Mexican.[26]

As the INS enforcement budget grew larger and larger during this period, the Supreme Court, swayed by arguments that the undocumented alien problem was worsening, gave more flexibility to INS enforcement strategies. First, in 1975, in *United States v. Brignoni-Ponce*,[27] the Court held that under certain circumstances, roving Border Patrol officers could stop motorists in the general area of the Mexican border for brief inquiry into their residence status if there was reasonable suspicion that passengers were undocumented. Next, in 1976, in *United States v. Martinez-Fuerte*,[28] the Court carved an exception to the Fourth Amendment's protection against unreasonable search and seizures by allowing the Border Patrol to set up fixed checkpoints located on major highways away from the Mexican border for purposes of stopping and questioning individuals suspected of being undocumented aliens. Then in 1984 in *INS v. Lopez-Mendoza*,[29] the Court held that even if the INS violated the Fourth Amendment's protection against illegal search and seizure in its apprehension of undocumented aliens, illegally obtained evidence could still be used against the aliens in deportation proceedings. (See Chapter 8.)

Affirmative Action for Western Europeans: "Diversity" in the 1980s and 1990s

By the end of the 1970s and through the 1980s, immigrant visa demands from Mexico remained high, and those from certain Asian countries surged. By 1990, immigrants from Mexico, the Philippines, India, Korea, and Chinese from China, Taiwan, and Hong Kong dominated legal immigration categories. Given the per country numerical limitations, Mexico and Asian countries shared (and continue to share) the largest backlogs in family reunification categories. This was especially true for preference categories reserved for siblings of U.S. citizens and relatives of lawful permanent resident aliens.

The modern-day nativists who see themselves as the protectors of the *true* American ideal did not stand by idly. Policy makers who enacted the 1965 amendments may have known that Mexican immigration would remain high under the new Western Hemisphere quota, but they did not predict that Asian immigration would reach such high levels.[30] The number of Asian immigrants began to increase in the early 1970s, then exploded in the late 1970s and 1980s, when Asian and Latin immigrants represented over 80 percent of all immigrants. In 1982, as part of a major legislative package, Republican Senator Alan Simpson of Wyoming initiated a crusade to eliminate the immigration category allowing U.S. citizens to be reunited with siblings and persisted in his efforts to abolish the category until his retirement in 1996. These efforts were a direct assault on Asians and Mexicans, who combined to make up the vast majority of siblings-of-citizen immigrants.

A second approach was implemented in 1986 to respond to the rising domination of Asians and Latinos in immigration totals in the 1980s. Although the country's population was still overwhelmingly white and of European descent, Congress added a little-publicized provision in the Immigration Reform and Control Act to help thirty-six countries that had been "adversely affected" by the 1965 changes. To be considered "adversely affected," a country must have been issued fewer visas after 1965 than before. Thus, the list included such countries as Great Britain, Germany, and France, but no countries from Africa, which had sent few immigrants prior to 1965. So the so-called diversity program (also known as the NP-5 program) was not about diversifying the country, which of course remained overwhelmingly white. It also was not about helping immigrants from countries that had little ability to voluntarily immigrate to the United States historically, for example, African nations. The "diversity" program was actually an affirmative action program for natives of countries who already made up the vast ethnic background of the country, such as western European countries. The program was about helping Europeans immigrate to an already Eurocentric country. In many respects, the philosophy of the so-called diversity program was the same philosophy of the national origins quota laws of the 1920s: help those groups immigrate whose ancestors had immigrated in larger numbers previously.

The new allocations were significant. The 1986 law provided an extra 5,000 such visas a year for 1987 and 1988, but the number increased to 15,000 per year for 1989 and 1990 through additional legislation. These visas were above and beyond the 20,000 visas that were already available for immigrants from each of the "diversity" countries under the preference system. But in order to qualify for the diversity visas, applicants did not have to have close relatives already in the United States or special job skills that would benefit the country. The program was a "first-come, first-served" worldwide mail registration program, benefiting the earliest-registered applicants and their immediate families, requiring them only to meet the nationality, health, and morals qualifications of immigration laws.

Part of the impetus for the "diversity" program was the fact that many Irish nationals who came to the United States were unable to fit into the regular immigration categories. They did not have close relatives who could petition for them, and many did not have special job skills. In the 1980s, a severe economic downturn in Ireland motivated many of its young professionals to look for work abroad. Ireland's gross domestic product (GDP) grew an average of only 1.8 percent each year from 1980 to 1985. Its national debt rivaled that of many Third World countries; in 1986, the debt stood at 134 percent of the gross national product (GNP).[31] Ireland's foreign debt, in per capita terms, was one of the highest in the world—three times as high as Mexico's. One out of every five Irish workers was out of a job by 1987, and the unemployment rate was worse in major cities such as Dublin.[32] For those who did work, the tax rate was a staggering 60 percent.[33] The economy was unable to support many young Irish professionals. One in three of the college-educated found employment abroad.[34] The figures were higher; for certain professions, for example, more than 70 percent of the architecture graduates took jobs overseas.[35]

Discouraged by the economy in Ireland, many of its young residents traveled to the United States, usually on temporary visas such as for tourism. Eventually, they overstayed their visas. By 1989, the Irish government estimated that perhaps 50,000 Irish nationals resided in the United States in undocumented status. But another organization, the Irish Immigration Reform Movement, set the figure closer to 150,000.[36]

The appeal for "diversity" in the immigration pool drew widespread support, even though the beneficiaries of the law were nationals of countries that had dominated immigration prior to 1965 and continued to comprise huge proportions of the ethnic makeup of the country. After all, the beneficiaries were largely white and English-speaking—just the stuff that made for good Americans in the minds of the mainstream. This editorial from the *Boston Globe* of September 26, 1988, was typical:

Immigration Injustice

Among the more urgent proposals that Congress should act on before it adjourns in October are two that would reopen the nation's door to immigrants from Ireland, Italy and other countries in Western Europe. The changes amount to unfinished business from the comprehensive recommendations of the 1986 Select Commission on Immigration and Refugee Policy.

Without depriving immigrants from other parts of the world of their chance to come to the United States, these measures would correct the adverse impact on Europeans that occurred when immigration rules were changed 23 years ago. The issue has a sense of immediacy because the major sponsor of the House version, Rep. Peter Rodino (D-N.J.), is retiring from Congress at the end of the year. Without him, efforts to pass a bill will be hobbled.

Inequities created under the 1965 act are denying entrance to tens of thousands of *Western Europeans, particularly those from Ireland and Italy*, where jobs are scarce. The American labor market, which needs their skills, is also being harmed.

The intent of the 1965 changes was to expand immigration opportunities for Asians and Latin Americans, who had been discriminated against under the old quota system. An unintended side effect put unreasonable limits on Western Europeans.

In the decade before 1965, about 71,000 Irish immigrants and 198,000 Italian immigrants entered the United States. Each year since then, 800 have entered from Ireland and 1,500 from Italy, although 100,000 immigrants are estimated to be living here illegally.

Rodino's bill, an outgrowth of efforts by Rep. Brian Donnelly (D-Mass.), is similar to one proposed by Sen. Edward Kennedy and Sen. Alan Simpson of Wyoming. The Senate version was approved on an 88–4 vote in April.

The bills would permit an additional 100,000 persons to immigrate here each year. A new category for "independent" immigrants would ease the preference now given the reunifying of families, as well as the labor preference given professionals.

Well-educated young Irish people are emigrating to European Common Market countries—soon to be strong competitors for America—says Thomas Flatley, a Massachusetts businessman and Irish immigrant. "Our loss of these immigrants," he says, "is those countries' gain."

As matters stand, the United States reaps none of the benefits of admitting young people who acquired expensive educations elsewhere. Those here under illegal status cannot work openly, so the country loses their income tax payments.

The Kennedy and Rodino bills could easily meld. Quick House action is needed to move the bills to a conference committee before another year is lost in rectifying this immigration injustice. (Courtesy of the Globe Newspaper Co., Boston, MA; emphasis added)

Interestingly, by 1988, "western Europeans" had come to include Irish, who were once vilified for their Catholic background, and Italians, who were once targeted in the anti-*southern* European national origins quota laws as well as for their presumed allegiance to the pope. What becomes evident in this 1988 editorial is that at last Irish and Italians had made it into the *real* American image.

So in 1988, Congress set aside an extra 20,000 visas to increase immigration diversity over a period of another two years. This time, the "OP-1" lottery for the visas was available to nationals of countries that were "underrepresented," namely, a foreign state that used less than 25 percent of its 20,000 preference visas in 1988. As a result, all but thirteen countries in the world were eligible despite lengthy visa backlogs faced by their nationals. Mexico, the Philippines, China, Korea, and India were among the countries that were excluded. Over 3.2 million applicants were received for the 20,000 visas.

Legislation in 1990 extended the diversity visa concept even more. Until October 1, 1994, a transition diversity program would provide 40,000 visas per year for countries "adversely affected" by the 1965 amendments, except that 40 percent of the visas were effectively designated for Irish nationals. True, displaced Tibetans residing in India or Nepal were also given extra numbers, but the overwhelming diversity beneficiaries would be white. After October 1, 1994, 55,000 diversity visas would be available annually in a lottery-type program to natives of countries from which immigration was lower than 50,000 over the preceding five years—certainly not Mexico, China, South Korea, the Philippines, or India. Under a complicated formula that weighs countries and regions of the world and uses relative populations, the State Department determines the distribution of lottery visas. A single state can never get more than 7 percent (3,850) of the total diversity visas available each year. In one early projection of the formula, the first year's regional distribution looked like this: Africa 20,900, Asia 6,380, North America 0, Europe 24,310, Latin America 2,530, and Oceania 880.

In order to take part in the lottery program in 1988, an applicant needed only to submit a letter with family and other biographical data. Under the 1994 diversity program, however, the applicant needed a high school education, or within five years of application, at least two years of work experience in an occupation that required at least two years of training or experience. That left out most Africans who wanted to immigrate.

The justification for special treatment of Irish nationals at various junctures of the diversity program was the recognition that under the primarily family-based immigration system, a special seed or pipeline category needed to be established. Only then could a significant number of people immigrate who could then take advantage of the family reunification categories by becoming U.S. citizens or filing under the category reserved for relatives of lawful permanent resident aliens. Of course, this was never afforded to Asian immigrants to make up for years of Asian exclusion laws. They had to slowly build up their pool of U.S. relatives who could petition for other relatives beginning after the 1965 amendments. Special treatment has never been afforded to Africans who seek to immigrate either, even though they too could benefit from a seed or pipeline category.

Debating Foreign Professional Workers

The historical tensions between employers and the native workforce over strategies of filling jobs with foreign workers (seen vividly in the agricultural industry) was highlighted in the battle over visas for skilled and professional workers in the 1980s and

1990s. Not coincidentally, the battle came at a time when those benefiting from most of the visas were not European; in fact, they were mostly Asian.

The battle also coincided with parallel attacks on the family immigration system—which had been the touchstone of the immigration laws since the 1965 amendments. Prior to 1990, 80 percent of the worldwide preference system quota of 270,000 was reserved for kinship provisions, and the category of immediate relatives of U.S. citizens was numerically unlimited. The effects of this priority were demonstrated vividly in the subsequent flow of Asian immigration, even though nations such as those in Africa and Asia, with low rates of immigration prior to 1965, were handicapped. In other words, the nations with large numbers of descendents in the United States were expected to benefit from a kinship-based system, and in 1965, less than a million Asian Americans resided in the country. Although the kinship priority meant that Asians were beginning on an unequal footing, at least Asians were on par numerically, in terms of the per country quotas. Gradually, by using the family categories to the extent they could be used and the labor employment route, Asians built a family base from which to use the kinship categories more and more. By the late 1980s, well over 90 percent of all Asian immigration to the United States was through the kinship categories, as with virtually all immigration to the United States. Table 6-1 shows the shift to greater reliance on family-based immigration categories for Chinese, Filipinos, Koreans, and Asian Indians.

The Select Commission on Immigration and Refugee Policy defended the family reunification system in its 1981 report: "The reunification of families serves the national interest not only through the humaneness of the policy itself, but also through the promotion of the public order and well-being of the nation. Psychologically and socially, the reunion of family members with their close relatives promotes the health and welfare of the United States."[37] After all, the system resulted in the entry of "ambitious, hard-working immigrants and their children" who provided a disproportionate number of skilled workers with a propensity for saving and investment.[38]

But others attacked the kinship system as nepotistic—perhaps not so coincidentally because mostly Asians and Latinos were benefiting—arguing that a skills-based system would be better for the country: "Nowhere else in public policy do we say not 'who are you and what are your characteristics?' but ask rather, as we do in immigration, 'who are you related to?' Current policy says: 'if you have the right relatives, we will give you a visa; if you don't have the right relatives, well, it is just too bad.'"[39]

The following like-minded statement from 1986 about undocumented migration reveals that the complaint was very much based on race:

> If the immigration status quo persists, the United States will develop a more unequal society with troublesome separations. For example, some projections indicate that the California work force will be mostly immigrants or their descendants by 2010. These working immigrants, *mostly nonwhite* will be supporting mostly white pensioners with their payroll contributions. *Is American society resilient enough to handle the resulting tensions. . . .*
>
> The American economy will have more jobs and businesses if illegal alien workers are allowed to enter freely and work in the United States. But the number of jobs and businesses alone is not an accurate measure of the soundness of economic development or

TABLE 6-1. Comparison of Entrants in Family Reunification Categories with Those in Occupational and Investor Categories, 1969 and 1985

Place of Birth	Relatives (%)		Occupational (%)		Investors (%)
	1969	1985	1969	1985	1969
China	60.9	80.9	20.8	15.8	4.5
India	27.0	85.9	45.0	12.6	26.8
Korea	64.0	89.2	23.2	7.6	11.6
Philippines	55.0	86.9	42.3	7.6	0.08

Sources: 1969 INS Annual Report, Tables 6, 6B, 7a, 40–48; 1985 INS Statistical Yearbook, Tables IMM 2.6, 3.1, 33–37.

quality of life. Tolerating heavy illegal immigration introduces distortions into the economy that are difficult to remedy, while imposing environmental and social costs that must be borne by the society as a whole.[40]

It seems apparent that this commentator's perception of a good "quality of life" without "environmental and social costs" is one with minimal tension from the presence of "nonwhite" "immigrants or their descendants." As an observer at the time recognized, "It may be fair to conclude that the problem masquerading as illegal immigration is simply today's version of a continuing American—in fact, human—condition, namely xenophobia."[41] As in the Asian exclusionary era, the complaints were not simply about the economy; they were about keeping people out who did not fit the right image.

In fact, the economic complaint was disingenuous. In the late 1980s and early 1990s, many economists and U.S. business leaders raised concerns over an ever-shrinking labor force. The problem was not necessarily a size shrinkage even though empirically the labor force was expected to be numerically smaller in the coming years. Rather, the problem was a "capacity" shrinkage. The fear was that the labor force was in danger of being ill-equipped to handle the technological changes that were transforming the working world. The reports suggested that these trends would inevitably result in an even greater decline in America's economic competitiveness. One such report that not only fueled much of the congressional debate on immigration policy, but also transformed the popular discussion on the changing American labor market was *Workforce 2000: Work and Workers for the Twenty-First Century* (1987), by William B. Johnston.

Workforce 2000 concluded that the emerging labor market in America contained a decreasing number of white males and an increasing number of females, both white and of color, and males of color. The report also concluded that the future labor force would be comprised of a very different racial mix, with a larger number of low-skilled or unskilled persons. This was dire news at a time when higher-skilled jobs were the fastest-growing category.

Studies assessed the composition of the labor market in the upcoming millennium. They revealed that not only would the appearance of the labor force change, but also that if the quality of education and training of the U.S. population continued at the same pace, the amount and quality of skills possessed by the labor force would degenerate by the year 2000.

The various pronouncements of the projected decline in the capacity of U.S. workers to perform future jobs adequately created a profound sense of impending doom among government leaders and captains of industry alike. Two major solutions were proposed and implemented to handle the problem.

The first, and most obvious solution to some, was to finally begin paying some attention to our long-neglected educational system. The Clinton administration attempted to squeeze extra dollars from the financially strapped federal budget to upgrade the nation's schools, but state systems were less inclined to pour more money into education than the federal government. In addition, although some American businesses took it upon themselves to reach out to communities and provide the additional resources needed to educate and train young people, they were the exception. At the time, U.S. corporations devoted only $30 billion annually to education and on-the-job training programs, just 1.4 percent of the nation's payroll. This contrasted sharply with the approximately $300 billion per year spent on plants and equipment.

A second solution to the prospect of a future workforce lacking essential skills—one that was increasingly being viewed with enthusiasm by big business interests and government powerbrokers alike—was immigration. That is, the "right" kind of immigration. Leaders saw immigration of ever-larger numbers of highly skilled immigrants as an immediate quick-fix to a thorny situation.

Business leaders took *Workforce 2000* and similar reports to heart and began to lobby Congress for an immigration-based solution. The legislative history of the Immigration Act of 1990 reveals that Congress appeared to acquiesce to the general perception that the lower level of skills among workers, rather than any actual decrease in the size of the workforce, presented the greatest threat to the economy. In addition, both Congress and business leaders had cause to be alarmed over the current state of the nation's workforce, let alone its future state. One study of the quality of America's domestic workforce stated that four million adults in the United States were unable to recognize letters and numbers, and twenty-seven million had basic skills below the fifth-grade level.

Furthermore, Congress must have believed that although the number of workers in the country were adequate to fulfill employers' needs, their abilities fell below par. So Congress acceded to employers' claims of increasing difficulty in locating qualified workers at a time of high unemployment.

More Visas for Permanent Workers

The beginnings of the legislation that ultimately became the Immigration Act of 1990 came in the form of Senate bill S. 358, whose primary sponsor was Republican Senator Alan Simpson, and House bill H.R. 4300, led by Democratic Congressman Bruce Morrison. Simpson had been a member of the Select Commission on Immigration and Refugee Policy that issued a report in 1981 calling for major changes in the immigration laws. After IRCA was enacted in 1986 to address the issue of undocumented migration through employer sanctions and legalization. (See Chapter 9.) Simpson turned his attention to legal immigration categories. At the time, although 20 percent of preference categories were available to labor employment immigrants (54,000), when the unrestricted immediate relative immigration categories were added to the total number of immigrants each year, less than 10 percent of immigrants who were entering each year were doing so on the basis of job skills.

Legal immigration continued to be dominated by Asians and Latinos even after "diversity" programs were being implemented to aid non-Asian and non-Mexican immigrants, and Simpson wanted the family immigration numbers reduced or at least managed. S. 358, which would establish a ceiling of 630,000 legal immigrants for three years, was approved by the Senate in July 1989. Of the total, 480,000 would be reserved for all types of family immigration and 150,000 would be set aside for immigrants without family connections but with skills or job-related assets. Yet after numerous markups and hearings, the House of Representative passed Morrison's H.R. 4300, a rather different bill, on October 3, 1990. The bill actually would cut family immigration more dramatically—thereby reducing the number of Asian and Latino family immigrants, providing 185,000 family-based visas and 95,000 employment-based visas annually.

As originally introduced, H.R. 4300 revamped most immigrant and nonimmigrant work visa categories. It created four categories, which would have priority within the 95,000 total visas for employer-sponsored immigrants. These aliens would also be exempt from the labor certification requirement, which had demanded that employers demonstrate the unavailability of U.S. workers. The bill would also allow up to 1,000 foreign investors to obtain a two-year conditional resident status by investing at least $1 million and creating ten new jobs for unrelated U.S. citizens or other workers. Critics noted that this would essentially allow foreign investors to buy citizenship. Employers could also sponsor other aliens provided they proved a shortage of U.S. workers.

The House bill was attacked for its "double temporary" requirement and the wholesale elimination of temporary work visas for professionals. The concern was that the spigot actually might be closed on foreign workers. Also, the possible elimination of H-1 nonimmigrant status for certain professions outraged immigration lawyers, who called it a "must-kill" provision. Another one of Morrison's more controversial suggestions was to tax employers who used alien employees. One early proposal required businesses to pay 15 percent of an alien's salary into a federal trust fund used to train U.S. workers. As introduced, the bill would impose a flat user fee dependent on the size of the company. This was opposed by businesses, but Morrison countered by arguing that the fees were "real bargains" and would provide an incentive for employers to hire U.S. workers. After furious negotiations, especially with fellow Democratic Congressman Howard Berman from Los Angeles, Morrison agreed to drop proposals that would have reduced the number of family-based visas.

As passed, H.R. 4300 would increase the number of legal immigrants to 775,000 a year from the prior 540,000. It would also speed the process of uniting families, attract more skilled workers, and create a new diversity category for immigrants from countries whose nationals had largely been excluded in the past. After passing the bill, the House changed the bill number to S. 358 to enable it to go to a joint House–Senate conference. However, many were opposed to the more liberal House bill and negotiated to cap legal immigration and place new measures to control illegal immigration, including tougher provisions against criminal aliens. The House conferees insisted on a sunset cap in the bill and wanted extra visas to go to relatives rather than to skilled workers. But Senator Simpson refused to agree, leading the *Wall Street Journal* to dub him a "one-man border control" and "Stonewall Simpson."[42] Eventually, compromises were reached and Congress passed S. 358.

Enacted on October 26, 1990, the compromise bill would allow 700,000 immigrants from 1992 to 1994 and 675,000 annually in subsequent years.[43] For the time being, proposals to cut back on family immigration were defeated. The Immigration Act of 1990 had responded to lobbying efforts by American businesses. It was a significant, and to some a revolutionary, revision of the focus of U.S. immigration law. After passage of the act, although the main thrust of immigration law continued to be family immigration, highly skilled immigrants would be deliberately encouraged to resettle in the United States more than ever before. In the long run, the number of employment-based visas would nearly triple, from 54,000 to 140,000 per year. Predictably, the bill met with a great deal of resistance from labor organizations. They were mollified, however, by the fact that the labor certification requirements remained essentially the same as they were prior to passage of the act, and were not streamlined even though an earlier House version of the bill had called for that.

Under the new law, which remains part of today's system, occupational visas were divided into five categories: (1) 40,000 visas for priority workers who possess extraordinary ability in the arts, sciences, education, business, or athletics, or outstanding professors and researchers, and certain multinational executives; (2) 40,000 visas for professionals holding advanced degrees or aliens of exceptional ability; (3) 40,000 visas for skilled workers, professionals with baccalaureate degrees, and unskilled workers for jobs for which qualified American workers are not available (only 10,000 visas can be issued for unskilled workers); (4) 10,000 visas for special immigrants; and (5) 10,000 visas for employment creation immigrants, specifically, investors of $500,000 to $3 million whose investments create at least ten new jobs.

To some, this policy favoring the "importation" of highly skilled immigrants to satisfy a growing vacuum in the labor pool created the danger of providing a way for U.S. leadership to escape the dilemma caused by the undereducation of Americans. They complained that a message was sent to low-income, undereducated communities that the U.S. government would rather bring in immigrants to fill skilled jobs than train available workers to fill them.

Most of the available immigrant visas are still reserved for relatives of U.S. citizens and lawful permanent resident aliens. However, the near tripling of occupational visas from 54,000 to 140,000 in the 1990 legislation signaled the beginning of a shift in the focus of U.S. immigration law from concern with family reunification toward a policy of importing skilled workers. In fact, before 1990, up to half of the 54,000 occupational visas could be used for unskilled workers who were not displacing American workers, but the figure for unskilled workers was reduced to 10,000 by the 1990 law.

The creation of the investor or employment-creation visa was also noteworthy. This category was designed for immigrants seeking to engage in a new commercial enterprise. The law requires that the investment be at least $1 million, but the amount is reduced to $500,000 if the enterprise is located in a targeted employment area, such as a rural area or any area that has experienced high unemployment of at least 150 percent of the national average rate. No fewer than 3,000 of the 10,000 visas are reserved for applicants whose enterprises will be located in targeted employment areas.

In the first year of availability, fewer than 200 applications were made for the 10,000 available investor visas. Immigration practitioners who worked with prospective investors offer several explanations. First, under U.S. tax laws, when a person becomes a lawful permanent resident of the United States, the person is taxed on her or his worldwide income. Most prospective investors have substantial income abroad from countries with very favorable tax laws, and they are reluctant to give that up for permanent resident status in the United States. Second, many potential investors balk at a regulatory requirement that their sources of income for the past ten years be disclosed. While this requirement was imposed to ferret out investors whose source of income was illegal drug trafficking, many legitimate investors prefer that the sources of their wealth remain confidential. Finally, many who would qualify for the investor category also qualify for less burdensome categories such as the intracompany transferee (L-1) category for those working for a multinational corporation; the L-1 category can be satisfied by a wealthy person who sets up a company that does business in more than one country. As a result, few takers for the new job-creation category have stepped forward, and most areas of high unemployment have not been helped.

While Simpson was disappointed that he failed to reduce the Asian- and Latino-dominated family categories, he was able to install an overall numerical cap. Furthermore, for Simpson, the new employment categories and expanded diversity programs could attract *real* American stock—those who were not Asian or Latino: "we [now] open the front door wider to skilled workers of a more diverse range of nationalities."[44]

More Visas for Temporary Workers: The H-1B Category

The Immigration Act of 1990 also implemented a new H-1B program that has proven to be quite popular with U.S. businesses, but also opposed by some who think businesses should hire available U.S. workers and groups that have seen the program used mostly by professionals from India and China.

Prior to 1990, an unlimited number of nonimmigrant H-1 work visas was available to individuals of "distinguished merit and ability."[45] This requirement was easily satisfied by professional-level employees. The law did not require the person to have an advanced degree or to be renowned in the field. In essence, all that was required was that the alien have at least a baccalaureate degree or its equivalent in a given field, and that the knowledge required for a particular job be a realistic prerequisite to entry into a particular field of endeavor.[46] As a result, tens of thousands of nonimmigrants entered annually in this H-1 professional category.

In 1990, the old H-1 program was replaced with the H-1B program for nonimmigrants entering "in a specialty occupation."[47] Like its predecessor, this provision provides a convenient way for professional workers to enter the country for temporary employment purposes. Again, the main requirement is at least a bachelor's degree in the particular specialty. But an important new requirement was added: the employer must submit a Labor Condition Application (LCA) to the Department of Labor, attesting that the foreign worker's employment does not adversely impact similarly employed U.S. workers. In other words, H-1B workers cannot be exploited and must be paid at least the prevailing wage in the industry; working conditions must match those of similarly employed workers in the same area of employment.

A critical difference, however, between the former H-1 program and the newer H-1B program has to do with numbers. The 1990 law imposed a limit of 65,000 on the number of aliens who could be given H-1B status each year. This number proved highly controversial and subject to much political struggle, as the quotas were easily reached in the late 1990s at the height of the high-tech boom. More than half of the visas were issued to nonimmigrants (mostly engineers) from India, and another 10 percent were issued to nationals of the Republic of China. Also, some 60 percent of the visas were issued for computer and systems analyst positions.

Led by the high-technology industry in the late 1990s, businesses lobbied Congress to increase the H-1B visa numbers. In spite of critics who argued unconvincingly that U.S. workers were available to fill these positions, in October 2000 Congress cleared the backlog of pending H-1B cases and increased the annual allotment to 195,000 for 2001, 2002, and 2003. These efforts proved unnecessary, as hundreds of high-tech industries went belly-up in 2001 and 2002, and the need for H-1B workers went dry. Fiscal year 2004 began with the 65,000 cap on H-1B visas reinstated.

Conclusion

Despite the overwhelmingly restrictive tenor of the 1952 legislation, a growing number of policy makers opposed the inherent bigotry and discrimination embodied in the immigration laws at the time. With the slow emergence of the global world economy by the early 1960s, President Kennedy understood the mutually dependent relationship among nations and that no one group of people should be singled out for preferential or adverse treatment by the United States.

With the 1965 amendments to its immigration policy, America was able to briefly shed its tarnished image in the world as one of the few developed countries that promoted backward and intolerant immigration policies. In using family relationships as the signifying factor for immigration settlement, one's country of origin was no longer a defining feature for admission. Detractors of the changes warned of an impending onslaught of non-western European immigrants. And in spite of the relatively egalitarian principles embodied in the 1965 amendments, even supporters did not believe (or perhaps hope for) a sea change in the ethnic background of new immigrants. The fact that Latino and especially Asian immigration expanded to impressive numbers beginning in the 1970s was disturbing to the gatekeepers of the *real* American ideal.

As soon as the numbers of Latin and Asian immigrants began to expand, restrictionist proposals appeared. Mirroring the uneasy relationship between Asians and white laborers in the early 1900s, Mexicans were now castigated as thieves of potential employment opportunities from rightful *American* workers. New numerical limitations were imposed on Mexicans by 1976, and calls for penalties on employers who hired undocumented workers began.

By the mid-1980s, aside from the passage of employer sanctions legislation (Chapter 9), inventive strategies were adopted to "even" things out for western European immigrants, whose numbers had drastically declined since 1965. Congress added a provision to assist countries that had been "adversely affected" by the 1965 amendments—and those countries just happened to be located in western Europe. The Irish were the biggest beneficiaries of this law. (Now it was fine to be a white Catholic as opposed to only a white Protestant.) The absence of close family relatives in the United States for prospective Irish immigrants was overcome with the creation of a special seed or pipeline category.

The diversity visa possibilities were not enough for those opposed to the large numbers of Asian and Latin immigrants. As a debate in the late 1980s raged over whether business and employment visas should be expanded, proposals were also made to reduce the Latin- and Asian-dominated family categories. The employment debate was reminiscent of the late 1800s and early 1900s, when employers wanted more cheap Asian or Mexican labor, and nativists and organized labor lobbied against it. In the modern version, big business prevailed in its desire for more skilled immigrant worker visas, but partly because congressional proponents viewed the new categories as a way of attracting non-Latin and non-Asian immigrants. Whatever reform came about, it was always with an eye toward what color or ethnic background qualified immigrants would bring, rather than simply what skills they could offer. The looks and ethnic background of prospective immigrants remained a test for which direction modern policy makers would take.

Part III

Defining Mexicans as Non-Americans

CHAPTER 7

Politicizing the Southwest Border

In the fall of 1994, Californians were in the throes of the debate over Proposition 187 and a U.S. senatorial battle between Democratic incumbent Dianne Feinstein and her free-spending Republican opponent, Michael Huffington. The central provisions of Proposition 187 would exclude undocumented immigrant children and the citizen children of undocumented immigrant parents from attending public schools in California. While the language of the proposition was not ethnic-specific, everyone knew that Mexican American children were the primary targets. The vast majority of Californians, including California Governor Pete Wilson and Congressman Huffington, supported the proposition. And even though Senator Feinstein ultimately announced her opposition to Proposition 187, she did so late in the campaign. But her statements in opposition to the referendum and campaign ads showing undocumented Mexicans dashing across the border made clear that she did not welcome the undocumented: "I read the polls and know that a majority of Californians support it. No way do I question the sincerity of working Californians, for I'm as fed up with the [undocumented alien] situation as they (are). But I believe Proposition 187 won't solve the problem, it'll only make it worse."[1] Today, the so-called illegal immigration problem has become synonymous with the control, or lack thereof, of the southwest border. As such, the "problem" is synonymous with Mexican migration, and Mexican immigrants are regarded as outside the construction of *real* Americans by many in the mainstream. The history of the border, labor recruitment, and border enforcement reveals the origin and perpetuation of this negative image.

The Republic of Texas and the Treaty of Guadalupe Hildalgo

What is now the southwestern United States was a destination of Spanish explorers a decade after Hernan Cortés's conquest of the Aztecs in 1519. Over the centuries, these early explorers were followed by settlers who located primarily in present-day New Mexico and to a lesser degree in areas that now comprise California, Texas, and Arizona. In 1821, Mexico took control of the entire territory (including all of California, Texas, New Mexico, and Arizona, as well as parts of Colorado, Utah, and Nevada) when it declared its independence from Spain. Within twenty-five years, however, present-day Texas had been annexed by the United States, and by 1849, the end of the Mexican-American War, the remaining areas were ceded to the United States.

Through the Louisiana Purchase of 1803, Texas had become a part of the United States, but in 1819 Texas was ceded to Spain in negotiations for Florida. Two years later, when Mexico became independent, the United States made two unsuccessful attempts to purchase Texas from Mexico. The settlement of Texas by 35,000 immigrants from the United States (including many slaveholders) finally led to the secession of Texas from Mexico. In November 1835, what was the northern part of the Mexican state of Coahuila-Tejas declared itself in revolt against Mexico's new centralist government. By February 1836, Texas declared its territory to be independent and that its border be extended to the Rio Grande rather than the more northern Rio Nueces that Mexicans recognized as the dividing line. Although Texans proclaimed themselves citizens of the Independent Lone Star Republic of Texas on April 21, 1836, following their victory over the Mexicans at the Battle of San Jacinto, Mexico continued to consider Tejas a rebellious province that they would reconquer someday.

The belief that American expansion westward and southward was inevitable, just, and divinely ordained was first labeled *manifest destiny* by John L. O'Sullivan, editor of the *United States Magazine and Democratic Review*. The annexation of Texas, O'Sullivan wrote in 1845, was "the fulfillment of our manifest destiny to overspread the continent allotted by Providence for the free development of our yearly multiplying millions."[2] In the 1840s expansionism reached a new fervor.

Fierce national pride spurred the quest for land. Subdued during hard times, it reasserted itself in the boom times of the 1840s. Americans were convinced that theirs was the greatest country on earth, with a special role to play in the world. As reform sought to perfect American society, so too expansionism promised to improve foreign lands. The acquisition of new territory, many Americans reasoned, would extend the benefits of America's republican system of government to the less fortunate and to those who were considered inferior.

In part, racism drove the belief in manifest destiny. Native Americans were perceived as savages best confined to small areas of the West. Latin Americans were seen as inferior peoples, best controlled or conquered. Thus, the same racism that justified slavery in the South and discrimination in the North supported expansion in the West. For some, expansion also offered a solution to the American race problem: free people of color, unwanted in the North and the South, could find refuge in distant territories. But racism also could limit expansion, for Americans did not look on Mexicans—whether Indian, European, African, or mestizo—with favor.

The establishment of an independent Texas and its annexation by the United States were major events. Soon after its independence, Texas sought annexation to the United

States. Sam Houston, president of the Texas republic, opened negotiations with Washington, but the issue quickly became politically explosive. Southerners favored annexing proslavery Texas; abolitionists, many northerners, and most Whigs opposed annexation. Given the political danger, President Jackson reneged on his promise to recognize Texas, and President Van Buren ignored the issue. But after Texas made overtures to the British, many in the United States feared that if Texas became an English ally, U.S. independence would be threatened. President Tyler, committed to expansion and eager to build political support in the South, pushed for annexation. Opposition remained strong, however, and the Senate rejected annexation in 1844. But after James Polk won the presidency on a Democratic platform calling for occupation of the Oregon Territory and annexation of Texas, the lame-duck Tyler proposed that Texas be admitted by joint resolution of Congress. The resolution passed. Mexico immediately broke relations with the United States, making war inevitable. In October, the citizens of Texas ratified annexation, and Texas joined the Union in December 1845.

Territorial expansion surged forward under President Polk. The annexation of Texas just before his inauguration strengthened his determination to acquire California and the Southwest (as well as Oregon). In an aggressive move, he ordered American troops to defend the border claimed but contested by Mexico, and he even attempted to buy a huge tract of land in the Southwest from the angry Mexicans. When that effort failed, Polk resolved to ask Congress for a declaration of war. During the process, Mexican and U.S. forces had already engaged in a bloody dispute on the disputed territory, and Congress recognized a state of war in May 1846. After U.S. troops were victorious in New Mexico and California, the war was taken to Mexico City, where a daring U.S. invasion was the decisive campaign of the war. The war was brought to an end when U.S. troops captured the Mexican capital.

Representatives of both countries signed the Treaty of Guadalupe Hidalgo in February 1848. The United States gained California and New Mexico (including present-day Nevada, Utah, and Arizona) and recognition of the Rio Grande as the southern boundary of Texas. This amounted to 55 percent of Mexico's territory. In return the American government agreed to settle the claims of its citizens against Mexico and to pay Mexico a mere $15 million.

The costs of the war included the deaths of 13,000 Americans and 50,000 Mexicans, plus Mexican-American enmity that endured into the twentieth century. The domestic cost to the United States was even higher. Public opinion was sharply divided, despite widespread hostility toward Mexicans. Southwesterners were enthusiastic about the war; New Englanders strenuously opposed it. Whigs in Congress charged that Polk, a Democrat, had "literally provoked" an unnecessary war and "usurped the power of Congress." The aged John Quincy Adams denounced the war, and a tall young, Illinois Whig named Abraham Lincoln questioned its justification. Abolitionists and a small minority of antislavery Whigs charged that the war was no less than a plot to extend slavery.

The 1848 treaty gave all Mexicans living in the ceded territory the option of remaining there and becoming U.S. citizens or of relocating within the new Mexican borders:

Article VIII

Mexicans now established in territories previously belonging to Mexico, and which remain for the future within the limits of the United States, as defined by the present treaty, shall be free to continue where they now reside, or to remove at any time to the Mexican Republic, retaining the property which they possess in the said territories, or disposing thereof, and removing the proceeds wherever they please, without their being subjected, on this account, to any contribution, tax, or charge whatsoever.

Those who shall prefer to remain in the said territories may either retain the title and rights of Mexican citizens, or acquire those of citizens of the United States. But they shall be under the obligation to make their election within one year from the date of the exchange of ratification of this treaty; and those who shall remain in the said territories after the expiration of that year, without having declared their intention to retain the character of Mexicans, shall be considered to have elected to become citizens of the United States.

Article IX

The Mexicans who, in the territories aforesaid, shall not preserve the character of citizens of the Mexican Republic, conformably with what is stipulated in the preceding Article, shall be incorporated into the Union of the United States, and admitted as soon as possible, according to the principles of the Federal Constitution, to the enjoyment of all the rights of citizens of the United States. In the meantime, they shall be maintained and protected in the enjoyment of their liberty, their property, and the civil rights now vested in them according to the Mexican laws. With respect to political rights, their condition shall be on an equality with that of the inhabitants of the other territories of the United States: and at least equally good as that of the inhabitants of Louisiana and the Floridas, when these provinces, by transfer from the French Republic and the Crown of Spain, become territories of the United States.[3]

Although some Mexicans moved to Mexico, most remained in what became U.S. territory. In the years immediately following the treaty, many Mexicans, especially those migrating from the annexed territories, thought of the territories as Mexico's. Mexicans and Americans paid little heed to the newly created international border, which was unmarked and wholly unreal to most. In essence, the boundary was at first an artificial one and did not effectively separate the new U.S. possessions from those south of the border. Mexicans continued to cross all along the border with the feeling that in reality nothing had changed. As a result, many border areas constituted one economic region. In these regions, miners, shepherds, and seasonal workers traveled in both directions to fill fluctuating labor demands. Unawareness of the border was a real force in posttreaty promotion access. Naïve obliviousness was encouraged from the outset by mutual economic advantage.

Recruitment and Migration of Mexican Laborers

Apart from Mexican gold seekers who migrated in 1849–50 (most of whom were driven away by white English-speaking miners), the first significant "modern-style" migration from Mexico began in the 1880s in response to the labor demand in railroads, mining, and agriculture. This movement is significant not for relative numbers, but for the distinctive promotional effort of U.S. industry that gave rise to it. Promotion of Mexican migration was part of a larger pattern of labor recruitment that began to emerge in the United States in the late nineteenth century.

Even with respect to European and Asian immigration during these early years, it would be simplistic to attribute the migration exclusively to political and economic disasters in the source countries. True, the federal government did little active promoting; from 1864 to 1868, employers were authorized to pay the passage and bind the service of immigrants. Individual states, however, actively developed programs to attract immigrants during the mid-nineteenth century. By the 1870s, competition for immigrants became so intense that a majority of states engaged promotional agents and offered other inducements. Private industry engaged in the same competitive promotion in source countries and domestic areas of high immigrant density. Historians in the early 1900s recognized the forces that induced this early migration: "Even more important than the initiative of immigrants have been the efforts of Americans and ship-owners to bring and attract them. . . . the desire to get cheap labor, to take in passenger fares, and to sell land have probably brought more immigrants than the hard conditions of Europe, Asia, and Africa have sent."[4]

Yet the arrival of immigrant labor brought with it a paradox: the immigrant was welcomed as a worker but rejected by being assigned an inferior status in the social structure. Established residents of the United States, themselves immigrants, perceived each succeeding immigrant group (especially Asians and Mexicans) as base and threatening to the American value system. According to these "nativists," new immigrants occupied the lowest-paid occupations because they were suited for them. Few nativists or even immigrants were willing to admit, especially at the time, that the role of independent entrepreneur—or any role above that of unskilled laborer in the United States—demanded more resources in 1840 than ever before and certainly more than those typically brought by poverty-stricken peasants. The resource gap between resident and new immigrant widened and the initial opportunity for skilled jobs decreased as mass production increased.

Relatedly, around the turn of the century labor turned on labor. Old labor blamed immigrant labor (primarily southern Europeans) for the former's low wages, poor working conditions, and unsatisfactory living standard. At the same time, old labor began to attack new labor for reluctance to enter unions, a curious twist in that, before 1870, nativists had attacked immigrants for organizing. This turn of events is thought by some to have been the product of the industrial employers' genius. There is evidence that whenever labor began to organize over wages and working conditions, employers would rush about the world, if necessary, to secure a new unorganized group of cheap migrant labor. Afterward, employers would join old labor's lament that new immigrant labor depressed wages and working conditions. Employers were quick to point out, "that's competition." It is little wonder that old labor attacked new labor; after all, "they" were the competition.

While both the international recruitment and fraternal antagonism of this larger pattern were, for the most part, indiscriminate by nature, they collaborated in their most repressive form in the whipsawing of Chinese immigrants. Active recruitment of Chinese labor during the gold rush was followed by old labor's animosity, an anti-Chinese crusade, and the Chinese Exclusion Act of 1882. (See Chapter 2.) There is substantial evidence that employers acquiesced in exclusionary acts that originated with the labor groups and that many who did were comforted by the prospect of their replacement by potentially more compliant new immigrants from Mexico.

Between 1880 and 1900, Mexican migration was insignificant in numbers. The Mexican population in the United States in 1900 was estimated at about 100,000. Migration during this period reflects, for the first time, the attributes of a mass movement. The pattern of relocation was distinct from that of the prior migration during the years 1850–80, and was remarkably similar to the forthcoming wholesale mass migration, both documented and undocumented. For instance, although many areas in Mexico provided migrant workers from 1880 to 1900, for the first time the central plateau, densely populated and poor, became a fertile source of recruits. And for the first time significant numbers of Mexicans began to travel regularly and seek employment throughout the southwestern United States and even in such places as Kansas City and Chicago.

In view of the surrounding circumstances, it is almost inconceivable that the emerging pattern of migration from Mexico was not, in significant part, attributable to recruitment and promotion. Before this period, migration had been largely restricted to the cross-migration in economically integrated border regions and to the excursions of certain Mexican miners, particularly from the state of Sonora. Despite substantial economic disparity between source regions in the central plateau of Mexico and destination regions in the southwestern United States, migration for other American jobs was virtually unknown. With the exclusion of the Chinese, widespread and long-distance Mexican migration began. Expansion of agriculture, particularly in the Rio Grande Valley of Texas and the central valley of California, created the demand. Large numbers of central Mexican workers found their way to jobs in the United States via an elaborate system of recruitment and support.

Employers had a self-interest in assuring a steady supply of cheap, willing labor. While immigration was, in part, a product of general economic conditions in Mexico, a complex and successful strategy of recruitment had existed long before 1900. American labor agents seem to have thought that men specially recruited from Mexico were better than those picked up by chance along the border. Furthermore, migration northward, particularly from Mexico's poor central plateau, was physically accommodated by the development of the railroad system built largely with American money.

In this period, the federal government played a role of *de jure* control and *de facto* passivity. In 1882, Congress, reacting to labor-protectionist demands, imposed a head tax of fifty cents on each immigrant entering the country. The 1882 act left the actual border inspection and collection of the head tax in the hands of existing state agencies that largely ignored the law. As a result, its enactment manifested an awareness of and acquiescence in recruitment, and fostered disrespect for the law among those involved in the immigration process.

The 1882 act also forbade admission to any person likely to become a public charge. This measure failed to satisfy domestic labor, and in 1885 and 1887 the federal government supplemented the act with contract labor laws prohibiting anyone from prepaying an immigrant's transportation to the United States in return for a promise to provide service. An 1888 amendment provided for the deportation of any laborer found to have entered in violation of the act within one year. On its face, this set of provisions effectively and severely restricted immigration.

Upon closer examination, however, foreign workers had not been boxed out; domestic labor had been outboxed. The contract labor laws contained a number of exemptions, including one for foreigners temporarily residing (and coincidentally working) in the United States. This exemption, coupled with lax enforcement by immigration officials along the Mexican border, undermined the protection ostensibly provided by the new laws.

What emerges from this brief account is American involvement in a pattern of recruitment designed to serve the proclivity of American employers to hire cheap, temporary laborers. At the same time, laws were adopted in response to domestic labor's demands, but these laws were ineffective, unenforced, or both. The practical effect was to permit continued disregard for the border and to cultivate deepening disrespect for the law. Poor people in Mexico benefited from the system; they needed the money. Their role as suppliers of cheap labor generated racial antipathy in domestic workers who expected their government to protect them from such competition. The most vital aspect of the process, at least for purposes of later analysis, is that Mexican workers grew dependent on wages earned in the United States. If anyone in this country worried about the consequences of dependence in the long run for workers, their families, and their dependents, those worries were not publicly expressed.

Near the turn of the century, several factors combined to increase migration from Mexico. Continued growth in mining, railroads, and agriculture, the latter stimulated by protective tariffs and by federally supported irrigation projects, expanded demand for cheap labor. Because forces similar to those that excluded the Chinese were now at work against the Japanese, the existing labor supply diminished. Many Japanese had been recruited in the 1890s to help fill the void left by Chinese exclusion, but restrictionist efforts resulted in the Gentlemen's Agreement of 1907–8, under which Japan agreed to issue no more passports to workers wishing to come to the United States. (See Chapter 2.) The resulting shortage of cheap labor triggered intensified recruitment in Mexico and increased immigration from southern and eastern Europe. The enhanced promotion in Mexico proved unusually successful due in part to the deepening poverty and increased social unrest of prerevolutionary (pre-1910) Mexico. As a result, between 1900 and 1910 the population of persons of Mexican descent living in the United States increased by approximately 49,000, nearly half the number of the total Mexican population in the United States only ten years earlier.

From 1910 to 1920, approximately 200,000 Mexicans were admitted into the United States. Many sought safety from the upheaval of the Revolution of 1910 and were admitted as economic refugees. During World War I others were actively recruited to fill severe manpower shortages resulting from American involvement in military service and the curtailment of the migration of cheap European laborers. So strong was the need for cheap labor that a provision of the 1917 Immigration Act, mandating a head tax and literacy requirement (see Chapter 3), was legally waived for Mexicans. Notably, the waiver was effected pursuant to a statutory provision authorizing, for temporary employment, the admission of various classes of workers, including agricultural workers. The "Ninth Proviso," as the statutory provision was commonly called, was later to serve as the authority for the admission of Mexican farmworkers during the Bracero program.

The 1917 act and the 1918 waiver in conjunction marked an important instance of self-serving manipulation of immigration law by the United States with respect to the admission of "temporary" Mexican labor. A *de jure* loophole for temporary labor had existed since the passage of the first Contract Labor Law in 1885 and was in fact used in the 1880s to bring Mexican migrants to the United States. However, the 1918 waiver was the first such instance involving a significant number of Mexican migrants. It took the combined effect of an increasingly vigorous restrictionist movement, a World War, and an amplified labor demand to focus attention on Mexico's labor resources.

There is also evidence that Mexicans were thought to be less troublesome than other potential immigrant groups. Mexican laborers were described as "not socially or industrially ambitious, like European and Asiatic immigrants"; they "can't do white man's work [and thus] compete little, if at all, with white labor."[5] Moreover, they were considered distinct from the southern blacks because they were not permanent, did not acquire land, and remained nomadic and outside of American civilization. The advantage of Mexican labor was summarized as follows: "His strongest point is his willingness to work for a low wage. . . . So long as the Mexican immigration is transient it is not likely to have much [negative] influence upon the United States."[6] The Dillingham Commission of 1911 concluded that Mexicans were undesirable as citizens but needed as cheap labor for the expansion of industry and the exploitation of natural resources.

Reports and other literature of the era reveal this country's attitude that Mexican laborers were useful but not the kind of people one would want as permanent members of the community. As long as Mexicans' participation in the workplace was economically efficient, their temporary presence in the United States was, apparently as a matter of national policy, to be encouraged and tolerated. But they were not regarded as potential members of the community.

Events in the decade after World War I provide evidence that American recognition of Mexican labor's value matured from appreciation into economic attachment. The 1918 *de jure* waiver by the federal government of the application of immigration law to Mexican labor was initially conceived as a wartime measure. Yet the close of World War I did not bring an end to the use of Mexican labor. Southwestern employers, primarily in agriculture, simply would not allow it. The temporary admission program's benefits, which included a financial windfall and few long-term legal responsibilities, were staggering. During the 1919–20 and 1920–21 seasons, the Arizona Cotton

Growers' Association spent approximately $425,000 recruiting and transporting Mexican workers. According to one official, the association's recruitment of Mexican workers saved the growers $2.8 million in picking costs by maintaining "as perfectly an elastic supply of labor as the world has ever seen." Industrial and agricultural representatives testified before congressional committees in the 1920s that Mexican labor had been a vital factor in the development of their enterprises.

In the face of a post–World War recession, an increasingly powerful domestic labor movement, and mobilized restrictionist sentiment, the success of Southwestern employers during the 1920s was remarkable. So too was their intricate and ingenious domestic strategy that had two compatible goals: first, gaining federal approval for continued immigration law exceptions for temporary Mexican labor, and second, keeping the migrant labor pool large, fluid, and unorganized. Employers argued that domestic workers, despite the recession, would not fill available jobs at any wage. Some jobs were seasonal or casual at best. For example, California agriculture operated through large-scale units producing specialized, labor-intensive crops. Demand for workers peaked at certain times; at other times, there was virtually no need for them. Other openings, such as second-hand jobs on the desert sections of railroad lines and unskilled work in desert mines and cement plants, were in highly undesirable locations. Other opportunities, such as working the sugar beet fields in Colorado, were, according to employers, simply unattractive to all except poor Mexicans. Colorado Congressman Edward T. Taylor explained:

> The American laboring people will not get down on their hands and knees in the dirt and pull weeds and thin these beets, and break their backs doing that kind of work. In fact there are very few people who can stand that kind of work. No matter how much they are paid, they can not and will not do it. That kind of labor is hard tedious work.[7]

Most available jobs were in fact arduous. Employers, through indifference or perhaps design, made these jobs more intolerable than they need have been, and drove off domestic workers. For example, conditions and facilities at migrant labor camps throughout the period were deplorable. Housing in the camps was generally makeshift and state standards were disregarded. In its 1927 Annual Report, the California Commission of Immigration and Housing found

> utter indifference and total disregard on the part of the operators of the camps as to how or where the Mexican employees lived, were manifest on all sides—a condition for which there was no excuse. . . . In addition to finding the camps in a deplorable condition, the director and county health officer . . . also brought to light the fact that many Mexican children who were infected with eye disease were attending the same schools as local children. Inspection showed that the camps from which the infected children came were invariably filthy hovels.[8]

Another committee concluded that the record "discloses, with monotonous regularity, a shocking degree of human misery."[9]

Finally, the employers' domestic strategy sought to capitalize on well-entrenched racist sentiment. The prevailing attitude was that these were Mexican jobs, just as they had once been Chinese and Japanese jobs, and that, being by nature brutally difficult, they were especially suitable for persons with the presumed mental and physical attributes of Mexicans. In short, the jobs were stigmatized as being beneath white Americans.

To ensure that the labor pool remained large and unorganizable, Southwestern employers stepped up their recruitment program in Mexico. Efforts to encourage a steady flow of workers from Mexico persisted despite the knowledge that most Mexicans were now entering without authorization and, that, according to immigration authorities, "many of the laborers never return[ed] to Mexico."[10] Moreover, employer strategy was flexible. When it appeared during the 1920s that strict quotas on Mexican immigration might be imposed despite organized employer resistance,[11] employers began recruiting workers from the Philippines. By 1930, 30,000 Filipinos were working in California alone, testimony to the employers' capacity to mobilize quickly and redirect their recruitment effort.

Judging from numbers and from the cooperation of the federal government, the employers' strategy worked. The best evidence available indicates that nearly half a million Mexican workers crossed the border during the 1920s. Although the waiver of 1918 was suspended immediately after the war, the federal government sought to minimize the negative impact on employers by issuing other orders permitting literate Mexican laborers to remain permanently upon paying a head tax. When an immigration limitation in the form of a national numerical quota system was temporarily adopted in 1921 and then permanently enacted in the Immigration Act of 1924, countries of the Western Hemisphere, including Mexico, were excluded. Displeased by these exclusions, restrictionists were somewhat appeased by the creation of a professional 450-man Border Patrol in that same year. Even this backfired in favor of employers. Policing what had once been a largely disregarded boundary, the Border Patrol was probably more effective in discouraging agricultural workers from returning to Mexico during the winter than it was in prohibiting initial undocumented entry.

While organized labor was displeased, its leaders were willing to reach a tacit political compromise with Southwestern employers. Organized labor did not want Mexicans employed in "white" industrial jobs, where unions were successfully battling for higher wages and better working conditions. As long as Mexicans were restricted to employment in Southwestern agriculture and other stigmatized jobs, where virtually no effort was being expended to organize workers or to improve working and living conditions, organized labor was willing to countenance their presence. Because their primary goals were compatible, Southwestern employers joined organized labor in condemning the use of Mexicans in industrial jobs, particularly as strike-breakers. An incidental but notable effect of this political alignment was the reinforcement of labor's notion that Mexican workers were either unorganizable or not worth organizing. Thus, for example, the American Federation of Labor barred Mexicans from its membership because it claimed Mexican competition was at the source of ongoing wage depression. Mexicans responded that because they lacked the clout to demand union rates, they had no choice but to work for lower wages. Meanwhile, employers, organized labor, and the American public in general seemed to have lulled themselves into the comforting assumption that the Mexican presence was temporary.

Efforts to extend the quota system to Mexico and other Western Hemisphere countries persisted after the passage of the 1924 act. The State Department opposed quotas as violative of the policy of Pan-American goodwill, adding, not coincidentally, that at the time 60 percent of all U.S. overseas capital investment and 34 percent of its foreign trade were with Western Hemisphere nations. Rather than risk economic retaliation if restrictionist efforts to impose quotas on the Western Hemisphere were realized, the State Department devised a clever palliative to decrease Mexican immigration. It simply required strict enforcement of existing immigration law, including old provisions like the head tax, the literacy test, the Contract Labor Law, and the prohibitions against immigrants likely to become public charges. The short-run result was sharply curtailed immigration; the long-run advantage was the continued retention of virtually unlimited federal flexibility for the future admission of temporary labor.

While the political strategy of Southwestern employers was shrewd and effective, the work of the federal government was equally adroit, satisfying at once labor and restrictionists' outcries and the employers' economic interests.[12] Mexican workers continued to serve as a good resonance to U.S. employers during the "Roaring Twenties." The decade's intricate trade-offs culminated in a viewpoint shared to some degree by all sectors, public and private: if Mexicans were needed for nonwhite jobs, their temporary presence was to be encouraged and accommodated; if not, they were to be kept out and if necessary driven out. Again, there was a notable absence of inquiry, much less concern, by U.S. leaders for the impact on the Mexican worker, his household, his pueblo, or his country.

Expulsion and the Bracero Program

After the stock market crash in October 1929, the bottom fell out of the economy and xenophobic notions surfaced almost immediately. Ridding the country of workers who were "no longer needed" became a priority. Undocumented Mexicans were rounded up and deported, but that was not enough for anti-Mexican forces. Exclusionists rallied public and private agencies at state and local levels to institute repatriation programs that encouraged documented Mexicans and U.S. citizens of Mexican descent to return to Mexico. The intent was threefold: to return indigent nationals to their own country, in this case Mexico; to save welfare agencies money; and to create jobs for *real* Americans.[13]

Unlike deportation, repatriation seldom involved the federal government, but the number of individuals affected was extraordinary. In Indiana, the repatriation program was financed largely by contributions from local businesses. Threats of physical violence induced many Mexicans to abandon jobs and long-established domiciles throughout the country. Trains, cars, trucks, and buses streamed southward from Los Angeles, Phoenix, El Paso, Denver, Kansas City, Chicago, Detroit, Pittsburgh, New York, New Orleans, San Diego, San Francisco, Portland, Seattle, and Fairbanks,

Alaska. During a five-month period in 1931, 50,000 Mexican nationals and their children were repatriated from Los Angeles alone. The U.S. Labor Department reported that two million returned to Mexico over a fifteen-month period.[14]

During the 1930s, poor white farmers from Oklahoma, Arkansas, and Texas, whose desperate migration to the Southwest has been passionately described, filled most of the slackened demand for labor in large agricultural enterprises. As the economy grew stronger with the approach of World War II, most of the "Okies" and "Arkies" relocated to better-paying industrial jobs. Their exodus and the new agricultural expansion renewed the domestic need for cheap labor. Under the authority of the Ninth Proviso, the federal government immediately moved, with almost amoral aplomb, to allow employers to initiate a new recruitment of Mexican labor.

Shortly thereafter, in 1942, the United States negotiated a treaty with Mexico in the form of the Labor Importation program, providing for the use of Mexicans as temporary workers in U.S. agriculture. The Labor Importation program is more commonly referred to as the Bracero program, a colloquial allusion to the "men of strength." Unlike previous measures, the treaty purported to regulate the employment of Mexicans as temporary agricultural workers through qualitative and quantitative provisions. Many of these provisions were mandated by new Mexican law enacted in response to the pernicious effects of the previous decade's repatriation; others were included to safeguard the two nations' national interests.

Braceros were tied to American private employers by contracts guaranteed by the federal government. The law qualitatively controlled transportation, wages, and working and living conditions. The treaty, supplemented and slightly amended by subsequent legislative acts and international agreements with Mexico, governed the emergency farm and industry program through December 31, 1947. Throughout the period, the federal government supervised the program and actively assisted U.S. employers in the recruitment of the Mexican workers.

From 1947, when the special wartime legislation expired, until 1951, when Public Law 78 was passed, the temporary worker program continued unabated, again pursuant to the authority of the Ninth Proviso. During these years the federal government abdicated its supervisory role. Contracts were made directly between employer and worker without government guarantees and absent qualitative and quantitative control. Taking advantage of the government's nonintervention, employers recruited more vigorously than before from the interior of Mexico and swiftly legalized undocumented workers already in the United States.

The Mexican government was not as pleased with the unsupervised program. Its displeasure was apparently outweighed, however, by the need to help alleviate domestic underemployment and to raise income. Some observers in the United States shared Mexico's displeasure, albeit for different reasons. A report issued by President Truman's Commission on Migratory Labor severely criticized administrative agencies for their failure to supervise adequately the postwar program. According to the commission's report, failure to administer the undocumented flow, wage rates, and working conditions adversely affected domestic labor.

Despite these concerns, Public Law 78, adopted in 1951, authorized the recruitment and employment of temporary Mexican workers by the United States. Shortly thereafter, the United States and Mexico reached a new international agreement that purported to replace the unsupervised program maintained since 1947 under the authority of the Ninth Proviso. Mirroring provisions of the 1942 agreement, the new one claimed to regulate and protect the interests of all concerned. Imported male laborers were to be provided with individual contracts supervised by the Farm Security Administration (FSA) that guaranteed minimum standards of housing (including laundry, bathing, toilets, and waste disposal), a minimum wage of $0.30 per hour, at least thirty days of work upon arrival, free transportation, and other essential living and labor criteria. With minor amendments, this new agreement served to implement the Bracero program until its termination in 1964.

The Mexican government had wisely insisted on minimum working standards for their citizens but could do little to monitor U.S. compliance with them. Evidence of this was demonstrated in the "El Paso Incident" in October 1948, when local INS officials unilaterally opened the U.S.-Mexican border at El Paso to eager migrant workers. Even though World War II had been over for three years, farmers' demands for cheap labor could apparently not be quenched in compliance with the agreement. Mexico City's response to such a blatant violation of the agreement was immediate abrogation. The State Department answered with a note of apology, but U.S. farmers continued to recruit undocumented workers even before the two countries reached another agreement.

Concern for migrant labor conditions on U.S. farms was justified. The FSA was drastically underfunded and provided, for example, that only two inspectors, headquartered at Portland, Oregon, were responsible for "monitoring all the Braceros working in Utah, Idaho, Oregon, Washington and Montana." There were countless testimonies of legally contracted Braceros who experienced widespread disregard for inadequate housing, food, health care, and even fair pay. The majority of recruits came from the rural, least developed, and more isolated regions of Mexico with very little, if any, background in English. This basic factor allowed farmer and recruiter manipulation of records and contracts, as well as contributed to the overall bewilderment of laborers. Climate was the most immediate challenge for many Braceros who arrived in regions such as the Northwest. Finding appropriate clothing for an Oregonian spring in southern Mexico proved difficult and growers were not expected to provide it.

Where the FSA lacked manpower, the black market compensated. Recruitment of undocumented workers and smuggling became commonplace from the very beginning of the Bracero program. Mexico's countless undocumented emigrants had even less leverage to push for realization of promises and lived under the constant threat of exposure. Undocumented residents granted farmers extended leverage to set arbitrary wages and demand longer hours over and above what the Bracero program legally allowed. While legally contracted Braceros could threaten to expose farmers' actions to authorities, undocumented workers knew such resistance would lead to deportation.

On balance, the program failed to achieve its professed goal of qualitatively and quantitatively controlling Mexican immigration. In addition, ill treatment, self-centered disregard, and broken promises characterized the program. Its failures bespeak an even greater disdain for Mexican workers than that suggested by the years of unregulated recruitment and employment. These failures were the product of the negligent, reckless, and sometimes malicious disregard for a national obligation explicitly assumed in the Bracero program. The United States not only did not fulfill its promise in the Bracero program; it never even properly equipped itself to do so.

In terms of servicing American economic interests, however, the program was without historical peer. In spite of the opposition of huge organizations such as the AFL-CIO to the migrant labor exploitation that was inherent to the Bracero program, it was renewed consecutively throughout the administrations of five U.S. presidents. Braceros constituted a quarter of the farm labor force in California, Arizona, New Mexico, and Texas, contributing not only to the vital food production of the period but also to increasing U.S. dominance in agriculture. As one administrator of the program observed, Mexican Braceros provided a "captive labor force . . . unnatural in our free competitive economy."[15] These men—for it must be remembered that Public Law 78 limited admission to adult males—were available to employers without the posting of a bond and with an exemption from social security and income tax withholding provisions. Braceros were the perfect workers for nonwhite jobs because their availability was controlled and predictable, and they did not place heavy social burdens on farm communities.

Despite all the economic advantages of the Bracero program, it did impose burdens on employers that could be avoided by using undocumented workers. While recruitment and transportation of legally contracted Braceros cost U.S. taxpayers about $450 apiece for the 4.5 million legal laborers, the program spurred the long-term migration of millions of undocumented workers (at no direct cost to taxpayers) who continued to support U.S. farming. By employing undocumented workers, an employer could save the $25 bond required for each documented worker and the $15 contracting fee imposed by the U.S. government, and could evade the minimum employment period, fixed wages, and other safeguards built into the official Bracero program. At the same time, legalized immigration seems to have removed psychological barriers that had reduced the willingness of Mexicans to seek work in the United States. Eliminating those barriers generated by the viciously effective repatriation of the 1930s probably affected undocumented as well as documented immigration. In any event, the rise in legal immigration associated with the Bracero program and the earlier activity under the Ninth Proviso coincided with a rise in undocumented migration. According to the official statistics of the INS, apprehensions of deportable aliens averaged less than 10,000 per year from 1934 to 1943. From 1944 to 1954 apprehensions rose, averaging greater than 277,000 per year with a high of 1,089,538 in 1954.

The suggestion that the legal program actually, though indirectly, encouraged undocumented immigration deserves elaboration because it bears on the general theme that the United States's acquiescence invited disrespect for law. The first person to note the relationship between the Bracero program and the undocumented migration of those years seems to have been Eleanor Hadley, who argued that the upsurge in undocumented migration was a response to Braceros' perhaps exaggerated accounts of the wages available in the United States. "The next year [Braceros] wanted to repeat their performance and their neighbors wanted to join," Hadley wrote. "The result was that there were many more Mexicans who wanted to come to the United States than there were certifications of need issued by the Secretary of Labor."[16] While Hadley's observations seem accurate in view of all that we now know of the phenomenon, they also seem unnecessarily circumspect. Hadley seems to assume that the Bracero program was the first instance of organized promotion, ignoring the impact of the many decades of *de facto* and *de jure* recruitment, and implicitly overlooking the fact that the majority of Mexicans recruited after the 1880s were undocumented.

It is entirely implausible to regard the United States's role in undocumented entry as unintentional, naïve, or innocent. Policy makers in the United States must have been aware that recruitment activities designed to promote the Bracero program would encourage poor Mexicans to believe the United States was a land of opportunity, thereby encouraging those who could not be admitted legally to enter without inspection. The relative attractiveness of undocumented entry was increased by the failure to enforce the promises that had been made in connection with the adoption of the Bracero program. U.S. policy makers relied on the tradition of migration to help win new recruits for their "qualitatively" controlled program. They must have been aware from past experience that the first wave of Braceros would be followed by increasing numbers of workers, documented and undocumented. Evidence indicates that policy makers knew particular regions in Mexico were primed for news of work opportunities, for the Bracero program focused its recruitment in the same areas that had been the target of earlier promotional efforts.

Although Eleanor Hadley may have unknowingly depreciated the value of hard-won tradition, she did note Congress's peculiar response to this "new" undocumented phenomenon. As the number of apprehended Mexican aliens grew during the Bracero program, Congress cut back funds for the Border Patrol, resulting in the retention of fewer patrol officers. Hadley characterized this response as "splendidly indifferent"; again, evidence suggests that the more accurate characterization is "splendidly suspicious." It was well known that undocumented workers benefited employers, although it is also true that "indifference" toward the undocumented flow helped the worker avoid red tape and fees.

While the message of work opportunities in the United States was being broadcast in villages throughout Mexico, lawmakers in the United States were avoiding the most obvious methods of discouraging undocumented migration, such as sanctioning U.S. employers of undocumented workers. When a provision outlawing willful importation, transportation, or harboring of undocumented aliens was debated prior to congressional passage of the Immigration and Nationality Act of 1952, an amendment was proposed that would impose criminal penalties for the employment of undocumented aliens if the employer had "reasonable grounds to believe a worker was not legally in the United States." Not only was the amendment soundly defeated, but the following was added to the final legislation: "For the purposes of this section, employment [including the usual and normal practices incident to employment] shall not be deemed to constitute harboring."[17] The defeat of the proposed employer sanctions caused the *New York Times* to observe:

> It is remarkable how some of the same Senators and Representatives who are all for enacting the most rigid barriers against immigration from Southern Europe suffer from a sudden blindness when it comes to protecting the southern border of the United States. This peculiar weakness is most noticeable among members from Texas and the Southwest, where the [undocumented Mexicans] happen to be principally employed.[18]

Opposition to employer sanctions in the 1970s and 1980s (when such laws were finally enacted) was based on concern for the civil rights of documented workers. Opposition to employer sanctions in 1951 and 1952, on the other hand (two years before *Brown v. Board of Education* and twelve years before the passage of the modern civil rights acts), reflects little more than indifference, if not insensitivity, toward documented Latinos. A careful reading of the earlier Senate debates suggests that profit-minded Southwestern employers led, and hypocritical members of Congress supported, opposition to imposing criminal sanctions on employers of undocumented aliens.

In 1954 over a million undocumented Mexicans were deported as part of an INS initiative dubbed Operation Wetback. Southwestern employers, who probably saw the operation as little more than a temporary setback, responded by making more extensive use of workers under the Bracero program. Federal government statistics indicate that, after remaining constant at about 200,000 from 1951 to 1953, the number of Braceros admitted increased by 105,000 during 1954 (the year of Operation Wetback), by another 100,000 in 1955, and leveled off at about 450,000 for the years 1956–59. As a result of effective Border Patrol enforcement, the number of undocumented aliens apprehended decreased gradually to a low of 30,272 in 1962. Some have attributed the rise in the number of Braceros from 1954 to 1959 to agriculture's growing confidence in the economic and political feasibility of the program. True only in part, this observation overlooks the fact that during these years enforcement of immigration law was so effective that the Bracero program was the only viable method to recruit workers.

That Operation Wetback could be mounted is, in itself, not inconsistent with the asserted political power of employers or with the contention that employers benefited from the undocumented worker program. Operation Wetback and the change of policy that it reflected followed Attorney General Herbert Brownell's 1953 tour of the border. Brownell's shock at the openness of the border and existing public sentiment proved temporarily more potent than the power of Southwestern employers. In view of the events that preceded and followed Operation Wetback, it seems unlikely that the lack of enforcement of immigration law was just the product of naïve laxity.

While Operation Wetback temporarily relieved national hysteria, criticism of the Bracero program mounted. In particular, organized labor continued to argue that Braceros depressed wages and working conditions. Labor's conviction was supported by government reports indicating that in Bracero-dominated areas the prevailing wage was set by Braceros and remained stationary. So strong was the criticism, President

Kennedy directed the secretary of labor to establish "adverse-effect" rates for each state employing Braceros. Adverse-effect rates were the minimum wage rates that employers had to offer and pay Braceros to prevent an adverse effect on wages of domestic workers similarly employed.

Despite the continuing assault on the Bracero program's legitimacy, the "emergency wartime measure" survived twenty-two years, until 1964, and employed nearly five million Mexican workers. The program's longevity is largely attributable to the political bond between employers, particularly in Southwestern agriculture, and congressional leaders. This bond, formidable throughout, was particularly so during the final decade of the embattled program; yet, as always, employer strategy remained flexible.

Probably contributing most to the program's ultimate termination was the sense that it was preventing normal interplay of labor supply and demand, infringing on employment opportunities for U.S. resident workers, and dragging down their wage levels. With each successive extension, proponents of the Bracero program faced greater opposition. Reduction of demand for Braceros after 1959 was related not only to mechanization in cotton and sugar beet production but also to tightened enforcement of program requirements. Tests for "adverse effect" were made more specific, and in early 1962 Bracero wage rates were raised sharply to a level determined to protect the wages of U.S. workers. When Public Law 78 came up for renewal in 1963, Congress decided to give it but one final year.

In 1963, when it became clear that the Bracero program would expire at the end of 1964, Southwestern employers and their congressional backers confidently pushed for the importation of Mexicans as H-2 or temporary alien workers under the provisions of the 1952 act. In so doing, the alliance simply aimed to reinstitute "temporary" and "discretionary" foreign labor programs available as early as the 1880s and as recently as 1947–51. The effort was defeated only by the narrowest of margins, and primarily due to the opposition of Secretary of Labor Willard Wirtz. His policy of preventing the importation of Mexican workers under the H-2 program continues, and the reasons underlying it remain unexamined to this day.

The defeat of the Bracero program was notable because from that point forward, cheap labor became exclusively undocumented. Employers, who had more extensively used the Bracero program during and immediately after Operation Wetback, now almost exclusively used the undocumented program after their defeat on the issue of the Bracero program and the H-2 workers provision. Whereas the 1950s and early 1960s revealed determined efforts to preserve the Bracero program, the period until 1986 evidenced a pernicious campaign to ensure the continued existence of the undocumented program. This well-documented campaign focused primarily on preserving immunity for those employing undocumented workers; numerous bills proposing employers' sanctions were defeated and delayed. The campaign was aware of public perceptions and of the advantages of the newly found concern for the civil rights of documented Latinos.

With immunity intact, employers had little to do after 1964 but reap the benefits of a century of promotion. Direct and indirect recruitment, though still undertaken, was most likely unnecessary. Tradition alone provided an adequate pool of potential workers. In addition, immigrant labor's traditional reliance on access to American wages was magnified by population growth and patterns of development in Mexico. Finally, to the extent that the border served as a barrier, employers learned to rely on the wily skills and self-interest of *coyotes* (commercial smugglers) and on the undocumented workers' knowledge of evasive tactics that had become an integral part of the migratory culture.

Direct and indirect recruitment has continued in spite of the implementation of employer sanctions legislation in 1986. As recently as 2001, researchers continued to identify organized groups of farm labor contractors who travel to Mexican cities and towns, where they offer loans and work guarantees to convince potential farm workers to cross the border into the United States. The process involves well-organized networks of contractors and contractor agents representing major U.S. agricultural companies. The headhunters are themselves often Mexicans who recruit in their own hometowns and farming communities, where it is not difficult to earn the trust of eager farm hands. One of the contractors' favorite tactics to attract workers is to offer them loans to help pay off debts, coupled with a pledge to find the person work north of the border. Due to the lack of willing farm hands in the United States, many U.S. companies are willing to foot the costs of illegally bringing the workers into the country.[19]

Conclusion

Under the Treaty of Guadalupe Hidalgo in 1848 the United States acquired much of the western part of today's nation. The treaty also marked the beginning of restrictionist policies that prevented the free flow of citizens both to and from the United States and Mexico.

In the later half of the nineteenth century, the significant immigration of Mexicans to the United States was initiated by individual U.S. states to attract cheaper and more "pliable" labor. As these states turned toward workers from Mexico, they began to rely less on older immigrants from southern and eastern Europe. These two immigrant groups, the new and the old, found themselves fighting over the same piece of the American pie. Employers encouraged disunity between the two labor groups in order to shield themselves from the brunt of a unified labor force. At the time, the Chinese carried the heaviest burden of oppression and discrimination, as epitomized by the exclusion law of 1882.

The most attractive feature of Mexican labor was its temporariness. Due to the proximity of Mexico to the United States, many in the United States promoted immigration policies that allowed Mexicans to remain here only as long as their labor was needed. Once their work was completed, they could then return to Mexico. Although this cultivated animosity between Mexicans and other laborers, U.S. employers reasoned that Mexican workers were merely doing work unsuitable for *real* Americans.

As the economy worsened poor white farmers were now willing to do agricultural work once limited to Mexicans; not until the economic growth spurred by World War

II and its aftermath did the United States and Mexico institutionalize the transient Mexican labor force in the form of the Bracero program. But the U.S. government did little to enforce the terms of the agreement that governed working conditions, and abuses were widespread. An increase in undocumented aliens also resulted because employers found undocumented migrants cheaper than those employed through the Bracero program. At the same time, as the number of Mexicans who crossed the international borders without inspection grew, funds for Border Patrols were reduced. But as political pressures expanded, in 1954 a concerted effort to deport workers forcibly back to Mexico embodied in Operation Wetback was launched. This resulted in employers doubling their efforts to obtain cheap Mexican labor through the Bracero program.

The Bracero program was officially terminated in 1964. What we today understand to be the crisis of undocumented aliens from Mexico had its official roots in the demise of the program. Employers became accustomed to cheap Mexican labor and were willing to ignore the fact that many employees were not legally residing in the country with proper immigration documents. Of course, once an undocumented worker was discovered by the INS, the worker, not the employer, had to deal with the ramifications.

CHAPTER 8

Patrolling the Border and Sweeping for Mexicans

Low-wage Mexican workers continued to (and still) respond to U.S. agriculture's recruitment and the availability of work in the Southwest (and later other parts of the country); attention to U.S. border enforcement and workplace raids, however, tended to increase when the U.S. economy sagged or when organized labor exerted pressure on immigration officials.

Table 8-1 illustrates that undocumented workers were recruited in large numbers during as well as after the Bracero program.

As their numbers increased, so did calls to "control the border" or "free up jobs for American workers." Clearly U.S. employers were not searching for would-be Americans but maintaining a pool of low-wage workers. Organized labor and others troubled by undocumented Mexican workers, on the other hand, sought new tools to keep out the undesirable Mexican laborer. Beefing up the Border Patrol along the southwest border and workplace raids became the strategies of choice.

TABLE 8-1 Mexican Braceros, Immigrants, and Undocumented Apprehensions, 1949–1974

	1949	1953	1964	1965	1970	1974
Braceros	107,000	201,380	177,736	20,284	0	0
Legal Immigrants	7,977	18,459	34,448	40,686	44,821	71,863
Undocumented Apprehended	233,485	676,602	43,844	55,349	277,377	709,959

Source: U.S. Immigration and Naturalization Service Annual Reports, 1949–1954 and 1964–1974.

Riding the Line: The Creation of the Border Patrol

Guarding its borders was not much of a priority for the United States until the late 1800s. What triggered this need was not a concern about Mexican or other Latin American immigration, but anxiety over surreptitious entries by Chinese. After the passage of the Chinese Exclusion Act of 1882, many Chinese laborers sought to steal their way across the United States–Mexico border. But by the early 1900s, as steamship passenger service from China to Mexico was terminated, border troubles with Mexico and the involvement of the United States in World War I changed the situation.

In 1917, Congress enacted the literacy test that required of all immigrants some knowledge of reading and writing in at least one language. (See Chapter 3.) Prior to 1917, Mexican laborers were admitted to work in the United States without much difficulty, but the literacy test became a huge obstacle. As a result, Mexican workers began to move illicitly across the border region and continued to do so even though a waiver of the literacy test was granted later to Mexican laborers. (See Chapter 7.) Attention to the United States–Mexico border increased in the aftermath of the Passport Act of 1918 and the passage of the Eighteenth Amendment to the United States Constitution. The Passport Act required all immigrants to present official papers attesting to point of origin, nationality, and identity. The enactment of the Eighteenth Amendment eventually led to laws that sought to halt all production, purchase, and conveyance of alcohol in the United States, thus driving consumer demand to find a supply south of the U.S. border with Mexico.

The first individuals charged with the responsibility of guarding the border were attached to the Customs Service and were referred to as "line-riders." By 1908, that function was shifted to the Immigration Service, a part of the Department of Commerce and Labor at the time. As the smuggling of alcohol increased along the border in 1920, mounted guards from the Immigration Service joined forces with the Customs Service line-riders as well as the Texas Rangers to aid in antismuggling efforts. As an exclusionary mood aimed at immigrants from southern and eastern Europe and all parts of Asia swept through the halls of Congress in 1921 and 1924 in the form of national origins quota laws (see Chapter 4), focus on the unlawful entry of migrants across the United States–Mexico border increased. A rider to the 1924 legislation provided new resources for an "additional land border patrol." These funds established what we know today as the Border Patrol,[1] with jurisdiction limited to the United States–Mexico border region. By the mid-1930s, the number of Mexicans moving across the border without inspection was steadily increasing.

The Border Patrol initially was composed of 450 male officers. These men were not subjected to any civil service-type of exam nor required to meet measurable qualifications. Some were Mounted Guard veterans; others were former Texas Rangers, sheriffs, or town marshals. Others were appointees culled from the Civil Service Register or qualified railway mail clerks. Most had been reared on ranches and owned all the arts of cowmen, including skill at tracking and the use of revolver and rifle.

World War II placed serious strains on the ranks of the Border Patrol, as many of the men were called into the armed forces. As a result, civil service exams were not used for new recruits, the training school lapsed, and new recruits were placed in the field with minimal training. By the 1950s, the candidate training program was reinstated and cars were substituted for horses. Greater focus was placed on the southwest border, as recruitment of undocumented Mexican workers by U.S. employers was stepped up.

Increasing Border Patrol Apprehensions and Resources

By the 1960s the flow of undocumented Mexicans was rapidly increasing and straining the resources of the Border Patrol. In 1962, after a severe drought in northern and central Mexico leading to high unemployment, U.S. officials estimated that the number of aliens who crossed the border without inspection increased by 41 percent and reported a 29 percent increase in the number of deportable Mexicans apprehended by the Border Patrol. In addition, U.S. wage rates attracted Mexican laborers. In lower Texas, for instance, cotton pickers were paid $2.50 per hundred pounds, while cotton pickers in Mexico were paid 75 cents.[2] Within two years, 59 percent of the deportable aliens arrested were Mexican, a 13 percent increase over 1963, attributable to the termination of the Bracero program.[3]

During this era, the Border Patrol used airplanes to monitor the border and seek out concentrations of aliens in places such as ranch areas. These strategies helped to locate over 4,000 deportable aliens in 1963.[4] By 1964, over 56,000 aliens were transported back to Mexico using an airlift in order to return people closer to their homes in southern Mexico. Another 54,000 were transported back to Mexico via train to Chihuahua.[5]

Attempts to smuggle aliens also increased at the time. In 1966, for example, three small boats of smuggled aliens were found in Mission Bay near San Diego; a rental truck was parked nearby waiting to take people to interior points of California. The aliens had paid $125 to $150 each.[6] In 1967, more aliens were found, concealed in trucks, as well as in new cars being freighted across the Canadian border.[7] In 1977, the INS established an Office of Anti-Smuggling to reduce alien smuggling in hopes of "immobilizing criminal conspiracies responsible for bringing in and transporting undocumented aliens."[8] No one knows, of course, how many similar attempts succeeded.

During the last four months of fiscal year 1977, 100 extra Border Patrol agents were sent to Chula Vista to augment the permanent force. During that period, about 145,000 aliens were apprehended, compared to 96,000 the previous year.[9]

Procedural restrictions on lawful residency disadvantaged Mexicans, thereby increasing the attraction of illicit entry. The ability to apply for lawful permanent resident status through adjustment of status without having to exit the United States was added by the 1965 amendments. Aliens, other than crewmen and natives of contiguous countries (i.e., Mexico and Canada) and islands, who had been admitted or paroled (i.e., entered with inspection), could apply for adjustment of status to permanent resident status without leaving the country to get an immigrant visa. The act specifically excluded any aliens born in any country of the Western Hemisphere.[10] In 1977, adjustment of status became available to Western Hemisphere immigrants if they qualified under an immigration category, but the provision does not apply to most undocumented Mexicans because the law requires that the person must have initially entered with inspection.[11] The procedural challenges to obtaining lawful permanent residence status contributed to the decision on the part of many undocumented Mexicans to simply enter without inspection even though they may have been able to qualify under a lawful immigrant category.

A different procedural option became available for some Mexican citizens crossing the U.S. border in 1966. Despite the increased fears of smuggling, the United States started to issue border-crossing cards to alleviate travel difficulties. Border, passport, and visa requirements were waived for Mexican nationals with border-crossing cards. These allowed individuals to remain in the United States for up to six months. The Mexican government reciprocated with a card valid from thirty days to six months.[12]

Today, the Border Patrol (formerly part of INS) is the mobile and uniformed enforcement arm of the Bureau of Immigration and Custom Enforcement of the Department of Homeland Security, responsible for protecting more than 8,000 miles of international land and water boundary. The Border Patrol contains twenty-one sectors, including nine southwest border sectors, sectors on the northern border, and those in Livermore, California; Miami, Florida; New Orleans, Louisiana; and Mayaguez, Puerto Rico.

In spite of general problems with the federal budget in the 1990s, money for immigration enforcement steadily increased. While a general federal hiring freeze was experienced in 1992 and 1993, in 1994 the Border Patrol was able to hire 350 new officers (300 were added to San Diego and fifty to El Paso, where the need was regarded as greatest), and 700 new positions were added in 1995. Close to 1,000 more were added in 1996.

The Border Patrol is engaged in a variety of activities, including boat patrol operations, antismuggling operations, and employer sanctions. Even before the creation of the Homeland Security Department, the Border Patrol was involved in intelligence work. It also has desert-area rescue teams, emergency response teams, canine units, drug awareness programs for schools, and scouting activities for youth, and is involved in the detection of aliens with criminal backgrounds. Of course, the Border Patrol is best known for border surveillance (or "linewatching"), transportation and traffic checks, and interior enforcement.

The purpose of transportation and traffic checks is to apprehend undocumented aliens who have penetrated the border area. Agents are assigned to "high traffic" areas such as bus and train terminals as well as specific highway checkpoint stations. The Supreme Court has ruled that fixed checkpoints away from the border are proper on roads shown to be highly traveled by undocumented aliens. Additionally, although agents in roving-patrol units cannot constitutionally search a vehicle for undocumented aliens simply for being in the general vicinity of the border, they can stop such motorists for brief inquiry into their residence status. About 15 percent of Border

Patrol officer time is spent observing traffic and using a "sixth sense" in determining which vehicles to stop due to likely transportation of undocumented immigrants. Agents claim that U.S. citizens of Mexican descent can be easily distinguished from undocumented Mexicans, insisting that clothes and haircut can tip off a person's alienage.

Border Patrol interior enforcement focuses on undocumented farm and ranch workers. Farm or ranch raids are usually based on tips that undocumented workers are at particular worksites. Each raid commonly results in the arrest of twenty-five to fifty aliens. Tips can also lead to Border Patrol arrests in towns and neighborhoods.

Though the Border Patrol is involved in myriad functions, patrolling the southern border is its primary task and that is where resources have been constantly added since the 1970s. In the late 1980s, an estimated 1.3 to 3.9 million undocumented crossings along the southern border occurred annually; 1.2 to 3.2 million were Mexicans crossing the southwest border. By the mid-1990s, some 88 percent of the Border Patrol's agents were stationed along the Mexican border, and southern border apprehensions accounted for 98 percent of all border apprehensions. And while the Border Patrol has always believed that the simple, large presence of an organized force would serve as a deterrent to some Mexicans contemplating an illicit crossing, a substantial portion of linewatch time has been spent in the apprehension and deportation of undocumented Mexican immigrants.

The apprehension aspect of linewatch operations continues to be a part of the Border Patrol routine. When deterrence does not work and persons suspected of surreptitious entry are observed, agents pursue and arrest. Although such agents usually work with partners, often pursuing individuals, sometimes four or five agents can effectuate the arrest of groups of up to seventy immigrants who have been detected in safe houses used by smuggling operations.

Once numerical limitations began being applied to Mexico in 1965 and in 1976 (see Chapter 6), waiting lists developed and there was more pressure for Mexicans to enter surreptitiously in response to available seasonal work and recruitment efforts by U.S. growers. Much of the public and policy makers reacted negatively to the illicit entries by Mexicans, and the rise of anti-immigrant sentiment in the 1970s was conspicuous. Although INS officials acknowledged that Mexicans did not make up the majority of undocumented aliens in the country, Mexicans were targeted by INS sweeps. In the mid-1970s, as exclusionists advanced a labor displacement theory, Congress considered an employer sanction law that was referred to as the Rodino Bill, named after Congressman Peter Rodino, a powerful immigration policy figure in Congress. (See Chapter 9.) Exclusionists persistently complained about undocumented workers coming across the United States–Mexico border, and the commissioner of the INS routinely alleged that twelve million undocumented aliens were in the United States. In 1977, for example, of the deportable aliens arrested by the INS, more than 90 percent were Mexican. Mexicans also continued to be the targets of highly publicized INS raids in the interior of the country.

Supreme Court Blessings to Target Mexicans

As the INS enforcement budget grew larger and larger, the Supreme Court, swayed by arguments that the undocumented alien problem was worsening, allowed more flexibility to INS enforcement strategies.

In 1973, the Supreme Court appeared to have put an end to the Border Patrol practice of "roving" near the United States–Mexico border to search vehicles, without a warrant or probable cause. In *Almeida-Sanchez v. United States*, INS officials unsuccessfully argued that as long as they were in the proximity of the border, their efforts in following and stopping cars located near the border was the "functional equivalent" of the border; on that theory, the Border Patrol felt that inhabitants of such vehicles were subject to the same intrusions as those at the border.[13] But within two years, the Supreme Court—overwhelmed by government claims of a crisis at the border—opened the door to stops by roving patrols near the border under certain circumstances.

In *United States v. Brignoni-Ponce* (1975), two Border Patrol officers were observing northbound traffic from a patrol car parked at the side of Interstate Highway 5, north of San Diego.[14] The road was dark, and they were using the patrol car's headlights to illuminate passing cars. They pursued Brignoni-Ponce's car and stopped it, saying later that their only reason for doing so was that its three occupants appeared to be of Mexican descent. The officers questioned the three occupants about their citizenship and learned that the passengers were aliens who had entered the country illegally. All three were then arrested, and Brignoni-Ponce was charged with two counts of knowingly transporting undocumented immigrants. At trial he moved to suppress the testimony of and about the two passengers, claiming that this evidence was the fruit of an illegal seizure because the officers did not have the authority to stop his car. The Court of Appeals agreed, holding that the Fourth Amendment, as interpreted in *Almeida-Sanchez*, forbids stopping a vehicle, even for the limited purpose of questioning its occupants, unless the officers have a "founded suspicion" that the occupants are aliens illegally in the country. The appellate court refused to find that Mexican ancestry alone supported such a "founded suspicion" and held that Brignoni-Ponce's motion to suppress should have been granted.

The Supreme Court agreed that a roving patrol generally should not be allowed to stop a vehicle near the Mexican border and question its occupants about their citizenship and immigration status, when the only ground for suspicion is that the occupants appear to be of Mexican ancestry. But the Court carved an important exception: patrolling officers may stop vehicles if they are aware of specific articulable facts, together with rational inferences, reasonably warranting suspicion that the vehicles contain aliens who may be illegally in the country and the occupants can be questioned. Any number of factors may be taken into account in deciding whether there is reasonable suspicion to stop a car in the border area. Officers may consider the characteristics of the area in which they encounter a vehicle. Its proximity to the border, the usual patterns of traffic on the particular road, and previous experience with alien traffic are all relevant. They also may consider information about recent illegal border crossings in the area. The driver's behavior may be relevant, as erratic driving or obvious attempts to evade officers can support a reasonable suspicion. Aspects of the vehicle itself may justify suspicion. For instance, officers say that certain station wagons, with large compartments for fold-down seats or spare tires, are frequently used for transporting concealed aliens. The vehicle may appear to be heavily loaded, it may have an extraordinary number of passengers, or the officers may observe persons trying to hide. The Court also acknowledged that trained officers can recognize the characteristic appearance of persons who live in Mexico, relying on such factors as the mode of dress and haircut.

The Court was willing to give more latitude to Border Patrol officers because of claims that undocumented Mexican migration was getting out of hand. The Court explained its reasoning, relying on figures provided by the government:

> The Government makes a convincing demonstration that the public interest demands effective measures to prevent the illegal entry of aliens at the Mexican border. Estimates of the number of illegal immigrants in the United States vary widely. A conservative estimate in 1972 produced a figure of about one million, but the INS now suggests there may be as many as 10 or 12 million aliens illegally in the country. Whatever the number, these aliens create significant economic and social problems, competing with citizens and legal resident aliens for jobs, and generating extra demand for social services. The aliens themselves are vulnerable to exploitation because they cannot complain of substandard working conditions without risking deportation. . . .
>
> The Government has estimated that 85% of the aliens illegally in the country are from Mexico. . . . The Mexican border is almost 2,000 miles long, and even a vastly reinforced Border Patrol would find it impossible to prevent illegal border crossings. Many aliens cross the Mexican border on foot, miles away from patrolled areas, and then purchase transportation from the border area to inland cities, where they find jobs and elude the immigration authorities. Others gain entry on valid temporary border-crossing permits, but then violate the conditions of their entry. Most of these aliens leave the border area in private vehicles, often assisted by professional "alien smugglers." The Border Patrol's traffic-checking operations are designed to prevent this inland movement. They succeed in apprehending some illegal entrants and smugglers, and they deter the movement of others by threatening apprehension and increasing the cost of illegal transportation.[15]

In 1976, the Court articulated a major exception to the Fourth Amendment's protection against search and seizure to accommodate the Border Patrol even further. The case, *United States v. Martinez-Fuerte*, involved the legality of a fixed checkpoint located on Interstate 5 near San Clemente, California, the principal highway between San Diego and Los Angeles.[16] The checkpoint is sixty-six road miles north of the Mexican border. Approximately one mile south of the checkpoint is a large black-on-yellow sign with flashing yellow lights over the highway stating "ALL VEHICLES, STOP AHEAD, 1 MILE." Three-quarters of a mile farther north are two black-on-yellow signs suspended over the highway with flashing lights stating "WATCH FOR BRAKE LIGHTS." At the checkpoint, which is also the location of a State of California weighing station, are two large signs with flashing red lights suspended over the highway. These signs each state "STOP HERE—U.S. OFFICERS." Placed on the highway are a number of orange traffic cones funneling traffic into two lanes where a Border Patrol agent in full uniform, standing behind a white on red "STOP" sign, checks traffic. Blocking traffic in the unused lanes are official U.S. Border Patrol vehicles with flashing red lights. In addition, there is a permanent building that houses the Border Patrol office and temporary detention facilities. There are also floodlights for nighttime operations.

The "point" agent standing between the two lanes of traffic visually screens all northbound vehicles, which the checkpoint brings to a virtual, if not a complete, halt. Most motorists are allowed to resume their progress without any oral inquiry or close visual examination. In a relatively small number of cases the "point" agent will conclude that further inquiry is in order. He directs these cars to a secondary inspection area, where their occupants are asked about their citizenship and immigration status. The average length of an investigation in the secondary inspection area is three to five minutes. A direction to stop in the secondary inspection area could be based on something suspicious about a particular car passing through the checkpoint, but in the three situations that were challenged in *Martinez-Fuerte,* the government conceded that none of the three stops was based on any articulable suspicion.

In the first situation, Amado Martinez-Fuerte approached the checkpoint driving a vehicle containing two female passengers. The women were undocumented Mexican aliens who had entered the United States at the San Ysidro port of entry by using false papers. They rendezvoused with Martinez-Fuerte in San Diego to be transported northward. At the checkpoint their car was directed to the secondary inspection area. Martinez-Fuerte produced documents showing him to be a lawful resident alien, but his passengers admitted being present in the country unlawfully. He was criminally charged with two counts of illegally transporting aliens.

The second situation involved Jose Jimenez-Garcia, who attempted to pass through the checkpoint while driving a car with one passenger. He had picked up the passenger by prearrangement in San Ysidro after the latter had been smuggled across the border. Questioning at the secondary inspection area revealed the illegal status of the passenger, and Jiminez-Garcia was charged with two counts of illegally transporting an alien.

The third case involved Raymond Guillen and Fernando Medrano-Barragan. They approached the checkpoint with Guillen driving and Medrano-Barragan and his wife as passengers. Questioning at the secondary inspection area revealed that Medrano-Barragan and his wife were undocumented aliens. A subsequent search of the car uncovered three other undocumented aliens in the trunk. Medrano-Barragan had led the other aliens across the border at the beach near Tijuana, Mexico, where they rendezvoused with Guillen, a U.S. citizen. Guillen and Medrano-Barragan were jointly indicted on four counts of illegally transporting aliens and four counts of inducing the illegal entry of aliens.

The defendants argued that the routine stopping of vehicles at a checkpoint was invalid because *Brignoni-Ponce* must be read as prohibiting any stops in the absence of reasonable suspicion. However, the Court recognized that maintenance of a traffic-checking program in the interior is necessary because "the flow of illegal aliens cannot be controlled effectively at the border." The Court noted the "substantiality of the public interest in the practice of routine stops for inquiry at permanent checkpoints, a practice which the Government identifies as the most important of the traffic-checking operations." The checkpoints (a similar one was in Texas) were located on important highways; in their absence such highways would offer undocumented aliens a quick and safe route into the interior. Routine checkpoint inquiries apprehend many smugglers and undocumented aliens who succumb to the lure of such highways. And the prospect of such inquiries forces others onto less efficient roads that are less heavily traveled, slowing their movement and making them more vulnerable to detection by roving patrols. Therefore, the Court held:

> A requirement that stops on major routes inland always be based on reasonable suspicion would be impractical because the flow of traffic tends to be too heavy to allow the partic-ularized study of a given car that would enable it to be identified as a possible carrier of illegal aliens. In particular, such a requirement would largely eliminate any deterrent to the conduct of well-disguised smuggling operations, even though smugglers are known to use these highways regularly.

Thus, fixed checkpoints, even though more than fifty miles away from the border, were constitutional. Again, the Court cited the importance of supporting the Border Patrol's efforts in enforcing immigration laws that were being violated by Mexicans.

> It has been national policy for many years to limit immigration into the United States. Since July 1, 1968, the annual quota for immigrants from all independent countries of the Western Hemisphere, including Mexico, has been 120,000 persons. Act of Oct. 3, 1965, § 21(e), 79 Stat. 921. Many more aliens than can be accommodated under the quota want to live and work in the United States. Consequently, large numbers of aliens seek illegally to enter or to remain in the United States. We noted last Term that "[e]stimates of the num-ber of illegal immigrants [already] in the United States vary widely. A conservative estimate in 1972 produced a figure of about one million, but the Immigration and Naturalization Service now suggests there may be as many as 10 or 12 million aliens illegally in the country." *United States v. Brignoni-Ponce, 422 U.S. 873, 878 (1975)* (footnote omitted). It is estimated that 85% of the illegal immigrants are from Mexico, drawn by the fact that economic opportunities are significantly greater in the United States than they are in Mexico.
>
> Interdicting the flow of illegal entrants from Mexico poses formidable law enforcement problems. The principal problem arises from surreptitious entries. . . . The United States shares a border with Mexico that is almost 2,000 miles long, and much of the border area is uninhabited desert or thinly populated arid land. Although the Border Patrol maintains personnel, electronic equipment, and fences along portions of the border, it remains rela-tively easy for individuals to enter the United States without detection. It also is possible for an alien to enter unlawfully at a port of entry by the use of falsified papers or to enter law-fully but violate restrictions of entry in an effort to remain in the country unlawfully. Once within the country, the aliens seek to travel inland to areas where employment is believed to be available, frequently meeting by prearrangement with friends or professional smug-glers who transport them in private vehicles.

In fiscal year 1973, 175,511 deportable aliens were apprehended throughout the nation by linewatch agents stationed at the border itself. Traffic-checking operations in the interior apprehended approximately 55,300 more deportable aliens. Most of the traffic-checking apprehensions were at checkpoints.

The Supreme Court majority was not concerned with the racial overtones of its decision even though the Border Patrol essentially was picking out those who looked Mexican for secondary inspection. A dissenting opinion by Justice William Brennan warned: "Every American citizen of Mexican ancestry and every Mexican alien lawfully in this country must know after today's decision that he travels the fixed checkpoint highways at [his] risk." But the majority indicated that it would encourage lower courts to act against the Border Patrol if there was evidence of "the misuse of checkpoints to harass those of Mexican ancestry."

Less than a decade later, in 1984, the Supreme Court made it quite clear that the Fourth Amendment's protection against illegal search and seizure was not available to aliens fighting deportation, even if INS officials acted illegally. In *INS v. Lopez-Mendoza*, Adam Lopez-Mendoza was arrested by INS agents at his place of employment, a transmission repair shop.[17] Responding to a tip, INS investigators arrived at the shop shortly before 8:00 A.M. The agents had not sought a warrant to search the premises or to arrest any of its occupants. The proprietor of the shop firmly refused to allow the agents to interview his employees during working hours. Nevertheless, while one agent engaged the proprietor in conversation, another entered the shop and approached Lopez-Mendoza. In response to the agent's questioning, Lopez-Mendoza gave his name and indicated that he was from Mexico with no close family ties in the United States. The agent then placed him under arrest. Lopez-Mendoza underwent further questioning at INS offices, where he admitted he was born in Mexico, was still a citizen of Mexico, and had entered this country without inspection by immigration authorities. While the arrest was illegal, the Supreme Court refused to exclude Lopez-Mendoza's admission that he was not a legal resident. It was important to the Court that deportation proceedings were civil rather than criminal proceedings, and the Court also felt that applying the Fourth Amendment exclusionary rule would have little deterrent effect on illegal police activity. In fact, the Court felt that excluding evidence after an illegal arrest by INS officials would have great societal costs.

> The first cost is one that is unique to continuing violations of the law. Applying the exclusionary rule in proceedings that are intended not to punish past transgressions but to prevent their continuance or renewal would require the courts to close their eyes to ongoing violations of the law. This Court has never before accepted costs of this character in applying the exclusionary rule.
>
> Presumably no one would argue that the exclusionary rule should be invoked to prevent an agency from ordering corrective action at a leaking hazardous waste dump if the evidence underlying the order had been improperly obtained, or to compel police to return contraband explosives or drugs to their owner if the contraband had been unlawfully seized.

Once again, the Court was also influenced by the perceived need to support INS activities to combat the problem of undocumented aliens.

> Immigration officers apprehend over one million deportable aliens in this country every year. . . . A single agent may arrest many illegal aliens every day. Although the investigatory burden does not justify the commission of constitutional violations, the officers cannot be expected to compile elaborate, contemporaneous, written reports detailing the circumstances of every arrest. At present an officer simply completes a "Record of Deportable Alien" that is introduced to prove the INS's case at the deportation hearing; the officer rarely must attend the hearing. Fourth Amendment suppression hearings would undoubtedly require considerably more, and the likely burden on the administration of the immigration laws would be correspondingly severe.

As the Court said, "There comes a point at which courts, consistent with their duty to administer the law, cannot continue to create barriers to law enforcement in the pursuit of a supervisory role that is properly the duty of the Executive and Legislative Branches." Effectively, the Court implied that point is reached when the issue of controlling the perceived problem of undocumented Mexicans is before the Court.

Thus, when it comes to the southwest border, the Border Patrol conducts three kinds of inland traffic-checking operations in an effort to minimize undocumented immigration. Permanent checkpoints, such as the one at San Clemente, are maintained at or near intersections of important roads leading away from the border. They operate on a coordinated basis designed to avoid circumvention by smugglers and others who transport the undocumented aliens. Temporary checkpoints, which operate like permanent ones, occasionally are established in other strategic locations. Finally, roving patrols are maintained to supplement the checkpoint system.

INS Sweeps for Mexicans

As the United States–Mexico border became more of an issue, enforcement of immigration laws against Mexican migrants was given higher and higher priority. Just as the recruitment of low-wage, undocumented Mexican workers by agricultural and other industrial interests continues, enforcement of the deportation laws against Mexicans continues as well. The scale of Operation Wetback in 1954, when over a million Mexicans were deported, seems overwhelming (see Chapter 7), but constant attention to the southern border and its containment for the past half century actually dwarfs the 1954 affair.

While 99 percent of the deportable aliens arrested in 1954 were Mexican, by 1962, less than a third were Mexican (8 percent were Canadian). Then the figures gradually increased. By 1976, 875,915 deportable aliens were arrested, and in 1977, the figure jumped to 1,042,215; 92 percent were Mexican.

Agriculture and other workplace sweeps for undocumented Mexican workers were common INS enforcement strategies in the last half of the twentieth century. Consider

Project Jobs or Operation Jobs, which occurred in April 1982, reminiscent of Operation Wetback and raids directed at Asian immigrants in the past. Five thousand people, primarily of Latin appearance, were arrested in nine metropolitan areas across the country. Critics of the raids charged that the operation was directed at Mexicans, whipped up antialien hysteria, and caused much fear in the Latino community, while providing no jobs for native-born citizens. Curiously, Operation Jobs was launched during the same week that restrictive legislation (the Simpson–Mazzoli Bill that contained employer sanctions provisions) was being marked up in the Senate subcommittee on immigration. The raids also coincided with Congress's consideration of additional funds for the INS. Operation Jobs highlighted what had been going on for many years—focused sweeps by the INS at locations with large numbers of persons of Latin descent.

The constitutionality of the operation was challenged in northern California in *International Molders' and Allied Workers' Local Union No. 164 v. Nelson*,[18] the facts of which are representative of what happened nationwide. During the operation, the INS and Border Patrol conducted approximately fifty workplace raids in northern California as part of a nationwide campaign. During these raids, agents arrived at various workplaces, such as the Petaluma Poultry Processors, Mammoth Lakes Lodge, and Pacific Mushroom Farm. The agents carried with them "warrants of inspection" authorizing entry into the nonpublic areas of particular premises. Typically, the warrants named one or more individuals thought to be undocumented aliens who were working at a specified location, but then went on to allow the INS to seek and seize unspecified and unlimited "others" on the premises who might also be undocumented aliens. During Operation Jobs, warrants were obtained for 8 of the approximately 50 raids. Although a warrant might list from 4 to 13 suspected undocumented aliens, as many as 70 people would be arrested, and few if any of these were the people named in the warrant. In the 8 warrant-based raids described in the case, 192 individuals were arrested. Of these, 179 were "others" not identified in the warrants. Of the 51 persons named in the various warrants, only 13 were found on the premises.

The typical INS warrant of inspection read:

I am satisfied that there is reasonable cause to believe that [several named persons] *and others* are illegally in the United States and are subject to deportation from the United States, and are located on the above-described premises during normal working hours.

WHEREFORE, YOU ARE HEREBY COMMANDED:

To search within a period of ten (10) days the place named above for the persons specified, *and others suspected of being illegal aliens* . . . and if such persons are found there to seize them. (Emphasis added)

The warrants said nothing about how the searches would be carried out, other than permissible hours of entry, or how INS agents would determine which persons were to be interrogated or seized as suspected "others." The warrants neither directed nor limited agents to the portions of the premises where the named suspects were likely to be found.

Officials admitted that they used the warrants to gain entry into workplaces for generalized searches for undocumented aliens. In many raids the INS agents made no particular effort to apprehend the suspects named in the warrants, but rather based their decisions as to which workers to question, detain, or seize solely on information or observation gained *after* they had entered.

The INS claimed that several of their raids were based on consent. The trial revealed, however, that typically INS agents arrived unannounced at premises that they selected for a raid, and requested permission to conduct the raid immediately. Although only the agent in charge made the request, the other agents who were to participate in the raid were already in position, often guarding each exit. At some raids there were twenty or more agents who were visible to both management and workers. Thus, when consent was requested, it was usually clear that the INS had both the intent and the ability to carry out the operation immediately.

At an April 1984 raid on Shamrock Technology, INS agents arrived at 5:00 P.M. and demanded consent from an office manager, the ranking company official present. Frightened, she telephoned her superior at home. The INS agent in charge allegedly told this second manager that if consent was not given for an immediate search, the INS would return and "close the shop." Feeling that he had no choice, the manager gave the INS consent to search.

At another raid, numerous INS agents went to the premises of Steak Mate without a warrant, allegedly intending to seek consent for entry. In their answer to interrogatories the defendants asserted that the Steak Mate survey was based on a consent entry. Yet there was no evidence that either manager on the premises gave consent, and one of the managers, Berry, testified that consent was neither requested nor given. Instead, the evidence suggested that INS vehicles and agents first entered at high speed onto the production areas of the premises, across the highway from the location of the office where the agents knew the managers were likely to be found. At that point the agents asserted a right to enter in order to chase suspects who were by that time fleeing.

In another instance, an INS agent entered a 7–11 store in San Jose on May 23, 1983, and asked the manager for consent to search nonpublic areas. When the manager, a naturalized citizen, refused and asked for a warrant, the agent allegedly told her that her citizenship would be revoked and her store closed down. The agent then accompanied her to a back room.

The court did not believe INS claims that many of its actions were taken due to "exigent circumstances," involving aliens who were fleeing.

At Neve Roses, twelve INS agents in six vehicles drove at high speeds into a driveway, which they blocked. Although agents claimed they entered the premises from the adjacent roadway only after they happened to observe fleeing workers, almost all work at Neve was performed inside greenhouses and closed rooms in which workers were not visible from outside the premises. A second raid at the same location transpired in a virtually identical manner.

In a raid at Petaluma Mushroom, eleven INS agents in several vehicles entered at high speed, again after allegedly observing fleeing workers. Petaluma's manager stated, however, that before the raid began there were no workers outside the closed rooms in which the mushrooms were cultivated and processed. The INS raided again weeks later, using four agents and two cars. One of those agents had participated in the earlier raid.

Once INS agents were on the premises, the court also felt that many agents routinely seized workers in violation of the Fourth Amendment. The court was well aware that the INS may question a worker on suspicion of mere alienage, may detain a worker on articulable suspicion of undocumented status, and may make an arrest if there is probable cause to believe that the person is undocumented. But there was considerable evidence that INS agents often questioned suspects in a detentive manner and even seized workers during raids before any questioning to establish articulable suspicion of undocumented status. Agents often were not inclined to allow suspects to produce documentation.

At Pacific Mushroom Farm on April 28, 1982, Rita Brambilla de Silva, Luisa Juarez-Esquivel, Evangelina Mendoza-Avalos, and Santos Gil Robles were seated in a mushroom shed taking a coffee break when approximately six agents entered and yelled in Spanish, "Don't move; you're under arrest; we're from Immigration." Agents then proceeded to direct workers into two groups for questioning: those who had "papers" and those who did not.

Workers from Pacific Mushroom who were seized were taken in handcuffs to vans and then loaded onto a bus that took them to a nearby beach for questioning. When one worker, Ramon Estrada, declined to answer agents' questions, agents allegedly hauled him off the bus, gave him a full body search, twisted his arm behind his back, grabbed his hair, and slammed him against an INS vehicle. The other workers witnessed this and were told that the same thing would happen to them if they refused to answer questions.

Another worker, Antonio Garcia Diaz, told agents he had papers and in fact produced those papers proving he was lawfully in the country. He was nevertheless forced into a van and then a bus. When Garcia declined to answer questions or sign papers before talking with his lawyer, he was forcibly removed from the bus and had his arm twisted behind his back. He feared that one agent was going to strike him until another intervened.

At Petaluma Poultry Processors on April 26, 1982, three different INS officers questioned Francisco Rivera as he continued working at his station on the poultry-processing line. The first and second agents examined Rivera's letter from an immigration judge directing him to report to Vancouver, Canada, on May 19 to pick up his permanent residency papers and were satisfied. The third officer, however, stated that he did not "recognize the judge's signature" and would have to take Rivera outside. Rivera was handcuffed, despite protestations that his papers were in order and he was not going to run, taken out of the building by his belt, placed in a van, and locked inside.

Agents were informed twice by different Petaluma Poultry managers that Rivera was not an undocumented alien. When Bill Cuppoletti, maintenance supervisor, told defendants that Rivera was a legal resident, an agent called him an "SOB," and told him to keep his mouth shut and to stay away. John Malone, Rivera's supervisor, also told agents that Rivera was in the country legally, but officers responded that they did not care.

Manager Cuppoletti also described two Latina women who were arrested and forced to walk back to back with tie wraps securing their arms. As they were being taken to the van, one of the women shouted to the agent that she had her green card. At the van, the tie wraps were cut with difficulty and both women produced their green cards.

Maria Socorro Araneta, a U.S. citizen and owner of a San Jose 7-11 store, was accosted in her store by an INS agent who demanded to see her papers. When Mrs. Araneta told him the date of her naturalization and explained that citizens are not required to carry papers, the agent told her that she was "obstructing justice" and remained in the store for more than an hour questioning Araneta and a friend.

Given these facts, the federal judge issued the following order against INS officials in northern California:

> Good cause appearing therefor, the Court preliminarily enjoins defendants and their officers, agents, and employees in the San Francisco District of the United States Immigration and Naturalization Service and the Livermore Border Patrol Sector as follows:
>
> 1. Each INS workplace entry, other than in public areas and open fields, must be based on at least one of the following: a valid warrant, a valid consent, or exigent circumstances not deliberately provoked by defendants' own conduct.
>
> 2. Every INS warrant must particularly describe each suspect to be questioned or seized pursuant to the particularity requirement of the fourth amendment. There must be probable cause to believe each such person is an alien illegally present in the United States. A warrant need not in every case identify the suspect(s) by name, but the warrant and its supporting affidavits must contain enough specific identifying information to assure that the search for that person is reasonably likely to result in finding that person.
>
> 3. A warrant may not provide that "others" may be searched and seized, if such "others" are unnamed or only conclusorily described by any supporting affidavits.
>
> 4. When possible, each warrant must describe the particular area(s) of the workplace where the suspect(s) are likely to be found, in light of the information available to the defendants.
>
> 5. Each warrant must provide that the agents executing the warrant, before searching any work area, must show the warrant to an authorized company representative, and ask that representative to produce the suspect(s) named or described in the warrant. Before the suspects are produced, agents may position themselves at exits and question or detain any workers attempting to flee. If the representative is unwilling or unable to produce those suspects within a reasonable time, agents may then enter the work area to search for the suspects. Such searches must be directed at finding the named or described suspects as quickly as possible, rather than for general questioning of the entire workforce. This does not preclude agents from questioning or detaining workers who attempt to hide or flee.
>
> 6. When agents have no warrant, but intend to obtain consent upon arrival at the worksite rather than ahead of time, they must not arrive or conduct themselves in a manner that would foreseeably provoke flight by workers, or that would leave a reasonable person with the belief that he had no choice but to consent to the raid. They must inform the representative of the nature and scope of the proposed survey. They may not expressly or impliedly suggest that the employer will face retaliation if he declines to consent.

7. Agents may not deliberately provoke flight by workers in order to justify entries onto workplace premises.

8. Absent a valid warrant or genuine exigent circumstances not deliberately precipitated by the agents themselves, agents may not detain workers without reasonable, articulable suspicion of illegal alienage. During non-detentive questioning, and before agents detain a worker, agents must give the worker a reasonable opportunity to produce his or her relevant documents, even if those documents are not on the worker's person but are in his constructive possession somewhere on the premises. Agents may accompany a worker who must retrieve his documentation.

9. Absent a valid warrant or genuine exigent circumstances not deliberately precipitated by the agents' own conduct, agents may not arrest a worker except upon probable cause, based on articulable facts and reasonable inferences drawn therefrom, that the worker is an alien unlawfully present in the United States and is likely to escape before a warrant can be obtained for his arrest.

A case in Illinois illustrates enforcement strategy by INS investigators that focuses on individuals with "Latin" appearance in both employment and nonemployment settings. In *Illinois Migrant Council v. Pilliod*,[19] the federal court of appeals upheld an order of a lower court critical of such INS tactics. The case involved six individuals and the Illinois Migrant Council (IMC), a nonprofit corporation, who brought a class action against officials of the INS. IMC was a community service agency that served as an advocate for illiterate migrant agricultural workers of Mexican heritage; the individual plaintiffs were U.S. citizens or permanent residents of Mexican descent. The plaintiffs alleged that INS officials were unconstitutionally stopping and questioning individuals simply on the basis of physical appearance, and without any basis for concluding that they were aliens.

One part of the case involved three street encounters between INS agents and four individuals. On September 18, 1974, plaintiffs Sandoval and Montanez were driving in Sandoval's car to the IMC office in Rochelle, Illinois. As they parked outside the office and were leaving the car, an INS car pulled alongside and the agents got out of their car. When Montanez was asked where he was born, he replied, "Mexico." He was asked for his identification and produced a satisfactory permanent resident alien card after being threatened otherwise with jail in Chicago. When Sandoval, a U.S. citizen of Mexican descent, was asked to produce identification, and refused to do so, the agents said they would have to take him to Chicago and forced him into the back seat of their car. He again refused to produce identification, but was ordered out of the car when he implied that he was a U.S. citizen.

During the first week of October 1974, plaintiff López was walking to his office at 19 West Jackson Boulevard in Chicago when he was asked by two strangers if he lived in the area. He responded "No" but said that he worked around there. Then he was asked where he was born. When he inquired why he was being interrogated, the agent said he was from the INS and flashed his identification. López then said that he was born in New Mexico. He is an American-born citizen of Mexican descent. At the time, he was attired in boots made in New Mexico, Levis jeans, an Illinois shirt, and a Mexican jacket.

Jose Ortiz, a member of the plaintiff class, stated that when he was walking with a friend on September 18, 1974, in Rochelle, Illinois, two INS agents stopped them and asked for Ortiz's papers. He was allowed to leave upon complying.

Other incidents involved "area control operations" conducted by agents without search or arrest warrants. At 4:30 A.M. on September 18, 1974, defendant Theodore Giorgetti, an INS employee, and thirty-two armed INS agents began simultaneous operations on preselected targets in Rochelle, Illinois. First, they knocked on the unlocked doors and entered two La Hacienda buildings where fifty-five female employees of the Del Monte Food Company were sleeping. The agents proceeded from bedroom to bedroom, demanding that the women occupants produce their papers. Afterward they left the buildings without making any arrests.

The agents also searched the Del Monte cottages where male immigrant employees resided. The INS agents used essentially the same method of operation in those cottages. When one of the residents, the same Jose Ortiz mentioned before, was unable to produce his green card evidencing legal residency, he was forced to accompany the INS agents on their search and was released only when another Del Monte employee assured them that Ortiz's papers were in order.

At the same time, an INS agent repeatedly kicked on the door of a small farmhouse near Rochelle occupied by Alonzo Solis, a U.S. citizen migrant worker. The agent tried to force his way into the house but desisted only when the Solis's child cried and Solis ordered him out. Solis dressed and showed the agent his "certificate" outside the house, whereupon the agent left.

At 5:00 A.M., INS agents also conducted similar operations at Del Monte plants 109 and 110. They questioned everyone who appeared to be of Latino heritage. Two Del Monte supervisors offered no resistance because they believed they had to allow the agents to search the plants.

In Mendota, Illinois, at 8:00 A.M. on September 26, 1974, defendant Giorgetti and thirty agents first went to the Motor Wheel plant. Nineteen employees were interviewed by Giorgetti, ten were arrested, and five of the ten were subsequently permitted to return to work. The agents then proceeded to several other industrial targets in Mendota and to hotels, boardinghouses, and private dwellings, resulting in the apprehension of 108 undocumented aliens, 104 of whom were still in detention at the time of the hearing below.

The court ruled that these INS enforcement strategies were improper, because a person should not be stopped by an INS agent unless the agent reasonably suspects that he or she is an alien illegally in the country, or at least that the person is an alien. Latin appearance alone is not sufficient basis for INS agents to stop and question.

While the rules outlined in the *International Molders' Union* and *Illinois Migrant Council* cases are still to be followed by INS officials, agents remain vigilant in their efforts to focus on Mexicans. One example of brazen INS strategies involved the sweep of an entire downtown area of a California town in conjunction with local law enforcement officials. On September 8, 1984, a raid of bars in the central valley town of Sanger, California, resulted in the deportation of 255 undocumented aliens. Five law enforcement agencies blockaded the main street downtown, swept through bars, and arrested forty people on criminal charges. Officers from the Fresno County Sheriff's Department, Sanger Police Department, Fresno Police Department, state Department of Alcoholic Beverage Control (ABC), and Border Patrol closed off downtown Sanger streets and entered sixteen bars. For the next two hours, they served thirty-five warrants and made forty arrests, mostly for misdemeanor offenses, while Border Patrol agents asked bar patrons for identification and arrested 255 undocumented aliens.

Officers entered bars and ordered that no one leave. An agent from ABC searched for liquor law violations and police officers attempted to serve individual arrest warrants on charges of B-girl activities, receiving stolen property, prostitution, gambling, and narcotics.

Meanwhile, a Border Patrol agent asked in English who had citizenship or legal residency documents. Those with documents were detained in another room for about forty minutes, while other patrons were searched and questioned. Of the hundred patrons in the bar, forty-seven were undocumented. One was arrested for having a concealed weapon. The other fifty-two patrons were detained although they were U.S. citizens or legal residents and were accused of no crime.

One bar owner (who was not cited for any wrongdoing) was appalled by what he saw: "Officers came in like Hitler's police or the police in South Africa. [Those suspected by the INS] were herded like cattle. I can't believe this can happen in the United States." What happened was clear to William Kennedy, an attorney with California Rural Legal Assistance, who investigated: "These are *racist raids*. There's no way to characterize them any other way. They're looking for *brown-skinned people*, not any others."[20]

Antonio Martinez fell prey to one of the more unusual INS enforcement strategies also directed primarily at Mexicans in southern California in 1993. Martinez received a letter from the INS and read it several times, getting an uneasy feeling each time. After two years of battling the INS to legalize his status so he could remain here with his American wife and daughter, the offer seemed too good to be true. Come to the Federal Building, bring some identification, and we'll give you a work permit good for a year, the letter said. How could the letter not be authentic? asked Martinez's wife, Ariel, a California native. It was written on INS stationery and said Martinez qualified under the "Immigration and Nationality Act of 1993."

In the end, Ariel's optimism and belief in the INS's credibility won out. On July 20, Martinez, his wife, and the couple's eighteen-month-old daughter drove to the INS office in downtown San Diego to pick up his permit. But instead of being welcomed by their adopted country, Martinez and dozens of others were promptly arrested and deported. The sting letter was sent to Martinez and more than 600 others, resulting in sixty apprehensions, though eighteen immigrants were released for a variety of technical reasons. Attorneys who saw the letter quickly determined that it was an INS sting because the law referred to in the letter does not exist. INS officials in San Diego said the operation targeted people who were under judges' orders of deportation, though several who received letters disputed this. After promising a work permit, the letter said: "Since this is a one-time event, failure to report to this office at this time will render you ineligible to receive your employment authorization."

INS officials avoided sending copies of the letters to immigrants' attorneys because they feared that the lawyers would alert their clients to the sting. They also said that two of the immigrants apprehended but later released were freed because they had pending appeals to their deportation orders. In addition, two others were released because they had become permanent residents. Four immigrants who received the letter were also released because they were "the right names but wrong persons."[21]

In border cities and areas, the INS has also engaged in some rather devious enforcement "sting" strategies. In the late 1980s in El Paso, Texas, the INS used a phony letterhead from "Argim" Ford. Argim is *migra* spelled backward, a Spanish word used by Mexicans to describe the INS. The bogus letters were sent to Spanish-surnamed individuals indicating that they might win a Ford Bronco if they showed up for a drawing. When letter recipients showed up, their immigration documentation was checked. Fifty-five of those who showed up turned out to be undocumented immigrants, and were deported.[22] There have even been reports of Border Patrol agents disguised as saguaro cacti waiting at the border to catch illicit border-crossers.

Other Workplace Strategies

INS workplace enforcement strategies were further emboldened by the Supreme Court in 1984. In *INS v. Delgado*,[23] INS officials, acting pursuant to warrants issued on a showing of probable cause that numerous unidentified undocumented aliens were employed at a garment factory, conducted two "factory surveys" of the workforce in search of undocumented aliens. A third factory survey was conducted with the employer's consent at another garment factory. During each survey, which lasted from one to two hours, INS agents positioned themselves near the factory exits, while other agents moved systematically through the factory, approaching most, but not all, employees at their work stations and, after identifying themselves, asking the employees one to three questions relating to their citizenship. The agents displayed badges, carried walkie-talkies, and were armed, although at no point during any of the surveys was a weapon ever drawn. If an employee gave a credible reply that he or she was a U.S. citizen or produced immigration papers, the agent moved on to another employee. During the survey, employees continued with their work and were free to walk around within the factory. Employees—who were U.S. citizens or permanent resident aliens, and who had been questioned during the surveys—and their union complained that the factory surveys violated their Fourth Amendment rights. They argued that the surveys constituted a seizure of the entire workforce, and that the INS could not question an individual employee unless its agents had a reasonable suspicion that the employee was an undocumented alien.

The Supreme Court disagreed with the plaintiffs, holding that the factory surveys did not result in the seizure of the entire workforce, and the individual questioning of the employees by INS agents concerning their citizenship did not amount to a detention or seizure under the Fourth Amendment. The Court ruled that interrogation relating to one's identity or a request for identification by the police does not, by itself, constitute a Fourth Amendment seizure. Unless the circumstances of the encounter are so intimidating as to demonstrate that a reasonable person would have believed he or she was not free to leave if he or she had not responded, such questioning does not result in a detention under the Fourth Amendment. In the Court's view, the entire workforce was not seized for the duration of the surveys, even though INS agents were stationed near the exits of the factory sites. The record indicated that the agents' conduct consisted simply of questioning employees and arresting those they had probable cause to believe were unlawfully present in the factory. This conduct should not have given employees any reason to believe that they would be detained if they gave truthful answers to the questions put to them or if they simply refused to answer. If mere questioning did not constitute a seizure when it occurred inside the factory, it was no more a seizure when it occurred at the exits.

The plaintiffs argued that the positioning of agents near the factory doors showed the INS's intent to prevent people from leaving. But the Court saw nothing in the record indicating that this is what the agents at the doors actually did. To the Court,

> The obvious purpose of the agents' presence at the factory doors was to insure that all persons in the factories were questioned. The record indicates that the INS agents' conduct in this case consisted simply of questioning employees and arresting those they had probable cause to believe were unlawfully present in the factory. This conduct should have given respondents no reason to believe that they would be detained if they gave truthful answers to the questions put to them or if they simply refused to answer.

One worker described an incident that occurred during the October factory survey at Mr. Pleat, in which an INS agent stationed by an exit attempted to prevent a worker, presumably an undocumented alien, from leaving the premises after the survey started. The worker walked out the door and when an agent tried to stop him, the worker pushed the agent aside and ran away. But the Court felt that this was "an ambiguous, isolated incident" failing to provide any basis on which to support the plaintiffs.

Likewise, as to workers inside the buildings, the Court felt that the mere possibility that they would be questioned if they sought to leave the buildings should not have resulted in any reasonable apprehension by any of them that they would be seized or detained in any meaningful way. The INS conduct simply did not create a psychological environment that made employees reasonably afraid they were not free to leave.

Conclusion

In the 1960s and 1970s, low-wage Mexican workers, including the undocumented, were constantly recruited to work in the United States. Although many may have qualified to become legal permanent residents of the United States, entry without inspection (EWI) became common for many of the workers. Of course, surreptitious entry could be dangerous and successful entry was uncertain, so many undocumented immigrants found themselves at the end of a yo-yo, moving back and forth from "almost" making it to the States and being redeported back to Mexico. Some immigrants were luckier; those with border-crossing cards were able to live in the United States legally. Nevertheless, even these "lucky" ones were restricted to a six-month maximum residency period.

Irrespective of economic swings since the 1960s, immigration enforcement funds have increased constantly. Most of the increases have been directed to Border Patrols in the southern region. These patrols sparked controversy when they extended beyond the border, to include "roving" Border Patrols and "fixed checkpoints." At first, the Supreme Court, the champion of American values and ideals, appeared to condemn such patrols, especially those that lacked a warrant or probable cause. But as immigration hysteria widened, the Supreme Court granted such patrols for special circumstances. These roving patrols could stop motor vehicles under suspicion that its passengers had entered the country without inspection. Since "reasonable suspicion" was never clearly delineated, the border patrols were permitted to use their own judgment in any situation. Even something as arbitrary as one's clothing or hairstyle could be used as an indication of immigrant status and, thus, constitute reasonable suspicion.

The defendants in *U.S. v. Martinez-Fuerte* challenged vehicle searches at checkpoints that were miles away from the border as improper in the absence of reasonable suspicion. But the Supreme Court ruled the fixed checkpoint procedures proper, noting the increase of undocumented Mexican immigration and its impact on American society.

Similarly, the Court upheld Border Patrol and INS intrusions into workplaces, where undocumented Mexican workers allegedly worked, overturning restraints imposed by lower courts. The Supreme Court in *INS v. Delgado* gave officials great leeway in its workplace raid strategies.

Despite the Border Patrol's greater authority the flow of undocumented Mexicans across the southwest border continued.

CHAPTER 9

IRCA: Penalizing Employers, as Amnesty Barely Survives

In the climate of heightened concerns over the number of undocumented workers (predominantly Mexican) in the United States in the 1970s and early 1980s, absurd estimates of from eight to twelve million undocumented aliens residing in the country were offered to demonstrate that INS efforts were ineffectual. Policy makers proposed addressing the situation from a different angle—by penalizing employers who were hiring undocumented workers, through what was called "employer sanctions." By 1986, employer sanctions had become part of the nation's immigration laws. The passage of the Immigration Reform and Control Act (IRCA) represented the culmination of years of social, political, and congressional debate about the perceived lack of control over the U.S. southern border. The belief that something had to be done about the large numbers of undocumented workers who had entered the United States from Mexico in the 1970s was reinforced by the flood of Central Americans who began to arrive in the early 1980s. While the political turmoil of civil war in El Salvador, Guatemala, and Nicaragua drove many Central Americans from their homeland, they, along with the Mexicans who continued to arrive, were generally labeled economic migrants by the Reagan administration, the INS, and the courts.

The idea of employer sanctions was not new. In 1952—when the immigration laws were overhauled to clamp down on subversives and Communists—a provision outlawing willful importation, transportation, or harboring of undocumented aliens was debated; one amendment proposed imposing criminal penalties for the employment of undocumented aliens if the employer had "reasonable grounds to believe a worker was not legally in the United States." Not only was the amendment soundly defeated, but the following was added to the final legislation: "for the purposes of this section, employment [including the usual and normal practices incident to employment] shall not be deemed to constitute harboring."[1] For the time being, we were not about to punish *real* Americans—employers—who might be benefiting from the labor of low-wage, undocumented workers. Beginning in 1971, legislative proposals featuring employer sanctions as a centerpiece reappeared and were touted as the tool needed to resolve the undocumented alien problem. By the end of the Carter administration in 1980, the Select Commission on Immigration and Refugee Policy portrayed legalization as a necessary balance to sanctions. However, the story of congressional support for IRCA is complicated. Although some broader-minded members of Congress may have wanted legalization to be implemented generously once enacted, Congress showed little support for legalization.

Within thirty years of the 1952 rejection of employer sanctions, most Americans were convinced that a crisis over undocumented immigration—especially undocumented *Mexican* migration—existed and that something had to be done. The power of employers to resist sanctions collapsed, and by 1986 federal employer sanctions were enacted as the major feature of reform. By a bare swing vote of only four members of the House of Representatives, legalization (or amnesty) provisions (one part for those who entered prior to 1982, and another for special agricultural workers) were also made part of the package to address the undocumented immigrant issue. Although on paper it appeared that a deal involving employer sanctions for amnesty had been struck, there was no political trade-off; IRCA would have gone forward if legalization were dropped by the House, and its effective implementation in the hands of an inept Immigration and Naturalization Service was seriously in doubt.

Legislative History of IRCA

More than a dozen years before the passage of IRCA, the California legislature, reacting to extreme anti-immigrant sentiment directed at undocumented Mexicans, enacted its own legislation in 1972 providing "no employer shall knowingly employ an alien who is not entitled to lawful residence in the United States if such employment would have an adverse effect on lawful resident workers." Employers could be fined $200 to $500 for each offense. When the California department of labor dragged its feet in implementing the law, the United Farm Workers (UFW) brought an action to force the labor department to enforce the law. Employers, especially agricultural interests, intervened in the case to oppose the law, but the case reached the U.S. Supreme Court, which ruled in *DeCanas v. Bica* that the law was constitutional.[2] The Court was deferential to arguments that undocumented workers were hurting U.S. workers:

> Employment of illegal aliens in times of high unemployment deprives citizens and legally admitted aliens of jobs; acceptance by illegal aliens of jobs on substandard terms as to wages and working conditions can seriously depress wage scales and working conditions of citizens and legally admitted aliens; and employment of illegal aliens under such conditions can diminish the effectiveness of labor unions. These local problems are particularly acute in California in light of the significant influx into that State of illegal aliens from neighbor-

ing Mexico. In attempting to protect California's fiscal interests and lawfully resident labor force from the deleterious effects on its economy resulting from the employment of illegal aliens, § 2805(a) focuses directly upon these essentially local problems and is tailored to combat effectively the perceived evils.

However, after winning the case, the UFW had second thoughts, dropped the matter, and never did return to the lower courts to force the implementation of the law.

By 1977, Representative Peter Rodino of New Jersey, at union prodding, was sponsoring a bill that included fines of $500 and up, and even jail sentences, for employers who knowingly hired undocumented aliens. The Rodino Bill had twice passed in the House—only to die in the Senate.

In 1978, Congress established the Select Commission on Immigration and Refugee Policy to study and evaluate immigration laws. The commission included members of the Carter administration, Congress, and the public, including Rodino and a representative from the AFL-CIO. Although its views were not unanimous, the commission report in 1981 recommended employer sanctions and legalization (amnesty) for undocumented aliens who were in the United States prior to January 1, 1980. Three of the commission's members, Senator Alan Simpson of Wyoming, Congressman Romano Mazzoli of Kentucky, and Rodino, set about to introduce legislation that incorporated many of the commission's recommendations. IRCA was clearly the result of their efforts.

A popular conception holds that the employer sanctions and legalization provisions like those found in IRCA somehow balanced one another. The *Los Angeles Times* had this view:

> [IRCA] is a well-intentioned effort to deal with a phenomenon that many Americans consider a serious problem—the presence of illegal immigrants in the United States. In the name of stemming the flow of people here from abroad, the law prohibits employers from giving them jobs, except under special circumstances. . . . These employer sanctions will go into effect June 1. The bill's restrictive intent is balanced by the amnesty program, which aims to help the illegals who have been in this country for at least five years.[3]

Indeed, in the 1970s and 1980s, the most visible legislative proposals paired the two concepts. If the country was going to be generous enough to legalize undocumented residents, then it would also close the door to future undocumented migrants by cutting off employment opportunities. The Select Commission on Immigration and Refugee Policy popularized the idea of "legalization" as part of the solution to the undocumented alien "problem," and recommended both employer sanctions and amnesty in its final report in 1981. The Simpson–Mazzoli proposal of 1982, which followed this final report and ultimately led to IRCA, employed the same prescription.

While strong congressional sentiment to respond to the perceived problem of undocumented aliens drove Congress to pass IRCA, congressional endorsement of the idea of "balancing" employer sanctions and legalization does not mean that there was strong support for legalization per se. Congress essentially concluded that with a flood of aliens crossing illegally and unchecked, the southern border was out of control. It was widely believed that the nation shared this fear. Accordingly, the House committee sponsoring the bill, the administration, and the INS agreed that IRCA was needed to stop the flow of aliens. "The major purpose of the Immigration Reform and Control Act [was] the control of illegal immigration to the United States. The major provisions of the Act all relate[d] to this purpose."[4]

Congress plainly acted out of a sense of urgency. Something—anything—had to be done to stem the tide of undocumented immigration, and IRCA seemed to be the only alternative. Said one representative, "To say that immigration reform is 'must' legislation does not begin to capture the compelling need for enactment of [this] bill before . . . Congress adjourns in a matter of days."[5] A doomsayer on the House floor predicted, "illegal immigration into this country is a national crisis, and if we don't act now to regain control of our borders we may forever lose the chance."[6] Passage of IRCA was necessary because the public was "demanding action now."[7]

Given this last-minute time pressure to get *anything* passed, many in Congress admitted IRCA's imperfections, but thought it the "least imperfect" bill possible.[8] IRCA, after all, was an assemblage of compromises. A few said the choice was between IRCA and no bill at all, or that it was "now or never" with the bill.[9] Later bills might be narrower and more restrictive, since the problem of undocumented immigration would worsen in the meantime. "Consider carefully," argued co-sponsor Representative Romano Mazzoli, "not whether there may theoretically exist a better bill, but whether the status quo—which is clearly unacceptable and intolerable—is preferable to the legislation before us."[10] Pleaded Representative Leon Panetta: "I do not know that this bill is going to work. We know that it is imperfect. Nobody can say it is going to work. But one thing is clear: the present situation is intolerable, and it must be responded to. Nobody can justify the situation as it exists today."[11] So great was the need to pass immigration legislation that quite a few congressional supporters admitted they had great trouble with the bill, and others may not have even known the bill's specific contents. Said one representative, "This bill is seriously flawed. . . . Amnesty is a provision that insults all the law-abiding people around the world waiting patiently, and legally, for their numbers to come up. . . . However, the need for control of illegals is growing. The problem is worsening daily. The need is great enough that I will vote for the bill in spite of its egregious faults. . . . This bill, flawed as it is, gives some promise of helping us to control our borders. On that basis, it deserves a try."[12] Similarly, Representative Edward Roybal spoke of the need for many to "hold their nose" from the stink of IRCA—for him the smelly part was employer sanctions—in order to vote for it.[13]

Legislative Intent

If Representative Roybal was correct that many members voted for IRCA solely on the basis of political necessity, any attempt to identify a single congressional "intent" is surely a senseless enterprise. Therefore, the argument that Congress mandated that the INS give the legalization aspects of the bill high priority and that it assume the most generous attitude possible must take into account the complex set of reasons—some having little to do with generosity—swirling in the minds of those who voted for IRCA.

Consider the range of reasoning behind legalization, especially the program for those undocumented who entered prior to 1982.

A logical starting point for determining legislative intent is the views of the original authors or the language of floor debates. Even though the version of legalization that was finally enacted differed from the original conception, the early goals and scope inform our search for legislative purpose. Of course, we must remain mindful that during the debates on IRCA, both supporters and opponents of the legalization program may have made exaggerations and misstatements that are not particularly helpful in our search.

An important early explication of a legalization program came from the Select Commission. In 1981 the commission submitted its final report, *U.S. Immigration Policy and the National Interest*. Among its recommendations was a legalization program giving amnesty to every undocumented alien who had entered the United States before January 1, 1980. The commission gave four reasons for legalization:

- Qualified aliens would be able to contribute more to U.S. society once they came into the open. Most undocumented/illegal aliens are hardworking, productive individuals who already pay taxes and contribute their labor to this country.
- Legalizing aliens would extend the protection of U.S. labor law and thus the new residents would no longer contribute to the depression of U.S. labor standards and wages.
- Legalization is an essential component of immigration reform and would allow the INS to target its enforcement resources on new flows of aliens.
- Legalization would provide statistical data about undocumented immigrants.[14]

A minority of commissioners supported two other reasons:

- Legalization would acknowledge that the United States has at least some responsibility for the presence of undocumented/illegal aliens in this country since U.S. law has explicitly exempted employers from any penalty for hiring them.
- Given this responsibility, alternatives to legalization—mainly deportation—would be unfair to the aliens.[15]

Some of the Select Commission's reasons for legalization appeared during the congressional debates; others, such as the desire for statistical data, dropped from the discussion. And the commission's legalization proposal was more generous than the program enacted, in that it included only a two-year cutoff period. Certainly, then, there is more to the question of congressional intent.

Several arguments used by legalization's supporters were strategic, and did not place much emphasis on the substantive importance of legalization. They help us to realize, however, that at least some support for legalization had more to do with procedural necessity than with substantive support for the concept.

The argument that Congress supported amnesty overwhelmingly is undermined by the presentation of legalization with employer sanctions as a unified, all-or-nothing choice. Some legalization supporters threatened that efforts to change or kill the provision would result in the death of the entire bill—a politically unacceptable possibility for members desiring to address the undocumented alien "problem." Proponents of legalization would not vote for an employer sanctions-only bill. As Representative Mazzoli, one of the legislation's main proponents, put it, "[Without legalization], I think we will have a very difficult time moving the rest of the bill"; and Representative Dan Lungren added: "I seriously believe that if [the legalization provisions are deleted], the bill will die."[16] The same argument was made in the Senate. Given this atmosphere—of a perceived desperate border situation leaving Congress with no choice but to pass legislation—it is hard to attribute to Congress a "generous intent" in its approval of legalization.[17]

The Opposition

While the comments of those opposing any legislation hardly provide a strong basis for determining congressional intent of a law enacted over such objections, they nonetheless are useful to keep in mind.

Opposition to legalization was so intense that the program narrowly survived in the House of Representatives. In the eleventh hour, on October 10, 1986, Representative Bill McCollum introduced an amendment to delete legalization completely from IRCA. The House defeated the amendment, thereby saving the legalization program, though by a vote of 199 to save it, 192 to kill it, with 41 absent. A swing vote of only four members would have reversed the result.

Pro-legalization sentiment in the House was by no means overwhelming. Opponents argued that it was unfair to prospective immigrants in all parts of the world who were on waiting lists and were seeking to immigrate lawfully. Many had been waiting for years. Legalization thus rewarded the "lawbreakers" who made their way into the nation illegally, and would have a "magnet" effect of drawing more undocumented migrants into the United States hoping to take advantage of the amnesty.[18]

The close vote on the McCollum amendment provided the basis for some legislators to argue that legalization need not be interpreted generously. To Senator Gramm, the House vote on the McCollum amendment showed there was "hardly a great mandate for legalization."[19] In the words of Representative E. Clay Shaw, the House vote "made a strong statement" that "we did not want to reward those who have violated our laws."[20] Even the author of IRCA in the Senate, Senator Alan Simpson, said that legalization "was probably the one thing in the bill—and there were plenty—that was least acceptable to the American people. Legalization only passed the U.S. House of Representatives by 7 votes. I do not think people ought to forget that."[21]

Justification

The major justifications advanced by legislative supporters of the program are obviously more relevant to understanding Congress's intentions. The four chief justifications were the lack of an alternative to legalization; the need to spread INS resources; the elimination of the underclass; and matters of equity.

How could Congress deal with the huge number of undocumented aliens living in the United States? Members of Congress only had a handful of alternatives: first, legalize some or all of the aliens; second, find and deport some or all of them; or third, do nothing. The second alternative would have required a huge effort to round up aliens, would probably have violated many civil rights and therefore engendered a slew of lawsuits, would have cost a fortune, and simply would never have worked. The third alternative was not possible since Congress was under pressure to do something about the perceived undocumented problem. Legalization was the only alternative.

Many legislators saw legalization as the only solution to the undocumented alien problem. The House Committee on the Judiciary said, "the alternative of intensifying interior enforcement or attempting mass deportations would be . . . costly, ineffective, and inconsistent with our immigrant heritage."[22] The bill's sponsors all made statements to the same effect. On the Senate side, Simpson argued that "the alternative to legalization is to go hunt for [aliens]. If you couldn't find them coming in how do you find them to get them out? The alternative to legalization is deportation."[23] The House sponsors concurred. Arguing against the McCollum amendment, Representative Peter Rodino said, "I would be no part of [the amendment to delete legalization] because, in my judgment, we cannot deport these people. We would not, I am sure, provide the money to conduct the raids. It would mean billions of dollars in order to try to deport them. . . . That is what the amendment asks us to do."[24]

Thus, in a real sense, this argument boiled down to a logistically realistic response to the "problem of undocumented aliens." Existing enforcement was failing and massive deportations would certainly never have worked. Thus, one could argue that the program had to be generous if the goal was to rid the country of undocumented aliens. Yet the cutoff date adopted for legalization was not generous, and the "no alternatives" argument was not the only reasoning offered to support legalization.

Another justification for legalizing undocumented residents was that this would allow the INS to stop concentrating its enforcement resources on locating and apprehending longtime residents and concentrate instead on enforcement of the border against newly arriving, undocumented aliens. This justification was first advanced by the Select Commission. Both Simpson and the congressional committees cited this rationale as well.

For some, legalization was the mechanism to address the fact that many undocumented aliens lived in what some described as an "underclass"—in poverty without the protection of labor or health laws. The Select Commission had complained of the existence of a "second-class" society. And many members of Congress hoped that legalization would eliminate the underclass.[25] The Senate report on IRCA noted:

> [Another goal of legalization] is to eliminate the illegal subclass now present in our society. Not only does their illegal status and resulting weak bargaining position cause these people to depress U.S. wages and working conditions, but it also hinders their full assimilation and, through them, that of legal residents from the same country of origin. Thus they remain a fearful and clearly exploitable group within the U.S. society.[26]

Upon signing the legislation, even President Reagan, who was more interested in the employer sanctions provisions of the law, expressed hope that the legalization program would remove people from "the shadows."[27]

The hope that legalization would eliminate the underclass found its greatest support among witnesses testifying during hearings. A delegation of religious leaders led the charge on this note in urging Congress to adopt legalization. A spokesman for the Mexican American Legal Defense and Education Fund (MALDEF) contended that "legalization is the only realistic and meaningful way to bring the undocumented population 'out of the shadows' and into the mainstream of American life with the minimum of disruption and expense."[28] Other witnesses simply assumed that Congress intended to eliminate this underclass.

Many lawmakers supported the legalization program because of the contributions that undocumented workers had already made to the country, and charged the nation with a responsibility to account for those contributions. This view was used to respond to complaints that legalization was not fair to prospective immigrants waiting in line abroad or that it might be a "magnet" for further unlawful entrants thinking they could cheat their way into the program. Indeed, the House report argued that legalization was "equitable" to the undocumented aliens working in the United States, and in President Reagan's words, "fair to the countless thousands of people throughout the world who seek legally to come to America."[29]

For others, it demonstrated "compassion" for those now part of American society, giving "dignity" and "honor" to those working illegally in America; in short, it was "necessary," "humanitarian," and the "American way."[30] Even INS commissioner Alan Nelson touted legalization as a compromise between a "humanitarian recognition of illegals who have significant equities in the U.S." and "fair and reasonable screening requirements that do not reward proven criminals."[31]

The Special Agricultural Worker Program

Evidence of the scope and intent behind the Special Agricultural Worker (SAW) legalization program is sketchy. The program made its way to inclusion in IRCA virtually without congressional debate and without any attempts to change it. Even its authors did not want to touch or discuss the SAW program.

The few comments relating to the SAW program during IRCA's legislative development appear mostly as unhappy criticisms of the legislative process. Representative F. James Sensenbrenner noted that the SAW program "was offered without hearings to determine its impact, and questions which were posed to determine 'how it would operate' were met with, 'That will have to be worked out later.'"[32] The same held true once the SAW program reached the floor: "Our biggest protest," said Representative Edward Roybal, "is the fact that no opportunity was really given to thoroughly debate this issue [of SAW changes in the conference report]."[33] Indeed, at the start of the House's final day of deliberation over H.R. 381—the House version of IRCA—the rules under which IRCA was debated provided a sort of "gag order" by preventing changes to the SAW program. Finally, those who wanted to raise questions about SAWs were stonewalled with statements that any attempts to change the program would have "killed" IRCA itself.[34]

Therefore, the record is relatively devoid of comments revealing the "intent" of the SAW program. Naturally, the program had its supporters and detractors. But few made statements revealing the intended scope of the program or the reasoning behind its structure. Several legislators viewed the SAW program as a compromise between growers and workers, probably meaning the program was not a blanket amnesty for agricultural workers. The prospects of sanctions created a need for a program that would provide a pool of legal agricultural workers. In fact, the timing of the implementation of sanctions in agricultural areas coincided with the end of the SAW application period. To placate concerns about the program, some said it was the "best" compromise Congress could get over the issue, that it was the key to getting compromises on IRCA altogether, and that while "every one on the floor" hated the SAW program, it was "part of the price you have to pay" for immigration reform.[35] As with the pre-1982 program, a legislator had to "hold his nose" over the SAW program to vote for IRCA.[36]

On the other hand, some saw it not as a compromise between agricultural growers and laborers, but rather between the growers and Congress. Representative Hal Daub dubbed the SAW program the "western growers buyout provision"; others said it existed only because of pressure from the growers' lobby for a cheap labor source. From this perspective, the SAW program was not at all an aid to farmworkers, but only a gift to growers. The INS explained the reasoning:

> The controversy over foreign agricultural workers was one of the reasons why immigration legislation failed in 1984 and why it almost derailed again in 1986. Growers have contended that many U.S. workers do not want to work in seasonal agriculture or live in rural areas. If employer sanctions were to be instituted, growers wanted some assurance that they could obtain sufficient workers lawfully so that their crops did not rot in the fields. Organized labor and farm worker rights organizations disputed the growers' assertions, pointing to high unemployment rates among domestic farm workers. They charged that growers were seeking to preserve a cheap labor force with few legal rights.[37]

No one seemed to think the SAW program was primarily for the benefit of laborers, although the legislative history makes it apparent that Congress was mindful not to reenact elements of the Bracero guestworker program from the 1950s. (See Chapter 7.)

Applicant Estimates

The anticipated number of applicants to IRCA's legalization program is relevant not only to understanding the opposition to and support for legalization, but possibly for measuring whether the program was implemented generously or not. For example, the concern that large numbers of applicants would apply probably created some political opposition to legalization. But those same large numbers, if not reached, might indicate that legalization was not implemented liberally. One suspects that smaller expected numbers would have resulted in less resistance to legalization, and also an easier target for INS to meet. Perhaps counterintuitively, support for legalization could have ensued from anticipated larger numbers if supporters saw the larger numbers as evidence that something had to be done.

Generally speaking, the total number of legalization applicants (almost three million pre-1982 and SAW) was smaller than expected, although the number of agricultural applicants (1.2 million) was larger than many expected.

The principal group of expected applicants for both the pre-1982 and agricultural worker programs were Mexican nationals. Demographers who scrutinized the 1980 census data concluded that 48 percent of the undocumented population was Mexican in origin. Farmworkers in particular, especially those in the Southwest, were overwhelmingly Mexican. Among the other groups who were expected to come forward, Salvadorans, Guatemalans, Filipinos, Chinese, and Polish nationals ranked highly. In addition to Mexican farmworkers, the typical applicants included Mexicans or Central Americans who had entered the United States without inspection prior to January 1, 1982, and nationals from Asia, Europe, and Africa who had overstayed or violated visitor or student visas prior to January 1, 1982.

Congress never offered a definite number of aliens who might be eligible for legalization. Taking the pre-1982 program as an example, all estimates ran in the millions, not the hundreds of thousands, but from there the estimates diverged wildly. Legalization supporters predicted between 1.5 million and 9 million potential applicants, while the opponents, assuming a chain migration of relatives, warned of 100 million new citizens within a decade. Given this range, some legislators suggested that there could be no congressional intent with respect to raw numbers because no reliable estimates existed, plain and simple.

Undoubtedly, Congress expected that at least a million aliens would be eligible for the pre-1982 legalization program. That, however, was only a starting point. From there, for many legislators, it was anybody's guess. Senator Gordon Humphrey explained: "I have been unable to find consistent estimates on the numbers of aliens who might be legalized . . . the number of relatives they might bring with them, and just as importantly, the number of aliens who would be encouraged to enter once these provisions are passed. All estimates range in the millions."[38] As a result, several legislators spoke only of unspecified "millions" as potential beneficiaries of the plan.

In spite of the obvious difficulties, some estimates were made, and they fell into two distinct categories. Some estimates predicted the number of applicants, while others attempted to count the number of eligible aliens. Not all eligible aliens would apply, and ineligible aliens might apply. Indeed, the number of aliens actually legalized represents a third prediction, because not every application would lead to legalization.

Consider the wide disparities between these different estimates in each category and between categories. The Congressional Budget Office (Budget Office), as part of its cost estimates of IRCA, derived a figure of 1.4 million likely applicants. The Budget Office estimate included 200,000 schoolchildren alone. As low as the overall number seems, the Budget Office received some criticism for being too liberal with its numbers. The next lowest estimate came from the Carnegie Endowment for International Peace, which predicted between 1.8 million and 2.6 million eligible aliens. The Department of Health and Human Services used basically the same method as the Budget Office, but came up with a range of 2.5 million to 3.3 million aliens eligible for amnesty. The INS predicted even more—between 2 million and 3.9 million aliens would be eligible. Finally, a group of religious leaders predicted between 3 million and 6 million eligible aliens.

During congressional debates, the few legislators who offered numerical estimates raised their sights even higher. Senator Phil Gramm guessed 4 million to 7 million amnesty recipients, and Senator Alan Simpson essentially agreed as did Senator James A. McClure.[39] Senator Joseph Biden sought the middle ground by guessing 5 million. On the House floor, Representative Bill Richardson predicted 3 million to 9 million and Representative Jack Fields predicted one million people in his home state of Texas alone.

The Budget Office derived its figure of 1.4 million using three principal figures:

Number of undocumented aliens in United States in 1986 (time of legalization program)	5,600,000
Percent of those who came to United States before January 1, 1982	× .40
Percent of those who would actually apply for legalization	× .60
Plus a fudge factor of aliens "with a history of employment who would be accepted"	+ 25,000
TOTAL	= 1,370,000

But the Budget Office's starting point for each figure was disputable. The first figure —the total number of undocumented aliens in the United States—was (and continues to be) a subject open to a great deal of speculation and debate. The Budget Office put the second figure, the percent of all aliens who would have been eligible for legalization, at 40 percent. But at the same time, the Department of Health and Human Services guessed 53 percent. In 1981 the Select Commission concluded that a 2-year cutoff period would have made 60 percent of all aliens eligible for amnesty, and a 3-year period would have reduced that percentage to 45. In fact, IRCA's cutoff period was more than 5 years.

The Budget Office's third prediction, the percentage of eligible aliens who actually would apply, was supported (or at least repeated) by Representative Daub. The 60 percent figure, however, referred to applications by families of eligible aliens, not to single young adults for whom legalization might not be as attractive. As a result, the overall number would be lower.

Given the wide range of predictions, from just over one million to upwards of six million or more, a single congressional "intent" with respect to the number of participants in the legalization program is impossible to identify. The most accurate assessment would be that Congress knew that millions of aliens would receive benefits, but not how many millions.

Even higher-range estimates of legalization recipients were bandied about by opponents of the concept. Of course, this was not unusual. As the Supreme Court has noted, opponents of bills often make less-than-realistic claims while trying to defeat passage.[40] The lowest estimate proposed by any opponent of the legalization program was 6 million to 12 million recipients. From there, figures climbed without ceiling and certainly without reason. Senator Orrin G. Hatch guessed 6 million to 16 million, and Senator Jesse A. Helms forecast anywhere from 6 million to 15 million. Representative Hal Daub said that "everyone is in agreement that you are going to have between 10 to 20 million people legalized if only half of those people come forward and take advantage of general amnesty."[41] Representative G. Taylor guessed 12 million to 20 million applicants, and Representatives Henry Hyde and F. Sensenbrenner opined that a third of the population of Mexico would use IRCA to legalize themselves in the United States. To make matters worse, argued the doomsayers, each legalization applicant would eventually petition for family members, thus creating a calamitous "chain migration" effect. Some estimated that within a decade, IRCA would add 70, 90, or 100 million new citizens to the United States.[42] Representative Bill McCollum assumed a 64 percent response rate (compared to the Budget Office's 60 percent rate), estimated that 2 million aliens a year would receive amnesty, and assumed that each alien would petition for an average of 7 family members. He therefore concluded that, over a decade, 100 million citizens would be added.

Finally, several legislators simply said there was no way of knowing the ramifications of legalization. "No one really knows how many aliens would be eligible for legalization,"[43] said one lawmaker during the debates. "We never could get any figures from anybody, and that was the frustrating part," observed Senator Alan Simpson after passage. Uncertainty existed about the total number of undocumented aliens in the country, the number of aliens entering and leaving every year, and the percentage of aliens who would be eligible for legalization. Indeed, the estimates of the Budget Office and the other organizations were all inherently unreliable and uncertain.

The trouble legislators had figuring out the number of applicants for the general legalization also infected debates on the agricultural worker program. Estimating that a quarter of all farmworkers were undocumented and that 60 percent would apply for legalization, the Budget Office projected that the SAW program would produce 250,000 legalized workers. Congressional estimates ranged from 200,000 to one million. Senator Simpson said the number would be "small" but agreed with a colleague that no one knew how many eligible workers existed.

What Legalization Entailed

IRCA contained two major amnesty or legalization provisions that had the potential of benefiting millions of undocumented aliens. The first provided permanent residence status to aliens who had resided in the United States since before January 1, 1982. The other afforded permanent residence status to farmworkers or special agriculture workers (SAWs) who had performed agricultural work for at least ninety days between May 1, 1985, and May 1, 1986.

Those who would commonly fall under the first program either entered by crossing the border without inspection prior to January 1, 1982, or entered on a visitor or student visa and worked without permission or overstayed the permitted length of stay prior to that date. No one knew exactly what nationalities the applicants would be, but policy makers, INS personnel, and community workers had a sense—grounded on INS apprehension statistics—that most would be Mexican. In fact, about 70 percent who ultimately applied under the pre-1982 program were Mexican; the next largest groups were Salvadoran (8.1 percent) and Guatemalan (3 percent). However, the percentages may simply reflect the results of publicity priorities of the INS and community-based organizations (CBOs). Demographers who scrutinized the 1980 census data prior to IRCA concluded that only 55 percent of the undocumented population was Mexican in origin.

Those qualifying under the farmworker program were also mostly expected to be Mexican. Indeed, Mexicans did predominate, with 81.6 percent of the SAW applications. Haitians received 3.4 percent, El Salvadorans 2 percent, and Guatemalans and Asian Indians 1.4 percent each.

Ultimately, 1.7 million applicants filed under the pre-1982 program and 1.2 million applied as SAWs. The number for the pre-1982 program was far below most estimates, while the figure for agricultural workers was higher than expected.

The procedures that INS established for legalization reflected the ambiguous support for a generous program. Some were complicated, others were straightforward, but none represented a bite-the-bullet, wipe-the-slate-clean amnesty. The simplest procedure for legalization would have merely asked applicants to register with name, birth, biographical data, and perhaps a completed fingerprint chart to check for criminality. Instead, each applicant faced a series of procedural requirements, most representing manifestations of complex eligibility and exclusion grounds.

Documentation

Each applicant had to provide evidence to support the claim of eligibility. Revealing either the INS's strict philosophy or its naivete about what typical applicants could be expected to produce, regulations proposed by the INS initially implied that every pre-1982 applicant had to submit a document for each month of residence. After a great outcry from CBOs over the difficulties that applicants would have in coming up with the required documents, however, the INS adopted the following philosophy in its instructions to field offices:

> Submission of voluminous documents is not necessary. Each day in the life of the applicant need not be documented. . . . Gaps in documentation for a certain period of time may be acceptable. However, if the entire family shows the same gap . . . the applicant may be requested to submit additional documentation to cover that period. The inference to be drawn from the documentation provided shall depend not on quantity alone, but also on its credibility and amenability to verification.[44]

Even under the new instructions, the demands of INS offices varied. As one staff member at a CBO saw it, "the documentation requirements varied greatly depending on the office and the adjudicator. The adjudicators varied too greatly, some asking applicants for a document for every quarterly period of residence, while others for only one document for every year. All of this was very frustrating . . . and many people were discouraged from applying."[45]

Pre-1982 applicants had to provide proof of identity, residence, and financial responsibility. Proof of Selective Service registration was required for males from the age of eighteen through twenty-six under the pre-1982 program. Otherwise, the applicant had to complete the registration form at the time of the interview. Agricultural program applicants had to provide proof of identity, financial responsibility, and evidence of qualifying agricultural employment.

To prove identity, the regulations suggested the following types of documents: passport, birth certificate, any national identity document bearing a photograph and fingerprint, driver's license, baptismal record/marriage certificate, or affidavit of a knowledgeable individual. If an assumed name had been used, additional evidence had to be submitted to prove the applicant's true identity.

To prove residence, the following types of documents were suggested: pay stubs, W-2 forms, letters from employers, utility bills, school records, hospital and medical records, letters from church, union or other organization officials, money order receipts, bankbooks, automobile license receipts, tax receipts, deeds, insurance policies, and affidavits.

As proof of financial responsibility, the applicant needed evidence of a history of employment (e.g., an employment letter, W-2 forms, or income tax returns), evidence of self-support (e.g., bank statements, stocks, or other assets), or an affidavit of support, completed by a responsible person in the United States, which guaranteed complete or partial financial support of the applicant.

Agricultural program applicants could establish proof of the requisite number of days of agricultural employment by submitting government employment records or any records maintained by agricultural producers, farm labor contractors, collective bargaining organizations, or other groups or organizations. If such primary sources of information were not available, applicants had to submit other evidence corroborating performance of qualifying employment. Such evidence might consist of worker identification issued by employers or collective bargaining organizations, or union membership cards or other union records such as dues receipts or work records (e.g., pay stubs, piecework receipts, W-2 forms, or copies of income tax returns certified by the IRS). It also might include affidavits by agricultural producers, foremen, farm labor contractors, fellow employees, or other persons with specific knowledge of the applicant's employment. All documents had to be submitted in the original, and any document in a language other than English had to be accompanied by a certified translation.

The documentation requirement was generally the most onerous for eligible applicants. For example, migrant farmworkers often could not obtain documentation for their work experiences. Pay records often were not matched to names; many of those that were only named a family or the head of a family. Payment often went to contractors who paid workers in cash without further records. Even when farmworkers received pay stubs, they often lost them in the process of migratory living. Even in non-farmworker cases, immigrants who had documents or letters from former employers, receipts, and other records often lost or destroyed them over the years. After all, keeping records, especially those relating to identity, was antithetical to life as an undocumented person. The prior use of false identities was also common among eligible applicants, exacerbating the nightmarish problem of collecting and straightening out records.

In order to meet the documentation requirement, prospective applicants typically had to pore over old documents, receipts, and records (if they were fortunate enough to have retained them over the years); contact friends and neighbors for possible letters; request documentation from past and former employers; visit schools and doctors' offices for verification of records; and seek old records from social service and governmental agencies.

Application

Each applicant had to complete a multipage application form and provide supporting documents. The forms for applicants who arrived before 1982 were four pages in length, while those for agricultural applicants were three pages long. The application forms were printed in English, and the only translation made available by the INS was a Spanish translation for the agricultural worker application.

Each application sought detailed information on a variety of topics. In addition to conventional biographical data, applicants were asked for other names and social security numbers they might have used; previous records or applications filed with the INS; absences from the United States; dates, places, and manner of previous entries to the United States; passport and visa history; dates and places of employment and residences in the United States; membership or affiliation with any clubs, churches, unions, or organizations; history of mental disorder, drug addiction, or alcoholism; arrests, convictions, pardons, or incarcerations; and receipt of public assistance.

The application could be filed in person, sent by mail to an INS legalization office, or filed in person at a particular community agency known as a qualified designated entity (QDE). If filing at a QDE, the applicant had an additional sixty days to submit the necessary documentary attachments. Each application had to be submitted with a filing fee of $185 per adult and $50 per child, up to a maximum of $420 per family. Every application required a completed fingerprint chart and two color photographs. Those applicants who did not have social security numbers had to submit a separate application for them. In addition, each applicant had to undergo a medical examination by an authorized physician, and submit a completed medical examination form.

Thus, applicants had to deal with a fairly lengthy application process that included finding a place to get fingerprinted and photographed, locating an authorized physician for a medical examination, coming up with a filing fee, and standing in line to file the application(s). The process was particularly difficult in cases where several family members applied, or where an applicant was not fully literate in English.

Interview

An interview was required of each applicant. Depending on the particular office, some interviews were scheduled at the time the application was filed, while other applicants waited to receive notice of the interview through the mail. Those who waited faced an additional problem if they moved. In spite of an appointment procedure at most offices, applicants commonly waited an hour or more in legalization office waiting rooms. Once the interview started, however, it usually lasted only a few minutes and consisted mostly of a review of the information in the application form and supporting documents. Stories of INS abuse and intimidation surfaced, especially in cases where the INS suspected fraud on the part of the applicants. For most applicants across the country, the interview was not a difficult experience.

Employment Authorization

Legalization applicants were granted permission to work. Upon filing the application with the INS, an applicant was generally given employment authorization if the interview could not be scheduled within thirty days. On the day of the interview, the applicant was issued temporary employment authorization for a period of six months. Once the final decision was made by the INS to grant the applicant lawful temporary resident status, the applicant was required to return within one month to the legalization office to be issued a more permanent card.

Permanent Residency Application

Within eighteen months of being approved for lawful temporary residency status, every pre-1982 applicant had to submit another application for permanent status and be prepared to show proficiency in English and knowledge of U.S. history and government or enrollment in an approved course of study. Most agricultural program applicants automatically became lawful permanent residents on December 1, 1990, and none had to meet the English and civics requirements for the permanent card. The form for agricultural workers at this stage was not complicated.

INS Approach during Legalization

Congress left implementation of legalization in the hands of two key players, the INS and CBOs. While many in the immigrant rights community were skeptical about the Service's ability to carry out the program, Congress felt it had little choice. After all, only the INS had the necessary combination of experience in immigration and the bureaucratic capacity to expand to meet the task. Congress was aware, however, that the Service's old enforcement attitudes might be difficult to reverse, and was concerned that the program would be severely crippled without the trust of a potentially suspicious immigrant community. Congress therefore authorized a deputization-like procedure for CBOs, enabling them to accept applications directly. This extension was novel and sensible. For many potential applicants, voluntary agencies were familiar, accessibly located, and known for their solid track record in other immigrant and refugee-related programs. As a result, voluntary agencies were perfectly positioned, both physically and culturally, to ease the experience for fearful clients. The bulk of the applications eventually were filed directly through the INS and community-oriented nonprofit programs, although many applicants benefited from the resources of other programs first. In addition, many applicants sought assistance from immigration consultant /notary publics, a number of businesses created to capitalize on legalization, and private attorneys.

Aspects of the INS response to legalization were severely criticized, and the INS responded with equal venom aimed at the actions of immigrant rights groups during legalization. However, close examination reveals that both sides deserve credit for positive achievements during the program. Congress handed the INS an enormous challenge. On the face of IRCA, the Service was given little time to prepare for legalization. Within six months of enactment, the agency had to construct a bureaucracy and open the doors for a program that was expected to serve millions. This work included everything from adding offices around the country and hiring more personnel to creating the proper forms and training both old and new employees on the new law and its procedures.

The INS did not fully anticipate the immediate challenge that IRCA posed. Although IRCA had been winding its way through Congress during 1986, several other, similar proposals had failed in the wake of the Select Commission report in the early 1980s. The IRCA bill had itself been declared dead that fall. The legalization program that seemed so unlikely in October 1986 sprang to life suddenly, and Congress expected it to be in full operation by May 1987.

INS Planning

The INS was not, however, caught completely off guard by IRCA. Early signs of congressional support for legalization stimulated some INS planning well before the act was passed. Legalization was a central proposal in the final report of the Select Commission in March 1981, as well as in the initial Simpson–Mazzoli legislative package in 1982. The INS assembled a task force to discuss implementation during congressional debates on immigration reform in 1982 and 1984, and convened a meeting of representatives from CBOs from across the country in 1983 for suggestions and input. By the end of 1984, the INS had completed an implementation plan. When IRCA was passed in 1986, many elements of the final implementation already had been worked out.

Within a month of IRCA's passage in November 1986, the INS introduced its preliminary plan to other government agencies, employers, unions, and immigrant service and advocacy organizations, and sought additional input. A December 1986 round-table discussion on implementation sponsored by the Carnegie Endowment for International Peace gave the INS another opportunity to consider its options. The Service listened to the views of other immigrant service agencies, and of officials from other countries that had tried legalization programs of their own.

Even with a plan in hand, however, the INS faced an immense implementation effort that included hiring and training of new staff, locating office space, and developing procedures for staff and applicants. The final substantive content of the law had to be learned and interpreted, and regulations had to be issued.

With a lead time of only six months, the INS encountered problems with the timing of its regulations. The Service began drafting regulations soon after the passage of IRCA, and distributed an informal draft to elicit comments from Congress and other interested parties in late January 1987. The INS published regulations for formal comment in mid-March, and promulgated final regulations on May 1, 1987—only four days before the doors to legalization opened. This process left little time for INS and community agency staff to learn exactly what would be required on opening day, especially since many of the proposed regulations had changed significantly after the comment period. The hurried process left several important issues unresolved until late in the program, including the INS's precise philosophy on documentation, procedures on employment authorization, the local INS's relationship with regional processing facilities (RPFs), and the structure of community outreach efforts by local INS offices. Several of these issues were never resolved.

These problems aside, the INS's willingness to seek input and its positive response to many of the comments were noteworthy. Recognizing that widespread cooperation was necessary for successful implementation, the INS felt it made "the maximum" effort to refine IRCA implementation plans and regulations in "the most open manner."[46] To its credit, the INS continued to seek and receive input from immigrant service organizations on many issues throughout the life of the program.

INS Structure

A multilevel INS bureaucracy implemented legalization. An assistant commissioner was appointed at the Central Office in Washington, D.C., to head up the legalization program. Each local district office set up one or more legalization offices (LOs) where applications were reviewed, applicants were interviewed, and adjudication recommendations were made. Four RPFs reviewed LOs' recommendations, granted and denied applications, and in some cases conducted investigations. The INS public information campaign was similarly divided, with large sums of centralized funds spent on a national scale, while regional and local offices devoted time to public awareness.

After considerable haggling, the regional and district offices retained a good deal of control over how legalization was implemented in their areas. After all, while the central office established regulations and a system-wide computer system, the bulk of the day-to-day work of implementing legalization was to be handled by the LOs and the

RPFs. They hired and trained staff, managed and set standards for initial application processing, and generally attempted to maintain communication between offices.

Legalization Offices.   The historical immigrant distrust of the INS meant that LOs had to be different if potential applicants were to participate. The INS's decision to deputize community agencies as QDEs was intended to address immigrant apprehensiveness, but the LOs had to perform adeptly as well. In order to lessen applicants' anxiety about approaching the INS, LOs were located away from regular INS offices, which were known to combine its prominent enforcement efforts with visa and naturalization functions. Trainers reminded staff that congressional proponents intended IRCA to be generously applied and emphasized that employees were to help immigrants determine how they could qualify. Applicant interviews were to begin with the explanation, "I'm here to help you with your application today."

Because the LOs, like most of the legalization apparatus, were completely new, it took significant efforts by INS—nationally, regionally, and locally—to organize and train the staff in only six months. Two thousand new workers had to be hired and trained, sites for 107 new offices located, acquired, designed, furnished, and equipped, and sixty million forms produced.

The task of hiring and maintaining 2,000 new workers was immense. Some LO supervisors were recruited from the ranks of INS retirees, but many workers were new to INS. Recruiting and hiring were difficult. Legalization jobs were temporary, salaries for new examiners were at low-range government levels, and applicants had to wait three or four months to pass FBI and other security checks. As of the May 5, 1987 start-up date, staffing was still not complete, and some regions suffered from high vacancy rates throughout legalization.

Thus, LO staff ended up being a mixed bag. Managers were described by some as "happy" to be in their position. However, some INS staffers who were transferred to the LOs retained an enforcement mentality. On the other hand, INS retirees who returned to work in the LOs were described as "sympatico," more friendly and sympathetic toward the applicants. Even some former Border Patrol officers were purportedly pro-amnesty. So in any given office, the staff likely included hardline INS staffers, and more beneficent new hires and retirees. Whatever their attitude, LO understaffing meant that employees worked very hard.[47]

Training of the LO staff was also complex. The idea was to provide the staff with two weeks of training under the coordination of the regional offices at the outset, and then to provide ongoing training as standards and procedures were modified. Indeed, training sessions were held across the country and, before the LOs opened, staff members were provided with agency operations instructions and field manuals. However, the law and the procedures were new, even for experienced INS personnel. Final regulations were not distributed until four days before the program began. Despite the training, therefore, the early days of legalization were plagued by inexperience and confusion and LO staff was bogged down in procedural, logistic, and even financial problems. The later, ongoing training during legalization was also spotty and weak. In addition, productive, informational intraregional conference calls were discontinued after the first several months.

In spite of these problems, LOs were credited with directly processing 71 percent of all applications, compared to 21 percent for qualified CBOs and 8 percent for private attorneys. This LO figure may be significantly inflated and misleading because many applicants received most of their assistance from community-based organizations (including deputized QDEs) and immigration consultant/notary publics, and then filed with the LO instead of a QDE. However, most applicants went directly to the LO for information and filing.

Thus, many applicants overcame their initial apprehension or fear, and first inquired about legalization at the INS. The majority of applicants found this system to be helpful. Certainly, during legalization, incidents of INS abuse and inhospitable treatment of applicants by INS personnel occurred. However, for those who went directly to the INS, it was not uncommon to find a helpful LO staff. Furthermore, as word of successful legalizations spread, anxiety over approaching LOs was eased in many quarters.

While much of their success in attracting applicants can be attributed to positive staff attitudes, several other factors gave LOs an edge over QDEs, voluntary agencies, and attorneys. Most applicants associated legalization with the INS, so that is where they turned to inquire and apply. QDEs generally charged a processing fee over and above the application fee charged at LO. Applicants needing work permits obtained them faster at LOs. Surprisingly, documentary requirements were often more rigorous at QDEs who sought to avoid having applications bounced back by the INS.

The LO funding scheme did, however, skew resource distribution, which affected service availability in certain districts and regions. Since legalization was to be self-funding, LOs received resources according to the number of applications processed. In spite of these problems, LOs generally established a public image that was quite good, relative to the prior image of the Service and its top leaders. Catholic Social Service agencies noted that the INS was following a course that varied considerably from the public posturing of some of its top officials. Many LO staff were courteous and helpful. LOs were located in immigrant communities with access to public transportation and many opened during evenings or on weekends. Finally, some LO staff members committed themselves to the legalization mission, bringing creativity and energy to the process.

Regional Processing Facilities.   The large numbers of applications that were processed through the LOs were not handled as quickly at the RPFs. Applications were forwarded to an RPF where security and record verifications were matched against INS records. Although this type of examination was not new to the INS, the 1.76 million pre-1982 applications received during the twelve-month window amounted to nearly four times the normal volume for the INS; an RPF logjam developed.

After eight months, less than 38 percent of all filed applications had been adjudicated. Chronic understaffing exacerbated the problems. More applicants than expected had prior INS or FBI files, each requiring a laborious verification process.

In addition to affecting the lives of applicants, slow RPF processing caused other problems. LOs and QDEs saw RPF decisions as a form of feedback on the adequacy of the applications filed. The cautious strategy employed by QDEs and other community agencies of requiring extensive documentation from applicants (which was time-consuming and discouraging to applicants) was in large part a response to the delay in feedback from the RPFs. The belief was that an extensively documented applicant would not be criticized for having "too much" documentation, particularly as a sampling of decisions on cases with "thinner" documentation was slow in developing.

Although applications were being handled slowly, fraudulent applications were rare. The RPF approval rate was about 95 percent.

INS Image

At the outset, even INS officials conceded that the INS had an image problem with the targeted undocumented immigrant population. Immigrants' rights advocates argued that LOs would be seen as no different from the INS Border Patrol, and preferred that a completely different government entity administer legalization. The INS argued that the "fear factor" was overblown by CBOs and immigrant rights groups, whose strongly negative feelings about the INS were not shared by the communities themselves.

A variety of sources confirm that fear was indeed a factor. In Massachusetts, one agency said many aliens thought the legalization program was a hoax or a trap. (Indeed, the INS has used such traps in its enforcement toolbag. See Chapter 8.) In the Southwest, "aliens were understandably apprehensive about the Service, which they have long perceived only as the group that was out to deport them. 'We knew there would be a certain amount of the "fear factor,"' says [an INS officer]. 'The Border Patrol, they're the cops,' and legalization was suspected by many of really being a sting operation."[48] Northern California INS officials also reported immigrant suspicion, and community workers found that mistrust prevented many filings by eligible aliens.

The image problem was exemplified by Harold Ezell, the controversial INS regional commissioner for the western region, home of most anticipated applicants. Prior to the passage of IRCA, Ezell was an outspoken opponent of "illegal" immigrants. He often invited television crews to the scene of INS workplace raids that he himself attended, and frequently charged that undocumented workers took jobs from Americans while exploiting the welfare system. While Ezell was apparently never personally involved in the physical mistreatment of aliens, he epitomized INS enforcement and symbolized the worst type of INS abuse of undocumented workers. Even his friends and church got into the act, helping to establish a vigilante-type border watch group called Americans for Border Control. Ezell's verbal attacks on Mexican migrants particularly ignited the ire of the Latino community, and stirred several spokespersons to call for his firing. Paradoxically, Ezell is "credited" by some in the INS with the passage of IRCA. They believe that had it not been for Ezell's media-grabbing enforcement antics, immigration issues would not have received the type of media attention and the level of importance necessary for the passage of major congressional legislation.[49]

Nevertheless, information from Los Angeles indicated that early predictions that the immigrant community could never trust the INS enough to apply directly in legalization offices were grossly exaggerated. The chief contractor for the INS public awareness effort went further, claiming that "fear factor" stories were just that—stories. After conducting "thousands of interviews with immigrants," he found that aliens actually trusted and respected the INS. Among those immigrants who thought themselves eligible for the program, "the INS received very high honesty levels [and the immigrants trusted] information from the INS more than they trusted information from the Church to tell them about the law." Perhaps because of the complexity of the process, however, "families would send out one person as a scout to test the water."[50]

Since the INS discounted a serious "fear factor," early in its program, it took few steps to increase its accessibility to the immigrant community or to spruce up its image, other than using QDEs as a buffer (which was mandated by Congress). Its major structural response was to establish LOs away from the main INS offices, in locations more accessible to most Latino communities. This was certainly not insignificant, but other INS "strategies" for increasing accessibility were quite passive. For example, in order to show that the program worked and to encourage the participation of others, one initial INS "strategy" was to let the alien community learn of early applicant "successes." This seemed sensible since "those with simpler cases, clearly eligible for legalization," were coming forward first, while others with more complicated cases were "hanging back, waiting to see how their families and friends fare[d] with the INS."[51] This approach succeeded to a degree. As word of individual successes spread, the INS was able to dissipate the "fear factor" and erase some of the early horror stories surrounding the program. However, the key to building trust occurred when people immediately got their temporary work authorizations. Even so, these strategies relied on undependable word of mouth, and were slowed by the extended turnover time in final approvals at the RPFs.

The INS also passively relied on the initial public awareness campaign to bolster its image. Officials believed that the simple process of providing legalization information to the alien communities in a straightforward manner (putting the word on the street, so to speak) would show a different side of the INS, and over time, fear would subside.

While these early "strategies" had some positive effect on the INS's image, initial regulations had a strong negative impact. Community organizations perceived that instead of welcoming aliens with open arms, the INS made its regulations difficult and restrictive, and generally showed a hostile attitude toward applicants.

Perhaps the INS found it difficult to transcend its traditional enforcement-centered ethic, or maybe it was simply not sensitive to the difficulties that bona fide applicants might have in meeting proposed requirements. Many reports that the Asian immigrant community was practically left out of the program support the notion that the INS was too nonchalant in its efforts to attract targeted communities, and may have been clueless about how to do so. These INS actions and inactions evoked tremendous criticism (and lawsuits) by immigrant rights organizations and members of Congress.

As a result, the INS eased aspects of the regulations and began a new, more successful campaign to overcome immigrant fears. One marketing approach incorporated the personal stories of successful applicants in the INS's paid advertisements. In Los Angeles, for example, local families appeared in Spanish-language television ads to describe their grant of amnesty. More important was a personal INS campaign to reach alien communities. This effort saved the day. Outreach by LO managers and district/regional staff members included extensive briefings, information seminars, talk-show appearances, and events to spread the word, and in some areas LOs opened regularly one night a week and advertised the openings as "Thursday Night Live." Ironically, Western Regional Commissioner Ezell was one of the most visible participants in this more personal INS outreach effort, and earned plaudits from many quarters. The U.S. Catholic Conference observed:

> Senior INS officials have been accessible and have earned respect that helped break down what some have called the "circle of fear" surrounding INS. The fear factor will never entirely disappear, but the personal effort and commitment given by many INS officials is reshaping INS' image in the public eye. . . . In the absence of an effective national publicity campaign, the places where the program has been more successful are the places where INS staff have aggressively, publicly sold legalization.[52]

As time passed, regulations were loosened, and RPF decisions on pre-1982 cases became more liberal. Skeptics charged that changes were due to lawsuits filed by community groups, rather than shifting INS attitudes. After all, the newly liberal INS positions on such matters as the reasons for lengthy absences abroad, reentries subsequent to 1982 with nonimmigrant visas, and the amount of documentation required were actually ideas and policies proposed by community groups at the start of legalization, but rejected by the INS.

Yet INS defenders could point to an institutional desire to reach eligible aliens. INS Commissioner Nelson asked LOs to be helpful to alien applicants, and training reflected these wishes. Of course, treating actual applicants well does not indicate a desire to maximize the number of applicants. Even in this cynical view, however, the INS would have known that its policies would have such an effect to some extent. The INS public awareness program contractor verified that officials were in fact very interested in increasing the number of applications. After all, legalization was supposed to be self-funding and a low number of applications would result in a funding shortfall. The INS wanted public information to ensure that all aliens at least knew of the program, regardless of whether or not they would apply.

Gradually, the immigrants' view of LOs, and to an extent of the entire INS, improved. The negative connection that immigrants initially made between the INS and its LOs proved beneficial to the entire INS in the long run. Over time, LOs were challenged to change applicants' minds about the INS by setting a "positive tone." Fear could not be entirely put to rest, "but the personal effort and commitment given by many INS officials [helped to reshape] the agency's image [not just that of LOs] in the public eye."[53]

Eventually, a confluence of events changed the amnesty applicants' image of the INS. The legalization program represented a completely "new ballgame," and the INS could claim to be the friend of undocumented immigrants. Neighborhood LOs worked. There were no uniformed Border Patrol officers at LOs, and the offices were described by many as open, clean, friendly, and accessible places. The "new look" image of the INS—amicable and service-oriented—made a big difference. Local outreach by LOs and district personnel was unprecedented. The LOs' attempt to reach out into the immigrant community was massive and inventive; for a period of time, 25 to 30 percent of all district staff were allocated to public relations appearances. As regional and LO staffs became personally involved and interested in the program, they took it upon themselves to perform the outreach that Washington headquarters was unwilling to do. An eventual loosening up of regulatory requirements, whether voluntary or a result of litigation, also attracted some applicants.

Efforts by Community Agencies

CBOs actively participated in the implementation of legalization. This participation emerged principally out of a sense of commitment to immigrant and refugee communities established long before the passage of IRCA. With its novel demand that the INS include CBOs in IRCA implementation, Congress formally institutionalized CBO participation in the QDE program.

In general it was assumed that community agencies were more accessible than the INS and better trusted, although perhaps less authoritative. Most observers, including many within the INS, agreed that many immigrants were apprehensive about the INS. If the program were left to the INS, they concluded it would not work. Congressional sponsors and others assumed that if immigrant service organizations processed the bulk of legalization applications, they would act as "buffers" between applicants and the INS.

After IRCA passed, CBOs and profit-making ventures shared one major goal: to get as many people legalized as possible. The patchwork of CBOs could help to achieve this goal in a variety of ways: engaging in community outreach and education, pressing the INS to be more responsive to the target communities, pushing the INS to be more liberal in its requirements and procedures, and suing the INS when its requirements and procedures violated the statute. A key way for CBOs to reach their goal was to provide direct services and to facilitate filings by serving as QDEs.

While 21 percent of the applications filed were with QDEs, the figure fell far short of the 50 to 80 percent that the INS and Congress expected from QDEs and other community agencies. During the first five months, only 15 percent of the total applications filed came through QDEs. As QDEs became more experienced with the process and their working relationship with the INS was hammered out, QDEs became more proficient and efficient at processing applications, and the proportion filed with QDEs slowly increased. Still, the 21 percent figure was surprisingly low to most observers, including staff members of CBOs.

One problem was that CBOs handled more of the later applicants who were likely to have complicated cases, involving documentation problems, lengthy absences, public charge issues, the need for expungement of misdemeanors, and the like. Also, the six-month lead time between IRCA's passage and the start of the program hurt CBOs in a number of ways. First, as in the case of the INS set up of LOs, the logistics of setting up an office structure and procedure to handle a large number of anticipated clients was difficult. Second, new and old personnel had to be trained on the legalization requirements and procedures. Third, CBOs had to wait for the INS to come up with interpretive regulations and new forms, a process that was not completed until just days before the legalization window opened on May 5, 1987. Fourth, for CBOs seeking QDE status from the INS, the application procedure and requirements were not immediately clear. Conditions for QDE status were still being hammered out during the application process. Indeed, the INS evaluated, selected, and certified 550 QDEs for 977 locations in the two weeks before May 5, 1987.

CBOs also were hampered by finding problems, the tardiness in INS issuance of regulations, and competition from profit-making ventures as well as LOs.

Legalization was difficult for QDEs with immigrant service backgrounds. They failed to file as many applications as expected, faced financial hardship, and constantly struggled with the INS. However, their high-quality assistance made it possible for people with complicated cases to apply. They insisted upon regulatory changes that made more people eligible for legalization, and removed bureaucratic barriers for many who were eligible to apply. In addition, their outreach was broader and more helpful than that of the Service. In these and other ways, QDEs were responsible for making legalization available to hundreds of thousands of people who would otherwise have been denied the security and opportunities it provided.

Employer Sanctions

Under IRCA, for the first time Congress prohibited employers from hiring workers who are not authorized to work in the United States, imposing civil and criminal penalties on violators. IRCA was the product of years of debate regarding the impact of undocumented immigrant workers on the United States. As part of the compromise that IRCA represented, amnesty (legalization) was granted to about three million undocumented aliens, and employers also became subject to penalties for new employment discrimination laws.

In response to intensive lobbying by civil rights advocates and concerned members of Congress who feared that employer sanctions would cause employment discrimination, protections were included in the law intended to safeguard against discrimination. In other words, IRCA contained provisions that attempted to ensure that employers would not use the new employer sanctions law as a pretext for discriminating against lawful immigrant workers. Prior to IRCA, private employers could require employees to be U.S. citizens, but after IRCA, employers had to hire a qualified immigrant job applicant, unless a citizen who was equally qualified applied for the job. Employers could be fined for such discriminatory hiring practices, as well as for requiring new immigrant employees to come up with more proof than necessary to establish eligibility to work.

IRCA's employer sanctions provisions placed great responsibilities upon the business community. Employers must verify that a new employee is authorized to work in the United States. The employer and the employee must complete an I-9 form. Employers who "knowingly hire" undocumented workers are subject to penalties, which can include fines ranging from $250 to $10,000 per unauthorized worker, as well as criminal penalties against the employer for pattern and practice violations.

IRCA mandated the General Accounting Office (GAO), the investigative arm of Congress, to conduct three annual studies from 1987 to 1989 to determine whether employer sanctions had resulted in "widespread discrimination." A "sunset" provision further stipulated that employer sanctions could be repealed if the GAO concluded that compliance caused employers to discriminate.

The first two status reports on employer sanctions by the GAO found that "one in every six employers in GAO's survey who were aware of the law may have begun or increased the practice of (1) asking only foreign-looking persons for work authorization documents or (2) hiring only U.S. citizens." In spite of the fact that almost 17 percent of employers admitted to practices that violated the discrimination provisions of IRCA, GAO concluded that the findings did not establish a pattern of "widespread discrimination," citing lack of conclusive evidence that the employer sanctions requirements were the cause of discrimination.

Upon the release of its second report, the GAO came under fire from both governmental and nongovernmental entities for using shoddy methodology in its evaluation of the possible discriminatory impacts of sanctions. The U.S. Commission on Civil Rights identified several problems inherent in both the methodology and the findings. For one thing, the commission argued that Congress needed to clarify the meaning of "widespread pattern of discrimination." Legal service providers and immigrant and refugee advocacy groups had been collecting evidence of IRCA-related discrimination since the law's inception. Organizations in New York, Chicago, San Francisco, Los Angeles, and Fresno established multilingual information and referral telephone hotlines upon the passage of IRCA to provide information to immigrants about the amnesty program and employer sanctions. Their experience revealed that employment discrimination as a result of employer sanctions was pervasive.

In 1989, a number of groups across the country began to compile information that they had received from individuals of mostly Asian, Latino, and Middle Eastern descent regarding discriminatory treatment they had experienced while seeking new employment or working in their current positions. Several civil rights organizations issued reports of the anecdotal evidence collected. While the reports documented disturbing accounts of discrimination, proponents of employer sanctions dismissed the data collected by advocacy groups as unreliable.

Eventually, some of the independent research could not be ignored by the GAO. A methodological survey of 416 San Francisco employers was conducted in San

Francisco, revealing that an overwhelming 97 percent of the firms regularly engaged in at least one employment practice that could be discriminatory under IRCA or other antidiscrimination laws. Another 53 percent reported that they engaged in three or more such practices. The research was submitted to the GAO in September 1989, and influenced the GAO's third report.[54]

The GAO significantly improved the research methodology for its third and final report. Its staff used both direct contact with employers and teams of job search testers. Its new findings showed that as a direct result of IRCA, 461,000 employers nationwide (10 percent) discriminated on the basis of national origin, and 430,000 employers (9 percent) discriminated on the basis of citizenship status. These findings meant that an estimated 2.9 million employees were discriminated against based on national origin, and 3.9 million based on citizenship status. The research found that rates of discrimination were somewhat higher in cities with high Latino or Asian populations: "Our survey suggests that persons of Hispanic and Asian origins may have been harmed by employers' citizenship discrimination practices." As part of the same report, the GAO contracted with Washington, D.C.-based Urban Institute to conduct a "hiring audit," by using a job applicant tester survey utilizing Latino and Anglo U.S. citizen college students to apply for a sample of 360 low-skilled, entry-level jobs in Chicago and San Diego. The study found that the Anglo testers received 52 percent more job offers and 33 percent more interviews than the Latino testers, and that overall, the Latino testers were three times as likely as Anglo testers to encounter unfavorable treatment.

Despite the GAO's findings of "widespread" IRCA-related employment discrimination and similar evidence by independent researchers, Congress did not repeal employer sanctions. The findings were routinely dismissed by anti-immigrant groups, Senator Alan Simpson (a co-sponsor of IRCA), and the AFL-CIO as insignificant or unreliable. Several bills to repeal employer sanctions were introduced in Congress in 1990 and 1991, but none reached the floor of Congress (in spite of bipartisan support from Senators Kennedy and Hatch).

Although employer sanctions were not repealed, the Immigration Act of 1990 did strengthen IRCA's antidiscrimination provisions. The law increased employer and employee education, added special agricultural workers to the category of protected workers, changed the penalties for discrimination to conform with those for employer sanctions penalties, made document abuse an unfair immigration-related employment practice, prohibited retaliation against those who file charges, made it easier to prosecute for document abuse by adding civil as well as criminal penalties, and eliminated the requirement that a noncitizen who makes a discrimination charge must have filed an official "declaration of intent" to become a citizen.

By the early 1990s, many members of Congress, most notably Senator Simpson, contended that no further employer education was necessary to decrease employment discrimination. In fact, Simpson argued at a 1992 Senate Judiciary Committee hearing that the employer sanctions provisions, both the documentation requirements and the antidiscrimination protections, were as familiar to employers as were the requirements to pay taxes.

While many politicians and business leaders claimed that compliance with employer sanctions had become a "regular part" of doing business in the United States, the experiences of immigrants and ethnic minorities suggested otherwise. Employer sanctions were often implemented and enforced selectively, discriminatorily, and as a means of intimidating undocumented workers who sought union representation or who complained about unfair labor practices, such as sexual harassment, wage and hour violations, and unsafe working conditions.

Only a fraction of U.S. employers and workers have received education from the Office of Special Counsel (OSC), which spent approximately $14 million on educational outreach between 1990 and 1996. OSC's education program did not begin in earnest until 1990, when it initiated a grants program, contracting with local groups to conduct educational campaigns. The OSC is located in Washington, D.C., with no branch offices. Between 1987 and 1996, the OSC received 4,868 charges of discrimination from workers, but only 145 formal complaints were filed by the OSC against employers, 83 of whom were fined for IRCA-related unfair employment practices. Distribution of INS's *Handbook for Employers* that explains the regulations and has pictures of acceptable documents also has been inadequate. Only two nationwide distributions of the handbook took place by 1996: one in 1987 and one in 1991.

Since 1990, no government-sponsored research examining the possibly discriminatory effects of employer sanctions has occurred. Lina Avidan's private survey of 422 employers in New York, Los Angeles, Chicago, and San Francisco conducted in 1992 revealed that 91 percent regularly engage in at least one employment practice prohibited under IRCA's antidiscrimination provisions, and 48 percent regularly engage in three or more. Half of the employers feel that the INS documentation requirements make it riskier to hire people who speak limited English, and more than a third (38 percent) feel it is riskier to hire Latinos, Asians, and people from the Caribbean.[55]

Although employer sanctions remain part of the immigration laws, by 2001, the concept had lost one of its ardent supporters. As organized labor, including the AFL-CIO, realized that its future viability rested solidly on the shoulders of immigrant workers, unions called for the repeal of employer sanctions and for the legalization of undocumented workers.

Conclusion

By the 1980s, contentious congressional debate over how to handle the problem of undocumented aliens, particularly Mexicans, took center stage. Clear support for employer sanctions was evident, but when IRCA was finally passed, support for legalization of undocumented immigrants was not as clear. The ambivalence over amnesty reflected the policy makers' desire to keep out undocumented Mexicans and not demonstrate any sign of approval for those already here.

Legalization applicants faced several challenges. Procedural hurdles discouraged many from even applying. The most difficult hurdle was obtaining documentation to prove the duration of time an applicant lived in the United States or worked in agriculture. Furthermore, each applicant was required to pay a filing fee as high as $420 per family—not an insignificant amount for many.

The implementation of legalization through INS and community agencies was inconsistent. Outreach efforts did not reach many eligible immigrants, the INS suffered from long-standing distrust in immigrant communities, and community service agencies miscalculated the needs of many applicants and suffered from bureaucratic problems themselves. Yet, important partnerships were formed, and the efforts INS officials finally implemented were impressive in many parts of the country. Most observers agree that the three million immigrants who benefited from legalization represent less than half of those who were actually eligible, and the ongoing employer sanctions provisions result in discrimination against lawful immigrants of color.

CHAPTER 10

The Dark Side
of Modern-day
Enforcement:
Operation Gatekeeper

The greater latitude granted to the Border Patrol by the Supreme Court, increased staffing of the Border Patrol, and the threat of employer sanctions after IRCA did little to deter the flow of undocumented migrants across the southern border in the late 1980s and early 1990s. Fear of apprehension was offset by the continued recruitment efforts by U.S. employers in Mexico, the relative imbalance in the economies of both nations, and the presence of relatives in the United States. U.S. border enforcement strategies shifted to deterrence rather than apprehension.

In Jaunary 1994, a year after President Bill Clinton took office, the Border Patrol embarked on a strategy of "control through deterrence" that has proven deadly. During the presidential campaign, Clinton was asked what he proposed to do about "illegal immigration." He had no plan, declaring that "immigration is the most complex issue facing the nation."[1] Early in 1993, his administration's Office of National Drug Control Policy commissioned Sandia National Laboratories, a federal government-supported facility devoted to research for the military, to study new methods to increase border security. The study recommended that the Border Patrol focus on preventing illegal entries rather than trying to apprehend the undocumented once they entered the country. The Sandia report recommended various measures to increase the difficulty of illegal entry, including the installation of multiple physical barriers, the use of advanced electronic surveillance equipment, and so forth.[2]

Around the same time in El Paso, Texas, the regional Border Patrol supervisor, Sylvestre Reyes, decided to station his agents in closely spaced vehicles, along the Rio

Grande, to intimidate would-be illegal entrants from even trying to cross. Although he had only half-hearted approvals from his superiors in Washington, Reyes's strategy, called Operation Blockade, had apparent dramatic short-term results: apprehensions of undocumented aliens plummeted within the El Paso sector, suggesting that migrants were being discouraged from entering.[3] This outcome was noticed by the media and Congress, and the INS soon found itself under great pressure to replicate what was immediately dubbed as the "successful" El Paso experiment, along other segments of the border, beginning with San Diego County. This set off a chain of policy decisions, leading to the establishment of "concentrated enforcement" operations along other parts of the border. The deadliest was Operation Gatekeeper.

The Development of Operation Gatekeeper

The San Diego Sector of the Immigration and Naturalization Service Border Patrol covers the section of the United States–Mexico border that historically has been the preferred site of entry for those entering the United States without inspection.[4] The sector contains sixty-six miles of international border.[5] Tijuana, Mexico's third largest city, lies directly south of San Diego, California, the sixth largest city in the United States.[6] A smaller Mexican city, Tecate, is situated in the eastern end of the sector.[7]

In 1994, over 450,000 apprehensions of illicit border-crossers were made in the San Diego sector (Table 10-1). This number far surpassed the sectors with the next highest apprehensions: Tucson (139,473) and McAllen, Texas (124,251). In the period prior to the end of 1994, undocumented border-crossers in the San Diego sector commonly entered in the western part of the sector near the city of San Diego. Often, many of these individuals traveled through private property, and some were even seen darting across busy freeways near the international border inspection station. Clearly, most of the illicit crossers entered along the fourteen-mile area from Imperial Beach (at the Pacific Ocean) to the base of the Otay Mountains.[8] Most of that stretch involves "easy terrain and gentle climbs," where the crossing lasts only ten or fifteen minutes to a pickup point.[9] Even individuals who were apprehended and turned back across the border were just as likely to attempt reentry in the westernmost part of the sector at the time.[10]

These highly visible border crossings resulted in tremendous public pressure on the INS to act. Residents of San Diego complained. Anti-immigrant groups demanded action. Politicians decried the lack of border control. Apparently, President Clinton now had an answer and an approach to the question of "illegal immigration." In his State of the Union address on January 24, 1995, Clinton signaled a renewed get-tough policy against undocumenteds, including "mov[ing] aggressively to secure our borders more by hiring a record number of border guards" and "cracking down on illegal hiring."[11] Knowing that Clinton faced reelection in 1996, administration officials hoped that a renewed enforcement effort against undocumented aliens would help shore up the president's support among voters in California, who overwhelmingly passed the anti-immigrant Proposition 187 in 1994.[12]

TABLE 10-1　Apprehension Statistics for the Southwest Border

SECTOR	FY 1994	FY 1995	FY 1996	FY 1997	FY 1998	FY 1999	FY 2000	Percent Change FY 99 to FY 00	Percent Change FY 94 to FY 00
California									
San Diego	450,152	524,231	483,815	283,889	246,092	182,248	151,681	−17	−66
El Centro	27,654	37,317	66,873	146,210	226,580	225,290	238,126	−6	761
TOTAL	477,806	561,548	550,688	430,099	472,672	407,538	389,807	−4	−18
Arizona									
Yuma	21,211	20,894	26,310	30,177	76,195	93,386	108,747	16	413
Tucson	139,473	227,529	305,348	272,397	387,406	470,449	616,346	31	342
TOTAL	160,684	248,423	331,658	302,574	463,601	563,835	725,093	29	351
Texas									
El Paso	79,688	110,971	145,929	124,376	125,035	110,846	115,696	4	45
Marfa	13,494	11,552	13,214	12,692	14,509	14,953	13,689	−8	19
Del Rio	50,036	76,490	121,137	113,280	131,058	156,656	157,178	0.3	214
Laredo	73,142	93,305	131,841	141,893	103,433	114,004	108,973	−4	49
McAllen	124,251	169,101	210,553	243,793	204,257	169,115	133,243	−21	7
TOTAL	340,611	461,419	622,674	636,034	578,292	565,574	528,779	−7	55
Southwest Border Totals	979,101	1,271,390	1,505,020	1,368,707	1,514,565	1,536,947	1,643,679	2	57

Source: Immigration and Naturalization Service.

Operation Gatekeeper was one of several operations that resulted from the Clinton administration's commitment to a new aggressive enforcement strategy for the Border Patrol. In August 1994, INS Commissioner Doris Meissner approved a new national strategy for the Border Patrol.[13] The heart of the plan relied on a vision of "prevention through deterrence," in which a "decisive number of enforcement resources [would be brought] to bear in each major entry corridor" and the Border Patrol would "increase the number of agents on the line and make effective use of technology, raising the risk of apprehension high enough to be an effective deterrent."[14] The specific regional enforcement operations that resulted included (1) Operation Blockade (later renamed Hold the Line), which commenced in September 1993 in the Greater El Paso, Texas areas; (2) Operation Gatekeeper, which commenced in October 1994 south of San Diego, California; (3) Operation Safeguard, which also commenced in October 1994 in Arizona; and (4) Operation Rio Grande, which commenced in August 1997 in Brownsville, Texas.[15] The idea was to block traditional entry and smuggling routes with border enforcement personnel and physical barriers.[16] By cutting off traditional crossing routes, the strategy sought to deter migrants or at least to channel them into terrain less suited for crossing and more conducive to apprehensions.[17] To carry out the strategy, the Border Patrol was to concentrate personnel and resources in areas of highest undocumented alien crossings, increase the time agents spent on border-control activities, increase use of physical barriers, and carefully consider the mix of technology and personnel needed to control the border.[18]

In the San Diego sector, efforts would be concentrated on the popular fourteen-mile section of the border beginning from the Pacific Ocean (Imperial Beach) stretching eastward.[19] That stretch had been the focus of some resources before Gatekeeper. Steel fencing and bright lighting were already in place in sections of this corridor, erected in part with the assistance of the U.S. military.[20] Yet because of the persistent traffic of undocumented entrants along this corridor, phase I of Gatekeeper continued to concentrate on increased staffing and resources along the fourteen-mile area.[21]

As the INS implemented its national border strategy, Congress supported these efforts; between 1993 and 1997, the INS budget for enforcement efforts along the southwest border doubled from $400 million to $800 million.[22] The number of Border Patrol agents along the southwest border increased from 3,389 in October 1993 to 7,357 by September 1998—an increase of 117 percent.[23] State-of-the-art technology, including new surveillance systems using electronic sensors linked with low-light video cameras, infrared night-vision devices, and forward-looking infrared systems for Border Patrol aircraft, were installed.[24]

Given these additional resources, Operation Gatekeeper buildup was impressive. Before Gatekeeper, the San Diego sector had 19 miles of fencing. By the end of 1999, 52 miles were fenced. Half of this fencing runs from the Pacific Ocean to the base of the Otay Mountains. Fourteen miles contain primary fencing (a 10-foot wall of corrugated steel landing mats left over from the Vietnam War). Two backup fences, each 15 feet tall, have been constructed. The first backup fence is made of concrete pillars. The second backup fence is made of wire mesh, with support beams. Both are topped with wire. Almost 12 miles of this stretch are illuminated by stadium lights. Some fencing has been erected on sections of the Otay Mountains, as well as around various East San Diego County communities along the border.[25] The Department of Defense's Center for Low Intensity Conflicts as well as the Army Corps of Engineers provided guidance to INS on the development of Gatekeeper features.[26]

In contrast, in areas other than San Diego, the construction was not as significant. The El Centro sector covers 72 miles of the border and is sparsely populated on the U.S. side and has only 7 miles of fence—all of it between the contiguous border cities of Calexico and Mexicali. Arizona has 17 miles of fencing—6 in the Yuma sector and 9 in the Tucson sector. That fencing was erected exclusively in the towns and cities. Texas has the Rio Grande River and 7 miles of fencing in the El Paso/Ciudad Juarez area—2 miles of primary and 5 of secondary. Thus, 73 miles of fencing has been erected on the 2,000-mile border, and the 66-mile San Diego sector has 72 percent of it, as well as 54 percent of the illumination.[27] The 144-mile long San Diego and El Centro sectors have almost a third of the Border Patrol agents stationed on the 2,000-mile southwest border.[28]

The Results of Operation Gatekeeper

In implementing its national strategy beginning in 1994, the INS made a key assumption about its "prevention through deterrence" approach: "alien apprehensions will decrease as [the] Border Patrol increases control of the border."[29] In other words, INS anticipated that as the show of force escalated by increasing agents, lighting, and fencing, people would be discouraged from entering without inspection so that the number of apprehensions naturally would decline. In fact, the Border Patrol predicted that within five years, a substantial drop in apprehension rates border-wide would result.[30] The deterrence would be so great that "many will consider it futile to continue to attempt illegal entry."[31] These assumptions and predictions have not been borne out.

Apprehension levels did not decline. The national enforcement strategies began with Operation Gatekeeper in San Diego and Operation Blockade in El Paso in 1994. True, the apprehension levels for those two sectors were considerably lower in 1998 than in 1993 (e.g., 531,689 apprehended in San Diego in 1993 compared to 248,092 in 1998).[32] However, the apprehension levels surged in El Centro, Yuma, and Tucson during the same period (e.g., from 92,639 to 387,406 in Tucson; from 30,058 to 226,695 in El Centro; and from 23,548 to 76,195 in Yuma).[33] In 1999, apprehensions at the California border fell by more than 65,000 from the previous year, but increased by more than 100,000 at the Arizona border.[34] The January 2000 apprehension figures along the Arizona border were 30,000 more than the previous January—a jump of 72 percent and 56 percent in the Yuma and Tucson sectors, respectively.[35] From 1994 to 1999, total apprehension statistics along the southwest border actually increased by 57 percent![36] The increase continues. In Arizona, 563,000 crossers were apprehended in 1999, but in 2000 the figure rose to 724,000.[37] And the number of apprehensions for all of fiscal year 2000, 1.64 million, was an all-time high, surpassing the Border Patrol's record year of 1986.[38] As Table 10-1 shows, in 1994, the apprehensions in the San Diego sector totaled 450,152, but dropped to 151,678 in fiscal year 2000. Meanwhile, as Gatekeeper pushed migrants east, the apprehension figure for the El Centro sector skyrocketed from 27,654 in 1994 to 238,127 in 2000. A clearer picture developed even more eastward. From October 1994 to September 2000, there were about 88,000 fewer apprehensions at the California border, but 564,409 more at the Arizona border and 188,168 more at the Texas border. In sum, after Gatekeeper sealed the westernmost section of the border, apprehensions in San Diego declined, but crossers moved east and overall apprehensions actually increased—substantially.

In short, the apprehension data confirm that what Operation Gatekeeper actually achieved was to move the undocumented foot traffic relatively out of the public eye. Empirical research demonstrates that undocumented Mexicans keep trying to enter until they are successful. In sending communities restudied since Gatekeeper began, most prospective migrants "said that they would only consider changing their destination within the United States (avoiding California, for example) rather than foregoing migration altogether." Migrants have learned quickly to avoid the heavily fortified areas and now cross "in places where their probability of apprehension is no higher than it used to be."[39] It is safe to say that border enforcement strategies initiated in 1994 were "affecting migration patterns, but not preventing unauthorized entry."[40]

The "prevention through deterrence" strategy also bolstered the smuggling industry. As the INS stepped up operations, most migrants turned to smugglers. This helps explain why most migrants attempting unauthorized entry succeed despite significantly more agents and technology on the border.[41] The INS did not foresee the extent of this effect. Former Commissioner Meissner said architects of a nationwide border crackdown expected that hostile terrain and deadly weather conditions in remote mountains and deserts along the 2,000-mile United States–Mexico frontier would act as a greater deterrent to illegal crossings than has been the case: "We knew there would be . . . changes in smuggling patterns. But it has been surprising to see how quickly that's happened and in the numbers that it's happened."[42] Yet, as early as 1995, the U.S. Commission on Immigration Reform noted that given the difficult terrain crossers faced after Gatekeeper, undocumented aliens "would need guides to cross such terrain, jacking up the cost of illegal entry."[43] In fact, get-tough campaigns like Operation Gatekeeper created new opportunities for sophisticated immigrant smuggling rings with ties to organized crime and drug traffickers. Tough policies benefited smugglers who had the transportation and communication capabilities to counter the INS's most zealous efforts.[44] Smugglers increased their fees and turned to more sophisticated smuggling tactics.[45] For example, in the Tucson sector, the smuggling fees increased from $1,000 in 1996 to $1,350 in 1998.[46] In the Douglas, Arizona area, in 1999 the typical charge to be smuggled through Douglas to Phoenix was $150; by 2001 the price range was $800 to $1,300.[47] Similarly, in San Diego, smugglers charged about $300 prior to Gatekeeper for help in crossing and transportation to Los Angeles; they charged $800 to $1,200 afterward.[48] In the view of one longtime observer:

The [smugglers] haven't priced themselves out of the market. Migrants desperate to get into the U.S. just take more time to save up what they need, or just borrow more money from relatives already based in the U.S. If they use a reasonably experienced [smuggler], most migrants can still get through on their first try. If they can't afford to use a [smuggler], many of the migrants must now try 3, 4, or 5 times.[49]

Increased use of fraudulent visas to gain entry also climbed. After the institution of Gatekeeper, southwest border port of entry inspectors apprehended a greater number of persons attempting fraudulent entry.[50] These attempts at ports of entry included the use of fraudulent entry documents and false claims to U.S. citizenship.[51] The increase in attempts to enter with fraudulent documents, at a time when apprehension rates were up as well, further suggested that the impetus to cross was severe.

Given increased apprehension rates, greater reliance on smugglers, and expanded use of fraudulent entry documents, one could hardly say that the INS did much to attain its primary goal of controlling the border through deterrence. While these results may say more about the will and desire of undocumented aliens to enter the United States than about any particular agency's inability to control the border, the INS clearly did not gain control through deterrence. Unfortunately, there were other costs.

Entering the Dark Side

The ineffectiveness of the INS in "controlling the border" after several years of a new strategy would be easy enough to dismiss in a "so what else is new" attitude were it not for a dark side of border enforcement that resulted from Operation Gatekeeper. Certainly, southwest border control always had an evil, racist dark side, with its targeting of Mexican migration during a thirty-year period when Mexicans made up far less than half the undocumented population in the United States.[52] However, the tragedy of Gatekeeper is the direct link of its prevention through deterrence strategy to an absolutely horrendous rise in the number of deaths among border-crossers who were forced to attempt entry over terrain that even the INS knew to present "mortal danger" due to extreme weather conditions and rugged terrain.[53]

As Operation Gatekeeper closed the Imperial Beach corridor, the border-crossing traffic moved east. Frustrated crossers moved first to Brown Field and Chula Vista, and subsequently to the eastern sections of the San Diego sector.[54] Before Gatekeeper began in 1994, crossers were just as likely to make their second try in the westernmost part of the sector; but that changed very quickly. By January 1995, only 14 percent were making their second try near Imperial Beach. The illicit border traffic had moved "into unfamiliar and unattractive territory."[55] Clearly, the increasing number of deaths due to dehydration and exposure was the result of concentrated efforts to block the normal, easier crossing points, forcing migrants "to take greater risks in less populated areas," as migration was redirected rather than deterred by Gatekeeper.[56]

The death statistics are revealing. In 1994, 23 migrants died along the California–Mexico border. Of the 23, 2 died of hypothermia or heat stroke and 9 from drowning. By 1998, the annual total was 147 deaths—71 from hypothermia or heat stroke and 52 from drowning (see Table 10-2). Figures for 1999 followed this unfortunate trend, and in 2000, 84 were heat stroke or hypothermia casualties. The total death count along the entire border for the year 2000 was 499 (see Table 10-3). Of those, 100 died crossing the desert along the Sonora–Arizona border.[57] In 2001, 387 deaths were counted, and more than 300 in the first nine months of 2002.

TABLE 10-2   Migrant Deaths by Causes

CAUSE	1994	1995	1996	1997	1998	1999	2000	2001
Hypothermia/ Heat Stroke	2	5	34	50	71	63	84	88
Drowning	9	30	10	22	52	30	33	31
Accident	11	21	15	16	20	18	22	13
Homicide	1	5	0	1	4*	2	1	2
TOTAL	23	61	59	89	147	113	140	21

Source: California Rural Legal Assistance Foundation.

TABLE 10-3   Migrant Deaths by Calendar Year

LOCATION	FY 1998	FY 1999	FY 2000
California			
San Diego	38	22	33
Calexico	109	91	107
TOTAL	147	133	140
Arizona			
Tucson	7	28	49
Nogales	3	4	15
Douglas	2	12	26
TOTAL	12	44	90
Texas			
El Paso	33	11	24
Del Rio	10	11	11
Eagle Pass	47	47	58
Loredo	43	76	85
McAllen	7	18	49
Brownsville	30	38	42
TOTAL	170	201	269
Southwest Border TOTALS	329	358	499

Source: California Rural Legal Assistance Foundation.

Why the radical surge in deaths? The new routes are death traps. The correlation between increasing deaths and Gatekeeper's closure of the westernmost corridors is clear. The Border Patrol chief stressed that although the distances migrants had to traverse in places like Texas were enormous, California had the "more difficult terrain." In fact, the San Diego and El Centro sectors encompass three of the four places considered by the Border Patrol as "the most hazardous areas," for example, East San Diego County, the Imperial Desert, and the All-American Canal. The fourth is Kennedy County in Texas.[58] The INS recognized the challenges of the new routes: rugged canyons and high desert, remote, desolate stretches, and risks of dehydration and exposure.[59] On the other hand, the 14-mile area from Imperial Beach to the base of the Otay Mountains, the less rigorous original route, is "easy terrain and gentle climbs." A typical crossing there lasted only 10 to 15 minutes from point of crossing to pickup point. The eastern mountain route crossings can last anywhere from 12 hours to 4 days.[60] The Otay Mountains are "extremely rugged, and include steep, often precipitous, canyon walls and hills reaching 4,000 feet." Extreme temperatures ranging from freezing cold in the winter to searing heat in the summer can kill the unprepared traveler.[61] The Tecate Mountains are full of steep-walled canyons and rocky peaks. Nighttime temperatures can drop into the 20s and snow can fall to altitudes as low as 800 feet. From mid-October to mid-April, there is a greater than 50 percent probability of below-freezing temperatures.[62] The All-American Canal parallels the border for 44 of its 85 Imperial County miles. It is unfenced and unlighted, 21 feet deep and nearly as wide as a football field. It has strong currents and is one of the most polluted rivers in the United States.[63]

Initially, the use of extreme climate and topography to prevent illegal entries was limited to California. The result was a much higher migrant death toll in California than in states like Texas, New Mexico, and Arizona, which also share borders with Mexico. Increasingly, however, illicit border-crossers from Baja, California, were being pushed into Arizona's Yuma desert, where they also began dying in unprecedented numbers. From the start, the goal was to push the undocumented foot traffic toward the terrain east of San Diego. By 1999, Gatekeeper had expanded as far east as Yuma, Arizona, and border-related deaths for Arizona soared from 18 in 1998 to 31 in 1999.[64] More than 100 people died in the first 10 months of 2000 crossing surreptitiously from Mexico to Arizona, already doubling the number who had died in all of the previous year.[65] Of the 106 deaths recorded in Arizona by October 2000, 65 were due to exposure to the heat, 3 from the cold, and 38 from a variety of causes, including drownings.[66] Environmental casualties along the Arizona border, like that of Vicente Ramirez Serrato whose body was recovered in the desert one mile north of the border on April 26, 2001, became commonplace.[67] Earlier that month, 400 undocumented immigrants turned themselves in to Border Patrol agents after being caught in a sudden, winter-like storm while crossing the Arizona desert; five suffering from hypothermia were transported to emergency rooms.[68]

Border Patrol agents acknowledged that the number of bodies recovered perhaps were only indications of a much larger death toll; many bodies simply may not have been discovered in the rugged territory.[69]

Government Response to Human Costs

The INS did respond to the rising number of environmental deaths. As the evidence of deaths resulting from Operation Gatekeeper became obvious in October 1997, INS officials launched "new humanitarian measures" like a "Stay Out, Stay Alive" public information campaign in Mexico, using posters and Spanish radio announcements to warn aliens about the dangers of crossing. The agency equipped twelve vehicles as emergency medical response units and certified fifty-six agents as emergency medical technicians (EMTs).[70] Also, "coolers of water, anti-dehydration liquids and food were stocked in Border Patrol vehicles and at processing centers."[71] An April 1998 INS Fact Sheet stated that vehicles had been equipped to respond to both hot and cold weather emergencies, and that all vehicles that patrol the waterways had been equipped with flotation devices.[72] Lifesaving was added to the list of border agent duties.[73]

By June 1998, officials announced a Border Safety Initiative to reduce injuries and prevent fatalities. Developed in cooperation with Mexican officials, the plan has three elements: prevention (inform and warn potential undocumented aliens of the realities and dangers of crossing the border at particular routes), search and rescue in hazardous areas, and identification of bodies.[74] The initiative, dubbed Operation Lifesaver, was billed as an "unprecedented border-wide public safety initiative . . . designed to reduce injuries and prevent fatalities."[75] Commissioner Meissner explained before a Senate subcommittee in July 1998, "we have an obligation to not only educate people about the dangers but also to assist those who don't heed these warnings."[76] The Mexican government signed on with a statement from Ambassador Jesus Reyes-Heroles about how the initiative "recognizes and advances our efforts to protect the rights and safety of migrants."[77]

Aircraft supplemented the 1998 safety initiative. On days when 100 degree temperatures were forecast, civil air patrol pilots were to fly over the deserts and mountains. The national commander said that they were "not there to enforce immigration laws or deter passage. We're here to help save lives."[78] However, a Border Patrol spokesperson told a Mexican newspaper that new helicopters, 50 percent quieter than other machines equipped with infrared scopes and the capability of lowering baskets, would be used to observe border-crossers as well as to respond to emergencies.[79] Another report by the Border Patrol indicated that the newest Huey helicopter addition would allow the San Diego sector's Search and Trauma Rescue Team to "rappel into steep canyons that we normally couldn't get to." The team would center its actions in "remote parts of eastern San Diego County, where dozens of illegal border crossers stranded in rugged terrain have died."[80] Pilots of the Huey helicopters confirmed that many migrants attempt to cross in extremely dangerous terrain.

The effectiveness of these rescue efforts was questionable. Heatstroke victims usually cannot be rescued in time. In August 1998, a month after the Border Safety Initiative began, thirty-three migrants died at the California border.[81] Migrants continued to die in San Diego and Imperial Counties at an alarming rate. In fact, 375 migrants died along the San Diego to Yuma corridor between June 1998 and January

2001, more than half of the six-year Gatekeeper death toll.[82] In the El Centro sector, where 80 percent of the deaths on the California border occurred, the ratio of deaths to rescues during 2000 was 1 to 3.[83] And in a sign of hypocrisy, private citizen Samaritans who were prompted to help needy migrants suffering from heat or cold were threatened with criminal charges for offering water or comfort.[84]

The INS response to the deaths—danger warnings in Mexico, more emergency vehicles, and the safety initiative—downplayed the link between the deaths and Operation Gatekeeper in INS enforcement circles and in the public image that INS projected. At her press conference announcing Operation Lifesaver, Commissioner Meissner absolved the INS of any blame: "It is not our border strategy that creates dangers at the border but instead it is smuggling that does so."[85]

The Immorality of Operation Gatekeeper

Given the harrowing conditions facing border-crossers, one has to wonder why the migration pattern continued, and even increased, after the institution of Operation Gatekeeper. The primary cause of the continued flow of undocumented migration from Mexico is economic. This is not a new observation,[86] but the timing of Operation Gatekeeper could not have been worse. On December 20, 1994, about two months after the institution of Gatekeeper, the Mexican peso was devalued, immediately plummeting 40 percent.[87] The devaluation, which came on the heels of an ill-fated privatization of eighteen state-owned banks in 1992, threw Mexico into its worst economic crisis since the Great Depression. A million people lost their jobs and thousands of borrowers stopped paying their loans as annual interest rates neared 100 percent.[88] Within six months, Mexico's annual inflation rate jumped to 90 percent, and 17 percent of the nation's 34 million workers could not find work for even fifteen hours a week.[89] Unemployment doubled and wages sank.[90] Within a year, the peso had lost 50 percent of its value.[91]

The attraction of the United States is obvious. The strong economy pays Mexican workers eight to nine times more than what they can earn in Mexico. As the Mexican consul in Douglas, Arizona, observes, "these are people trying to get a better job so they can provide for their families, so they can improve their lot."[92] Specific aspects of the Mexican economy—lost value of the peso, cuts in federal spending, increased taxes, and slow job growth—have increased the pressure to migrate north.[93] Extreme poverty has exacerbated the situation. In 1993, 31 percent of Mexicans were considered extremely poor; by 1996 the figure was 50 percent.[94]

The situation calls into question the likely effectiveness of the installation of fences and rigorous terrain on reducing migrant traffic. The reality is that people desperate for work go where they can find work. Even Border Patrol officials acknowledge that the "challenge" of border control in the Gatekeeper area of operation is the high motivation of most of the aliens crossing there, who "travel hundreds of miles over several days from interior sections of Mexico on their way to find jobs in cities throughout the

U.S."[95] The migrants and their smugglers have a higher motivation to enter than the Border Patrol has to close down the border. Human rights advocates who have interviewed the migrants sense a desperation to cross and warn, "if we mined the border, people would be blown to pieces trying to avoid the land mines as they continued to come."[96] As one agricultural economist observes, "lots of folks still are successful at illegal entries. Most have invested enough to getting in that even three of four apprehensions does not discourage them."[97] Given the current economic realities, even though the risks have increased, the potential gain from successfully crossing the border will always be greater than having nearly nothing back home. In a sense, the only choice for many crossers is to attempt the journey. Quite possibly crossers are not aware of the severe risks involved in crossing the border over treacherous terrain in the freezing cold of winter or the searing heat of summer. Or perhaps they know of the risks, but figure that the risks are outweighed by the benefits of crossing.[98]

Assigning Responsibility

Whose fault is it that hundreds of migrants have died along the California–Mexico border since the implementation of Operation Gatekeeper? In assigning responsibility, arguing that the migrants themselves should know better is unsatisfactory once the impetus for crossing is understood. Singling out smugglers as the culprits ignores the fact that Gatekeeper has produced the market for high-priced smugglers. Pointing to the failure of employer sanctions ignores the nature of the economy in which these migrants work. In the end, policy makers and those who have decided to enforce the laws through the Gatekeeper strategy have much to answer to and deserve close scrutiny.

The Migrants

Are the migrants themselves at fault for attempting to cross in spite of harrowing circumstances? Perhaps they should know the risks, or perhaps they do know them and accept them. As we have seen, the domestic crisis has forced Mexico's poorest citizens to leave their homes because they cannot earn enough, even when they have jobs, to feed their families.[99] Family motives and historical patterns impel others. Migrants have no choice: the potential benefits of crossing outweigh the risks given what little benefit there is in staying home. These are victims we should be hard pressed to blame.

Smugglers

The chief INS response to the question of "who's to blame?" is "the smugglers." INS officials, and even Mexican authorities, have pointed fingers at smugglers when it comes to migrant deaths. For example, Former Commissioner Meissner's attempt to deflect criticism over the deaths placed the blame squarely on the smugglers' shoulders.[100] The Border Patrol says smugglers paid by the migrants fail to warn their customers adequately of the harsh conditions and the long journey through the desert. The Tucson sector chief similarly argues that the culprits are the smugglers, who falsely tell people the trips will be short and that little water will be needed.[101] Even the U.S. ambassador to Mexico has called for Mexico to take tougher action against smugglers "who don't think twice about leaving an immigrant to die in the desert."[102]

Are the smugglers really to blame? True, Operation Gatekeeper has bolstered smuggling fees and has made smugglers indispensable to many who want to enter.[103] And smugglers should not be glorified. They are not providing a "humanitarian service." Rather, smuggling is an "increasingly lucrative business that is being carried out in a more and more heartless way."[104] Yet it is Gatekeeper that has led to the environment that breeds expanded use and reliance upon smugglers.[105] Without Gatekeeper, the use of smugglers would decline. So blaming the smugglers begs the question and smacks of scapegoating. The smugglers may be opportunistic money grubbers, but they merely act in response to the crossing market. Thus, one could argue that Gatekeeper is more of the problem than are the smugglers.

Congress and Employer Sanctions

Blame for continued migration might also be placed at the feet of Congress. Responding to public complaints about undocumented migration, Congress simply threw more border enforcement funds at the issue, while encouraging migration with weak employer sanction laws. Certainly many who support, as well as many who oppose, Gatekeeper claim that the failure to prosecute employers for hiring undocumented workers is a problem. Between 1992 and 1997, the number of INS fines levied against employers decreased from 2,000 to 888, and the amount of fines levied decreased from $17 million to $8 million.[106] Further, the Department of Labor had only 900 investigators to enforce workplace requirements such as minimum wage laws in 7 million U.S. workplaces in 1995.[107] Broadly speaking, however, criticism of weak employer sanction laws is misplaced. Enforcement of employer sanctions will not deter undocumented migration. U.S. employers' need for low-wage workers is too strong, and migrant motivations for entering are too great.

The conventional wisdom goes like this: if the country seriously enforces the laws that make it illegal for employers to knowingly hire undocumented workers, employers will stop hiring undocumented workers, undocumented migrants will get the message and stop migrating, and environmental deaths at the border will disappear. The Clinton administration argued that to control illegal immigration effectively, the federal government must "remove the magnet of illegal employment that draws illegal aliens" to the United States.[108] INS Commissioner Meissner said that border enforcement should be coupled with workplace disincentives.[109] The U.S. Commission on Immigration Reform (USCIR) similarly argued that since "employment opportunity is . . . the principal magnet which draws illegal aliens to the United States," the best thing to do is improve the system of employer sanctions enforcement, and labor standards enforcement should be enhanced as well.[110] USCIR's executive director observed that as a "nation we have a basic ambivalence about workplace enforcement."[111] Thus, Clinton's border czar Alan Bersin complained: "We have not been given the tools—as a matter of deliberate policy—to have effective worksite enforcement. . . . Because people can show an employer phony documents, there's no reliable way to correctly identify [the immigration status of] people seeking work."[112] Similarly, although the *San Diego Union-Tribune* applauded efforts that resulted in fewer crossings in urban areas, its editors were troubled by the environmental deaths, concluding that as "long as we continue to hire illegal aliens, we will continue to have rampant illegal immigration."[113] Wayne Cornelius, a longtime observer of the border, also notes that "work site enforcement is without doubt the weakest element of the current U.S. strategy for controlling illegal immigration."[114] In his view, "large numbers are still getting in, and because of low employer sanctions enforcement, they are just as employable today as they were before the current build-up of border enforcement capabilities began."[115] A binational body of experts chimed in, suggesting that the United States should assess the extent to which the demand of U.S. employers can be reduced through enhanced enforcement of labor standards, including wage and hour requirements, child labor prohibitions, and employer sanctions.[116] Even representatives of the California Rural Legal Assistance Foundation, ardent critics of Operation Gatekeeper, while not supporting employer sanctions, note the inconsistencies of U.S. policies: "During the last five years the INS has done virtually nothing to counteract the employer magnet that pulls migrants here—the undeniable hypocrisy of its immigration policy. For example, since the start of Gatekeeper, only a half-dozen employers of undocumented laborers have been prosecuted in either of California's border counties,"[117] and "the agency devotes only two percent of its enforcement man-hours to enforcing immigration laws at the work site."[118]

Could the employment of undocumented workers really be stopped? What would it take? Would the enforcement of employer sanctions really deter the employment of undocumented workers and their continued migration? I doubt it. The fortitude, drive, and unbelievable desire to migrate north among border-crossers given the economic disparities, family ties, and tradition are factors that cannot be discounted lightly. And the labor market that relies on such workers is ingrained in our economy. In sum, assuming that employer sanctions will discourage further migration and the hiring of undocumented workers is unrealistic and simplistic. Employer sanctions enforcement, even with greater resources, faces insurmountable challenges.

Employer sanctions create additional problems as well. Many employers use employer sanctions as an excuse to discriminate. (See Chapter 9.) The General Accounting Office has reported that nearly one-fifth of employers discriminate against foreign-appearing or foreign-sounding job applicants because of employer sanctions.[119] This is too much of a price to pay for a regime that has little incentive to discourage the hiring of undocumented workers anyway.

INS and Other Officials: Deeper into the Dark Side

In assigning responsibility for the increase in environmental deaths, the individuals or agency that enforce Operation Gatekeeper have to be considered. Arguably, the border enforcers who implement Operation Gatekeeper are merely following congressional will, and perhaps the will of the people, in places like San Diego. However, two facts are hard to avoid. First, strong evidence suggests that government officials knew human costs would result from the new border strategy, even before Gatekeeper was instituted. Second, the fact that INS and other officials have continued Gatekeeper in spite of the human costs presents a more serious problem.

A deeply troubling aspect of the deaths that have resulted from Operation Gatekeeper is that INS officials knew of the life-threatening circumstances that the more eastern routes posed to potential crossers and that increased environmental deaths would result. As the INS developed the Gatekeeper plan to cut off the westernmost corridor—the foundation for the operation—it published its *Strategic Plan for 1994 and Beyond* in August 1994. The Strategic Plan makes clear that the planners knew:

> The border environment is diverse. Mountains, deserts, lakes, rivers and valleys form nat-
> ural barriers to passage. Temperatures ranging from sub-zero along the northern border to
> searing heat of the southern border effect [*sic*] illegal entry traffic as well as enforcement
> efforts. Illegal entrants crossing through remote, uninhabited expanses of land and sea
> along the border can find themselves in mortal danger.[120]

Besides the blazing-hot days and freezing-cold nights, the planners assumed that many migrants would not be deterred by the prospect of going over a mountain or crossing a desert.[121] They were well aware of the nuances in push-pull factors that control border crossing, recognizing that "twenty percent are women and children who are attempting to reach their husbands and/or fathers who are already in the United States. Most of the aliens encountered are poor, are looking for work and have incurred transport and smugglers fees."[122] Although the peso was not devalued until four months later, the 1994 Strategic Plan indicated INS awareness that Mexico's government institutions and economy were under significant "stress from its lower socio-economic strata."[123] This stress was manifested in increasing instances of social unrest and undocumented immigration caused by rapid population growth in Mexico's lower socioeconomic groups, great disparity in the standard of living and chances for upward mobility in Mexico versus the United States, and the significant population of unemployed and underemployed in Mexico.[124] In other words, prior to the institution of Operation Gatekeeper, INS officials knew that the eastward terrain was life-threatening and that migrants would attempt to cross it rather than stop coming.[125]

Even assuming that some INS officials did not anticipate that migrants would brave the perils of the eastward routes, soon after the implementation of Operation Gatekeeper this became obvious. In the early stages of Operation Gatekeeper, some Border Patrol staff informed the U.S. Commission on Immigration Reform that the purpose of shifting surreptitious entries to the eastern county was to give the Border Patrol greater advantage for apprehension, and that there was a deterrence value apart from a short-term increase in apprehensions to the shift eastward: "It was evidence that the terrain itself was a deterrent because many of the illegal aliens crossing in Imperial Beach had neither the physical ability nor the financial resources to tackle the much more difficult crossing in the east."[126] Moreover, a few years after the institution of Gatekeeper, some officials expressed shock that record numbers continued to cross through East County's Laguna Mountains: "The idea was, the terrain[s] so difficult that they would not attempt it. But it didn't happen."[127]

By the end of 1995, and even more so at the end of 1996, crossings had increased, environmental deaths had surged, and the Mexican economy was collapsing.[128] Yet the INS crusade continued. Phase II began in the spring of 1996, when the INS extended Gatekeeper to cover the entire sixty-six miles of border in the San Diego sector. In the words of Bersin, migrants would be "forced to enter into a much more inhospitable terrain," for example, the Tecate Mountains.[129] An INS progress report issued in the fall of 1997, at the beginning of Phase III, acknowledged, "forced out of Imperial Beach, potential illegal crossers encounter considerable personal adjustments as they move eastward toward Tecate or Mexicali."[130] INS commissioner Meissner explained, "the next real step in moving east gets you into the desert and [like the mountains, it is] very formidable territory."[131]

The connection between INS efforts and increased environmental deaths became so obvious that denial was not feasible. Instead of expressing remorse, official comments seem to treat the deaths as necessary incidents of war. Bersin summed up the policy as "forc[ing] migrants into much more inhospitable and rugged places," casually going on to say that "the difficulty of passage is evidenced in the increased number of accidents and fatalities involving illegal entrants."[132] In its 1997 booklet *Operation Gatekeeper: Three Years of Results at a Glance*, the Border Patrol acknowledged, "illegal border traffic has changed, the result of cold hearted smugglers [who] have led their unsuspecting clients into perilous situations, sometimes resulting in tragedy in the harsh heat of summer and the freezing cold of winter."[133] Recognizing that migrants seldom carry more than a day's supply of food or water,[134] Border Patrol officers searching for migrants via air surveillance observe: "As they become more heat stressed and susceptible to the environment . . . they'll be wandering. You'll see them dropping clothes, personal effects, things of that nature. Perhaps the next point you'll see them is disrobing, taking their clothes off."[135] In its 1999 review of the Border Patrol strategy, the General Accounting Office observed:

> The objectives of the strategy were to close off the routes most frequently used by smugglers and illegal aliens (generally through urban areas) and shift traffic through the ports of entry that inspect travelers or over areas that were more remote and difficult to cross. With the traditional routes disrupted, INS expected that illegal alien traffic would either be deterred or forced over terrain less suited for crossing, where INS believed it would have the tactical advantage.[136]

> Shifts in apprehensions have been associated with a change in the causes and locations of alien deaths along the border.[137]

Thus, the INS and other officials simply regarded environmental deaths as casualty-of-war-like statistics. This is troubling, as it indicates that INS officials are aware that their policies have resulted in avoidable deaths. In any other context, maintaining an operation with the full knowledge that deaths will result might very well involve criminal liability on the part of directing officials.[138] Instead, government officials have threatened to prosecute private citizens for harboring undocumented aliens if they offer help to migrants who may need water or a warm fire.[139]

The Racism of Gatekeeper and Police Power

Conflicts that are at bottom about race often get masked by language about "problems." The problem in this case is that of people coming across the border who have been excluded from the *real* American construct of the mainstream. Problematizing undocumented migrants allows us to demonize them,[140] and, in turn, to render the inherent racism invisible. But in fact, the migrants involved are human beings—Mexican human beings. The focus of the U.S. immigration policy is on Mexico–United States border enforcement, where Congress has spent over a billion dollars implementing Operation Gatekeeper alone.[141] Yet only half of the estimated five million undocumented aliens in the United States come to the country via illicit border entries; the other half are visa overstays—students, tourists, temporary workers—from all over the world.[142]

With Gatekeeper, the stories of human existence, struggle, and difficulty are solved by police power. When we ask "how is this possible?" the question feels naïve because that lost human existence is viewed through a very particular racial lens and does not have a powerful meaning or resonance. Border enforcement is viewed as the exercise of a conceptual sovereign right against a faceless mass. The enforcement of this sovereign right enables us to dehumanize the entity—the horde in popular terms—in a manner that allows us to ignore racial implications. Thus, in the popular image, the Border Patrol is eliminating a problem. But in a humanized image, the Border Patrol is eliminating people.

Some well-meaning attempts to rehumanize migrants are only somewhat helpful. For example, descriptions of those who are dying as our future yard workers, busboys, or farm workers appear accurate.[143] But these depictions actually encode racism. Such depictions are so stereotypical that they completely fail to convey what brings the people across the border, what their lives become once they are here, or who they are. They contribute to a sense that these individuals are disposable.[144] They ignore the nuanced personalities of individuals, allowing them to remain nameless and faceless. By categorizing migrants in our social and economic structure as our future yard workers, they are placed in a conventional subordinated position through what might generously be labeled "unconscious racism."[145] Thus, these depictions are a direct product of a very passive but real racism.

The danger of using police power against people who are seeking a better life should trouble us. Gatekeeper represents pervasive use of police power against human beings seeking productive lives who are involved in nonviolent activity. Although Operation Gatekeeper directs the police force against an unpopular nationality group, race has disappeared from the discourse. Instead, the conversation presents itself as being about turning a "nuisance" and "annoyance" in the urban areas of San Diego into "an improvement in quality of life," by moving the migrants out of the public's view. Two related concepts are in play. First, the public generally is inured to police force. Second, the public is immune from it when it is invisible. In the instance of Gatekeeper, the public becomes inured to the use of police power (essentially violence) to do everything for it as long as it is not noticed. The public is similarly so accustomed to discourse about convenience and quality in (middle-class, white) life, that its normalcy is not challenged. This latter problem is very old and, perhaps, is not much more pervasive than before. But now it exists in tandem with the deadly policies of Gatekeeper that make middle-class complacency especially dangerous, problematic, and lethal.

Reconsidering Operation Gatekeeper: "Withdrawing from Vietnam"

Given the immediate intractability of the economic imbalance, the billions of dollars invested in border-control measures with little if any impact on apprehension rates, and most of all the resulting deaths, we have to ask why the American public permits the strategy to continue and whether Operation Gatekeeper really makes sense. As to the first question, the American public apparently allows the situation to continue because Mexican migrants do not fit the image of *real* Americans, even before September 11, 2001. As to the second question, avoidable deaths have resulted from this major undertaking, raising serious moral issues. Should time and money be spent elsewhere to address the question of illicit border crossing? The crossings are the manifestation of the forces of economic imbalance, family ties, and history. Gatekeeper's attempt to address the symptoms—crossings—has done little to address the root causes, with tragic results. Beefing up Gatekeeper, in effect militarizing the border, has only ensured that the tragedy will continue. Yet the United States continues to spend up to $2 billion a year on the "deterrence" strategy along the southwest border.[146] As a former INS general counsel later conceded, Operation Gatekeeper does not "deter the way we thought it would. Operation Gatekeeper has become our Vietnam, mistakenly thinking that if we added just a little more [to the buildup], then a little more, that we would get results."[147] On the surface, Gatekeeper has given the impression of addressing the problem. People are crossing surreptitiously, so fences are erected and patrols are beefed up. But crossers continue to enter, simply shoved out of sight toward more treacherous routes. Understanding the phenomenon of border crossing reveals that Gatekeeper has been a popular, conventional response that does little to address the long-term goal of assisting Mexico out of its poor economic times. In fact, Gatekeeper was constructed during one of Mexico's most dire economic eras, contributing to Gatekeeper's ineffectiveness. Gatekeeper demonstrates little understanding of the tradition of migrant Mexican workers who benefit economically and psychically from their movement into the United States, but who also benefit U.S. society. We would do better by acknowledging the needs of the workers, their families,[148] and the industries involved, and determining how to facilitate the movement in a manner that is sensitive to various interests.

Migrant border deaths raise important ethical questions. The persons who die are the citizens of Mexico, other countries in Latin America, and elsewhere. The policies that lead to those deaths are set by another country, the United States. The United States claims sovereign authority to control its own borders. Yet to do so creates conditions leading to a high number of death among migrants. If these were U.S. citizens who were dying, mortality rates this high would doubtless raise considerable controversy. The extreme physical measures of border enforcement epitomized by Gatekeeper have not succeeded in deterring undocumented immigration. Rather, they have placed human beings in mortal danger. Subjecting crossers to hazardous conditions raises questions of moral responsibility. Gatekeeper's successful movement of migrant foot-traffic out of the public eye is not a legitimate reason for maintaining a strategy that claims lives.

Assuming for the sake of argument that undocumented migration to the United States is bad,[149] the continuation of the Operation Gatekeeper enforcement strategy remains problematic. Given the fact that many undocumented immigrants will continue to risk everything, including their lives, to gain entrance into this country, the number of environmental deaths will remain high as long as the crossers are pushed into life-threatening terrain. The inevitability of these gruesome deaths should give us pause as a civilized nation. If behavior we dislike is nonetheless going to happen, why cruelly increase the suffering when it occurs? Might we not tolerate one evil, at least in the eyes of certain policy makers and certain segments of the public, in order to avoid a greater evil?[150]

Consider the possible analogy with needle exchange or teen contraception programs. Most would argue that a reasonable societal goal is to eliminate all injection drug use. Proponents of needle exchange programs argue that injection drug use will continue with or without access to sterile needles and syringes, so clean ones should be supplied to reduce the spread of AIDS. Similarly, the likely societal goal regarding sexual behavior is to delay intercourse until marriage or at least until an age of responsibility. Yet, since sexual intercourse among the young will not cease if access to contraceptives is withheld, proponents of providing contraceptives to teens seek to provide them with contraception to avoid teen pregnancies. We can imagine that the contraception programs work in some cases. And empirical studies on needle exchange programs have definitely found them to be successful. The incidence of HIV infection among needle exchange participants decreased by a third, while the existence of such programs does not result in increased drug use among participants or the recruitment of first-time drug users.[151]

Another analogy can be drawn between the profit-gouging alien smugglers and drug dealers. Drug sellers are "simply more highly motivated than those who are paid to stop them. Drug sellers make enormous profits—much more than they could make at legal jobs—and they are willing to risk death and long prison terms to do it."[152] As we have already seen, alien smugglers and their clients may be more highly motivated than the Border Patrol. And the alien smugglers make large profits, not only risking their own lives, but also the lives of the immigrants that they smuggle.

Whether immigrants cross the border over relatively flat land with normal temperatures or rocky, mountainous terrain or deserts with extreme temperatures, they will still cross.[153] Do we really want to make things worse by forcing them through the latter terrain, knowing that some of them will die as a result?[154] Or should we accept the notion—as we have with needle exchange programs—that even while we seek to stop an activity, we should try to minimize the suffering of those whom we would stop? Reverting to pre-Gatekeeper enforcement strategies would be no less effective, in terms of apprehensions and deterrence, but would result in far fewer deaths. The less dangerous routes to entry would be reopened and the need for high-priced smugglers reduced.

Understanding the economic and social situation in Mexico and the nature of the relationship between Mexicans and the United States enables us to formulate better approaches to border crossing. Addressing push-pull factors should be the priority, not militarizing the border in response to the results of push-pull factors. Like it or not, Mexico and the United States not only share a border, but also a long social, economic, and political history. The Fox administration in Mexico presents opportunities for the United States to address meaningfully economic and social challenges in Mexico. Recognizing that family reunification is a major reason for border crossing suggests that special visas facilitating permanent or seasonal reunification are in order. Understanding the long-standing tradition of back-and-forth migration for seasonal employment and the needs of U.S. employers should lead us to seriously consider how to facilitate this phenomenon. For the amount of money and time we have spent on Operation Gatekeeper, our strategies can be much more creative and relevant than simply hiring more Border Patrol officers.[155] Thus far, U.S. border policies have not reflected an understanding of the reason for undocumented migration.[156]

A Moral Outrage

The issue presented by Operation Gatekeeper is not whether the United States has a right to control its border. Rather, the issue is whether the United States has abused that right with a strategy designed to maximize the physical risks, thereby ensuring that hundreds of migrants would die. In its second response to the Inter-American Commission on Human Rights, the U.S. government said that "every state has a sovereign right to control entry into its territory and to take *effective and reasonable* steps to prevent unlawful, unauthorized entries."[157] Is Gatekeeper effective and reasonable?

By adopting an explicit policy that maximizes physical risks that everyone knows will result in deaths, can the policy truly be regarded as reasonable? The primary question that policy makers need to consider is how many human lives we are willing to sacrifice with current enforcement policy. Immigration officials have entered into a dubious moral arithmetic—how many migrant lives are we prepared to lose to keep the problem out of the national spotlight?

Motivations for continued migration call into question the likely effectiveness of a program such as Gatekeeper if the goal is to discourage border-crossers. Beyond the economic situation in Mexico, a socio-cultural phenomenon is at play. The phenomenon is the long, historical travel patterns between Mexico and the United States, coupled with the interdependency of the two regions. Migration from Mexico is the manifestation of these economic problems and social phenomena. The militarization of the border represented by Gatekeeper does nothing to address these phenomena. Instead, it is killing individuals who are caught up in the phenomena. Gatekeeper represents a false *practical* solution to moral questions raised by the flow of migrants pushed and pulled by economic and social factors. The migrants have become objectified, problematized, and demonized,[158] allowing proponents to skirt the moral questions. Thus, Gatekeeper has moral implications in an abstract way (as in "what kind of people are we to permit such things to happen to") and in a concrete way (the death toll and the hardship for Gatekeeper's victims, and the attitude of those who enforce it, and live with it).

The dark side of Operation Gatekeeper reveals "knowledge" of the high probability of deaths on the part of the U.S. government officials. The INS has knowingly created a death trap to control the southwest border. Shifting apprehension statistics disclose that crossers have not been discouraged from continuing to enter. The push-pull factors that continue to drive undocumented migration do not appear to be subsiding. The safest routes to cross the border surreptitiously have been foreclosed. INS officials recognize that the terrain over which crossers are now forced to enter poses threats of mortal danger. Yet instead of retreating from its life-threatening strategy, the INS forges on, creating even greater physical challenges for crossers. The INS response is to develop lifesaving operations in the environmental hazard zone it has created. Operation Gatekeeper is not simply a law enforcement operation that has created a harsh result. Gatekeeper is a law enforcement operation that imposes a death sentence on individuals—principally Mexicans—who simply are seeking a better life because of economic imbalance or seeking to be with family. Operation Gatekeeper is a moral outrage, and our nation has lost its soul in supporting it.

Conclusion

Ignoring the long economic and social history and to stem the flow of undocumented aliens along the United States–Mexico border near San Diego, the Clinton administration implemented Operation Gatekeeper in the 1990s. Fixed checkpoints and roving border patrols were not sufficient; a physical wall between the United States and Mexico was deemed necessary at this location. A new war on immigration was waged, but the timing increased the stakes. Mexico was in the throes of a major economic crisis. Many Mexicans were determined to seek economic opportunities in the North, no matter how dangerous the road to get there.

Unfortunately, the war seems to have no conclusion. The INS thought that with the combination of fencing and increased spending on border patrols at the most frequently traveled routes, undocumented immigration would slow, if not come to a complete halt altogether. But migrants were not deterred, and began looking for other areas to penetrate the border. However, the new areas of travel were risky; they were more dangerous and life-threatening. Given the challenges, more migrants turned to costly smugglers to help them across the border.

In spite of the aid of smugglers, the new routes were simply too dangerous for many border-crossers, and deaths among the migrants surged. The INS could not plead ignorance to the growing number of casualties that followed its new strategies. The number of migrant deaths increased 600 times from 1994 to 2000; a number that could be attributed to Operation Gatekeeper's pushing of surreptitious entries toward more treacherous eastward routes. While the INS could argue the deaths could not be anticipated at its initial Gatekeeper planning stages, once the pattern became known, officials did not terminate Operation Gatekeeper and consider more humane ways of addressing the movement of migrants from Mexico. In essence, they adopted a "hear no evil, see no evil" position. And as economic imbalance between the United States and Mexico continues, surreptitious entries continue, and the United States knowingly keeps pushing the migrants into Gatekeeper's death trap.

Why do policy makers, the Border Patrol, and the American public allow these avoidable deaths to continue? Why is there no outcry? Our nation has allowed the moral outrage of Operation Gatekeeper to continue because we have defined Mexican migrants outside of the scope of becoming real Americans. Operation Gatekeeper represents the worst manifestation of defining America through immigration policy.

Part IV

Deporting and Barring Non-Americans

CHAPTER 11

Removal

As we have already seen in the context of rounding up and deporting Mexicans, removal is a prime instrument for implementing immigration laws. Certainly, immigration laws aimed at stopping the undesirable at the border are partially effective, as were historical state laws designed to make the unwanted uncomfortable. But for those who have made it past the port of entry and with whom we become uncomfortable or whom we subsequently realize are not "one of us," the remedy is removal.

Development of Deportation Laws

The nation's first deportation and expulsion provision related to political ideology. As noted in Chapter 1, the authority to expel or deport certain aliens from the United States was the Alien Friends Act (part of the Alien and Sedition Laws). This act authorized the president to deport aliens "dangerous to the peace and safety of the United States" during peacetime. Part of four laws enacted in 1798, this act and a corresponding naturalization act were aimed largely at Irish immigrants and French refugees who had participated in political activities critical of the Adams administration. Although one of the four laws—the Sedition Act—was used to attack political critics of the Adams administration,[1] no alien was ever deported under the Alien Act, and its provisions expired in 1800.[2]

Not until ninety years later, in 1888, did another deportation statute appear. This time the provision was economic and labor related. The initial federal limitation upon immigration prohibited the importation of Asian slave labor prostitutes and alien convicts pursuant to legislation enacted in 1862 and 1875.[3] In 1882 the classes of inadmissibles were increased to include the mentally ill, those liable to become public charges, and Chinese laborers. (See Chapter 2.) In 1885 and 1887, Congress enacted contract labor laws aimed at the practice of importing cheap foreign labor under contracts that depressed the labor market in the United States. An 1888 amendment allowed the deportation within one year of aliens who had entered in violation of the contract labor laws. As the first deportation statute since 1798, it was the direct ancestor of later legislative developments.

The first general provision authorizing the deportation of aliens was not enacted until 1891. The law provided that any alien who entered in violation of the law was subject to deportation. This meant that an alien who entered in violation of the immigration laws could be deported. By then, federal limitations on immigration prohibited the importation of oriental slave labor, and the entry of prostitutes, certain criminals, the mentally ill, polygamists, those suffering from certain diseases, those likely to become public charges, and, of course, the undesirable Chinese laborers. Under the deportation provision, a person falling within one of these grounds of exclusion, who somehow escaped detection at entry, could be deported if discovered later. In 1903, the statute of limitations for deportation was increased to three years after entry, except for a two-year period for public charges.[4] The Immigration Act of 1903 was primarily designed to codify existing law although it increased the inadmissible classes to include epileptics, those who had one attack of insanity within five years of entry or two or more attacks of insanity, beggars, anarchists, and importers of women prostitutes. A few years later, the 1907 Immigration Act extended the classes of excludables to include imbeciles, feeble-minded persons, those suffering from tuberculosis, as well as those with a physical or mental defect that might affect their ability to earn a living, and those who had committed a crime involving moral turpitude.

In 1907, the Dillingham Immigration Commission was appointed that made recommendations, eventually leading to the Immigration Act of 1917. (See Chapter 3.) This law added to the list of excludables illiterates, persons of constitutional psychopathic inferiority, alcoholics, those who had suffered an attack of insanity, and, of course the racially barred Hindus and other Asiatics who had been deemed unfit to be part of America. However, aliens who entered in violation of the immigration laws only could be deported within five years after entry. Others who could be deported, with some limitations, included aliens who were sentenced to a year's imprisonment for a crime involving moral turpitude committed within five years after entry, those sentenced twice to a year or more for crimes involving moral turpitude, those advocating the overthrow of the government by force and violence, and those practicing or connected with prostitution were declared deportable irrespective of length of their residence.

The Passport Act of May 22, 1918, authorized the president to impose additional conditions upon the exit and entry of aliens during wartime. The Anarchist Act of October 16, 1918, amended in 1920, authorized the exclusion and expulsion of anarchists and others whose activities were "prejudicial to the public interest or would endanger the welfare or safety of the United States." The language of these deportation provisions was expanded to include those whose "acts of interference with foreign relations" of the country or "possession in time of war of explosives" could be established. Narcotics offenders became deportable in 1922.

Under the 1924 national origins quota law, immigrants who entered the United States without visas and those who overstayed the period of their admission were made subject to deportation without time limitation, without regard to their length of residence, and without regard to their family ties. Previously, such a drastic deportation policy was reserved only for prostitutes, anarchists, subversives, narcotic violators, and criminals. The harshness of the deportation proceedings corresponded with the intent of the quota law to keep the ethnic composition of America from changing. (See Chapter 4.)

However, the major provisions related to deportation were contained in the details of the 1952 act. Generally, they authorized expulsion of aliens who entered unlawfully, nonimmigrants who overstayed their allotted time, and aliens guilty of certain misconduct in the United States, such as criminals, subversives, Communists, narcotics violators, prostitutes, and violators of registration and reporting requirements.

The 1952 act also provided avenues for relief from deportation such as suspension of deportation (subject to congressional approval—an approach later ruled unconstitutional), voluntary departure, adjustment of status, and stay of deportation. Fair hearing procedures were also established before a special inquiry officer.

The 1952 law for the first time eliminated time limitations on deportation. For sixty-five years prior to the 1952 act, there had been a statute of limitations on deportation proceedings. For example, the 1888 amendment allowed the deportation within one year of aliens who had entered in violation of the contract labor law; if more than a year had passed, the person could no longer be deported. Beginning in 1917, there was a general five-year period limiting the institution of deportation proceedings after improper entry, except for deportable offenses committed in the United States, subversive aliens, and entry in violation of quota requirements or with improper visa.

In general, all statutes of limitations were eliminated under the 1952 act, and deportation proceedings could be brought at any time, no matter how remote from the alleged improper entry or activity. In three instances, the law did retain a type of time limitation. The statute specified that these grounds of deportation must have occurred "within 5 yrs of entry": institutionalization at public expense for mental disease, status as a public charge (such as a welfare recipient), conviction of violations of the provisions relating to alien registration.

In 1996, Congress changed the terminology of the laws and the term *removal* is now used to describe the deportation or expulsion of an alien from the United States. Congress has established a list of categories of deportable aliens. An alien falling into any one of these categories is subject to removal proceedings and banned from the country. The most common classes of deportable aliens include the following:

- Aliens who at the time of entry or adjustment of status were inadmissible
- Nonimmigrants (e.g., students and tourists) who have failed to maintain nonimmigrant status, such as by working without authorization, or who have violated their status, such as by staying longer than permitted
- Aliens who have, within five years of any entry, assisted in or encouraged the smuggling of another alien into the United States

- Aliens who were parties to sham marriages
- Aliens who have committed crimes involving moral turpitude
- Aliens who have committed an aggravated felony
- Aliens convicted of narcotics offenses
- Drug addicts
- Aliens who have been convicted of an offense relating to firearms or destructive devices
- Aliens convicted of a crime of domestic violence, stalking, child abuse, child neglect, or child abandonment
- Aliens who have committed immigration document fraud
- Aliens who have engaged in terrorist activity, sabotage, espionage, or criminal activity that endangers public safety or national security
- Aliens who, within five years of entry, have become public charges from causes not shown to have arisen since entry
- Aliens who have voted in violation of any federal, state, or local laws

After realizing that many Nazi war criminals had actually escaped to the United States using assumed names or by concealing their backgrounds, in 1980 Congress added a provision to explicitly address the situation. Under the law, an alien is deportable if he or she was associated with the Nazi government of Germany between 1933 and 1945 and ordered, incited, assisted, or participated in the "persecution of any person because of race, religion, national origin, or political opinion."

Some grounds of deportation can be waived, while relief such as cancellation of removal or asylum may be granted in other situations. In general, however, the most serious grounds of deportation are those related to aggravated felonies and narcotics offenses. Individuals falling within those grounds usually have few options in removal proceedings.

Although the U.S. Supreme Court has acknowledged the severity of deportation, by noting that removal "may result . . . in loss of both property and life; or of all that makes life worth living,"[5] the Court consistently reminds observers that deportation proceedings are civil rather than criminal in nature. As such, the strict due process rights that are afforded to criminal defendants, such as the right to counsel at government expense and a "beyond the reasonable doubt" burden on the government, are not provided to aliens facing removal. Congress has vast power in the area of deportation laws.

As Congress broadened the grounds for deportation, the number of deportation cases increased. But the primary historical focus has been on those who simply do not meet the ideal of who constitutes an American: large numbers involving ethnic or racial groups, as well as those whose views do not comport with American ideals. Today, the vast majority of deportable aliens apprehended are from Mexico who have entered without inspection (see Chapters 8 and 10). However, other examples that reflect the enforcement of deportation grounds directed at unpopular groups are easy to locate.

Chinese Exclusion Era

Chinese laborers were excluded from the United States from 1882 to 1924, and all Chinese were excluded from 1924 to 1943. Thus, most Chinese confrontations with U.S. immigration officials came in the context of exclusion, where they were being barred from entering the United States, rather than in the removal or deportation context. One of the more onerous examples involved the revocation of "section 6" certificates. After the first Chinese Exclusion Act was enacted in 1882, Chinese immigrants who were already in the United States were issued certificates of identity (issued under section 6 of the 1882 act). The idea was that an individual with a section 6 certificate could depart and return to the United States. But the Scott Act of 1888 expanded the exclusion laws and prohibited the entry of all Chinese laborers, including those who had left the United States temporarily with valid return certificates. The constitutionality of the Scott Act was upheld in *The Chinese Exclusion Case* of 1889. A Chinese lawful resident laborer had left the United States in 1887 to visit China carrying a valid section 6 reentry certificate. While he was at sea, the Scott Act was passed; when his boat docked, the laborer was not permitted to reenter. The Supreme Court upheld his exclusion, ruling that Congress's power to regulate immigration was a matter of sovereignty. The Scott Act was held to be constitutionally permissible protection against aggression by a foreign national.[6]

There were many Chinese who entered under false pretenses and were deported after their true status was discovered.

Confronted with the blatantly racist exclusion laws, Chinese were forced to migrate illegally if they wanted to come to the United States. Their gambits were many. A legion entered after the enactment of the exclusion laws under false citizenship claims. A Chinese laborer might assert, for example, that he had been born in San Francisco and that his birth certificate had been destroyed in the 1906 earthquake. Then he would claim, after various trips to China, that his wife there had given birth to children (usually sons) who automatically derived U.S. citizenship through him. In fact, the children were often fictitious, and the few immigration slots were given or sold to others in China. They came to be known as "paper sons." Some who had valid claims of entry would simply sell their identity to another. Since merchants, students, and teachers were exempted from the exclusion laws until 1924, laborers entered with falsified evidence of membership in one of those classes. Thousands of others, including wives, sneaked across the Canadian or Mexican border. In fact, the Border Patrol was established in response to surreptitious entries of Chinese. Any estimate of how many Chinese entered through any of these means would be speculative, but undocumented family members (living or deceased) are mentioned so often in casual conversation with older Chinese Americans that the practice was undoubtedly widespread at one time.

Tom Ung Chal v. Burnett (1928) is an example of a deportation involving a Chinese resident whose undocumented status apparently was discovered.[7] Chal asserted that, having been born in Honolulu, he was a U.S. citizen. He claimed that he was taken to

China by his mother in 1902 when he was ten months old, and he remained there for twenty years. In 1924, he returned to Hawaii and was admitted as a U.S. citizen based on his assertions. In 1927 deportation proceedings were instituted against Chal, on the grounds that he had obtained admission to the United States by false and fraudulent representations as to his citizenship. The federal court of appeals was troubled by discrepancies between Chal's testimony in January 1924, when he was admitted to the Hawaiian Islands, and his testimony in 1927. In 1924 he testified that his only sister had died in 1916. In 1927 he testified that she was still living. He contended that he accompanied his mother to China in 1902 on the ship *Hongkong Maru*. But the manifests and departure records of that steamer failed to list Chal's mother any time during that year, or any name that even remotely resembled hers. In brief, the only evidence supporting his claim was his own statement that his mother had told him what had happened, and the statements of other Chinese persons that she had told them the same thing. As a result, Chal was deported to China.

Immigration inspectors grew to distrust Chinese Americans. Consequently, besides the Border Patrol, the government used other enforcement tools against alleged offenders, such as a notorious holding camp on Angel Island in the San Francisco Bay. Between 1910 and 1940, about 50,000 Chinese were confined—often for months and years at a time—in Angel Island's bleak wooden barracks, where inspectors would conduct grueling interrogations. The extensive carvings of prose and poetry on the barracks' walls bear eloquent testimony both to the immigrants' determination and to the pain they endured. Across the country, raids on private homes, restaurants, and other businesses were also favored by the authorities. Initiated at the turn of the century, raids were resurrected in the 1950s to capture and deport supporters of the new communist regime in mainland China.

Many Chinese Americans lived in constant fear of immigration authorities. Many Chinese did have something to hide, and the Chinese as a community faced an intense level of deportation scrutiny and monitoring. Even those with nothing to hide were forced to look constantly over their shoulders. A "confession program" offered by immigration authorities in the 1950s for those Chinese desirous of clearing up their immigration histories (since names and family trees had been confused by earlier false claims) made matters worse. The program was purportedly a trade-off for the raids during the Red Scare and was promoted in some quarters as an amnesty program. In fact, it offered only a weak assurance that if a confessed Chinese was eligible for an existing statutory remedy, the paperwork would be processed. Some might be married to a citizen through whom immigration was possible, others who had entered illegally prior to June 1940 could be eligible for a relief termed "registry," and still others could apply for suspension of deportation if extreme hardship and good moral character could be demonstrated. But many who admitted past fraud were not eligible and were deported. Relatively few Chinese went through the confession program, because they feared immigration authorities. And if they confessed, their action might affect others with whom they had conspired. For example, of 1,419 Chinese who "confessed" in 1962, another 3,000 were exposed who had entered the same way.[8] In the San

Francisco area, the principal residence for most Chinese Americans at the time, only about 10,000 Chinese came forward during the program.

Deporting "Radicals"

The 1918 law providing for the deportation of alien anarchists was a direct reaction to the Russian Revolution of 1917 and the increasingly effective efforts in the United States to organize workers. The big "Red Scare" of 1919–20 resulted in a nationwide crusade against left-wingers whose Americanism was suspect.[9] In one major use of the law, 249 "radicals" were deported, including the prominent labor organizer Emma Goldman.

In 1893 Goldman was tried and convicted for inciting to riot and was imprisoned on Blackwells Island for telling a crowd of more than a thousand mostly unemployed people at New York's Union Square that they should demand work from the rich; if the rich denied them work, they should demand bread from the rich; and if they were denied bread too, they should "take" bread from the rich; it was their "sacred right."[10] Although Goldman was best known as a labor organizer, it was her call to draft resistance that led to her deportation. She and Alexander Berkman were convicted of violating the Espionage Act because they made speeches and distributed literature opposing compliance with the Selective Draft Law of May 18, 1917. The Supreme Court affirmed the conviction, finding that Goldman overtly conspired to induce persons to disobey the law by failing to register.[11] They were convicted in New York and sentenced to serve two years in prison and fined $10,000 each. Goldman had immigrated as a child. The FBI researched her record, anarchist beliefs, and citizenship status, looking for grounds to deport her. Her arrest had been recommended even though her citizenship, which was purportedly obtained through her parents who received citizenship, might protect her from deportation. By this time she had resided in the United States for twenty-two years.

After serving the two-year term at the Missouri State Penitentiary, Goldman learned that the government had instituted deportation proceedings against her under the 1918 law. She and more than 200 others, "scores of them working men still in their working clothes, many of them men who had been arrested at their jobs, were whisked off for deportation without their families."[12] Goldman resisted deportation, arguing that she was a U.S. citizen. She also was married to a U.S. citizen. But, according to Goldman, authorities found her immigrant parents and terrorized them into saying their naturalization forty years previously had not been in order. Goldman and Berkman were deported, along with 249 others, to Russia. Goldman was a native of Russia, having fled czarist Russia.

When she arrived in Russia, Goldman gave this statement: "Thirty five years ago I fled out of Russia and found a sanctuary in the United States from the opposition of Czarism. Now I am returning to my former home, a member of the first party of political prisoners ever exiled from a land which once typified freedom to all Europe."[13]

After a few years in Russia she moved to Canada, disappointed with the new Russian regime:

> The political institutions in Russia today are worse than under the Czar. There is not one breath of freedom of thought, of action or of initiative in Russia. . . . I found there was not the slightest semblance of any free initiative on the part of the Russian people. Instead, I found a Russian dictatorship which added to the many evils of Czardom.[14]

The Palmer Raids

At the height of industrial unrest in the country in 1919, not long after the enactment of the 1918 deportation act aimed at anarchists, millions of workers went on strike to win union recognition. Most of the movement occurred in immigrant-dominated workforces of the coal, steel, meatpacking, and transportation industries. Employers strongly resisted these efforts, using a variety of tools. The deportation law was viewed as a method of dividing the workers, to raise the heat against the foreign-born and to paralyze the most militant. A heated political and administrative conflict occurred when Justice Department and Labor Department leaders interpreted the immigration laws differently. Secretary of Labor Wilson and Assistant Secretary Post believed the laws, which denied judicial rights to aliens and left their fate in the administrative hands of the secretary of labor, were poorly written and ambiguous. They believed that aliens should face deportation only if they openly advocated violent overthrow of the government. Justice officials, led by Attorney General Mitchell Palmer, viewed simple membership in a radical organization as a deportable offense.

At the end of April 1919, twenty-nine bombs were mailed anonymously to prominent Americans, including Attorney General Palmer. This coincided with May Day (May 1, 1919), the annual labor holiday celebrated by the working class. The bomb mailings served as the catalyst for the "Palmer Raids."

Apparently, even before the bombs, Palmer had contemplated a massive roundup effort. News of his plans were leaked to the media in early May:

> The expected roundup of anarchists and other radicals who are agitating for the overthrow of this government did not begin yesterday. The authorities, it was explained yesterday, were moving slowly but thoroughly, and when the time came every person suspected of activities directed against the government, its officials, or other persons prominent in the public or private life of the country would be seized. In making arrests it is understood that the authorities will act with the expectation that all agitators of alien citizenship will be deported, while those of American citizenship will be held for criminal prosecution in the Federal courts.[15]

Supported by the looming threat of violence epitomized by the anonymous bombs, Palmer convinced Congress to increase his budget for the specific purpose of detecting and prosecuting persons committing crimes against the United States. He set up the "Radical Division" in the Department of Justice's Bureau of Investigation.

On the grounds of exposing "aliens" and "Communists," the Department of Justice focused on a number of independent unions, and its efforts often assisted employers in breaking strikes. The Radical Division established a spy apparatus, sending its operatives out as spies and as agent provocateurs.

Preparations for a major roundup of "radicals," many of whom had been suspects since the start of the bomb hysteria, began in September 1919. The technique—sudden and spectacular raids, first developed on a local scale—was tested in the form of "experimental" raids on November 7, 1919, in order to gauge public reaction as well as prepare the public for such actions. The raids took place in eighteen cities, aimed at meeting rooms of the Union of Russian Workers.

> Armed with warrants for dangerous agitators whom Federal agents have trailed for months the raiders swarmed into the Russian People's Hall in New York and into similar gathering places of alleged "reds" in Philadelphia, Newark, Detroit, Jackson, Mich., Ansonia, Conn., and other cities, broke up meetings, seized tons of literature, and herded the group of foreign men and women into various offices for examination, whence many of those proved to be the most sought after of the radicals found their way into cells.[16]

And the raids were violent: "Thirty-three men, most of them with bandaged heads, black eyes or other marks of rough handling were taken to the immigration offices at Ellis Island, while 150 others were set free."[17] Attorney General Palmer explained that "drastic methods" were necessary, and that a number of the leaders in Ansonia had been arrested on deportation warrants.[18]

The main raids took place the evening of January 2, 1920, in fifty-six cities across the country. Palmer and his right-hand man, J. Edgar Hoover, had 3,000 persons arrested and jailed in one night. The *New York Times* reported on the raids:

> The action, though it came with dramatic suddenness, had been carefully mapped out, studied, and systematized. Every agency was ready, and every operative at his post. For months the Department of Justice men, dropping all their work, had concentrated on the Reds. Agents quietly infiltrated into the radical ranks, slipped casually into centers of agitation, and went to work, sometimes as cooks in remote mining colonies, again as steel workers, and when the opportunity presented itself, as agitators of the wildest type. Although careful not to inspire, suggest, or aid the advancement of overt acts or propaganda, several of the agents, "under-cover" men, managed to rise in the radical movement, and become, in at least one instance, the recognized leader of the district.[19]

These raids also were not peaceful:

> Meetings wide open to the general public were roughly broken up. All persons present—citizens and aliens alike without discrimination—were arbitrarily taken into custody and searched as if they had been burglars caught in the criminal act. Without warrants of arrest men were carried off to police stations and other temporary prisons, subjected there to secret police-office inquisitions commonly known as the "third degree," their statements written categorically into mimeographed question blanks, and they were required to swear to them regardless of their accuracy.[20]

The Radical Division maintained detailed records on tens of thousands of individuals.

> In order that the information obtained upon the ultra radical movements might be readily accessible for use by the persons charged with the supervision of the investigations and prosecutions, there has been established as part of this division a card index system, numbering over 200,000 cards, giving detailed data not only upon individual agitators connected with the ultra-radical movement, but also upon organizations, associations, societies, publications and special conditions existing in certain localities. . . .
>
> Biographies are prepared of all authors, publishers, editors, etc., showing any connection with an ultra-radical body or movement. Stenographic reports of speeches made by individuals prominent in the various movements are properly filed and together with articles in any one of the newspapers or publications referred to above, are digested or briefed and made available for immediate reference.[21]

While there was popular and political support for the roundups, the courts were critical of Department of Justice's procedures violative of due process. In *Colyer v. Skeffington* (1920),[22] twenty aliens who were affiliated with the Communist Party brought petitions for habeas corpus after they were taken into custody pursuant to a raid on January 20, 1920. Bail was fixed at $5,000 to $10,000. The case involved the legality of the government's deportation under the Anarchist Act of 1918, that authorized the deportation of any alien anarchist, irrespective of time of entry. After the hearing, the federal court was convinced that none of the aliens were in any way involved, by the use of bombs, guns, or other weapons, in plans of injuring persons or property, much less being anarchists. Bail was reduced to $500. The court held that although the government had every right to exclude or expel aliens for the safety and independence of the nation, deportation solely on the grounds that aliens were members of the Communist Party was invalid for deportation when the Department of Labor violated due process against the aliens. The court was critical of the methods used in many of the related raids:

> I refrain from any extended comment on the lawlessness of these proceedings by our supposedly law-enforcing officials. The documents and acts speak for themselves. It may, however, fitly be observed that a mob is a mob, whether made up of government officials acting under instructions from the Department of Justice, or of criminals, loafers, and the vicious classes.
>
> Necessarily a raid of this kind, carried out with such disregard of law and of properly verified facts, had many unexpected and some unintended results. For instance, in a hall in Lynn 39 people were holding a meeting to discuss the formation of a co-operative bakery. About half of them were citizens. But the Lynn police, acting under the instructions of the Department of Justice, raided this hall and arrested the entire 39, held them over night in cells at the police station, and then had them docketed as "suspects" and 38 of them discharged.
>
> There were also incidents of the arrests of women under conditions involving great hardship. For instance, the witness Mrs. Stanislas Vasiliewska, the mother of three children, aged 13, 10, and 8, was arrested in a hall in Chelsea, taken in the police patrol wagon with her eldest girl to the police station, and both put with another woman into one cell. About

midnight they took her child and sent her home alone to a remote part of the city. Mrs. Vasiliewska was taken the next day to the wharf, where, with Mrs. Colyer, she was confined for about 6 hours in a dirty toilet room. She was then taken to Deer Island, where she was kept 33 days. Such treatment of women by the Department of Justice contrasts with that contemplated by rule 22 . . . when women are taken by the Department of Labor, which has a lawful right to arrest alien women.

The witness Minnie Federman was arrested at her home at 6 o'clock in the morning. Several men, showing her no warrant, entered her room where she was in bed. She was told to get out of bed and dress, which she did in a closet. Then she was taken in a police wagon to the police station after they had searched her premises, apparently for I.W.W. literature. When they found that she was a naturalized citizen, she was allowed to go.

In Nashua, a hall was raided and about 13 women taken, 6 or 7 of whom were released at the police station; 5 of them were kept from Friday night to Saturday afternoon in one cell, without a mattress.

It was under such terrorizing conditions as these that these aliens were subjected to questionnaires, subsequently used as, and generally constituting an important part of, the evidence adduced against them before the immigration inspectors. Pains were taken to give spectacular publicity to the raid, and to make it appear that there was great and imminent public danger, against which these activities of the Department of Justice were directed. The arrested aliens, in most instances perfectly quiet and harmless working people, many of them not long ago Russian peasants, were handcuffed in pairs, and then, for the purposes of transfer on trains and through the streets of Boston, chained together. The Northern New Hampshire contingent was first concentrated in jail at Concord and then brought to Boston in a special car, thus handcuffed and chained together. On detraining at the North Station, the handcuffed and chained aliens were exposed to newspaper photographers and again thus exposed at the wharf where they took the boat for Deer Island. The Department of Justice agents in charge of the arrested aliens appear to have taken pains to have them thus exposed to public photographing.

Private rooms were searched in omnibus fashion; trunks, bureaus, suitcases, and boxes broken open; books and papers seized. I doubt whether a single search warrant was obtained or applied for. There is some hearsay or inferential evidence as to obtaining so-called "gun warrants" in Worcester and Lawrence. At the trial the court stated that, if such warrants had been issued, a certified copy of the records should be produced. No such record evidence was produced. I therefore doubt the truth of this inferential evidence. But, if it was true, these "gun warrants" were obtained by an abuse of process—most likely by the use of knowingly false affidavits. "Gun warrants" could not be legally obtained or used for the purpose of searching for and seizing documentary evidence.[23]

When these officials arrested and scheduled deportation for one of the first groups of more than 300 aliens in December 1919 (the group that included Emma Goldman and Alexander Berkman), Labor Secretary Wilson, who believed some of the detainees were deportable, ordered a stay of deportation for aliens having families (who could not be deported even voluntarily under the immigration laws). All aliens arrested and taken to immigrant stations other than Ellis Island were spared, but officials at Ellis Island, collaborating with Palmer and Hoover, ignored Wilson's order and allowed 249 persons, including Goldman and Berkman, to be deported.

After Wilson became ill, Assistant Secretary Post took immediate steps to correct the illegal and unethical actions of his subordinate. He told J. Edgar Hoover to cease interrogating aliens detained at Ellis Island unless approved by an official board of inquiry sanctioned by the secretary of labor or himself. Immigration officials, citing lack of evidence and a low percentage of "guilty" findings of those previously arrested, began refusing warrant requests from Justice officials.

This battle between the two departments continued into the summer of 1920, but it was clear that the Labor Department would not let Ellis Island become an oppressive site, shrouded in secrecy. When Attorney General Palmer ordered his agents to censor the mail of detained aliens on Ellis Island, Labor Department Solicitor Rowland B. Mahany informed him that censorship in peacetime would not be tolerated. Palmer withdrew all but a token force of agents from Ellis Island and other immigrant stations. By mid-1920 the Red Scare had abated, and Post, who faced a congressional impeachment hearing for his stand against injustice, commented, "We have been going through a state of hysteria. Folks will look back with regret for having made fools of themselves, but there is nothing like a panic to make fools of us all."[24] But by then, the victims rounded up by the Palmer raids totaled about 6,000. Eventually Post's perspective prevailed, and Congress criticized Palmer for his excesses.

Deportation of Japanese Immigrants During World War II

Although the Alien Enemy Act of 1798 was enacted at the urging of the nation's second president, John Adams, he never used its provisions to deport anyone. In fact, its provisions were roundly criticized. (See Chapter 1.) But during World War II, pursuant to the authority conferred upon him by the Alien Enemy Act of 1798, Franklin D. Roosevelt on December 7, 1941, issued Proclamation No. 2525, which concerned Japanese alien enemies. While the internment of over 120,000 Japanese Americans, most of them citizens by birth, is well documented, the separate incarceration of Japanese aliens pursuant to the Alien Enemy Act is less discussed. Following this first proclamation, many Japanese immigrants who were suspected of being dangerous to the country were placed in various zones within the continental limits of the United States. Almost four years later, on July 14, 1945, FDR issued Proclamation No. 2655, known as the Alien Removal Proclamation, which provided in part:

> All alien enemies now or hereafter interned within the continental limits of the United States pursuant to the aforesaid proclamation of the President of the United States who shall be deemed by the Attorney General to be dangerous to the public peace and safety of the United States because they adhered to the aforesaid enemy governments or to the principles of government thereof shall be subject upon the order of the Attorney General to removal from the United States and may be required to depart therefrom in accordance with such regulations as he may prescribe.

Japanese aliens, who were suspected of being dangerous, were brought before the Alien Enemy Hearing Board and the Repatriation Hearing Board. If an alien was deemed a danger to the public peace and safety of the United States because of adherence to the principles of a government with which the United States was at war, the attorney general ordered the person to depart from the country within thirty days. If the person failed to depart, he or she would be deported. This process was upheld in *Ex Parte Zenzo Arakawa v. Clark* (1947).[25]

Some Japanese Americans who were U.S. citizens elected to renounce their U.S. citizenship and seek deportation to Japan.[26] The renunciations were valid only if they were done freely and the person who sought renunciation was mentally competent.[27]

Almost forty years later, in the 1980s, evidence was unearthed that the U.S. military actually had no evidence that Japanese Americans were a danger to the national security of the United States during World War II. In fact, decades-old criminal convictions of Fred Korematsu and Gordon Hirabayahi for violating curfew and internment orders were tossed out by federal courts on the grounds that the federal government had lied and committed fraud in securing their convictions.

Nazi War Criminals

Even before Congress added the 1980 section providing for the deportation of Nazi war criminals, the Department of Justice established the Office of Special Investigations (OSI) to search for such war criminals who had somehow managed to enter the United States, usually by falsifying their background information at the end of World War II. By 1980, the OSI consisted of 50 persons, including 20 lawyers and 5 professional historians. It had already investigated 470 cases, but within 20 years, the OSI had managed to extradite just over 50 individuals, mostly low-level concentration camp guards. Two—Feodor Fedorenko and John Demjanjuk—were accused of serving at extermination camps whose sole purpose was to kill Jews.

The Fedorenko Case

In October 1949, Feodor Fedorenko applied for admission to the United States as a displaced person. The Displaced Persons Act (DPA) of 1948 enabled European refugees driven from their homelands by World War II to emigrate to the United States without regard to traditional immigration quotas. He was admitted to the United States under a DPA visa that had been issued on the basis of his 1949 application, telling investigators from the Displaced Persons Commission that he had been a farmer in Sarny, Poland, from 1937 until March 1942, and that he had then been deported to Germany and forced to work in a factory in Poelitz until the end of the war, when he fled to Hamburg. Fedorenko was issued a DPA visa, and sailed to the United States, where he was admitted for permanent residence. He took up residence in Connecticut and for three decades led an uneventful and law-abiding life as a factory worker.

In fact, Fedorenko was born in the Ukraine in 1907. He was drafted into the Russian Army in June 1941, but was captured by the Germans shortly thereafter. After being held in a series of prisoner-of-war camps, he was selected to go to the German camp at Travnicki in Poland, where he received training as a concentration camp guard. In September 1942, he was assigned to the Nazi concentration camp at Treblinka in Poland, where he was issued a uniform and rifle and where he served as a guard during 1942 and 1943. The infamous Treblinka concentration camp was a "human abattoir" at which several hundred thousand Jewish civilians were murdered. After an armed uprising by the inmates at Treblinka led to the closure of the camp in August 1943, Fedorenko was transferred to a German labor camp at Danzig and then to the German prisoner-of-war camp at Poelitz, where he continued to serve as an armed guard. He was eventually transferred to Hamburg, where he served as a warehouse guard. Shortly before the British forces entered that city in 1945, Fedorenko discarded his uniform and was able to pass as a civilian. For the next four years, he worked in Germany as a laborer.

In 1969, Fedorenko applied for naturalization at the INS office in Hartford, Connecticut. He continued to conceal his wartime service as a concentration camp armed guard in his application. His petition for naturalization was granted, and he became an American citizen on April 23, 1970. Eventually, he moved to Miami Beach and became a resident of Florida, where the OSI caught up with him, eventually successfully moving to strip him of his citizenship and having him deported in the early 1980s.

Even though more than thirty years had elapsed since Fedorenko's service for the Nazis, the government's witnesses at trial included six survivors of Treblinka who claimed that they had seen Fedorenko commit specific acts of violence against inmates of the camp. Each witness made a pretrial identification of him from a photo array that included his 1949 visa photograph, and three of the witnesses made courtroom identifications. One witness, Eugeun Turowski, testified that he saw Fedorenko shoot and whip Jewish prisoners at the camp. Another, Schalom Kohn, testified that he saw Fedorenko almost every day for the first few months Kohn was at Treblinka, that Fedorenko beat him with an iron-tipped whip, and that he saw Fedorenko whip and shoot other prisoners. The third witness, Josef Czarny, claimed that he saw Fedorenko beat arriving prisoners, and that he once saw Fedorenko shoot a prisoner. Gustaw Boraks testified that he saw Fedorenko repeatedly chase prisoners to the gas chambers, beating them as they went. Boraks also claimed that on one occasion, he heard a shot and ran outside to see Fedorenko, with a gun drawn, standing close to a wounded woman who later told him that Fedorenko was responsible for the shooting. Sonia Lewkowicz testified that she saw him shoot a Jewish prisoner. Finally, Pinchas Epstein testified that Fedorenko shot and killed a friend of his, after making him crawl naked on all fours. Based on this dramatic testimony, Fedorenko was stripped of his citizenship and eventually deported to Russia, where he was executed as a war criminal.[28]

The Demjanjuk Case

The Demjanjuk case proved much more difficult for the OSI. In the late 1970s, the OSI arrested John Demjanjuk, an autoworker from Cleveland, claiming that he was "Ivan the Terrible," one of World War II's most notorious and malevolent practitioners of genocide. The OSI alleged that he drunkenly beat Jews as they entered the gas chambers at Treblinka, then turned on the gas himself before heading out to rape local girls. At his denaturalization trial, several survivors of Treblinka testified about its horrors. Each of the witnesses recalled a Ukrainian named "Ivan" who not only herded the Jewish prisoners into the gas chambers, but also activated the motors that gassed the Jews. The savage cruelty of this notorious man earned him the special nickname among the camp's Jewish inmates, "Ivan Grozny," or "Ivan the Terrible." The evidence linking Demjanjuk to this notorious Ivan at Treblinka consisted of photographic identifications made by the six witnesses both before and at trial. No in-court identification was attempted by the government. All the pretrial photographic identifications except for one were conducted overseas. Several different photospreads were shown individually to each of the witnesses by different investigators on various dates. Two photographs of Demjanjuk were utilized in these identification sessions. Each witness was shown a photospread containing his picture taken from his 1951 application for an immigration visa. In 1951, Demjanjuk was thirty-one years old. Each witness picked out Demjanjuk's visa photograph and identified him as the man known as Ivan at Treblinka. In addition to the visa picture, five of the six witnesses were also shown another photospread containing the picture of Demjanjuk found on the training camp card; four of the witnesses picked out the photograph from the card and again identified Demjanjuk's picture as that of Ivan. The fifth witness, Rajchman, failed to identify his training camp picture in a pretrial confrontation, but did so at trial. Based on this evidence, a federal judge stripped Demjanjuk of his U.S. citizenship in 1981.

By the time of the 1981 Demjanjuk trial, the OSI was under tremendous political pressure to prove its worth. And it went forward with the case, despite growing misgivings among some in the office. One of the reasons for doubt was that by 1981, the OSI had learned of a sworn deposition given to the KGB in 1949 by another Ukrainian, Ignat T. Danilchenko, who was captured by the Nazis and said he served with Demjanjuk not at Treblinka but at Sobibor, Flossenburg, and a nearby camp called Regensburg. The government neither introduced the Danilchenko statement at trial nor turned it over to the defense for six years.

Demjanjuk's story, which also shifted repeatedly over the years, though not as much as the government's, was that he fought for the Soviets, was held in two POW camps after being captured, and was then sent by the Germans to fight his former army with a band of other Ukrainians in Austria. Never, he maintained, did he serve at a concentration or extermination camp.

In 1986 Demjanjuk was deported—not to his home country of the USSR, which likely would have charged him with treason, but to Israel, which would try him for war crimes. The trial was Israel's first against a Nazi since 1962, when an unrepentant Adolf Eichmann was found guilty and hanged for administering the Holocaust. With Demjanjuk, soft-spoken and awkward, described by prosecutors as the devil in disguise, the trial served not only as a Holocaust tutorial for a generation of Jews born after the war but also as a reminder of how many war criminals continued to live freely.

The Israeli tribunal found Demjanjuk guilty and in 1988 sentenced him to die as Eichmann died, at the end of a rope.

Even as Demjanjuk's trial was winding down, however, so too was the Soviet Union. And from a Ukrainian state archive emerged the depositions of thirty-seven Treblinka guards captured by the Red Army at the end of the war. Every one of them identified another man, Ivan Marchenko, as Ivan the Terrible.

It soon became clear that Demjanjuk was almost certainly not Ivan the Terrible.

Israel's Supreme Court freed Demjanjuk in 1993. In its decision, the court said there was considerable evidence that Demjanjuk was indeed a Nazi collaborator who served at Majdanek, Flossenburg, and Sobibor, but that since the allegations were that he was Ivan of Treblinka, he had not had a chance to defend himself on these other allegations. He was allowed to return to the United States. Prison workers were building his gallows when the call came to set Demjanjuk free.[29]

A Special Master appointed by the federal court of appeals found recklessness on the part of the prosecution during the 1981 U.S. proceedings, and in 1998 the district court vacated the original denaturalization order. In 1999, the OSI filed a complaint based on new evidence showing, for example, that Demjanjuk was a guard at three other concentration camps. OSI alleged that as a Ukrainian farm boy drafted by the Soviet army and quickly wounded and captured by the Nazis, he was pressed into service as a guard at the Nazi camps. And when he emigrated to the United States in 1948, the government says, he lied to conceal that fact. In February 2002, the federal court agreed and once again stripped Demjanjuk of his U.S. citizenship. Polish officials are considering extraditing Demjanuk to face war crimes charges in their country.[30]

The 1979 Roundup of Iranian Students

On November 4, 1979, Iranian militants invaded the U.S. embassy in Tehran and took approximately sixty-five U.S. citizens hostage in order to force the United States to meet hostage holders' demands. As part of his response to the crisis, President Carter on November 10, 1979, directed the attorney general to identify any Iranian students in the United States who were not in compliance with the terms of their entry visas, and to take the necessary steps to commence deportation proceedings against those who had violated applicable immigration laws and regulations. On November 13 the attorney general issued a regulation requiring all postsecondary Iranian students to report within thirty days to their local INS office to "provide information about residence and maintenance of nonimmigrant status."[31] This was a significant action, because the largest group of foreign students in the United States at the time was Iranian.

As Iranian students began to report to local INS offices throughout the country, the impact was evident. Many students were found to be technically out of status. Some were not registered for the minimum amount of course credits required. Some were working without authorization. Others were attending some classes at schools that were not the principal school to which they had been admitted. As a result, thousands of Iranian students were deported or ordered to leave immediately.

A challenge to the regulation was filed, but ultimately proved unsuccessful. The lower federal district court ruled that the attorney general had violated the Iranian students' rights to equal protection by focusing on a specific nationality group; the court perceived no "overriding national interest" that would justify the regulation and found that the regulation as a response to the Iranian student attack on the U.S. embassy in Tehran did not support a "legitimate national interest." But the court of appeals disagreed. Using a deferential standard, the court found a rational basis for the regulation. The court gave great weight to an affidavit submitted by the attorney general that explained that the regulation was issued

as an element of the language of diplomacy by which international courtesies are granted or withdrawn in response to actions by foreign countries. The action . . . is a fundamental element of the President's efforts to resolve the Iranian crisis and to maintain the safety of American hostages in Tehran. Distinctions on the basis of nationality may be drawn in the immigration field by the Congress or by the Executive. So long as such are not wholly irrational, they must be sustained. . . . Any rule of constitutional law that would inhibit the flexibility of the political branches of government to respond to changing world condition should be adopted only with the greatest caution.[32]

One of the court of appeals judges went on to explain in a separate opinion that under certain circumstances legal resident aliens become our enemy:

Under our law, the alien in several respects stands on an equal footing with citizens, but in others has never been conceded legal parity with the citizen. Most importantly, to protract this ambiguous status within the country is not his right but is a matter of permission and tolerance. The Government's power to terminate its hospitality has been asserted and sustained by this Court since the question first arose.

War, of course, is the most usual occasion for extensive resort to the power. Though the resident alien may be personally loyal to the United States, if his nation becomes our enemy his allegiance prevails over his personal preference and makes him also our enemy, liable to expulsion or internment, and his property becomes subject to seizure and perhaps confiscation. But it does not require war to bring the power of deportation into existence or to authorize its exercise. Congressional apprehension of foreign or internal dangers short of war may lead to its use. So long as the alien elects to continue the ambiguity of his allegiance his domicile here is held by a precarious tenure.

That aliens remain vulnerable to expulsion after long residence is a practice that bristles with severities. But it is a weapon of defense and reprisal confirmed by international law as a power inherent in every sovereign state. Such is the traditional power of the Nation over the alien and we leave the law on the subject as we find it.[33]

Prior to the takeover of the embassy in Tehran, Iranian students in the United States had received much different treatment. On April 16, 1979, the INS commissioner issued a directive to INS district offices that action should not be taken, prior to September 1, 1979, to deport Iranian nationals who indicated an unwillingness to return to Iran because of the instability of the conditions then existing in that country. Nonimmigrant Iranian nationals who accepted the deferred voluntary departure were informed that they would not be reinstated to a nonimmigrant status upon expiration of the departure period. On August 9, 1979, the INS, in consultation with the secretary of state, extended the September 1, 1979 departure date until June 1, 1980. A nine-month extension was granted because a large proportion of Iranian nationals in the United States were students enrolled in nine-month programs. But after the November 4 takeover of the embassy in Tehran and the subsequent directive to all Iranian students to report to INS, a directive rescinding the June 1980 deferred departure was issued. Each Iranian who had received the benefit of deferred departure was to be notified of the revocation and that departure was required on or before thirty days from date of the notice.

In *Mahdjoubi v. Crosland* (1980),[34] Iranian students challenged the directive revoking the deferred departure dates that the INS had previously granted to them. However, the federal court of appeals found that the directive was within the scope of the president's stated policy, and rejected the students' contentions. Because the INS commissioner was implementing the president's foreign policy, the court felt that the directive fell within the foreign affairs function of the executive branch, excusing it from requirements of the Administrative Procedures Act.

John Lennon and the Nonpriority Program

Although various INS regimes enforced deportation provisions fairly rigorously, at times the equities or political ramifications presented by certain cases would soften even the most hard-nosed INS enforcement agent. Until the 1970s, immigration officials maintained a low-profile, almost secret, "nonpriority program," where deportable aliens were allowed to remain in the country because of special circumstances. This program was exposed in the midst of the government's attempt to deport John Lennon, the legendary member of the Beatles.

After the Beatles broke up, Lennon and his wife, artist Yoko Ono, traveled to New York in August 1971 to seek custody of Ono's daughter by a former marriage to a U.S. citizen. At the time of entry, INS authorities were aware that Lennon had pleaded guilty to possession of one-half ounce of hashish in Great Britain in 1968. Officials temporarily waived what was deemed to be a ground of excludability because of that conviction. Lennon's temporary visa was eventually extended to February 29, 1972. During his stay, he performed at rallies organized to protest the United States's involvement in the Vietnam War. His activity caught the attention of President Richard Nixon, who ordered INS officials to make sure that Lennon was removed from the United

States. Soon after Lennon's visa expired in March 1972, deportation proceedings were instituted against Lennon and Ono. Although they had filed applications for lawful permanent residence, INS officials did not act on the applications, choosing instead to seek deportation, in part based on the British conviction that they had earlier ignored.

While the proceedings were pending, Lennon's attorney, Leon Wildes, brought an action against the INS, arguing that Lennon and Ono should not be deported, and instead be allowed to remain in the same manner that Wildes and other immigration lawyers had heard was possible in the officials' discretion. As part of the lawsuit, Wildes discovered the existence of the "nonpriority program." Nonpriority status was essentially an administrative halt to deportation; the deportable alien would be allowed to stay and the case had the lowest possible priority for INS action. Traditionally, the status was accorded to aliens whose departure from the United States would result in extreme hardship. The family courts had awarded Lennon and Ono custody of the child. However, the father absconded with the child and could not be found. In the midst of the frantic search for the child, Lennon and Ono were subjected to expulsion proceedings. They argued that the equities involved in their search for the child justified the application for nonpriority status.

What Wildes unearthed about the government's nonpriority program was surprising to many. He was allowed to examine 1,843 cases and found that nonpriority status could apply in virtually any circumstance where a grave injustice might result from removal. Nonpriority had been granted to aliens who had committed serious crimes involving moral turpitude (including rape), drug convictions, fraud, and prostitution. Nonpriority had been given to Communists, the insane, the feebleminded, and the medically infirm. Often there were multiple grounds of deportability. Family separation, age (both elderly and young), health, and economic issues were important factors that officials considered.[35]

After the revelation of the existence of the secret nonpriority program, the INS formalized the process publicly, publishing guidelines for requesting "deferred action" from INS authorities. Local INS district directors had the authority to grant a deportable person deferred action, permitting him or her to remain in the country indefinitely. The primary considerations district directors would use in deciding whether to grant deferred action included (1) the likelihood of ultimately removing the alien, including physical ability to travel, or availability of relief; (2) the presence of sympathetic factors that might lead to protracted deportation proceedings or bad precedent from the INS perspective; (3) the likelihood that publicity adverse to the INS would be generated because of sympathetic facts; and (4) whether the person was a member of a class whose removal was given high priority, for example, dangerous criminals, large-scale alien smugglers, narcotic drug traffickers, terrorists, war criminals, or habitual immigration violators.

Lennon ultimately won his deportation battle with the INS even though authorities did not grant him deferred action or nonpriority status. The question in Lennon's case was whether his 1968 British conviction for possession of cannabis resin rendered him an excludable alien under an immigration law that applied to those convicted of illicit possession of marijuana. In *Lennon v. INS* (1975),[36] the court of appeals held that Lennon's conviction did not fall within this law. His deportation saga began three years earlier.

The day after Lennon's visa expired, March 1, 1972, the New York district director of the INS, notified Lennon and Ono by letter that, if they did not leave the country by March 15, deportation proceedings would be instituted. On March 3, Lennon and Ono filed "third preference" petitions as a first step toward becoming lawful residents of the United States. At the time, third preference was given to "qualified immigrants who . . . because of their exceptional ability in the sciences or the arts will substantially benefit prospectively the national economy, cultural interests, or welfare of the United States." (First and second preferences were reserved for certain relatives of U.S. citizens and lawful permanent residents.) Rather than ruling on these applications, the INS instituted deportation proceedings three days later. Lennon and Ono were therefore unable to apply for permanent residence. After waiting two months, they filed suit in federal district court for an injunction compelling the INS to rule on their petitions. The strategy worked, and under pressure from the federal court, INS officials approved the preliminary third preference petitions.

The battle was far from over. Since deportation proceedings had been initiated, Lennon and Ono had to pursue the next step toward permanent status from the immigration judge. On May 12, 1972, ten days after the INS finally approved their preliminary petition for third preference status, Lennon and Ono applied to the immigration judge for permanent residence. During the hearing, letters from many eminent writers, artists, and entertainers, as well as from John Lindsay, at the time the mayor of New York, were submitted to show that, were the applications approved, Lennon and Ono would make a unique and valuable contribution to this country's cultural heritage. The government did not challenge Lennon's artistic standing, but instead contended that his 1968 guilty plea made him an excludable alien, thus mandating the denial of his application. Lennon countered by arguing that he was not excludable under the law since he had not been convicted of violating a law forbidding *illicit* possession. Under British law, Lennon urged, guilty knowledge was not an element of the offense. The immigration judge filed his decision on March 23, 1973. Since Yoko Ono had once obtained permanent resident status in 1964, he granted her application. But, because he believed that Lennon was an excludable alien, the immigration judge denied Lennon's application and ordered him deported.

The court of appeals did not agree with the immigration judge. The court felt that U.S. immigration laws related to marijuana possession required the individual to have knowledge that he or she was in possession of the substance. The language of the British statute under which Lennon was convicted was deceptively simple: "A person shall not be in possession of a drug unless . . . authorized." Analysis of British law as it existed in 1968 when Lennon was convicted made guilty knowledge irrelevant. A person found with tablets that he reasonably believed were aspirin would be convicted if the tablets proved to contain heroin. Therefore, a conviction under the British statute could not be used for marijuana exclusion under U.S. immigration laws.

Marriage Fraud Amendments

In 1986, the Immigration Marriage Fraud Amendments (IMFA) were adopted following intense media coverage that portrayed immigration-related marriage fraud as pervasive. The claim was that many prospective immigrants would enter into fraudulent or sham marriages with U.S. citizens in order to obtain lawful permanent resident ("green card") status. Congress was influenced by the media pressure as well as INS "statistics" showing that 30 percent of immigration-related marriages were fraudulent and by a comparative study suggesting that conditional status was an effective means of controlling fraudulent immigration.[37] According to INS Commissioner Nelson, marriage fraud posed a significant threat to the integrity of the immigration system because marriage was the easiest and most frequently used means of obtaining permanent resident status. The legislation was enacted, even though the State Department did not support the adoption of INS-backed measures, arguing that most fraudulent cases were detected at the visa interview stage and suggested that proper enforcement of existing law rendered legislative amendment unnecessary.

Under IMFA, in order to obtain lawful residence status through marriage to a U.S. citizen, the marriage must remain viable for two years. Procedurally, the couple file paperwork on behalf of the prospective immigrant after the marriage, and again two years later. At both stages, separate interviews of the husband and wife by INS interviewers may be conducted to verify the validity of the marriage. A person who is found guilty of attempting to obtain an immigration benefit through a sham marriage is permanently barred from immigrating to the United States.

After the passage of IMFA, INS "statistics" that were used to justify the amendments came under serious question. In 1988, an independent study of the INS's statistical methodology pointed out that the INS did not use cases in which fraud was actually demonstrated, but derived its estimates from the personal judgments of investigators, formulated after preliminary investigation. Second, the survey base was extremely small, comprising only one-twentieth of one percent of the immigration petitions filed during fiscal year 1984. Third, although purportedly a random sample, the INS survey selectively excluded certain petition types.[38] Then in a lawsuit that was filed, the INS admitted that the 30 percent figure had no statistical foundation. It turns out that the 30 percent was a projection by an INS regional office about how many cases they would investigate where fraud was suspected. So it was just a matter of how many cases would be investigated, not how many were actually fraudulent.[39]

The enactment of IMFA also had an all-too-familiar racial aspect. The hearings and debates categorized the types of marriage fraud. In one, the nonresident alien pays a citizen or legal permanent resident for marriage. In the other, a nonresident alien "marries a U.S. citizen only to abandon the spouse following receipt of a green card."[40] Those who spoke characterized the second type of marriage fraud as more pernicious. Most of the immigrants who obtain resident status by marriage to a citizen or legal permanent resident are women. So according to the hearings and debates, immigrant women constituted a threat to the integrity of law and citizenship.

While participants in the hearings and floor debates did not mention this fact per se, they did repeatedly use mail-order brides to illustrate the problems with the then-existing law and the more "invidious" type of marriage fraud. Mail-order brides are figuratively Asian in popular representations and disproportionately Asian and Pacific Islander in fact.[41] As such, echoes of the 1875 Page Law enacted to exclude Chinese prostitutes can be detected in IMFA. Both statutes restrict the immigration of Asian women and both, to different degrees, were intended to do so. IMFA, like the Page Law, defined the morality of immigrant Asian women in terms that simultaneously construct and condemn a dangerous sexuality.[42]

Indefinite Detention

Although the primary focus of the Immigration Act of 1990 was on the debate over the number of visas for kinship categories versus employment categories (see Chapter 6), Senator Alan Simpson insisted on stronger provisions to deal with aliens convicted of crimes as well. The compromise included portions of S. 3055 sponsored by Simpson, which would speed deportations of criminal aliens. Section 501 expanded the definition of "aggravated felony" to include illicit trafficking in any controlled substance, money laundering, and any crime of violence with a five-year imprisonment imposed. Aliens convicted of aggravated felonies would have expedited deportation hearings and would not be released from custody while in deportation proceedings.[43]

The 1990 enforcement provisions stemmed from Congress's belief that aliens in deportation proceedings and those convicted of crimes had too many rights.[44] Congress also presumed that aliens and their attorneys unnecessarily delayed deportation proceedings through frivolous motions and appeals. After the passage of the 1990 act, other acts of Congress further limited the rights of aliens convicted of aggravated felonies through the Immigration and Technical Corrections Act of 1994, the Antiterrorism and Effective Death Penalty Act (AEDPA) of 1996, and the Illegal Immigration Reform and Immigration Responsibility Act of 1996.

In the summer of 2001, the Supreme Court addressed the issue of indefinite detention of aliens. In *Zadvydas v. Davis*,[45] the Court heard consolidated cases of two aliens. One was Kestutis Zadvydas, who had a long criminal record, including possession with intent to distribute cocaine and attempted burglary. The second alien, Kim Ho Ma, was convicted of manslaughter, an aggravated felony. Ma had been admitted to the United States as a refugee from Cambodia as a child. Both were ordered deported and detained. The INS continued to keep both Ma and Zadvydas in custody because their home countries refused to take them. Eventually Ma was released because there was no realistic chance that Cambodia would accept Ma. The issue was whether the statute authorized the attorney general to detain a removable alien indefinitely, as the confinement was potentially permanent. However, in March 2002,

Cambodia agreed to begin accepting Cambodian nationals who had committed deportable offenses in the United States, and in October 2002, Kim Ho Ma was removed to Cambodia. The removal occurred in spite of the fact that Cambodia continues to commit serious human rights violations and families, such as Ma's, were survivors of the infamous Killing Fields genocide. Many Cambodian deportees entered the United States as infants and toddlers, and their parents suffer from post traumatic stress disorder and have not been given the tools to raise their children in such a radically different culture.

The Court held that the statute implicitly limited the detention to a reasonable period necessary to bring about the alien's removal from the United States, and did not permit indefinite detention. In interpreting the statute, the Court noted that a statute permitting indefinite detention of an alien would raise a serious due process problem. Although the government argued that the statutes had two regulatory goals—(1) to ensure the appearance of aliens at future proceedings and (2) to prevent danger to the community—the Court found these goals unpersuasive in part because the dangerousness rationale was not accompanied by some other special circumstance that would justify detention. Since the confinements were civil in nature, the Court reasoned that the only circumstance present was the aliens' removable status itself, which bore no relation to the aliens' dangerousness.

The government argued that alien statutes could justify indefinite detention, citing *Shaughnessy v. United States ex rel. Mezei* (1953).[46] That case involved an alien who was refused admission and indefinitely detained on Ellis Island because the government could not find a country to accept him. The Court there held that the detention was constitutional. However, the *Zadvydas* Court distinguished the old case by noting that the due process clause applies to all persons inside the United States and since the aliens had already entered, it applied to them as well.

However, the Court noted that if there were clear congressional intent to grant the attorney general power to hold aliens ordered removed indefinitely, the Court would be required to give the statute effect. But in this case, legislative history did not clearly demonstrate a congressional intent to authorize potentially permanent detention. As such, the Court provided a loose guideline of no more than six months as the "reasonable time" an alien could be detained.

Conclusion

During the 1950s, as the Red Scare infiltrated the daily lives of all Americans and as McCarthyism entered the English vocabulary, the U.S. government broadened the country's deportation policy and executed extremely harsh restrictions. For instance, the 1952 act removed time limitations on deportation, so no matter how long an immigrant had lived here, if he or she was found to be undocumented, the person could, and usually would, be instantly uprooted. To counteract these drastic effects, Congress did create some exceptions for hardship or persecution-type situations.

In addition to the deportation of groups like the Chinese, who had long been the focus of immigration restrictions, the deportation laws were also used as a means to rid the country of other "undesirables" such as labor organizers and "communist sympathizers." A classic example of that policy, the Palmer Raids in the early 1900s, aimed at "radical organizations," were conducted as modern-day Spanish Inquisitions, where mere suspicion ruled the day. In spite of criticism from some circles, hundreds of people were deported.

For many, the absence of a statute of limitations in the deportation laws was validated when former Nazi war criminals were discovered in the United States decades after World War II. Although time limitations may not bar the use of such removal laws, the passage of time has made prosecution of some alleged Nazi criminals difficult. Faded memories, aging, and the death of potential witnesses has drawn the validity of some of these actions into question.

Most recently, as the United States has initiated removal of individuals such as Kim Ho Ma to places like Cambodia, the morality of the removal authority is brought into question when used to deport individuals to places where human rights violations continue to occur and the deportees originally entered as infants and toddlers.

CHAPTER 12

The Politics of Asylum

The United States takes considerable pride in its long history of providing refuge to foreign nationals displaced by the ravages of war or persecuted by totalitarian governments. Since George Washington's 1783 expression of open arms to the "oppressed and persecuted,"[1] to the admission of Kosovo refugees in 1999, two centuries of similar statements from leaders and citizenry alike have helped to project, even if they did not always accurately reflect, a certain national generosity of spirit.

Refugees and freedom fighters from around the world took such statements at their word. The anti-Mexican government journalist Ricardo Flores Magon fled to the United States, where he founded the Mexican Liberal Party in 1906. In January 1911, he and his brother directed the uprising of Baja California, Mexico, and seized the towns of Mexicali and Tijuana. Also around the turn of the century, Chinese revolutionary Sun Yat Sen entered the United States and began raising funds for rebellion. In 1905, three Korean political exiles fled here to avoid persecution after an abortive coup. Between 1910 and 1918, 541 Korean refugee students fled Japanese persecution. Indian refugees began arriving in 1908, using the United States as the base from which to lead anti-British activities. Expelled from Palestine in 1915, Polish-born David Ben-Gurion traveled to New York. After World War I, he returned to the Middle East and organized support for the future Jewish nation of Israel. The list of refugees to the United States who gained notoriety include Albert Einstein, Thomas Mann, Madeleine Albright, Marc Chagall, and numerous artists, ballet stars, and athletes.

On the surface, U.S. refugee and asylum policies appear generous. But closer examination reveals that those policies, too, have been manipulated to define the acceptable American and, especially, to reject the unacceptable.

Ad Hoc Policies Prior to 1980

Thousands of refugees, sometimes hundreds of thousands, have been escorted here by an array of congressional acts that, on an ad hoc basis, superseded the national quota systems. Prominent among these was the 1948 Displaced Persons Act,[2] which enabled 400,000 refugees and displaced persons to enter, most of whom were from Europe.[3] The 1953 Refugee Relief Act[4] admitted 200,000 refugees, including 38,000 Hungarians and about 2,800 refugees of the Chinese Revolution.[5] In 1959, thousands of Hungarian "freedom fighters" were permitted to enter the United States as refugees, and later were able to apply for lawful permanent resident status.[6] Refugee-escapees were admitted under the act of July 14, 1960, from France, Germany, Belgium, Austria, Italy, Greece, and Lebanon. The law was extended indefinitely by the act of June 28, 1962.[7]

Refugee migration to the United States finds its origin in the noble pursuit of humanitarian-oriented foreign policy objectives. Refugee sympathizers invariably invoke the need to respond compassionately to those in other countries confronted with life-threatening crises. In passing the Displaced Persons Act, Congress explicitly adopted the definition of the terms *displaced person* and *refugee* set forth in the 1946 Constitution of the International Refugee Organization.[8]

> It is the historic policy of the United States to respond to the urgent needs of persons subject to persecution in their homelands, including, where appropriate, humanitarian assistance for their care, and maintenance in asylum areas . . . admission to this country of refugees of special humanitarian concern to the United States, and transitional assistance to refugees in the United States.[9]

The rhetoric notwithstanding, refugee law and policy has reflected the tensions between humanitarian aims and practical domestic and international concerns. These tensions—evident over the years in even the least obvious situations—make plain the link between refugee and immigration policy. In the 1930s, for example, the United States turned away thousands of Jews fleeing Nazi persecution, in large part because of powerful restrictionist views against certain ethnic, religious, and racial groups. Congress and U.S. consular officers consistently resisted Jewish efforts to emigrate and impeded any significant emergency relaxation of limitations on quotas.[10]

The plight of European Jews fleeing Nazi Germany aboard the ship *SS St. Louis* in 1939 is a horrific example of how restrictionist views were manifested toward refugees at the time. In a diabolical propaganda ploy in the spring of 1939, the Nazis had allowed the ship, carrying destitute European Jewish refugees, to leave Hamburg bound for Cuba, but had arranged for corrupt Cuban officials to deny them entry even after they had been granted visas. It was the objective of Nazi propaganda minister Joseph Goebbels to prove that no country wanted the Jews. The *St. Louis* was allowed to discharge only twenty-two passengers and was ordered out of Havana harbor. As it sailed north, it neared U.S. territorial waters. The U.S. Coast Guard warned it away. President Franklin D. Roosevelt had said that the United States could not accept any more European refugees because of immigration quotas, as untold thousands had already fled Nazi terror in Central Europe and many had come to the depression-racked United States.[11]

Nearly two months after leaving Hamburg, and due to the efforts of U.S. Jewish refugee assistance groups, the ship was allowed to land in Holland. Four nations—Great Britain, Holland, Belgium, and France—agreed to accept the refugees. Two months later, the Nazis invaded Poland and the Second World War began. Over 600 of the 937 passengers on the *St. Louis* were killed by the Nazis before the war was over. When the United States refused the *St. Louis* permission to land, many Americans were embarrassed; when the country found out after the war what had happened to the refugees, they were ashamed.

Maintaining a generally restrictive immigration policy during this era, the United States did accept an estimated 105,000 refugees from Nazi Germany in the 1930s (including such luminaries as Albert Einstein); but many more—primarily Jews—were refused entry, and were forced to return to Europe and oblivion. But during the war, the Roosevelt administration brought fewer than 1,000 Jewish refugees out of Europe.[12] A 1939 refugee bill would have rescued 20,000 German children had it not been defeated on the grounds that the children would exceed the German quota.

The Roosevelt administration's record on Hitler's "Final Solution" could not have been more indifferent. Initial reaction to evidence of genocide in Europe was denial. By June 1942, the State Department had reliable reports about the Nazis' systematic extermination of the Jews. Even then, after learning from U.S. officials in Switzerland that Nazis were already killing 6,000 Jews per day at one site in Poland alone, the State Department in February 1943 instructed the officials not to transmit any more information of this kind.[13]

When news of Nazi death camps became public in late November 1942, civic and religious groups began urging President Roosevelt to rescue those Jews still alive, but he refused. Some speculate that he did not want to bring Jewish refugees to the United States for fear he would lose the votes of Jew-haters and immigration opponents in the 1944 election. He also supported the British government, which, under Winston Churchill, bitterly opposed rescuing Jews. The British were afraid that if Jewish refugees demanded entry into Palestine, it could precipitate an Arab rebellion.[14]

As if collectively to deny the tensions between humanitarian aims and practical domestic and international concerns, policy makers showed every sign through the early 1970s of being pleased with their system of policies, laws, and ad hoc decisions. As they saw it, whenever large numbers of deserving refugees appeared, new legislation could be enacted or existing laws and regulations manipulated. That sort of flexibility in a legal regime was, to their minds, to be unashamedly admired. It also permitted policy making consistent with their political preference for refugees from communism.

A closer look at the basic structure of the system and the policies that informed it bears witness to this ideological bias. Consider the 1952 McCarran–Walter Act, which granted the attorney general discretionary authority to "parole" into the United States any alien for "emergent reasons or for reasons deemed strictly in the public interest."[15] Although the original intent was to apply this parole authority on an individual basis,[16] the 1956 Hungarian refugee crisis led to its expanded use to accommodate those fleeing communist oppression.[17] The parole authority was also used to admit more than 15,000 Chinese who fled mainland China after the 1949 communist takeover[18] and more than 145,000 Cubans who sought refuge after Fidel Castro's 1959 coup.[19] Following the fall of the Batista government in Cuba on January 1, 1959, anti-Castro Cubans fled to the United States by the thousands, reaching a rate of 1,500 per week. They entered in a variety of methods: by common carrier, small boats, commandeered aircraft, and even across land boundaries after getting from Cuba to Mexico. The numbers did not readily subside. In fact, in 1962, 125,800 Cubans were inspected, up from 62,500 in 1961. On May 23, 1962, President Kennedy directed that steps be taken to parole in the United States several thousand Chinese from Hong Kong, to assist in alleviating conditions in that colony caused by the influx of persons fleeing from Communist China.

Using the parole authority, the attorney general also permitted over 400,000 refugees from Southeast Asia to enter between 1975 and 1980.[20] By 1980, 99.7 percent of the more than one million refugees admitted under the parole system were from countries under communist rule.[21] These figures betray any claim that refugee policy was based solely on humanitarian considerations.

The preference afforded refugees from communist countries is also reflected in the 1965 reforms, when Congress created the first permanent statutory basis for the admission of refugees. Incorporating prior refugee language into a seventh preference category, conditional entry was provided for refugees fleeing communist-dominated areas or the Middle East. Immigration controls were manifest as well in this category, since it included a worldwide annual quota of 17,400 and a geographic restriction that limited its use through 1977 to countries outside the Western Hemisphere. Until its repeal in 1980, the seventh preference was used by tens of thousands of refugees fleeing China, the Soviet Union, and other communist societies.

Shortly after the creation of the seventh preference, the United States agreed in 1968 to the United Nations Protocol Relating to the Status of Refugees.[22] The protocol obligated compliance with the guidelines established by the United Nations Convention Relating to the Status of Refugees.[23] The ideological and geographic restrictions of the seventh preference, however, were inconsistent with the ideologically neutral protocol, so the United States attempted to jury-rig compliance by using the attorney general's discretionary parole authority.[24] But that authority did not conform to the protocol's principles of neutrality either.

Few complaints about refugee policies and laws were registered on the floors of Congress during most of the 1970s. Some liberal observers did challenge the bias favoring refugees from communist countries, but mostly as it affected applications for political asylum filed by individuals who had already gained entry. As for the greater numbers seeking refugee status from abroad, policy makers seemed satisfied with the status quo. Rather than being disingenuous, this attitude was entirely consistent with their sense of humanitarianism.

After 1975, policy makers became less complacent as Asians began entering in increasing numbers under existing guidelines. Only about 2,800 Chinese benefited before then from the 1953 Refugee Relief Act. Through 1966, about 15,000 were admitted under the parole provision. These low numbers were not perceived as threatening, since the seventh preference category restricted Chinese refugees through its annual worldwide limitation of 17,400 that had to be shared with others. Indeed, until it was repealed in 1980, only 14,000 who fled mainland China were able to take advantage of the seventh preference.

Following the military withdrawal from Vietnam in April 1975, however, the flow of Asian refugees increased markedly almost overnight. Invoking numerical restrictions in the midst of a controversial and devastating war would have been unacceptable; too many understood such inflexibility as morally treacherous and politically high priced. Consequently, the attorney general on several occasions used the parole authority to permit Asians to enter—the first time it was so employed since the 1965 amendments.

Initially, the United States merely wanted to evacuate from Vietnam fewer than 18,000 American dependents and government employees.[25] Immediately before the fall of Saigon in April 1975, however, former employees and others whose lives were threatened were included. These evacuees included approximately 4,000 orphans, 75,000 relatives of American citizens or lawful permanent residents, and 50,000 Vietnamese government officials and employees. Mass confusion permitted many who did not fit into these categories to be evacuated as well.[26] Between April and December 1975, the United Status thus admitted 130,400 Southeast Asian refugees, 125,000 of whom were Vietnamese.[27]

The exodus did not stop there. By 1978 thousands more were admitted under a series of Indochinese Parole Programs, authorized by the attorney general. The number of Southeast Asian refugees swelled to 14,000 a month by the summer of 1979.[28] Following the tightening of Vietnam's grip on Cambodia, several hundred thousand "boat people" and many Cambodian and Laotian refugees entered between 1978 and 1980.[29] In fact, annual arrivals of Southeast Asian refugees had increased exponentially: 20,400 in 1978; 80,700 in 1979; and 166,700 in 1980.[30]

In general, the flow of Southeast Asians was poorly coordinated. The executive branch repeatedly waited until the number of refugees in the countries of "first asylum" (those refugees entered first) reached crisis proportions before declaring an emergency. Only then would a new parole program be instituted.[31] Attacks on the inconsistent treatment of refugees and calls for a consistent policy became commonplace. Many were uncomfortable with the attorney general's considerable unstructured power to admit tens of thousands of refugees under the parole mechanism. Others were genuinely concerned with the government's erratic response to the plight of Southeast Asian refugees.[32] Dissatisfaction with ad hoc admissions provided the impetus for reform and, ultimately, the passage of the 1980 Refugee Act.[33]

The new refugee law was an attempt by Congress to treat refugee and immigration policies as separate and distinct. A major catalyst for the new refugee law was a disturbing anxiety felt by some members of Congress that thousands of Southeast Asians would destabilize many communities.[34] Concerns about controlling immigration have dominated Refugee Act applications ever since.

Ideological and Racial Enforcement
of the 1980 Refugee Act

The enactment of the Refugee Act of 1980 was enormously important. The United States became a party to the United Nations Protocol Relating to the Status of Refugees in 1968, and the legislative history of the 1980 act reveals that it was intended to bring U.S. law into conformity with the protocol. The law eliminated dogmatic language in the prior statute that gave special preference to those fleeing from communist-dominated countries or counties of the Middle East. The new law also established the position of U.S. coordinator of refugee affairs, with the rank of ambassador-at-large.[35] Liberal co-sponsors of the legislation, like Senator Ted Kennedy and Congresswoman Elizabeth Holtzman, heralded the legislation as replacing the old approach that used "geographic and ideological criteria [that was] inherently discriminatory."[36] Yet, soon after the passage of the act, the vivid contrast in the treatment of Haitians, who were being turned away from the shores of south Florida, and Cubans, who were being greeted with open arms, reaffirmed that the nation's refugee policy would continue to be used in a selective manner to define the nation from a particular political perspective.

The law provided a framework for processing two related groups of applicants: refugees and asylees. The basic difference is that a refugee must apply for refugee status abroad, and if granted, may then enter the United States. An asylee is generally someone who enters the United States as a nonimmigrant, applies for asylum, and is deemed eligible. Both asylees and refugees must demonstrate a "well-founded fear of persecution" on account of race, religion, nationality, membership in a particular social group, or adherence to a certain political opinion.

The statute provided that each year the president, after consultation with Congress, would establish the number of refugees that could enter the United States and from which regions of the world. The refugee quota for 1980 was 234,000, but over the years, the quota declined. By 1983 the quota was 90,000, but increased to over 100,000 in 1995. In order to qualify, a refugee applicant must fall into one of the geographic regions of the world that the president and Congress have designated as areas from which individuals may enter as refugees. These areas generally include Africa, East Asia, Europe, Latin America and the Caribbean, the Near East, and South Asia. Special considerations have existed for persons in Vietnam, Cuba, and the former Soviet Union. Asylum, on the other hand, theoretically can be granted to unlimited numbers and to individuals from any country. In practice, until the 1990s no more than 5,000 asylum applications were approved each year, usually less than a third of all applications.

Ten years after the enactment of the law, the INS began to implement a new system for handling asylum applications. Seven asylum offices were opened across the country in Newark, Miami, Chicago, Houston, San Francisco, Los Angeles, and Arlington. An initial corps of eighty-two specially trained asylum officers was recruited to adjudicate all affirmatively filed asylum applications. The officers reported directly to INS headquarters in Washington, D.C., rather than to local INS district directors. The officers were trained by instructors from the INS, the United Nations High Commissioner for Refugees, the private immigration bar, the Canadian asylum office, Amnesty International, Human Rights Watch, and the State Department's Bureau of Human Rights and Humanitarian Affairs. Eventually, the size of the corps grew to over 150 officers.

An applicant who was unsuccessful before an asylum officer, or who had not applied until being arrested for being in the country in violation of the immigration laws (e.g., someone who overstayed a student or visitor visa, or who entered without inspection), could apply for asylum before an immigration judge in the context of a deportation proceeding.

While the asylum approval rates were quite low in the 1980s, there was some increase in the 1990s after the end of the cold war. During the cold war, the asylum process was criticized for purportedly reflecting U.S. foreign policy goals. But in the 1990s, rates of asylum approval remained high for applicants from communist or former communist countries. Natives of noncommunist Syria had the highest overall asylum approval rate (73 percent). The next highest approval rates were the People's Republic of China (52 percent), the former Yugoslavia (50 percent), Cuba (49 percent), Ethiopia (44 percent), Russia (44 percent), and Ukraine (40 percent).

By contrast, the asylum approval rate for Haitians was only 21 percent, even though many Haitian asylum applicants had already been prescreened at Guantanamo Bay, Cuba, and found to have a credible fear of persecution. Certainly more applicants from some countries were winning asylum by the early 1990s than under the old system. For example, in the mid-1980s the asylum approval rate for Salvadorans and Guatemalans was less than 3 percent. In fiscal year 1992, the approval rate for Salvadorans was 28 percent, and for Guatemalans 21 percent. But for 1993, the rates fell to 5 and 7 percent, respectively.[37]

Well-Founded Fear

Besides political bias against applicants from certain countries, the major hurdle for asylum applicants proved to be establishing a "well-founded fear of persecution" to the satisfaction of asylum officers and immigration judges. In the 1987 precedent-setting case INS v. Cardoza-Fonseca,[38] the Supreme Court interpreted the "well-founded fear" standard of proof in asylum cases generously, essentially holding that considering what is at stake, the applicant should be given the benefit of the doubt. In technical terms, the Court ruled that an asylum seeker need not prove that it is more likely than not that he or she will be persecuted if deported.

Prior to 1980, most asylum seekers who made their way across the nation's borders surreptitiously or by entering on nonimmigrant visas had only one recourse: to apply for a statutory form of relief referred to as "withholding of deportation." For many years, the Board of Immigration Appeals and immigration courts required that withholding applicants had to demonstrate a "clear probability" of persecution in order to qualify. The Supreme Court reviewed the "clear probability" standard three years prior to the *Cardoza-Fonseca* case in *INS v. Stevic* (1984).[39] In that case, the Supreme Court held that to qualify for withholding, the "clear probability" standard required an alien to demonstrate that it is "more likely than not" that the alien would be subject to persecution in the country to which he or she would be returned. By using the "more likely than not" language, the Supreme Court determined that the standard of proof most common in civil cases—preponderance of the evidence—was to be applied in withholding of deportation cases, but the Court did not discuss the standard of proof for asylum.

When *Cardoza-Fonseca* reached the Court three years later, the government argued that the "well-founded fear" standard that Congress attached to the new asylum provision in 1980 should be governed by the "clear probability" standard of the withholding provision that existed prior to the 1980 reforms. The Supreme Court disagreed:

> Congress used different, broader language to define the term "refugee" as used in [the new asylum provision] than it used to describe the class of aliens who have a right to withholding of deportation. . . . The Act's establishment of a broad class of refugees who are eligible for a discretionary grant of asylum, and a narrower class of aliens who are given a statutory right not to be deported to the country where they are in danger, mirrors the provisions of the United Nations Protocol Relating to the Status of Refugees, which provided the motivation for the enactment of the Refugee Act of 1980.[40]

In construing the meaning of "well-founded fear," the Court recognized that the eligibility determination turns to some extent on the subjective mental state of the alien as well as the objective evidence presented. Thus, "one can certainly have a well-founded fear of an event happening when there is less than a 50% chance of the occurrence taking place."[41] To emphasize that the standard must not require rigorous proof that persecution will definitely result if the applicant is deported, the Court noted:

> There is simply no room in the United Nations' definition for concluding that because an applicant only has 10% chance of being shot, tortured, or otherwise persecuted, that he or she has no "well-founded fear" of the event happening. . . . A moderate interpretation of the "well-founded fear" standard would indicate "that so long as an objective situation is established by the evidence, it need not be shown that the situation will probably result in persecution, but it is enough that persecution is a reasonable possibility."[42]

After the Court's announcement of a generous standard for asylum seekers in *Cardoza-Fonseca*, immigrant and refugee rights advocates looked forward to a higher and consistent approval rate for asylum applicants irrespective of political bias that the United States might have toward certain countries. That never happened.

The hope for a uniform, generous standard for determining well-founded fear after *Cardoza-Fonseca* was never attained. The decision-making process in the asylum arena continued to have inconsistent results. In the 1990 documentary film, *Well-Founded Fear*, a core of asylum officers clearly do not apply the deferential standard announced by the Supreme Court in *Cardoza-Fonseca*. Instead, the officers seem completely focused on questions of credibility that provide a convenient vehicle for imposing a preponderance of the evidence (more-likely-than-not) standard of proof.

Consider the words of one asylum officer from the film, Kevin:

I [did not grant asylum and] referred the case to the immigration judge. I found [the applicant] not consistent. There were things in there that were inconsistencies [in] his testimony. There was a time when he said he was brought by two men into a van, and drove around town for two hours during which time he was beaten. And then this is where the inconsistency was. He said "no, no no, there was three of them . . . one was driving and two were in the back with me." So that was enough for me. . . . But, you know, that inconsistency again, if that was in another case, maybe I wouldn't have clung onto it, I may have saw past it. But for some reason in this case I didn't. That's because I found him not to be credible. . . .

This is maybe the 450th time that I've interviewed a similar case, because I've had this experience, I'm seeing it totally different. Totally different story. You sat in on one case that I had, and I made a credibility determination. First he said there were two people in the van, then he said there were three, and I determined that this person wasn't credible. Aside from the horrible story that he was detained and beaten. . . . And I've referred people [to the immigration judge], women who have told me that they were raped, and that they've been abused. And I didn't [grant] because they didn't fall within the framework of what it takes to get asylum. I did it because I found that they weren't credible. . . . And I know in the beginning, as I said earlier, that I used to grant a whole lot more, but after you do this for awhile you become much more critical, and you become much more, very aware of inconsistencies, and I hope that's what it is, right? I mean I know that it could just be the fact that you're just very jaded. And how do you know where one begins and the other ends? If I admitted that I was jaded, wouldn't I then be saying that I shouldn't be doing this job anymore? So I say that I have a more acute understanding of credibility issues.

One of the more sympathetic asylum officers, Mary-Louise, confided:

How do you decide whether someone is telling the truth or not? It's not simple. You're never sure, that's the problem. If you are pretty sure that it's not the truth, then at least you're in the comfortable position that the decision is based on something that's real. But, in a case like this when it's just plain fuzzy, I have to talk to somebody else about it, to get another perspective. That's life, it's real life. We're dealing with real people, in real situations; yes, they stay fuzzy forever. And we still have to make a decision, based on fuzziness!

Another sympathetic officer, Gerald, explains why he did not approve the claim by an Algerian applicant:

I think that the woman's telling the truth, and I think Algeria's a dangerous place, but she didn't establish a well founded fear of future persecution to me. She had lived there for a significant length of time since her last trouble. There was *confusion over dates*, which I couldn't get past. And basically I didn't think that she established a well-founded fear. That combined with a lack of past persecution made me refer the case. (Emphasis added)

These examples illustrate the constant focus on credibility by asylum officers. In essence, the officers asked: "prove to me that you are telling the truth, before I will grant your asylum claim." While this is seemingly reasonable, in the asylum context the approach raises serious questions. These comments (as illustrated vividly in the film) reveal the total absence of consideration of the impact that posttraumatic stress disorder has on refugees. The officers demonstrated no understanding of how the trauma and threat of persecution can result in seemingly inconsistent accounts of historical events, dates, and experiences. Immigration practitioners and crisis counselors know that several meetings are often necessary to bring out the full details of the traumatic experiences that asylum applicants have withstood.

The demand for precise testimony at the risk of being deemed not credible is the equivalent of demanding proof that something is more likely than not to be true—the standard rejected in *Cardoza-Fonseca*. Certainly, officers should be determining whether or not the applicant's story is believable, but that is only part of the task. Given available resources, one would think that the asylum corps has more at its disposal than the application and testimony before it in individual cases. Human rights reports, State Department reports, independent sources, and public information are readily available to adjudicators searching to verify claims. Demanding precision in testimony seems more than what was required in *Cardoza-Fonseca*, where the Court seemed satisfied with evidence that a reasonable possibility of persecution exists. The natural impulse for adjudicators to want to be convinced that what is being alleged is truthful or not is not what the Court demanded in *Cardoza-Fonseca*.

Asylum officer Gerald made this statement in *Well-Founded Fear* after interviewing an applicant for the second time:

> I have to go back and look at . . . how well I think the explanations stand up. So I've got that, which I didn't have before. He testified to the same things on two different occasions. I need to go back and to compare . . . whether he said the same things. So I feel a whole lot better about it now than I did before I interviewed him the second time. This is still not a case . . . whatever I decide, it's not going to be a case that I, I'm sure of. I mean there are some that you feel pretty confident of when you're—but this is not one of them. I think that . . . if nothing surprises me, I'll probably grant the man.

The first part of this statement is typical of asylum officers and immigration judges in their concern over the issue of credibility: "I need to go back to compare . . . whether he said the same things." The second half of the statement is another key, however. This is not a case he is "sure of." This is not a case about which he feels "pretty confident." Yet, he will "probably grant" the application. This is perfectly consistent with the spirit of the asylum statute and the well-founded fear standard of proof. As noted in *Cardoza-Fonseca*, the decision maker does not have to be convinced that the applicant will be persecuted. A showing that persecution is more likely than not to happen is not required. As long as a reasonable possibility of persecution occurring is demonstrated—even a 10 percent chance—that is sufficient; they need not be "pretty confident" that persecution will occur; they need not be "sure" that persecution will occur. Thus, granting this claim should not be a problem for Gerald even if he is not "sure" or is not "pretty confident" that persecution will occur, as long as he feels better about the information provided.

The Board of Immigration Appeals (which reviews decisions of immigration judges) appeared to be adopting the approach to asylum mandated by the Supreme Court's *Cardoza-Fonseca* decision, at least with respect to applicants who only have their own testimony to go on. In *Matter of Mogharrabi* (1987),[43] the BIA explained that an asylum applicant need not always present corroborating evidence of the claim because given the circumstances, such evidence is impossible to obtain in most cases. This standard was codified in the regulations: "The testimony of the applicant, if credible, may be sufficient to sustain the burden of proof without corroboration."[44] *Matter of Mogharrabi* established the reasonable person standard for asylum cases, finding that well-founded fear exists if a reasonable person in like circumstances would fear persecution. *Mogharrabi* is often cited as the applicable standard. Yet, when it purported to apply the standard to facts of individual cases, the BIA appeared to be applying a standard of proof that was much more demanding than the reasonable person standard.

Consider the typical scenario. The decision maker (either the asylum officer or the immigration judge) listens to the applicant, looks at the application, and denies the application because the judge or officer simply does not believe the applicant. Perhaps that makes sense to the casual observer, but that is not the intent behind the humanitarian nature of asylum as recognized by the Supreme Court in *Cardoza-Fonseca*. As Paragraph 196 of the United Nations Handbook explains:

> It is a general legal principle that the burden of proof lies on the person submitting a claim. Often, however, an applicant may not be able to support his [or her] statements by documentary or other proof, and cases in which an applicant can provide evidence of all his [or her] statements will be the exception rather than the rule . . . if the applicant's account appears credible, he [or she] should, unless there are good reasons to the contrary, be given the benefit of the doubt.

Put differently, if nothing contradicts the applicant's statements and the statements, if taken to be true, establish a well-founded fear of persecution, then asylum should be granted. If the person "appears credible," then he or she should be afforded "the benefit of the doubt."

The BIA often denies asylum claims by upholding findings that the applicant lacks credibility (negative credibility findings) based upon minor inconsistencies and perceived discrepancies.[45] For example, in *Matter of Y—B—* (1998),[46] the BIA noted that in the asylum application completed prior to the hearing, the applicant stated that he had been "badly mistreated by the Mauritanian army" but failed to mention the arrest and detention he later described in testimony at the hearing. In other words, the application did not contain all the information that was brought out at the hearing, and that formed the basis of the BIA's ruling that the applicant was not credible. The problem with that position is that none of the statements made by the applicant were inconsistent. In fact, many applicants who complete their own applications merely summarize their claims on the application form, and elaborate on the summary at their hearing.

Furthermore, anyone who has interviewed an asylum applicant knows that if more time is spent with an applicant (often over a period of weeks or months), more details are unearthed, in large part because of the applicant's difficulty or hesitance in coming forward with all the information due to posttraumatic stress disorder.

In *Matter of A—S—*(1998),[47] a majority of the BIA was satisfied with an immigration judge's finding that the applicant is not credible if the immigration judge's finding is "reasonable." But the dissent points out that there is a problem with that type of approach in asylum cases because it means that an outcome favorable to the applicant could have been reasonable as well. And in asylum, if a reasonable person would fear persecution, then the well-founded fear standard is satisfied. So the analysis should not be whether the immigration judge's finding is reasonable; the focus should be on whether a ruling in favor of the applicant is reasonable; if so, the standard has been met.

Besides the well-founded fear standard problem, some adjudicators demonstrate a bad taste for asylum claims. The outcomes of asylum applications have varied widely from one immigration judge to another. Wide disparities in asylum approval/denial rates among immigration judges have been found. Data (obtained via the Freedom of Information Act [FOIA]) from the Department of Justice detailed the asylum approval/denial rates of immigration judges across the country over a five-year period. Some judges granted two-thirds or more of the asylum applications before them, while others granted fewer than 5 percent. In one district where two immigration judges handled every asylum case for four states, the approval rate for both judges was less than 4 percent. Disparities among nationalities of asylum seekers and from region to region were also apparent.

The negative attitude of some immigration judges toward asylum seekers is also telling—certainly not in the humanitarian spirit of the law as suggested in *Cardoza-Fonseca*. Consider the case of Mumin Ibrahim, who spent four years in INS custody after arriving at New York's Kennedy Airport from Somalia in December 1994. He fled Somalia after rival clansmen had murdered his parents, two brothers, and a sister. Another sister was gang raped in front of him. He was detained and tortured. Yet, as Ibrahim recounted those horrific experiences to a visitor in 1998 in the Lehigh County, Pennsylvania jail, he saved his harshest words for the immigration judge who had been assigned to evaluate his case. "I've never been in court before in my life," he said. "The judge wasn't neutral. He tried to intimidate me. I would rather die in Somalia than go before him again."

Seven months later, the BIA spared Ibrahim. In spite of its rigorous credibility standards the BIA overturned the judge's decision that Ibrahim lacked credibility. The BIA did not bother to send the case back to the judge; instead, the BIA granted the man asylum and ordered him freed. The judge in question was Donald V. Ferlise, the same immigration judge who had ruled that Fauziya Kassindja of Togo was not credible when she told her story of female genital mutilation. He was overturned in that celebrated case as well. Ferlise granted fewer than 15 percent of the asylum cases before him.

Discouraging Haitians, Guatemalans, and Salvadorans

In addition to the questionable strict interpretation of the asylum standard, U.S. and INS officials have used other means of discouraging, or at least not accommodating, certain potential asylum applicants. Consider the plight of Haitian refugees in the 1980s.

In response to the repressive Duvalier regime that caused political and economic havoc in Haiti in the 1970s, many Haitians fled to the United States seeking refuge. Large numbers sought asylum once they reached the shores of Florida. A backlog developed, so INS officials implemented an accelerated program to deal with the situation. The program—termed the "Haitian program"—embodied the government's response to the tremendous backlog of Haitian deportation cases that had accumulated in the INS Miami district office by the summer of 1978. By June of that year, between 6,000 and 7,000 unprocessed Haitian deportation cases were pending in the Miami office. These staggering numbers were not the result of a massive influx of Haitians to south Florida over a short period. Although significant numbers of Haitians had entered the United States from Haiti and the Bahamas in the spring of 1978, the backlog was primarily attributable to a slow trickle of Haitians over a ten-year period and to the confessed inaction of the INS in dealing with these aliens.

Many officials provided input in the planning process of the Haitian program. Assigned by the deputy commissioner of the INS with the task of assessing the Haitian situation in Miami, INS Regional Commissioner Armand J. Salturelli submitted the recommendation, among others, that processing could be expedited by ceasing the practice of suspending deportation hearings upon the making of an asylum claim. Salturelli acknowledged that this would contravene internal operations procedures, but suggested that those procedures should be canceled or "at least be suspended insofar as Haitians are concerned." One July 1978 report from the Intelligence Division of INS to the associate director of enforcement advised in absolute terms that the Haitians were "economic" and not political refugees and, in belated recognition of the obvious, warned the Enforcement Division that favorable treatment of these Haitians would encourage further immigration. Associate Director of Enforcement Charles Sava later visited Miami to find space for holding an increased number of deportation hearings and to discuss with Miami personnel the processing of Haitians. Out of those discussions arose recommended deterrence measures, which Sava outlined in a letter to Deputy Commissioner Noto. These included detention of arriving Haitians likely to abscond, blanket denials of work permits for Haitians, swift expulsion of Haitians from the United States, and enforcement actions against smugglers.

Planning of the Haitian program culminated in a memorandum sent on August 20, 1978, by Deputy Commissioner Noto to INS Commissioner Leonel J. Castillo. The memo explained the basic mechanics of the accelerated processing already being implemented in the Miami district office. Among the specifics set forth were the assignment of additional immigration judges to Miami, the instructions to immigration judges to effect a threefold increase in productivity, and orders for the blanket issuance of show cause orders in all pending Haitian deportation cases.

In accordance with the goal of high productivity demanded of the Miami office, Acting District Director Gullage issued a memorandum to all personnel in the office, stating, "processing of these cases cannot be delayed in any manner or in any way. All supervisory personnel are hereby ordered to take whatever action they deem necessary to keep these cases moving through the system." The Haitian cases were processed at an unprecedented rate. Prior to the Haitian program only between one and ten deportation hearings were conducted each day. During the program, immigration judges held fifty-five hearings per day, or approximately eighteen per judge. At the program's peak the schedule of deportation hearings increased to as many as eighty per day.

At the show cause or deportation hearing, the immigration judges refused to suspend the hearing when an asylum claim was advanced, requiring the Haitians instead to respond to the pleadings in the show cause order and proceed to a finding of deportability. The order entered by the judge allowed the Haitians ten days to file an asylum claim with the district director, then ten days to request withholding of deportation from the immigration judge if the asylum deadline was not met. Failure to seek withholding in a timely manner effected automatic entry of a deportation order.

Deportation hearings were not the only matter handled during the Haitian program. Asylum interviews also were scheduled at the rate of forty per day. Immigration officers who formerly had worked at the airport were enlisted as hearing officers for these interviews. Prior to the program such interviews had lasted an hour and a half; during the program the officer devoted approximately one-half hour to each Haitian. In light of the time-consuming process of communication through interpreters, only fifteen minutes of substantive dialogue took place. Consistent with the result-oriented program designed to achieve numerical goals in processing, the Travel Control section in the Miami office recorded the daily totals of asylum applications processed. The tally sheet contained space only for the total number of denials; there was no column for recording grants of asylum.

Hearings on requests for withholding deportation also were being conducted simultaneously with asylum and deportation hearings, at several different locations. It was not unusual for an attorney representing Haitians to have three hearings at the same hour in different buildings; this kind of scheduling conflict was a daily occurrence for attorneys throughout the Haitian program. The INS was fully aware that only about twelve attorneys were available to represent the thousands of Haitians being processed, and that scheduling made it impossible for counsel to attend the hearings. It anticipated the scheduling conflicts that in fact occurred. Nevertheless, the INS decided that resolving the conflicts was "too cumbersome for us to handle" and adopted the attitude that everything would simply work out.

Under these circumstances, a federal court of appeals concluded that the INS had knowingly made it impossible for Haitians and their attorneys to prepare and file asylum applications in a timely manner. The court found that adequate preparation of an asylum application required between ten and forty hours of an attorney's time. The court further estimated that if each of the attorneys available to represent the Haitians "did nothing during a 40 hour week except prepare [asylum applications], they would have been able to devote only about 2 hours to each client."

The results of the accelerated program adopted by INS are revealing. None of the over 4,000 Haitians processed during this program were granted asylum.

In the end, the federal court struck down the accelerated program as a violation of procedural due process. The government was forced to submit a procedurally fair plan for the orderly reprocessing of the asylum applications of the Haitian applicants who had not been deported.[48]

Poverty and infant mortality rates in Haiti ranked the highest in the Western Hemisphere, and the flow of refugees continued. But rather than recognize the crisis and the assistance that the refugees needed, the United States sought new strategies for denying asylum. The government's new brainstorm was that if the Haitians could be turned away on the high seas before they reached U.S. shores, they could not then seek asylum.

On September 29, 1981, President Ronald Reagan authorized the interdiction of vessels containing undocumented aliens from Haiti on the high seas. The president based this action on the argument that undocumented aliens posed a "serious national problem detrimental to the interests of the United States," and that international cooperation to intercept vessels trafficking in such migrants was a necessary and proper means of ensuring the effective enforcement of U.S. immigration laws. By executive order, the Coast Guard was directed "to return the vessel and its passengers to the country from which it came, when there is reason to believe that an offense is being committed against the United States immigration laws." The Coast Guard's interdiction was only allowed outside the territorial waters of the United States.

In *Haitian Refugee Center v. Gracey*,[49] a federal court upheld the actions of the president, holding that the president has inherent authority to act to protect the United States from harmful undocumented immigration. Since the program was carried out pursuant to an agreement with Haiti, this was further indication that the action came within matters of foreign relations that should not be disturbed by the court. The court ruled that the action did not violate the United States's obligations under the Refugee Act of 1980 or the country's obligations under the United Nations Protocol Relating to the Status of Refugees.

At the height of civil turmoil in Guatemala, El Salvador, and Nicaragua in the 1980s, thousands of migrants from those countries also sought refuge in the United States. The cold war affected the treatment that these refugees received. After the left-leaning Sandinistas (led by Daniel Ortega) took control in Nicaragua, the United States supported rebels (known as the *contras*) who were trying to regain power. Reagan administration officials commonly referred to these rebels as *freedom fighters*. Nicaraguans who fled their country during that period were given asylum at a higher rate than most, and deportation was not enforced against Nicaraguans who were denied asylum or who simply wanted to remain in the United States. On the other hand, the United States had good relations with the right-wing governments of Guatemala and El Salvador. The rebels in those countries were referred to as *guerrillas* who engaged in terrorist tactics. Refugees fleeing the civil strife in Guatemala and El Salvador were quickly labeled "economic migrants," who were generally denied asylum and deported. As in the case with Haitians, an INS strategy was implemented to discourage these entrants from applying for asylum as well.

In a typical year like 1986, the INS apprehended 1.8 million undocumented aliens. The Border Patrol accounted for 94 percent of the total apprehensions. Mexican nationals accounted for 94 percent of the undocumented aliens arrested while Salvadorans comprised 1.1 percent of the total INS apprehensions in 1986. A lawsuit filed against the INS in the 1980s, *Orantes-Hernandez v. Smith*,[50] revealed that immigration officials engaged in a strategy that foreclosed the opportunity to apply for asylum for arrested Salvadorans.

Generally, after aliens were apprehended, either Border Patrol agents or INS officers processed them. INS processing of detained aliens consisted of an interrogation combined with the completion of various forms, including Form I-213, "Record of Deportable Alien," and the presentation of Form I-274, "Request for Voluntary Departure." Although the arrested Salvadorans were eligible to apply for political asylum and to request a deportation hearing prior to their departure from the United States, the vast majority of Salvadorans apprehended signed voluntary departure agreements that commenced a summary removal process. Once a person signed for voluntary departure in the course of INS processing, he or she was subject to removal from the United States as soon as transportation could be arranged. A person given administrative voluntary departure in this manner never had a deportation hearing, the only forum before which the detained person could seek political asylum and mandatory withholding of deportation.

The *Orantes-Hernandez* court found that the widespread acceptance of voluntary departure was due in large part to the coercive effects of the practices and procedures employed by the INS and the unfamiliarity of most Salvadorans with their rights under U.S. immigration laws. INS agents directed, intimidated, or coerced Salvadorans in custody who had no expressed desire to return to El Salvador to sign Form I-274 for voluntary departure. INS agents used a variety of techniques to procure voluntary departure, ranging from subtle persuasion to outright threats and misrepresentations. Many Salvadorans were intimidated or coerced to accept voluntary departure even when they had unequivocally expressed a fear of returning to El Salvador. Even when an individual refused to sign Form I-214, "Waiver of Rights," INS officers felt that they could present the person with the voluntary departure form.

The court also found that INS processing officers engaged in a pattern and practice of misrepresenting the meaning of political asylum and of giving improper and incomplete legal advice, which denied arrested Salvadorans meaningful understanding of the options presented and discouraged them from exercising available rights. INS officers and agents routinely advised Salvadorans of the negative aspects of choosing a deportation hearing without informing them of the advantages of other options. Without informing them that voluntary departure could be requested at a deportation hearing, INS officers advised detainees that if they did not sign for voluntary departure they could be formally deported from the United States, and that such a deportation would preclude their legal reentry without the pardon of the attorney general.

INS officers and agents routinely told Salvadoran detainees that if they applied for asylum they would remain in detention for a long time, without mentioning the possibility of release on bond. Similarly, without advising that an immigration judge could lower the bond amount and that there were bond agencies that could provide assistance, INS agents regularly told detainees that if they did not sign for voluntary departure they would remain detained until bond was posted. Some agents told individuals the monetary bond amount they could expect or the bond amount given to other Salvadorans, without telling them that the bond amount ultimately depended upon the circumstances of the individual.

INS officers commonly told detainees that if they applied for asylum, the application would be denied, or that Salvadorans did not get asylum. INS officers and agents made it seem that Salvadorans ultimately would be deported regardless of the asylum application. INS officers and agents misrepresented eligibility for asylum by saying that it was only given to guerrillas or to soldiers. INS processing agents or officers further discouraged Salvadorans from applying for asylum by telling them that the information on the application would be sent to El Salvador, and stating that asylum applicants would never be able to return to El Salvador. INS processing officers also used the threat of transfer to remote locations as a means of discouraging detained Salvadorans from exercising their rights to a hearing and to pursuing asylum claims.

Furthermore, INS agents often did not allow Salvadorans to consult with counsel prior to signing the voluntary departure forms, although they acknowledged that aliens had this right. Even those Salvadorans fortunate enough to secure legal representation were often unable to avoid voluntary departure, as the INS's practice was to refuse to recognize the authority of counsel until a formal notice of representation (Form G-28) was filed. Due to the rapid processing of Salvadoran detainees, it was often physically impossible for counsel to locate a client and file Form G-28 before the client was removed from the country.

In conclusion, the *Orantes-Hernandez* court noted:

> The record before this Court establishes that INS engages in a pattern and practice of pressuring or intimidating Salvadorans who remain detained after the issuance of an OSC to request voluntary departure or voluntary deportation to El Salvador. There is substantial evidence of INS detention officers urging, cajoling, and using friendly persuasion to pressure Salvadorans to recant their requests for a hearing and to return voluntarily to El Salvador. That this conduct is officially condoned, even in the face of complaints, demonstrates that it is a *de facto* policy. The existence of a policy of making daily announcements about the availability of voluntary departure, coupled with the acknowledgement that the policy is designed to free-up scarce detention space, supports the conclusion that INS detention officers make a practice of pressuring detained Salvadorans to return to El Salvador. This conduct is not the result of isolated transgressions by a few overzealous officers, but, in fact, is a widespread and pervasive practice akin to a policy. . . .

This pattern of misconduct flows directly from the attitudes and misconceptions of INS officers and their superiors as to the merits of Salvadoran asylum claims and the motives of class members who flee El Salvador and enter this country.

Thus, the court ordered INS and Border Patrol officers to stop their threatening and misleading behavior revealed in the case.

The bias that INS officials and asylum corps officers exhibited toward Guatemalan and Salvadoran asylum applicants was further exposed in *American Baptist Churches v. Thornburgh* (1991),[51] a class action filed on their behalf. As the *New York Times* reported on the case:

Such applications have long presented the Government with an embarrassing choice. The United States supports the Governments of El Salvador and Guatemala, and at the same time it is asked by asylum applicants to find that they have a "well-founded fear of persecution" if they are returned home. Every approval of an application for political asylum thus amounts to an admission that the United States is aiding governments that violate the civil rights of their own citizens.

Since 1980 the Government has denied 97 percent of applications for political asylum by El Salvadorans and 99 percent of those by Guatemalans. During the same time, applications for political asylum by Eastern Europeans, Nicaraguans and residents of other countries have a high percentage of approval. For example, 76 percent of applications by residents of the Soviet Union were approved, as were 64 percent of those by residents of China.[52]

A settlement was reached requiring the INS to readjudicate the asylum claims of certain Salvadorans and Guatemalans who were present in the United States as of 1990, and who had sought immigration benefits. The case, known as the "*ABC* litigation," began in 1985 as a nationwide class action on behalf of Salvadorans and Guatemalans. The plaintiffs alleged that the INS and the Executive Office of Immigration Review were biased in their asylum adjudication process for those two nationalities. Under the settlement, Salvadorans were eligible for new asylum interviews. New asylum interviews for *ABC* class members began on April 7, 1997.

But although INS officials may have been forced to provide some procedural safeguards to applicants, many potential asylum applicants were thwarted in other ways. Holding asylum applicants in custody with high bonds (or with any bond for some indigents) discouraged many applicants. Beyond that, INS engaged in a policy of transferring detainees to remote areas of the country where little, if any, pro bono legal assistance was available. The *Orantes-Hernandez* court was critical of that procedure when an attorney-client privilege had already been established. But in *Committee of Central American Refugees v. INS*, (1988)[53] a federal court refused to stop transfers of Guatemalan and Salvadoran refugees to remote areas of the Southwest, especially if there was some free legal services available in those areas:

Aliens detained at El Centro [California] or Florence [Arizona] have ample opportunity to bond out, obtain counsel, and apply for political asylum. If the alien has requested a bond redetermination, a hearing is scheduled shortly after his arrival at the facility. Before the bond hearing, the alien can arrange for an attorney to provide representation in-person or by telephone. The judge will consider, on an equal basis, all equities possessed by the alien anywhere in the United States. An alien's bond may be paid at an INS office anywhere in the country; bonds are paid at the San Francisco District Office for El Centro detainees on a daily basis. After an alien has bonded out of either El Centro or Florence, the immigration court will routinely grant a motion for change of venue to the court with jurisdiction over the alien's new location.

If a detainee at El Centro or Florence is not represented at his initial bond redetermination hearing, the IJ provides a list of free legal services available and strongly recommends that the alien find an attorney. Legal services lists are also posted at each facility. After furnishing the list, the judge continues the bond hearing and calendars the hearing on the Order to Show Cause (also known as a "master calendar hearing" or "status call") for a fixed date. When an El Centro detainee is represented, his bond and deportation hearings are scheduled on a separate calendar for the pertinent attorney.

The problem was that legal services in El Centro and Florence are very limited.

On the other hand, in *Louis v. Meissner* (1981),[54] the INS practice of transferring Haitian asylum applicants from Florida to various remote parts of the country was stopped. Seven hundred Haitians were transferred to a former army base in a remote area of Puerto Rico; fifty to a facility in the West Virginia coal fields; and 200 to Kentucky. All of these facilities were in desolate, remote, and hostile areas, with a paucity of legal support, lacking Creole-speaking individuals to act as translators. Some of the facilities had no telephones. Many of the detainees were not advised on the procedure to file asylum claims; some were given inaccurate or misleading information. In contrast, they were removed from Miami, a city with a substantial immigration bar and volunteer lawyers. However, INS did not give up on the strategy, and a few years later in the mid-1980s erected a thousand-bed Alien Detention Center in Oakdale, Louisiana, away from any area that might have attorneys who could represent detained aliens.[55] Around the same time, facilities in Florence, Arizona—a remote part of the state—were also established, which became the subject of the *Committee of Central American Refugees v. INS* case.[56]

Legislative Restraints in 1996

The creation of the asylum officer corps in 1990 enabled the INS to process applications at a higher rate. As the corps expanded and became more experienced, its efficiency increased. As Table 12-1 illustrates, from 1991 to 1993, the numbers of approvals were in the 2,000 to 5,000 range per year, but after that, the number of approvals steadily increased. The table also illustrates the relatively high volume of applications that was received each year from 1992 to 1995—reaching close to 150,000 in 1995.

In spite of the limitations on asylum resulting from such strategies as strict interpretations of the "well-founded fear" standard, interdiction on the high seas, detention, and transfers to remote locations in many cases, as the number of asylum applications

TABLE 12-1   Asylum Officer Corps Adjudications, 1991–2000

Year	Cases Received	Cases Completed	Cases Approved	Cases Denied	Cases adjudi- cated	Percent Approved
1991–95	593,609	205,161	31,661	70,055	137,307	23
1991	56,310	16,552	2,108	4,167	6,275	34
1992	103,964	21,996	3,919	6,506	10,425	38
1993	142,680	31,970	5,053	17,610	22,664	22
1994	143,225	46,527	8,133	28,183	36,336	22
1995	147,430	88,116	12,448	13,589	61,607	20
1996–2000	327,686	412,770	63,305	11,045	228,837	28
1996	116,882	105,000	13,505	2,358	61,672	22
1997	76,827	117,001	10,162	2,304	52,634	19
1998	49,110	79,629	9,930	3,017	42,416	23
1999	38,091	52,712	13,159	1,620	34,218	38
2000	46,776	58,428	16,549	1,746	37,897	44

increased, critics of the asylum system grew louder. They charged that applicants who had no real fear of persecution, but who simply were seeking a way to remain in the United States and to obtain employment authorization, were abusing the system. Ultimately, a segment on the television show "60 Minutes" on March 14, 1993, proved to be a catalyst for changing asylum policies and procedures.

The story emphasized the fact that Sheik Omar Abdel-Rahman, who was allegedly connected to the World Trade Center bombing in 1993, had applied for political asylum. The tone of the story was set at the beginning of the program when the preview quoted a representative of the immigration restriction group, Federation of American Immigration Reform (FAIR): "Every single person on the planet Earth, if he gets into this country, can stay indefinitely by saying two magic words: political asylum." That preview made it seem that asylum seekers can effortlessly create a new life—whether they are persecuted or not. That impression was reinforced throughout the program by continual references to the "two magic words" even though the program ultimately recognized that asylum seekers could stay in the United States only until the INS gets around to hearing their claims. FAIR was the only independent organization quoted in the story, even though FAIR is widely known to oppose political asylum and advocates other restrictionist views toward immigration. The one-sided program did not include different perspectives.

The facts presented in the story also were erroneous. For example, the story claimed that of the 100,000 applications filed each year, only 1 or 2 percent of the applications were legitimately fleeing persecution. In fact, in 1992, immigration courts approved 19 percent of the applications before them, and the asylum officer corps approved 38 percent.

Soon after the report aired, lawmakers examined the asylum process and declared that the system needed to be changed. They charged that the asylum system was out of control. Detractors argued that many asylum seekers were using the system as a short-cut to permanent residency. Stories of the World Trade Center bombers were cited to illustrate that asylum seekers were not to be trusted and were unworthy of protection. They asserted that most refugees were economic migrants rather than victims of political persecution.

Before Congress enacted legislation, the INS itself responded to the concerns in January 1995 by making significant changes to asylum procedures. The new regulations essentially speeded up the process by streamlining procedures. More asylum officers and immigration judges were hired. The new regulations also eliminated the automatic grant of a work permit when an asylum application was filed. Permits would not be granted unless the applicant received asylum or the INS did not act on the application for 180 days. Consequently, the prospect of receiving work authorization, long perceived as a magnet for frivolous asylum claims, was eliminated.

The INS changes had tremendous effect. New applications declined by more than 60 percent. In 1994, before the reforms took effect, more than 140,000 affirmative asylum applications were filed with INS. In 1996, the year after the regulations took effect, the number dropped to 116,000. The processing time was reduced to about 60 days (compared with at least several months in most districts prior to the changes). The number of asylum cases completed annually almost doubled.

In spite of these effective regulatory changes, Congress proceeded to make even more radical changes. The Illegal Immigrant Reform and Immigrant Responsibility Act (IIRAIRA), enacted in September 1996, created procedures to remove aliens appearing at the border without proper documentation and required that anyone desiring asylum must file within one year of entering the country. Both the Clinton administration and the refugee rights community strenuously opposed any deadline. Their opposition succeeded only in lengthening its duration from thirty days (as originally proposed) to one year.

Before IIRAIRA, a person could apply for asylum at any time. The lack of a deadline made sense because many obstacles prevent most refugees from applying for asylum immediately after entering the United States. Refugees usually flee without their property or savings and often must spend their first weeks or months in search of food, shelter, and basic social services. Frequently, they do not speak English. Many have been traumatized by recent imprisonment or torture and by separation from their homeland and family. Many are in poor mental and physical health. Few know about American asylum law. When they learn about it, they discover that a very detailed personal narrative to prove that the applicant really has a well-founded fear of persecution must accompany a successful asylum application. The filing must include pages of evidence to corroborate the facts alleged in the narrative, such as birth and marriage certificates, arrest records, affidavits of eyewitnesses, and records from refugee camps. These records may take months or years to compile. Even if friends or family members can obtain copies of documents, hostile governments may intercept international mail. Therefore, many applicants hesitate for a long time before asking others to put themselves at risk by requesting corroborating records. Representation is not readily available. In the years before IIRAIRA was enacted, fewer than half of the successful asylum applicants represented by volunteers from the Lawyers Committee for Human Rights applied for asylum within their first year in the United States.

The expedited procedures were designed to remove aliens who arrived in the United States without proper travel documents or who were suspected of carrying documents procured by fraud. A single immigration officer at an airport or other port of entry screens individuals to determine whether they intend to apply for asylum or fear persecution. If the officer thinks that the person does not fear persecution, the officer can order the person summarily removed from the country and bar the person from reentering the country for five years, without any further hearing or judicial review. This power is so unprecedented that former INS Commissioner Doris Meissner conceded it lacks normal due process protections to guard against abuses.[57] This provision marked a radical change from prior law; the new procedures gives lower-level INS inspections officers one of the most powerful and awesome authorities entrusted to the INS: the authority to remove an individual from the United States. The INS has now deported numerous refugees who have suffered past persecution or have a well-founded fear of persecution upon returning to their home country without giving them an opportunity to apply for asylum protection. The Lawyers Committee for Human Rights and other organizations have discovered many stories of such deportations, including cases in which the aliens had explained to INS inspectors that they were afraid to return home. In one case, a U.S. citizen, Sharon McKnight, mistakenly was subjected to expedited removal back to Jamaica, where she had been visiting![58]

Those persons arriving who do express fear or want to apply for asylum immediately are transferred to a detention center. They may be placed in handcuffs, even shackles, at the airport, then transported to detention centers or jails. Although they are not charged with any crimes, they remain locked up at least until asylum officers can conduct extensive interviews to determine whether the applicants have a "credible fear" of persecution.[59] This policy alarms officials of the United Nations High Commission for Refugees. "People risk their lives to flee persecution, get here, and bang— the doors slam," said Washington representative Karen Abu Zayd. "This is not what America should be."

Immigration officials have broad authority to decide who stays locked up and who does not. As a result, some asylum seekers are confined far beyond the finding that they have a "credible fear" of persecution; some stay locked up for months, even years, before officials determine that they have a "well-founded fear" of persecution if sent back home. Although aliens in deportation and asylum proceedings have the right to counsel, counsel is not provided at government expense as in the case of the criminal justice system. Therefore, asylum seekers who have no funds to retain counsel are forced to go it alone, unless free legal services are available. Unfortunately, the availability of free legal services for asylum seekers (and other aliens facing removal) is extremely limited. Thus, many applicants are left to navigate the process in a language (English) that is foreign to them, without any legal assistance.

If the asylum officer determines that the person does not have a credible fear of persecution, then the person must affirmatively request a review by an immigration judge.

There is no right to judicial review. The review before an immigration judge is expedited and limited. That is, the review must be concluded no later than seven days after the credible fear determination and need not even be conducted in person; it can be conducted by telephone or video connection. Counsel cannot be present, no evidence can be submitted, and no witnesses can be called.

The effect of IIRAIRA on the number of asylum applications filed is obvious in Table 12-1. By 1999, fewer than 40,000 applications were received.

Politicizing Asylum

Although the 1980 Refugee Act removed the ideological-specific language of refugee policy, in practice, applicants from communist-dominated countries continue to be treated more favorably. The annual refugee allocations agreed upon by the president and Congress always set aside more slots for nationals of the former Soviet bloc, East Asia, and Cuba. In fact, without much congressional opposition, presidents have continued to favor refugees from communist countries while consistently ignoring pleas of those from U.S. allied countries. Furthermore, as to those individuals who flee to the United States and apply for asylum, Cubans are treated much better than Haitians, Nicaraguans are favored over Salvadorans and Guatemalans, and approval rates for applicants from the People's Republic of China, the former Yugoslavia, Russia, and Ukraine consistently run high.

But to say that every applicant from a communist-dominated country will be granted asylum would be inaccurate—especially when significant numbers are involved. For example, although the refugees from communist countries are favored under the refugee system, the allotment for Asian refugees has declined dramatically. The executive branch and Congress established a limit of 234,000 refugees for fiscal year 1980. Of that number, the Carter administration designated 169,000 places for Southeast Asia, 33,000 for the Soviet Union, 19,500 for Cuba, and 1,000 for the remainder of Latin America. By 1985, the total number of refugees allotted by the Reagan administration dropped to 70,000, with 50,000 reserved for East Asia. For 1992 under the Bush administration, the total was increased to 142,000, primarily to accommodate an increase to 61,000 for the former Soviet Union. The number for East Asians remained at 52,000, despite dire circumstances in Asian refugee camps. By 1998 under the Clinton administration, the total number was down to 83,000, with 14,000 for East Asia and 51,000 for Europe.

Humanitarianism has occasionally taken precedence over the drive to control. Consider the 1982 and 1987 legislation concerning "Amerasian children." Designed to enable Southeast Asian children whose natural fathers were U.S. servicemen to enter more easily, the legislation allowed them the exceptional option of either filing on their own behalf or having an immigration visa petition filed for them. Other prospective family-based immigrants cannot petition on their own behalf. The consequences of this technical accommodation have not been insignificant. A large number of children were fathered by servicemen in Korea, Vietnam, Laos, Cambodia, and Thailand over a period of decades, where the children suffered racial discrimination and ostracism in their native lands that led to inadequate housing, substandard medical care, and nutritional deficiencies. By October 1991, over 18,000 Amerasians (mostly from Vietnam) had benefited from the law and migrated to the United States.

But when boatloads of Chinese from Fujian Province began arriving in 1992 and 1993, asylum was definitely not automatic. At first, this created a dissonant situation for the INS. After all, Chinese were fleeing from communism; but the situation seemed somehow different. Two incidents that occurred in late 1992 only days apart demonstrated the dilemma. In one, a Cuban commercial pilot commandeered a flight and landed in Miami. All aboard who wanted asylum, including the pilot, were welcomed with open arms, and none were taken into custody. Yet, a few days later, a boatload of Chinese seeking asylum landed in San Francisco Bay, and every single person on board who could be rounded up was incarcerated. Many applied for asylum, arguing that they feared persecution because of their opposition to China's one-child-per-family birth policy or because they had supported the protesting students at Tienanmen Square in 1989. It was the nature of these claims that critics labeled outrageous, citing the Chinese as perfect examples of how the asylum system was being exploited. After several Chinese boats arrived—particularly the highly publicized *Golden Venture* in New York Harbor in 1993—critics were able to rally great public and political support for their cause, and asylum and undocumented immigration played on the front page for some time after that. Ironically, a coalition of Chinese asylum supporters and right-to-life proponents were able to convince Congress in 1996 to add an automatic asylum eligibility provision for those Chinese fleeing China's one-child policy.[60]

Although Cubans fleeing the Castro regime generally have been greeted generously, one incident shortly after the passage of the 1980 Refugee Act illustrates that the generosity does not extend to all would-be Cuban refugees. The Mariel boatlift began as a small-boat exodus of several thousand Cubans who were welcomed in the United States as refugees from the Castro government in 1980. After President Carter offered an "open arms" welcome to the initial group, the numbers swelled to 125,000, including individuals that Castro had released from Cuba's prisons and mental institutions, and Americans became increasingly upset at the numbers. Some 2,500 criminals and mental patients were estimated to fall within this group. All of the refugees were called "Marielitos" for the Mariel port of Cuba from which most were launched to sea.

Initially, the exodus was called a "freedom flotilla," but it was downgraded to "boatlift" when criminals and others that Castro called "misfits" turned up among the masses of refugees. Many of the refugees were forced to leave spouses and children behind. Many who were criminals or who committed crimes after arriving in the United States have been held in detention for years and years. Others have been subjected to racial discrimination because they are black.

Cubans who entered as part of the Mariel boatlift differ in many ways from the two waves of Cuban exiles that came to the United States in the 1950s and 1960s. In the first wave, 1959–62, 200,000 Cubans came in an organized airlift. More than 90 percent were white, middle-aged, and well-educated. They had benefited from the system that preceded the Castro government and have established themselves in the social, business, and political life in the United States. For the most part they came in family units.

In the second wave, 1965–70, 270,000 people arrived, first by boat then in a more organized airlift. They were also mostly white, but 24 percent were black or mulatto. These were largely educated and many worked at trades and came from Cuba's working class. Again, most came with their families.

In the case of the Mariel refugees, the large majority were blue-collar workers, less educated, and younger males. They had a higher level of divorce than those before them. About 20 percent were not allowed to bring their families, and 20,000 males were separated from their wives. Most of the Mariel refugees spoke only Spanish and about half were black.

Conclusion

U.S. refugee and asylum policy has always been influenced by political, ethnic, and racial considerations. From the country's failure to rescue Jews during World War II to the institutional barriers erected for Guatemalan, El Salvadoran, and Haitian applicants, evidence of bias in our asylum policies is clear. Favoring those fleeing communism until too many of a particular ethnic group, such as Southeast Asians, have arrived has become engrained in our approach to refugee admissions. Even in the area of asylum, our policies are implemented in ways that are not generous toward those who would not fit the real image of who an American is.

Although the Refugee Act of 1980 was intended to bring U.S. law into compliance with United Nations agreements, formally canceling preference to those fleeing former communist or Middle East regimes, special treatment continues. Think only of the nation's strong embrace of the educated Cubans fleeing Fidel Castro's communist rule, in contrast to our rejection of Haitian immigrants fleeing a so-called democratic country.

The government's attempt at a more uniform and independent asylum decision-making process by establishing an asylum adjudication corps has not helped. Officers often fail to comprehend basic problems, such as the fact that some cultures understand times and dates differently than Americans. Unaware of these cultural differences, the officers treat these inconsistencies as proof that potential asylees are lying about their experiences. Furthermore, the officers, untrained in recognizing the symptoms of posttraumatic stress disorder, lack the capacity to appreciate fully the reasons for the applicant's inconsistencies as to events, dates, and experiences. Instead, the officers demand precision as to dates and will only grant asylum for those applicants who provide precise information, demanding more than is required by the generous well-founded fear standard contemplated by the refugee law.

Legislation in 1996 further reduced one's chances of being granted asylum. Procedures were created that expedited the removal of aliens at the border who lacked proper identification; today asylum applications must be filled no later than one year after entering the country. As for those stopped at the border, the process allows one officer to make the ultimate decision as to whether one's fear of persecution is valid. If the officer is not satisfied, the asylum seeker is quickly removed. No judicial review of the officer's momentous decision is possible.

Epilogue: Two Americas

"USA! USA!"

Within hours of the terrorist attacks on September 11, 2001, Americans of Muslim, Middle Eastern, and South Asian descent found themselves targets for acts of hate and racial profiling. In Bridgeview, Illinois, s suburb of Chicago, 300 protestors, many waving American flags and chanting "USA! USA!" marched on a mosque. One nineteen-year-old demonstrator exclaimed, "I'm proud to be an American and I hate Arabs and I always have."[1] In Huntington, New York, a seventy-five-year-old man tried to run over a Pakistani woman in the parking lot of a shopping mall. He then followed the woman into a store and threatened to kill her for "destroying my country."[2] Near San Diego, a Sikh woman was attacked by a knife-wielding man, shouting, "This is what you get for what you've done to us."[3] A Sikh family was followed out of a restaurant by two white men who screamed at them, "Go back to your country,"[4] Soon, arrests were made of individuals who were racially profiled, and by October, over 1,100 suspicious individuals, mostly Arab Americans, were detained, without access to family or counsel.[5] By November, the Department of Justice developed a list of 5,000 Middle Eastern men, between the ages of eighteen and thirty-three, who were to be "voluntarily" interviewed.[6] Although the men were supposed to have entered on nonimmigrant visas after January 2000,[7] numerous reports indicated that law enforcement officials were also contacting lawful permanent residents and U.S. citizens of Arab descent.[8]

In contemplating this targeting of Muslim, Middle Eastern, and South Asian Americans by private individuals and official government policies after September 11, a clear theme emerged. In spite of the fact that these people have been part of the fabric of our country for some time, in the eyes of many, those among us of Muslim, Middle Eastern, and South Asian background are not *real* Americans.

The fact that hateful acts and words of private citizens are followed up with official regimes of detention and profiling only reaffirms the subordination of the victims through suspicion of loyalty. The government imprimatur helps to "marginalize" the victims in U.S. society.[9]

Although Ahmad Namrouti, a Jordanian American grocery store owner, had been victimized by teenage vandals upset because they could not buy cigarettes, being targeted with a fifteen-pound brick because he was "Arab" and "Islamic" after September 11 is a substantively different situation. This time, Namrouti was de-Americanized and subordinated for not fitting the perpetrator's image of a *true* American. In the perpetrator's mind—the mind of a vigilante racist—Namrouti is forever foreign, notwithstanding his status as a U.S. citizen. The message was clear to him, and he put his store up for sale, intending to return to Jordan rather than endure such persecution.[10]

The message is one of exclusion: "You Muslims, Middle Easterners, and South Asians are not true Americans." Certainly, de-Americanization is a process that involves racism, but unlike the racism directed at African Americans, with its foundations in the historically held beliefs of inferiority, de-Americanizers base their assault on loyalty and foreignness.[11] In the minds of the private actors, who are nothing more than lawless vigilantes,[12] self-appointed enforcers of true Americanism, their victims are *immigrants* or *foreigners* even though they may in fact be citizens by birth or through naturalization. Irrespective of the victim community's possible long-standing status in the country, its members are regarded as perpetual foreigners. The victim community is forever regarded as *immigrant* America, as opposed to simply part of America and its diversity.

What has been happening to Muslims, Middle Easterners, and South Asians in the United States in the wake of September 11 is a process of ostracism from the American community—a de-Americanization process—that we have witnessed before. The process often involves two aspects: (1) the actions of private individuals and (2) official government-sanctioned actions. On the private side, the process involves identifying the victims as foreigners, sometimes mistakenly, other times simply treating the person as a foreigner knowing otherwise. De-Americanization is a twisted brand of xenophobia that is not simply hatred of foreigners, but also hatred of those who in fact may not be foreigners but whom the vigilantes would prefer being removed from the country anyway. In fact, we have seen this process not long ago with respect to Arabs and others of Middle Eastern descent following the 1995 bombing of the federal building in Oklahoma City. Immediately after that attack, media and officials wrongly speculated that an Islamic terrorist might have been responsible.[13] The culprit turned out to be a white supremacist, Timothy McVeigh.[14] The official side of the process involves laws or enforcement strategies that broadly focus on the entire group either without adequate basis or at least in an overly broad manner.

"Ching Chong, Chinaman"

Asian American history is replete with examples of the de-Americanization of its members by vigilante racism. For some, the ostracism started immediately. Consider the poignant autobiography of Mary Paik Lee, a Korean immigrant, who described her family's arrival in San Francisco harbor in 1906:

> As we walked down the gangplank . . . young White men were standing around, waiting to see what kind of creatures were disembarking. We must have been a very queer-looking group. They laughed at us and spit in our faces; one man kicked up Mother's skirt and called us names we couldn't understand. Of course, their actions and attitudes left no doubt about their feelings toward us.[15]

Throughout their early life in the United States, Lee and her family were greeted with "For Whites Only" signs everywhere. Public restrooms, theaters, swimming pools, and barber shops were off limits.[16]

Unfortunately, other private, vigilante acts of racist comments and hate crimes directed at Asian Americans are easily located. While many often think such actions are a thing of the past, the similarity between blatantly racist acts from a hundred years ago and today is troubling. As they have been recently, turban-wearing Sikhs were victimized historically. When they arrived in the 1800s, Sikh men continued to wear turbans, because not cutting their hair is a requirement of their religion. As a result, they endured being called "ragheads."[17] Fast forward to the 1980s, and in New Jersey, home to the largest population of Asian Indians in the United States, a gang of hoodlums who victimize Asian Indian Americans pride themselves in calling themselves the "dot-busters" in apparent jest of the fact that many Asian Indian women of the Hindu faith wear a bindi, or marriage mark, on their foreheads.[18]

Similar acts, both past and present, can be found in incidents targeted against East Asians as well. In the mid-1800s, Chinese miners were subject to wanton abuse. An 1862 California legislative committee developed a list of eighty-eight Chinese miners who were murdered in what the committee labeled "a wholesale system of wrong and outrage practiced upon the Chinese population in this state, which would disgrace the most barbarous nation upon earth."[19] In the 1870s, the homes of many Chinese living in California's Sacramento Valley were burned down.[20] In 1885, 600 unarmed Chinese coal miners were fired upon in Rock Springs, Wyoming; 28 were killed and 15 wounded.[21] In 1913, 15 Korean fruit pickers in Riverside County, California, were threatened by a crowd that forced them to leave town.[22] Similarly, in a San Joaquin County, California town in 1921, 58 Japanese laborers were rounded up by armed men and forced out of town.[23] In 1930, a mob of 400 attacked the Northern Monterey Filipino Club near Watsonville, California, killing one Filipino and injuring dozens more.[24]

One of the more notorious, de-Americanizing, vigilante hate crimes of our time involved the 1982 murder of Vincent Chin, a young Chinese American man who lived near Detroit, Michigan.[25] Chin, who was out with friends celebrating his upcoming wedding, was confronted by Ronald Ebens and Michael Nitz, two unemployed auto workers. Ebens made racial and obscene remarks toward Chin, calling him a "Chink" and a "Nip" and making comments about foreign car imports: "It's because of you little M—f—that we're out of work."[26] The Court of Appeals noted that Ebens "seemed to believe that Chin was Japanese" and may not have distinguished Asians of "Japanese and Chinese descent since there is testimony to show he made references to both."[27] A fight ensued and in the end, Chin was beaten to death by a baseball bat-wielding Ebens, while Nitz restrained Chin.[28] Chin, who was a native of China, was adopted at the age of six by a Chinese American couple and became a U.S. citizen in 1965.[29] Yet he was targeted because he represented Japan and its automobile manufacturers in the eyes of the culprits.

Even more recently, de-Americanizing acts have been directed at Chinese Americans. In the midst of an international crisis in April 2001, when a U.S. spy plane had to land on Chinese soil and China would not immediately release the plane,[30] many Americans took their frustration out on Chinese Americans. A radio station disc jockey in Springfield, Illinois, suggested boycotting Chinese restaurants.[31] Another commentator called people with Chinese last names from his local telephone book to harass them.[32] Pulitzer Prize-winning cartoonist Pat Oliphant ran a cartoon portraying a buck-toothed Chinese waiter yelling at a customer (depicted as Uncle Sam), "Apologize Lotten Amellican!"[33] The American Society of Newspaper Editors was entertained by the renowned satirical group Capitol Steps, featuring a white man dressed in a black wig and thick glasses impersonating a Chinese official who gestured wildly as he said, "Ching, ching, chong, chong,"[34] Perhaps this apparent license to poke fun at Chinese Americans should not be surprising. Even before the two-week spy plane incident, a poll found that a quarter of all Americans hold "decisively negative views," and another 43 percent hold "somewhat negative attitudes" toward Chinese Americans.[35]

Historical vigilante private actions designed to deny Asian and other immigrants of color membership in the community found support from xenophobic officialdom. For example, laws often required Chinese to live outside the city limits,[36] or a local ordinance would bar laundries of wooden construction when officials knew only Chinese businesses would be affected.[37] California barred Chinese from testifying in court,[38] while several states prevented all Asian immigrants from owning land or marrying whites.[39] Of course, Congress got into the act as well. In 1870, Chinese immigrants officially were told that they could never become Americans. In the post–Civil War era, Congress moved toward granting naturalization rights to residents of African descent. As the legislation progressed, Senator Charles Sumner of Massachusetts moved to add Chinese immigrants to the list of those who could be naturalized, a right that constitutionally was reserved for "free White men."[40] But the amendment failed, and Chinese were specifically excluded from the right to naturalize.[41] The message to Chinese immigrants—that they could never be real Americans—was based on the view that Chinese were so different that they could never assimilate and adopt real American values. That sentiment was later recognized by the Supreme Court in upholding aspects of the Chinese exclusion laws:

[The Chinese] remained strangers in the land, residing apart by themselves, and adhering to the customs and usages of their own country. It seemed impossible for them to assimilate with our people or to make any change in their habits or modes of living. As they grew in numbers each year the people of the coast saw, or believed they saw, in the facility of immigration, and in the crowded millions of China, where population presses upon the means of subsistence, great danger that at no distant day that portion of our country would be overrun by them unless prompt action was taken to restrict their immigration.[42]

Of course, the internment of Japanese Americans during World War II is a prime example of their de-Americanization through official action. The ease with which internment was accepted by the general public illustrates a history of hostility toward Japanese Americans dating back to the early 1900s.[43] After the bombing of Pearl Harbor on December 7, 1941, the bigotry and fear that had informed earlier anti-Japanese laws became a panic. Japanese Americans suddenly became suspected of acts of sabotage and treason. Though no acts were ever proved, the civilian government acceded to unprecedented military orders that subjected all West Coast Japanese first to curfews and then forced evacuation into detention camps. Eventually, 120,000 Japanese Americans, most of them citizens, were interned in camps scattered across the country.[44]

More recently, Chinese American scientist Wen Ho Lee lost his job and was jailed for nine months before a former government counterintelligence chief acknowledged that racial profiling had occurred.[45] The government dropped all but one charge against Lee, and the federal judge handling the case ordered Lee released and apologized to him.[46] Even the *New York Times* acknowledged that its reporting on the case was flawed and "fell short" of its standards.[47] As a result of the de-Americanizing profiling of Chinese American scientists at government labs, many feel ill at ease working at labs and others have felt pressured into quitting.[48]

These official acts essentially condoning private vigilante actions do much to solidify the image of people of color with immigrant roots as perpetual foreigners. This encourages private individuals to engage in discriminatory acts and reinforces their hostility. As such, people of color became prime targets for de-Americanization by vigilante racists.

"We Know an American When We See One"

De-Americanization of people of color such as Asian Americans and Latinos finds its roots in the historical immigration exclusionary and enforcement policies directed at Asian and Latin immigrants. The Chinese exclusion laws were followed by analogous provisions directed at Japanese, Asian Indians, Filipinos, and the rest of the so-called Asiatic Barred Zone.[49] Mexicans have been subjected to roundups like that of braceros in the 1950s called Operation Wetback, shortchanged visas by Congress in the 1970s, and subjected to expanded INS powers to arrest courtesy of the Supreme Court in a series of cases in the 1970s and 1980s.[50] In the early 1900s, in a prequel to de-Americanization, Mexican immigrants were subjected to government-sponsored Americanization programs. Family planning was a key ingredient, out of fear that uncontrolled Mexican population growth would contribute to Anglo "race suicide."[51] A goal was to cure the habits of the stereotypical "lazy Mexican" and replace the Mexican penchant for fried foods, substitute bread for tortillas, and serve lettuce instead of beans.[52] More recently, unconstitutional Immigration and Naturalization Service (INS) procedures in the 1980s intended to disadvantage Haitian, Guatemalan, and El Salvadoran asylum applicants were exposed by federal courts.[53] (See Chapter 12.)

Even though immigration categories no longer permit blatant racial and ethnic discrimination, selection policies and philosophies of the past have set the tone for much of the de-Americanization that goes on today.[54] Immigration policies, especially after 1965,[55] have permitted the entry of immigrants from many parts of the world, and naturalization rules now permit immigrants, irrespective of ethnic background, to become U.S. citizens. So Americans come in all different shades and from all ethnic backgrounds. Yet, the words of the Supreme Court more than eighty years ago perhaps best capture who many Americans—certainly vigilante racists—continue to regard as *true* Americans. In 1923, the right to citizenship through naturalization continued to be limited, as it had since 1870, to "White persons" and those of "African descent." That year, in *United States v. Bhagat Singh Thind*,[56] the Court was confronted with a case involving an immigrant from India, who was a high-caste Hindu of full Indian blood, who wanted to be naturalized. Thind offered convincing ethnological evidence that high-class Hindus belong to the Aryan race, and that the Aryans came to India around 2000 B.C. Thus, Thind could establish a personal, scientific line of descent from Caucasian ancestors. The Court acknowledged that the phrase *white persons* and the word *Caucasian* are synonymous. But the unanimous Court essentially threw up its arms and held that there was no way that Congress intended to extend naturalization rights to any immigrants from India:

> What we now hold is that the words *"free White persons" are words of common speech,* to be interpreted in accordance with the understanding of the common man, synonymous with the word "Caucasian" only as that word is popularly understood. *As so understood and used, whatever may be the speculations of the ethnologists, it does not include the body of people to whom the appellee belongs.* It is a matter of familiar observation and knowledge that the physical group characteristics of the Hindus *render them readily distinguishable from the various groups of persons in this country commonly recognized as white. The children of English, French, German, Italian, Scandinavian, and other European parentage, quickly merge into the mass of our population and lose the distinctive hallmarks of their European origin.* On the other hand, it cannot be doubted that *the children born in this country of Hindu parents would retain indefinitely the clear evidence of their ancestry.* It is very far from our thought to suggest the slightest question of racial superiority or inferiority. *What we suggest is merely racial difference, and it is of such character and extent that the great body of our people instinctively recognize it and reject the thought of assimilation.*[57]

When the Court wrote "'free White persons' are words of common speech. . . . As so understood and used, whatever may be the speculations of the ethnologists, it does not include the body of people to whom the appellee belongs," it essentially said that, irrespective of science, a Hindu from India was not white. When the Court wrote "It is a matter of familiar observation and knowledge that the physical group characteristics of the Hindus render them readily distinguishable from the various groups of persons in this country commonly recognized as white," it might as well have substituted the word *American* for *white*.

When the Court wrote "the children of English, French, German, Italian, Scandinavian, and other European parentage, quickly merge into the mass of our population and lose the distinctive hallmarks of their European origin," it was essentially limiting the ethnic backgrounds of who could become a real American to those who could merge into the masses, namely, English, French, German, Italian, Scandinavian, and other Europeans.[58]

When the Court wrote "the children born in this country of Hindu parents would retain indefinitely the clear evidence of their ancestry, [and w]hat we suggest is merely racial difference, and it is of such character and extent that the great body of our people instinctively recognize it and reject the thought of assimilation," it appeared to endorse a vision of *true* Americans being able to reject certain races with which to commingle.

In other words, the Court was saying to Thind, "We know an American when we see one, and you're not one." The Court endorsed a Eurocentric vision of Americanism that has endured in the psyche of much of the country. This Eurocentric vision, dominant throughout history, still pervades America, as is evidenced by the thoughts and actions behind the recent vigilante crimes.

In addition to recent de-Americanization and subordination crimes and pranks of vigilante racists fueled by a Eurocentric immigration history aimed at Asian Americans, Latinos have suffered as well. Private citizens were behind California's Proposition 187 in 1994, an initiative designed to bar immigrant and citizen children from public schools and other public benefits, primarily aimed at Latinos.[59] Sadly, hate is also apparent. Near San Diego, California, seven high school students were arrested for beating five Latino migrant workers with pipes. Police said the students attacked the workers because "they didn't like Mexicans."[60] In Van Nuys, California, a woman was charged with murder and hate crimes after using her car to run down and kill a Latino man, because she hated "persons of Latino origins."[61] And once again, official support has exacerbated matters. The Supreme Court's endorsement of sweeping Border Patrol tactics (see Chapter 8) has resulted in incidents such as the detention of Eddie Cortez, the mayor of Pomona, California, a U.S. citizen, who was stopped by agents more than a hundred miles from the border and ordered to produce proof of citizenship because he looked Latino.[62] Prominent English-only advocate Linda Chavez, also a U.S. citizen, was detained at the United States–Canada border because agents did not believe she was a lawful resident of the United States due to her appearance.[63]

The Eurocentric vision of America is the driving force behind vigilante racist attacks on what is perceived as *immigrant* America. To the perpetrators, this is about an exclusive membership limited to *real* Americans.

Sadly, the de-Americanization process is capable of reinventing itself generation after generation. We have seen this exclusionary process aimed at Jews, Asians, Mexicans, Haitians, and those of other descent throughout the nation's history. De-Americanization is not simply xenophobia, because more than fear of foreigners is at work. This is a brand of nativism cloaked in a Eurocentric sense of America that combines hate and racial profiling. Whenever we go through a period of de-Americanization like what is currently affecting South Asians, Arabs, Muslim Americans, and people like Wen Ho Lee, a whole new generation of Americans sees that exclusion and hate are acceptable; that the definition of who is an American can be narrow; that they too have license to profile. Their license is issued when others around them engage in hate and the government chimes in with its own profiling. This is part of the sad process of unconscious and institutionalized racism that haunts our country.[64]

The War on Terrorism

A few weeks before the terrorist attacks of September 2001, Mexico's President Vicente Fox delivered a stirring address, demanding legalization (amnesty) for undocumented Mexicans in the United States by the end of the year. President Bush and members of Congress responded with sincere pledges that the issue would be given serious attention. In February 2000, the AFL-CIO, proponents of employer sanctions in the Immigration Reform and Control Act of 1986, called for the repeal of those penalties, realizing that the laws actually hurt immigrant workers who represent the future of the organized labor movement in the United States; the union also supported the call to legalize undocumented workers.[65] These and other issues that would have eased restrictive immigration laws were on the front burner of the immigration policy debate on September 10, 2001.

The terrorist attacks of September 11, 2001, changed all that.

As soon as investigations revealed that the hijackers of the jet planes that flew into the World Trade Center towers and the Pentagon were Muslim and Arab foreigners, President Bush's War on Terrorism expanded its scope to include sweeping legislative and enforcement tools that targeted immigrants.[66] Instead of determining how to go about legalizing migrants, the immigration debate shifted its attention toward better ways to track, monitor, arrest, prosecute, and deport foreigners who may or may not have been a threat to national security. U.S. legislators' focus quickly evolved from decreasing immigration penalties in order to secure a stable labor force to hiring more Border Patrol agents, improving background checks on visa applicants, and overhauling the INS.[67]

In its investigation of the attacks, the administration detained between 1,500 and 2,000 people, mostly foreigners, under unprecedented secrecy. Attorney General John Ashcroft justified their detention by calling them "suspected terrorists," but none were charged with involvement in the September 11 attacks. With the exception of four individuals indicted on support-for-terrorism charges in late August 2002, no one was charged with any terrorist act.[68] Those arrested on immigration charges—the vast majority—had effectively "disappeared." Their cases were not listed on any public docket, their hearings were closed to the public, and the immigration judges were instructed to neither confirm nor deny that their cases existed, when or if asked. As Ashcroft explained, "Aggressive detention is vital to preventing, disrupting or delaying new attacks."

But two federal district courts and a court of appeals held the practice unconstitutional. The Sixth Circuit Court of Appeals criticized the attorney general for "seek[ing] to uproot people's lives, outside the public eye, and behind a closed door," reminding us that "democracies die behind closed doors."[69]

The administration repeatedly insisted that it opposed racial or ethnic profiling, but simultaneously undertook numerous measures predicated on little more than a foreign citizen's Arab country of origin. Eight thousand foreigners were called in for interviews based solely on the fact that they were recent male immigrants from Arab countries as the deportation of Arabs was made a priority. In addition, supplemental plans were implemented to fingerprint and register noncitizens from Arab nations. In February 2002, the INS announced that it would soon begin apprehending and interrogating thousands of undocumented Middle Eastern immigrants who apparently ignored deportation orders, seeking ways to prosecute anyone who had ties to terrorism. The results of these interviews would be compiled in a new computer database to facilitate future monitoring of these individuals.

These tactics were part of INS efforts to locate an estimated 314,000 foreign nationals, known as "absconders," who ignored court orders to leave the country. But the effort would initially be limited by order of the Department of Justice. Officials from the department said that the operation would focus first on about 6,000 immigrants from countries identified as al Qaeda strongholds, though the vast majority of absconders are Latin American. The "Absconder Apprehension Initiative" was billed as one of the Justice Department's wide-ranging efforts to thwart terrorism by increasing its focus on domestic intelligence gathering.[70]

In actuality, "absconders" are not the only noncitizens the government is after. In December 2002, immigration officials mandated that everyone with a temporary visa from Iran, Iraq, Libya, Syria, and Sudan had to register. This led to the unexpected detention of at least 450 individuals on immigration violations (mostly minor), many who had nearly completed the process for legal residency. Citizens of fifteen other countries, including North Korea, Saudi Arabia, Indonesia, Pakistan, and North African nations, had to register by January or February 2003. In all, officials screened about 7,500 noncitizens under this effort.[71]

The USA Patriot Act, enacted within six weeks of September 11 with little opposition, contains several provisions reserved for noncitizens. The act authorizes the attorney general to detain noncitizens without a hearing; bars foreign citizens from entering the country based solely on their speech; and authorizes deportation based on any support to a disfavored group, without any requirement that the support be connected to a terrorist act. Had this law been in place in the 1980s, it would have authorized the government to deny entry to those who publicly endorsed the African National Congress, and would have empowered the attorney general to detain and deport anyone who contributed to Nelson Mandela's lawful antiapartheid political activities. After all, until the ANC defeated apartheid in South Africa, our State Department designated it as a terrorist organization.[72]

Under Patriot Act amendments to preexisting emergency power laws, the president can designate any organization or individual a terrorist and thereby freeze all attendant assets and criminalize all transactions with the person or group. President Bush used these powers to shut down three of the nation's leading Muslim charities. Two were closed without any charges at all, simply because they were "under investigation." The third, the Holy Land Foundation, was designated a terrorist organization, not based on charges that it had engaged in or even supported terrorist activity, but simply on the charge that it was connected to Hamas. The foundation was given no notice or hearing prior to its designation, and when it filed suit after the fact, the federal court denied it any opportunity to produce evidence supporting its innocence.[73]

In some situations, the Bush administration attempted to bypass certain processes by imposing "military justice." The president asserted the authority to hold people in military custody incommunicado, without any individualized hearing into the basis for their detention, without access to a lawyer, and without judicial review. He set up military tribunals in which detainees could be tried, and ultimately executed, without independent judicial review and without anyone outside the military, including the defendant, ever seeing the evidence on which the conviction rested.

Defense Secretary Donald Rumsfeld claimed that even if a defendant managed to prevail in such a trial, the military would not release the person, but would hold him or her until there were no longer any terrorist organizations of potentially global reach left in the world, or more simply, for the rest of their lives. When the president introduced the concept of military justice through a military tribunal order in November 2001, he assured Americans that it would only apply to "noncitizens." Yet by the summer of 2002, the administration asserted the authority to detain under military custody two U.S. citizens—Yasser Hamdi, a citizen captured in Afghanistan, and Jose Padilla, arrested at O'Hare Airport on suspicion that he might be planning to set off a radioactive "dirty bomb." The military claimed that simply by attaching the label *enemy combatant*, the president could authorize the indefinite, incommunicado incarceration of any U.S. citizen he chose, without judicial review.

In August 2002, the *Wall Street Journal* reported that high-level administration officials advocated even broader reliance on this power, suggesting the creation of a special camp to house citizen "enemy combatants." Not coincidentally, President Bush's plan to establish a new Department of Homeland Security (DHS), also unveiled in the summer of 2002, included as a top priority the total inclusion of the Immigration and Naturalization Service within the new department. Homeland Security Director Tom

Ridge called approval of the department "the next critical step" in the war against terrorism.[74] Indeed, soon after Republicans took over control of Congress in the November 2002 elections, the DHS bill was enacted; the INS has been subsumed into the new defense-against-terrorism-first department.

Even where military process is not available, Attorney General Ashcroft implemented a plan to speed up the review process in deportation cases. He restructured the Board of Immigration Appeals (which reviews decisions of immigration judges) by instituting a one-judge review (in place of the prior three-judge panel) and reducing the board from twenty-six members to eleven to somehow "increase its efficiency." (Critics charged this was a way for Ashcroft to get rid of certain Clinton administration appointees.) Ashcroft also eliminated "de novo review," ordering the BIA to accept the factual findings of the lower court, unless the case presents "novel or complex issues." The plan also barred the introduction and consideration of new evidence before the BIA.[75]

America's Continuing Diversity

In an odd manner, the tragic events of September 11 served as a reminder that the United States is a nation of immigrants that has grown more and more diverse since the 1965 amendments to the country's immigration laws. As the nation reeled from the attacks, we regrouped in incredible demonstrations of unity and patriotism. Yet, an ugly aspect of that regrouping targeted immigrant communites of Arab Americans, American Muslims, Sikhs, and Pakistani Americans. And these communities are growing. The Arab American population numbers over a million. Hundreds of thousands of other Americans of Middle Eastern descent, such as those from Iraq and Iran, have settled in the United States. They contribute to the diversity fueled by immigration—a diversity that is led by growing numbers of Latin and Asian immigrants.

Nathan Glazer's 1985 description of the United States as the "permanently unfinished country" continues to be apt.[76] With the number of foreign-born residents in the United States increasing by 13 million during the 1990s, a primary lesson from the 2000 census is that our nation continues to be a land of immigrants. The foreign-born population numbers 30.5 million, 11 percent of the total. In particular, the census story reveals changes in the past decade that reflect increasing numbers of residents of Latin and Asian descent in new parts of the country. Asians and Latinos have reached a stunning 58 percent in population growth rate over the past ten years nationwide.[77]

The rise in Latinos outstripped overall population growth throughout the country.[78] Data from the 2000 census showed explosive growth in the Latino population outside the nation's urban areas as Latinos helped to fill increasingly available low-wage jobs in the 1990s. They came in droves to work in meatpacking plants in Minnesota and Nebraska, tend crops in Kentucky, and manufacture carpets in Georgia mills.[79] The numbers are further evidence of how thirty-plus years of massive Latino immigration continues to alter the nation's demographic landscape. Half of all Latinos live in Texas and California, and 77 percent (27.1 million) live in seven states: California, Texas, New York, Florida, Illinois, Arizona, and New Jersey (listed in order from the largest to the smallest Latino populations). In fourteen other states scattered throughout the country, the percentage of Latinos as part of the overall population doubled in the 1990s. Those states are Alabama, Arkansas, Delaware, Georgia, Indiana, Iowa, Kentucky, Minnesota, Mississippi, Nebraska, North Carolina, Oregon, South Carolina, and Tennessee.[80] The dramatic surge in the nation's Latino population was due mainly to a 53 percent increase in the number of people of Mexican heritage. Mexican Americans make up 58 percent of the nation's 35.3 million "Hispanics," by far the fastest-growing segment of the United States' Latino population.[81]

Asian American growth almost matched Latino growth in the 1990s. Their presence is most visible in big and powerful states like Texas, New York, New Jersey, Virginia, Maryland, Illinois, Ohio, and Pennsylvania, where they prefer to cluster in huge numbers in capital cities, where jobs are available and generally recession-proof.[82] Even in a place like Kentucky, the 2000 census found a 75 percent population increase in Asian Pacific Americans since 1990, and an even greater 173 percent increase in the Latino population.[83] In Louisville, more than a third of the residents will likely be foreign-born by the year 2010.[84]

The type of diversity that immigration has engendered is not limited to racial lines. Consider the religious diversity that has ensued in a traditional "Bible Belt" city like Nashville, Tennessee, where one can now find six Buddhist communities, five Jewish congregations, five Islamic mosques, a Baha'i center, a Hindu temple and a Hindu ashram, or teaching abode, plus assorted Sikhs and Jains. In Nashville, two categories of new religious expression are apparent: the Christian and the non-Christian. Enclaves of Laotian Buddhists, Kurdish Muslims, and a scattering of Jains, practitioners of an ancient Indian philosophic tradition, can be found, but also 4,000 Korean Protestants, Armenian Christians, and an Eastern Orthodox coffeehouse/chapel.[85] In Bowling Green, Kentucky, the population of 50,000 includes 4,000 Muslims.[86]

Immigration-driven growth is not limited to a few states. In fact, the recent census shows that in the past decade the foreign-born population grew far more slowly in states with the largest immigrant populations, such as California, New York, and Texas, than in a group of nineteen new growth states.[87] The nineteen new growth states—those with the fastest-growing immigrant populations in the 1990s—include Alabama, Arizona, Arkansas, Colorado, Georgia, Idaho, Iowa, Kansas, Kentucky, Maryland, Mississippi, Nebraska, Nevada, North Carolina, Oklahoma, Oregon, South Carolina, Utah, and Virginia. During the 1990s, the foreign-born population grew by a dramatic 95 percent in the new growth states, compared to only 23 percent in traditional immigrant destination states of California, New York, Florida, Texas, New Jersey, and Illinois.[88]

Even traditional immigrant destinations have become more diverse. For example, in New York City, while Chinese Americans remained the largest Asian Pacific American group, Asian Indian Americans grew 80 percent (to 170,899) in the 1990s, while Bangladeshi Americans surged 285 percent to 19,148.[89] The city's Mexican American population grew from 62,000 in 1980 to about 300,000 in 2000.[90]

Information about particular states suggests that issues pertaining to cultural pluralism, race relations, and defining who is an American are real questions in many communities across the nation. Consider these examples.

Colorado's Latino population nearly doubled in the past decade. They make up more than a third of Denver's population.[91] Roughly one-fourth of the state's 724,000 students are Latino, many of them Mexican immigrants.[92] In Denver, Latino and Asian American communities are booming, and businesses in thriving immigrant enclaves do well.[93] Merchants and workers in some neighborhoods find it increasingly necessary to use three languages—English, Spanish, and an Asian language, often Korean.[94] Jeremiah Kong, a native of Seoul, South Korea, owns La Plaza Mexicana, a 26,000-square-foot building with eighteen shops selling everything from auto parts to furniture that cater to Spanish-language immigrants. Eight of the shop owners are Korean; the others are Latino, both U.S.-born and Mexican immigrants. His workers are also Spanish-language immigrants. So, for Kong to deal with his employees, he tends to use "Spanglish"—a combination of English and Spanish. Estella Jaime, a native of Mexico who has worked for Kong for more than three years, now also understands a few Korean phrases.[95] The state's Latino population grew 73 percent and Asians by 68 percent.

Iowa's Latino population has grown by roughly 29,000, a leap of roughly 90 percent, since 1990. The 61,500 Latino residents are the state's largest minority group. Iowa's Asian population has grown by 11,300 since 1990, an increase of 44 percent.[96] In all of Iowa's 99 counties, Latino population growth during the 1990s outpaced the overall population rise (or declined more slowly in counties that lost people). Latino growth ranged from Clarke County (up 1,842 percent) to suburban Dallas County right outside Des Moines (up 1,112 percent).[97]

North Carolina led the country in Latino growth, up 394 percent over the decade, followed by Arkansas, Georgia, Tennessee, and Nevada. In Siler City, North Carolina, Latinos made up 4 percent of the town's 4,808 people in 1990. By 2000, they constituted 39 percent of the city's 6,966 residents, drawn by jobs at chicken-processing plants and textile mills.[98] Oklahoma's Latino population doubled in the 1990s; Mexicans make up three-quarters of the total.[99] In Oklahoma City, schools experienced an eightfold increase in the number of students who consider English a second language.[100]

Kentucky's population increased by nearly 10 percent during the 1990s, topping 4 million for the first time at 4,041,769.[101] The Asian American and Latino growth in the state was even greater: 75 percent for Asian Americans (to almost 30,000) and 173 percent for Latinos (to approximately 60,000).[102] In Louisville, more than a third of the residents will likely be foreign-born by the year 2010.[103]

Consider these other immigrant-driven statistics. One of every four residents of Arizona is now Latino. In Tennessee, the Latino population nearly tripled in ten years and now accounts for 2 percent of the state population. The number of Asians almost doubled, though the state remains 80 percent white and 16 percent black. The Latino population also tripled in Alabama, Georgia, and Minnesota, while at least doubling in states like Utah, Idaho, Indiana, Oregon, Kansas, South Carolina, and Mississippi. In New Hampshire, the Latino population grew by 81 percent and the Asian Pacific Islander community by 74 percent. In Utah, Asians are the second-largest minority group following Latinos. In Massachusetts, the Asian population increased nearly 70 percent, while Latinos grew almost 50 percent. The Asian population doubled in South Dakota.[104]

The effect of immigration on the census is obvious: the population throughout the country is becoming more diverse. And this immigration-driven growth in diversity will likely continue.

Conclusion

As the history of U.S. immigration policies has demonstrated, the line between alien and citizen has often been disregarded. One need think only of the internment of Japanese Americans during World War II, and the Palmer Raids during the Red Scare era that was the precursor to the McCarthy era communist witch hunt. The search for "enemy aliens" all too often has metamorphosed into the harassment and detention of U.S. citizens. While the internment of Arab Americans after September 11 did not occur, virtually all those caught up in the Justice Department's preventive detention campaign were Arab or Muslim. The detention of 1,500 to 2,000 Arabs and Muslims as "suspected terrorists" reveals that ethnic identity has been the code word for enforcement, in spite of the fact that nearly all of those incarcerated ultimately had no connection to terrorism whatsoever.

This latest chapter in the nation's history of immigration policy is consistent with a pattern established long ago. In times of stress or crisis, policy makers and those who enforce those policies express a vision of America that excludes bodies of people, based on skin color, ethnicity, or political belief. We certainly must and should attempt to exclude and ferret out those who would do us harm through intelligent law enforcement. But engaging in over-inclusive, over-reaching tactics in the name of homeland security bears little resemblance to an open society of which we can be proud. Ironically, President Bush maintained that the terrorists attacked us because "they hate our freedoms." But sweeping government implementation of the Patriot Act and private vigilante racism should give us pause about just who is threatening our freedom. Regular official warnings of potential al Qaeda attacks breed public fear that foment today's alien crackdown, as similar stereotypes did in the past. Not surprisingly, citizens and residents of color are uncomfortable and new headlines like "Fear Keeps Immigrants in Hiding" result.[105] Yet as with any era when our policy makers and law enforcers engage in sweeping action, they do so in the face of resistance and criticism from segments of our society that view things differently.

The chapters of U.S. immigration policy that have attempted to define America are numerous: the Asian exclusion laws beginning in the late 1800s; the 1917 literacy law; the Palmer Raids; national origins quotas of the 1920s; heightened political and social exclusions of the 1952 act; the clampdown on asylum applicants through the 1980s and 1990s are important examples. But each example faced some resistance—even presidential vetoes—from Americans who saw things differently.

Throughout U.S. history, the country and its people have been constantly challenged with the question: who is an American? At times, the question has been answered narrowly, at times broadly. The question was answered narrowly when Africans were not regarded as full persons at the founding of the nation. The question was answered narrowly when Asian immigrants were excluded and denied the right to citizenship through naturalization. The question was answered narrowly when children of Native Americans were taken from their families and placed into schools where the goal was to "kill the Indian in him, and save the man." The question was answered narrowly when immigration quota laws restricted southern and eastern Europeans, Catholics, and Jews. The question was answered narrowly when Japanese Americans were interned. The question is answered narrowly each time a hate crime occurs or a racial epithet is hurled. The basis for narrowly defining the community of Americans at times is asserted as questioning loyalty; at other times, the basis is unassimilability; sometimes, it is just plain discomfort with difference or racism.

Other times, the question, who is an American, has been answered broadly. When naturalization rights were extended to those of African descent in 1870, when the Chinese exclusion laws were repealed in 1943, when the 1964 Civil Rights Act was enacted, when the immigration quota system was repealed in 1965, the question was answered broadly. When hate crimes legislation is enacted and perpetrators of hate crimes are prosecuted, the question is answered broadly. When George W. Bush appointed the most racially diverse cabinet ever, the question was answered broadly. In the wake of September 11, the question was answered broadly again by President Bush when he visited a mosque to demonstrate support of American Muslims, and when Attorney General John Ashcroft spoke out against racial profiling.[106] The question is answered broadly when any American reaches out to another American from a background that we have been conditioned to distrust, dislike, or ostracize.

Beginning at an early age we encounter a good deal of discourse about the virtues and strengths of our pluralistic society. A typical fifth grade social studies textbook, *America Will Be,* begins with a chapter entitled "A Nation of Many Peoples," and the first paragraph contains this passage: "From the earliest times, America has been a land of many peoples. This rich mix of cultures has shaped every part of life in the United States today." The authors continue: as a "pluralistic culture, life is exciting. People work, join together, struggle, learn, and grow."[107]

Few would deny—at least publicly—the aspirations and optimism contained in this sentiment. The public face of American pluralism—dominated by politicians, professionals, and community leaders as we have seen after September 11—is mostly positive. Certainly one can point to statements of outliers such as Louisiana Congressman John Cooksey (in referring to American Muslims with turbans, he said that anyone wearing "a diaper on his head and a fan belt wrapped around the diaper" ought to be "pulled over for extra questioning at airports") or perpetrators of hate crimes (recall the Huntington, New York, man screaming, "[I am] doing this for my country" as he attempted to run down a Pakistani woman with his car),[108] but those statements are publicly criticized and labeled as out of the mainstream. In this America, most leaders speak proudly of our diversity and the strength it brings to the nation.

In spite of the sentiment expressed publicly, there is and, as we have seen from our history lesson, always has been cause for concern over another America, where private sentiment about pluralism and diversity remains Eurocentric. From private conversations among truck drivers ("A lot of [folks] are saying, 'If you can't speak American, go back to where you came from'")[109] to the fact that fully one-third of all Americans favored the internment of Arab Americans following the events of September 11, the broad vision of an American appears problematic for many.[110] Attitudes about immigration reveal much about attitudes toward pluralism. When I speak at public forums on immigration policy, the fervor and rabidity of many of the restrictionists in the audience suggests that a strictly Eurocentric vision of America remains dominant in the minds of many. Some of these individuals are simply racists, representing extreme views. Yet I worry about people of goodwill who seem enamored of anti-immigrant zealots. Those zealots do the nation further harm and disfavor by emboldening the misguided who would embrace the hateful rhetoric and act rudely and even violently.

In our liberal society that enables immigrants and refugees from most parts of the world to enter, being an American is not a function of race or ethnicity. Perhaps a famed Filipino American writer put it best when he wrote that "America is in the heart."[111] Yet for reasons of racial or ethnic bias, questions of loyalty, or simply discomfort with difference, Americans of non-European descent are stigmatized or ostracized—even demonized—to the point of *de facto* losing their status as Americans, or even being welcomed members of the society. Depending on the circumstances and the conditions, the power to "de-Americanize" entire racial or ethnic groups can be controlled not only by policy makers, but by moblike actions and even individual actions or words. For each time a misguided person acts or speaks in terms that mark the subject as unwanted or "not one of us," a message of expatriation has been delivered. Broad, official government targeting of racial or ethnic groups only emboldens these racist vigilantes. The tragedy is that intransigent views of who cannot possibly be Americans, such as migrant Mexicans attempting to cross the border, lead us to tolerate avoidable deaths at the hands of Operation Gatekeeper.

Changes in practices and policies reflecting a broader vision of America are possible, but require persistent challenge to programs that are premised on a narrow vision of who an American is. On the local and private level, as the power to *de facto* disenfranchise clearly exists in the hands of a few, the ability to influence the views of such power holders who remain open-minded through education and experience is also clear. Stories of good-hearted people, who are open to new visions of community after getting to know their new neighbors, provide hope that our society has the capability of forging a broad, accepting notion toward Americans of different backgrounds and cultures.

Our nation's immigration and refugee policies tell us much about ourselves, including whom we tolerate, much less respect. We have a choice between two Americas—one narrow and one broad. One choice is closed-minded, resistant to continuing changes that will continue to breed tension and violence. The other is one that embraces change and encourages integration in the hopes of building a stronger, better community. The choice we make, individually, locally, and nationally, will tell us much about ourselves as a country, as a community, and as human beings.

Appendix

TABLE A-1: Immigration by Region and Selected Country of Last Residence, Fiscal Years 1820–2000

Region and Country of Last Residence	1820	1821–1830	1831–1840	1841–1850	1851–1860	1861–1870	1871–1880	1881–1890
All countries	8,385	143,439	599,125	1,713,251	2,598,214	2,314,824	2,812,191	5,246,613
Europe	7,690	98,797	495,681	1,597,442	2,452,577	2,065,141	2,271,925	4,735,484
Austria-Hungary						7,800	72,969	353,719
Austria						7,124	63,009	127,681
Hungary						484	9,960	127,681
Belgium	1	27	22	5,074	4,718	6,734	7,221	20,177
Czechoslovakia								
Denmark	20	169	1,063	539	3,749	17,094	31,771	88,132
France	371	8,497	45,575	77,262	76,358	35,986	72,206	50,464
Germany	968	6,761	152,454	434,626	951,667	787,468	718,182	1,452,970
Greece		20	49	16	31	72	210	2,308
Ireland	3,614	50,724	207,381	780,719	914,119	435,778	436,871	655,482
Italy	30	409	2,253	1,870	9,231	11,725	55,759	307,309
Netherlands	49	1,078	1,412	8,251	10,789	9,102	16,541	53,701
Norway-Sweden	3	91	1,201	13,903	20,931	109,298	211,245	568,362
Norway							95,323	176,586
Sweden							115,922	391,776
Poland	5	16	369	105	1,164	2,027	12,970	51,806
Portugal	35	145	829	550	1,055	2,658	14,082	16,978
Romania							11	6,348
Soviet Union	14	75	277	551	457	2,512	39,284	213,282
Spain	139	2,477	2,125	2,209	9,298	6,697	5,266	4,419
Switzerland	31	3,226	4,821	4,644	25,011	23,286	28,293	81,988
United Kingdom	2,410	25,079	75,810	267,044	423,974	606,896	548,043	807,357
Yugoslavia								
Other Europe		3	40	79	5	8	1,001	682
Asia	6	30	55	141	41,538	64,759	124,160	69,942
China	1	2	8	35	41,397	64,301	123,201	61,711
Hong Kong								

Region and Country of Last Residence	1820	1821–1830	1831–1840	1841–1850	1851–1860	1861–1870	1871–1880	1881–1890
India	1	8	39	36	43	69	163	269
Iran								
Israel								
Japan						186	149	2,270
Korea								
Philippines								
Turkey	1	20	7	59	83	131	404	3,782
Vietnam								
Other Asia	3		1	11	15	72	243	1,910
America	387	11,564	33,424	62,469	74,720	166,607	404,044	**426,967**
Canada	209	2,277	13,624	41,723	59,309	153,878	383,640	393,304
Mexico	1	4,817	6,599	3,271	3,078	2,191	5,162	1,913
Caribbean	164	3,834	12,301	13,528	10,660	9,046	13,957	29,042
Cuba								
Dominican Republic								
Haiti								
Jamaica								
Other Caribbean	164	3,834	12,301	13,528	10,660	9,046	13,957	29,042
Central America	2	105	44	368	449	95	157	404
El Salvador								
Other Central America	2	105	44	368	449	95	157	404
South America	11	531	856	3,579	1,224	1,397	1,128	2,304
Argentina								
Colombia								
Ecuador								
Other South America	11	531	856	3,579	1,224	1,397	1,128	2,304
Other America								
Africa	1	16	54	55	210	312	358	857
Oceania	1	2	9	29	158	214	10,914	12,574
Not specified	300	33,030	69,902	53,115	29,011	17,791	790	789

(continued)

TABLE A-1 (Continued)

Region and Country of Last Residence	1891–1900	1901–1910	1911–1920	1921–1930	1931–1940	1941–1950	1951–1960	1961–1970
All countries	3,687,564	8,795,386	5,735,811	4,107,209	528,431	1,035,039	2,518,479	3,321,677
Europe	3,555,352	8,056,040	4,321,887	2,463,194	347,566	621,147	1,325,727	1,123,492
Austria-Hungary	592,707	2,145,266	896,342	63,548	11,424	28,329	103,743	26,022
Austria	234,081	668,209	453,649	32,868	3,563	24,860	67,106	20,621
Hungary	181,288	808,511	442,693	30,680	7,861	3,469	36,637	5,401
Belgium	18,167	41,635	33,746	15,846	4,817	12,189	18,575	9,192
Czechoslovakia			3,426	102,194	14,393	8,347	918	3,273
Denmark	50,231	65,285	41,983	32,430	2,559	5,393	10,984	9,201
France	30,770	73,379	61,897	49,610	12,623	38,809	51,121	45,237
Germany	505,152	341,498	143,945	412,202	114,058	226,578	477,765	190,796
Greece	15,979	167,519	184,201	51,084	9,119	8,973	47,608	85,969
Ireland	388,416	339,065	146,181	211,234	10,973	19,789	48,362	32,966
Italy	651,893	2,045,877	1,109,524	455,315	68,028	57,661	185,491	214,111
Netherlands	26,758	48,262	43,718	26,948	7,150	14,860	52,277	30,606
Norway-Sweden	321,281	440,039	161,469	165,780	8,700	20,765	44,632	32,600
Norway	95,015	190,505	66,395	68,531	4,740	10,100	22,935	15,484
Sweden	226,266	249,534	95,074	97,249	3,960	10,665	21,697	17,116
Poland	96,720		4,813	227,734	17,026	7,571	9,985	53,539
Portugal	27,508	69,149	89,732	29,994	3,329	7,423	19,588	76,065
Romania	12,750	53,008	13,311	67,646	3,871	1,076	1,039	2,531
Soviet Union	505,290	1,597,306	921,201	61,742	1,370	571	671	2,465
Spain	8,731	27,935	68,611	28,958	3,258	2,898	7,894	44,659
Switzerland	31,179	34,922	23,901	29,676	5,512	10,547	17,675	18,453
United Kingdom	271,538	525,950	341,408	339,570	31,572	139,306	202,824	213,822
Yugoslavia			1,888	49,064	5,835	1,576	8,225	11,604
Other Europe	282	39,945	31,400	42,619	11,949	8,486	16,350	11,604
Asia	74,862	323,543	247,236	112,059	16,595	37,038	153,249	427,642
China	14,799	20,605	21,278	29,907	4,928	16,709	9,657	34,764
Hong Kong							15,541	75,007
India	68	4,713	2,082	1,886	496	1,761	1,973	27,189

Region and Country of Last Residence	*1891–1900*	*1901–1910*	*1911–1920*	*1921–1930*	*1931–1940*	*1941–1950*	*1951–1960*	*1961–1970*
Iran				241	195	1,380	3,388	10,339
Israel						476	25,476	29,602
Japan	25,942	129,797	83,837	33,462	1,948	1,555	46,250	39,988
Korea						107	6,231	34,526
Philippines					528	4,691	19,307	98,376
Turkey	30,425	157,369	134,066	33,824	1,065	798	3,519	10,142
Vietnam							335	4,340
Other Asia	3,628	11,059	5,973	12,739	7,435	9,551	21,572	63,369
America	**38,972**	**361,888**	**1,143,671**	**1,516,716**	**160,037**	**354,804**	**996,944**	**1,716,374**
Canada & Netherlands	3,311	179,226	742,185	924,515	108,527	171,718	377,952	413,310
Mexico	971	49,642	219,004	459,287	22,319	60,589	299,811	453,937
Caribbean	**33,066**	**107,548**	**123,424**	**74,899**	**15,502**	**49,725**	**123,091**	**470,213**
Cuba				15,901	9,571	26,313	78,948	208,536
Dominican Republic					1,150	5,627	9,897	93,292
Haiti					191	911	4,442	34,499
Jamaica							8,869	74,06
Other Caribbean	33,066	107,548	123,424	58,998	4,590	16,874	20,935	58,980
Central America	**549**	**8,192**	**17,159**	**15,769**	**5,861**	**21,665**	**44,751**	**101,330**
El Salvador					673	5,132	5,895	14,992
Other Central America	549	8,192	17,159	15,769	5,188	16,533	38,856	86,338
South America	**1,075**	**17,280**	**41,899**	**42,215**	**7,803**	**21,831**	**91,628**	**257,940**
Argentina					1,349	3,338	19,486	49,721
Colombia					1,223	3,858	18,048	72,028
Ecuador					337	2,417	9,841	36,780
Other South America	1,075	17,280	41,899	42,215	4,894	12,218	44,253	99,411
Other America				31	25	29,276	59,711	19,644
Africa	**350**	**7,368**	**8,443**	**6,286**	**1,750**	**7,3672**	**14,092**	**28,954**
Oceania	**3,965**	**13,024**	**13,427**	**8,726**	**2,483**	**14,551**	**12,976**	**25,122**
Not specified	14,063	33,523	1,147	228		142	12,491	93

(continued)

TABLE A-1 (*Continued*)

Region and Country of Last Residence	1971–1980	1981–1990	1991–2000	1997	1998	1999	2000	Total 181 years, 1820–2000
All countries	4,493,314	7,338,062	9,095,417	798,378	654,451	646,468	849,807	66,089,431
Europe	800,368	761,550	1,359,737	122,358	92,911	94,373	133,362	38,460,797
Austria-Hungary	16,028	24,885	24,882	1,964	1,435	1,518	2,024	4,367,664
Austria	9,478	18,340	15,500	1,044	610	727	997	1,844,446
Hungary	6,550	6,545	9,382	920	825	791	1,027	1,677,142
Belgium	5,329	7,066	7,090	633	557	522	827	217,646
Czechoslovakia	6,023	7,227	9,816	1,169	931	895	1,415	155,617
Denmark	4,439	5,370	6,079	507	447	387	556	376,491
France	25,069	32,353	35,820	3,007	2,961	2,664	4,093	823,407
Germany	74,414	91,961	92,606	6,941	6,923	7,442	12,372	7,176,071
Greece	92,369	38,377	26,759	1,483	1,183	4,061	5,138	730,663
Ireland	11,490	31,969	56,950	932	907	806	1,279	4,782,083
Italy	129,368	67,254	62,722	2,190	1,966	1,681	2,695	5,435,830
Netherlands	10,492	12,238	13,308	1,197	1,036	881	1,466	387,540
Norway-Sweden	10,472	15,182	17,893	1,517	1,344	1,284	1,977	2,163,847
Norway	3,941	4,164	5,178	391	327	358	513	758,897
Sweden	6,531	11,018	12,715	1,126	1,017	926	1,464	1,259,523
Poland	37,234	83,252	163,747	11,729	8,202	8,487	9,773	770,083
Portugal	101,710	40,431	22,916	1,690	1,523	1,078	1,402	524,177
Romania	12,393	30,857	51,203	5,276	4,833	5,417	6,521	256,044
Soviet Union	38,961	57,677	462,874	48,238	28,984	32,740	43,807	3,906,580
Spain	39,141	20,433	17,157	1,607	1,185	1,074	1,406	302,305
Switzerland	8,235	8,849	11,841	1,302	1,090	885	1,349	371,280
United Kingdom	137,374	159,173	151,866	11,950	10,170	8,663	14,532	5,271,016
Yugoslavia	30,540	18,762	66,557	9,913	7,264	7,077	12,213	202,828
Other Europe	9,287	8,234	57,651	9,113	9,970	6,811	8,517	239,625
Asia	1,588,178	2,738,157	2,795,672	258,561	212,799	193,961	255,860	8,814,852
China	124,326	346,747	419,114	44,356	41,034	29,579	41,861	1,33,490
Hong Kong	113,467	98,215	109,779	7,974	7,379	6,533	7,199	412,009

Region and Country of Last Residence	1971–1980	1981–1990	1991–2000	1997	1998	1999	2000	181 years, 1820–2000
India	164,134	250,786	363,060	36,092	34,288	28,355	39,072	818,776
Iran	45,136	116,172	68,556	6,291	4,945	5,042	6,505	245,407
Israel	37,713	44,273	39,397	2,951	2,546	2,538	3,893	176,937
Japan	49,775	47,085	67,942	5,640	5,647	4,770	7,730	530,186
Korea	267,638	333,746	164,166	13,626	13,691	12,301	15,214	806,414
Philippines	354,987	548,764	503,945	47,842	33,176	29,590	40,578	1,530,598
Turkey	13,399	23,233	38,212	4,596	4,016	2,472	2,713	450,539
Vietnam	172,820	280,782	286,145	37,121	16,534	19,164	25,340	744,422
Other Asia	244,783	648,354	735,356	52,072	49,543	52,717	65,746	1,766,074
America	1,982,735	3,615,225	4,486,806	359,619	298,156	312,324	397,201	17,554,354
Canada & Netherlands	169,939	156,938	191,987	15,788	14,295	12,948	21,475	4,487,572
Mexico	640,294	1,655,843	2,249,421	146,680	130,661	146,436	171,748	6,138,150
Caribbean	741,126	872,051	978,787	101,095	72,948	70,386	85,875	3,681,964
Cuba	265,863	144,578	169,322	29,913	15,415	13,289	19,322	918,032
Dominican Republic	148,135	252,035	335,251	24,966	20,267	17,745	17,441	845,387
Haiti	56,335	138,379	179,644	14,941	13,316	16,459	22,004	414,401
Jamaica	137,577	208,148	169,227	17,585	14,819	14,449	15,654	598,727
Other Caribbean	134,216	128,911	125,343	13,690	9,131	8,444	11,454	905,417
Central America	134,640	468,088	526,915	43,451	35,368	41,441	62,708	1,346,543
El Salvador	34,436	213,539	215,798	17,741	14,329	14,16	22,332	490,465
Other Central America	100,204	254,549	311,117	25,710	21,039	27,025	40,376	856,078
South America	295,741	461,847	539,656	52,600	44,884	41,112	55,392	1,789,945
Argentina	29,897	27,327	26,644	2,055	1,649	1,578	2,485	157,762
Colombia	77,347	122,849	128,499	12,795	11,618	9,769	14,191	423,852
Ecuador	50,077	56,315	76,592	7,763	6,840	8,903	7,658	232,359
Other South America	138,420	255,356	307,921	29,987	24,777	20,862	31,058	975,972
Other America	995	458	40	5		1	3	110,180
Africa	80,779	176,893	354,939	44,668	37,494	33,740	40,969	689,084
Oceania	41,242	45,205	55,845	4,855	4,403	4,299	5,962	260,467
Not specified	12	1,032	42,418	8,317	8,688	8,771	16,453	309,877

Source: 2000 INS Statistical Yearbook, 6.

Notes

Introduction

1. *Woman 113th Border Crosser to Die*, SAN DIEGO UNION-TRIBUNE, September 15, 1998.
2. *72 Illegals Rescued on the Mountain*, LA VOZ, March 31, 1998.
3. *3 Illegal Immigrants Die in Winter Storm*, SAN FRANCISCO EXAMINER, March 7, 2000.
4. *Shifting to the East: U.S. Fights to Close Gaps from Otay to Jacumba*, SAN DIEGO UNION-TRIBUNE, May 26, 1996.
5. Joyce Vialet, *A Brief History of U.S. Immigration Policy* 6 (Library of Congress, 1980).
6. Suzy Platt, ed., *Respectfully Quoted: A Dictionary of Quotations Requested from the Congressional Research Service* 169 (U.S. Government Printing Office, 1989).
7. Since the intent of this text is to review racial and political subtexts of U.S. immigration policy, the tragic treatment of Native Americans by the United States is not covered. The well-documented movement to "Americanize" many Native American children by taking them from their homes to extract the "savage" from them is, however, consistent with the themes of this book that there has been an image of what a "real" American is that has driven much immigration policy. This is also not a book about involuntary migration, especially of the 350,000 African slaves who were brought to areas that became part of the United States. Again, slavery and the constitutional inferiority imprinted on those of African descent demonstrate that they too were not regarded as "real" Americans (or humans, for that matter).

Chapter 1. The Western European New World and the New Americans

1. Thomas A. Bailey, David M. Kennedy, and Lizabeth Cohen, *The American Pageant* 2–3 (11th ed., Boston: Houghton Mifflin, 1998).
2. Joyce Vialet, *A Brief History of U.S. Immigration Policy* (Library of Congress, 1980).
3. *Americans All*, OMAHA WORLD-HERALD, July 4, 2001, at 10.
4. New York Convention, at 5.
5. As Gerald Newman points out, colonial and state quarantine measures targeted acute diseases that applied to a "state's own citizens as well as to aliens and citizens of other states." Gerald L. Newman, *The Lost Century of American Immigration Law (1776–1875)*, 93 COLUMBIA L. REV. 1833 (1993), at 1860.
6. Id.

7. Id.

8. Id.

9. 8 U.S.C. § 1182(a)(15) (1980).

10. Newman, *Lost Century*. The right to travel between states clearly was not a concept that the poor enjoyed as fundamental during this period. In article IV of the Articles of Confederation, "paupers, vagabonds and fugitives from justice" were excepted from the equal enjoyment of the privileges and immunities of citizens.

11. Id. at 1866–74.

12. 1 Stat. 103–104.

13. The period of residence was changed to five years on January 29, 1795, and the person was asked to renounce allegiance to any foreign government or nobility ("declare in court their intention to become citizens of the United States and to renounce any allegiance to a foreign prince, potentate, state, or sovereignty three years before admission as citizens")—a requirement that remains part of the law today. The residency requirement was increased to fourteen years under the unpopular Alien and Sedition Act of 1798, but cut back to five years on April 14, 1802. Jack Wasserman, *The Immigration and Nationality Act of 1952—Our New Alien and Sedition Law*, 27 TEMPLE L. QUARTERLY 62 (1953).

14. In an act of 1705, if a person brought up in the Christian religion denies the being of a God, or the Trinity, or asserts there are more Gods than one, or denies the Christian religion to be true, or the scriptures to be of divine authority, he is punishable on the first offense by incapacity to hold any office or employment ecclesiastical, civil, or military; on the second by disability to sue, to take any gift or legacy, to be guardian, executor, or administrator, and by three years' imprisonment, without bail. A father's right to the custody of his own children being founded in law on his right of guardianship, this being taken away, they may of course be severed from him and put, by the authority of a court, into more orthodox hands.

15. 11 S.&R. 394, 26 Pa. 342.

16. New York Convention, at 10.

17. Id. at 17.

18. Dillingham Commission.

19. J. A. Leo Lemay, *Benjamin Franklin: Writings* 374 (New York: Library of America, 1987).

20. Clinton Rossiter, ed., *The Federalist Papers* 94 (New York: Mentor, 1961).

21. Merrill Peterson, ed., *Thomas Jefferson: Writings* 1097 (New York: Library of America, 1984).

22. John Adams, Inaugural Address In the City of Philadelphia, March 4, 1797, found at <http://www.bartleby.com/124/pres15.html>.

23. John C. Miller, *Crisis in Freedom: The Alien and Sedition Acts* 75 (Boston: Little, Brown, 1951).

24. Id.

25. Id. at 147–48.

26. *Worcester v. State of Georgia*, 31 U.S. 515, 542–43 (1892).

27. Alexander Hamilton, Excerpts from the Treasury Secretary's "Report on Manufactures," 1791 <http://www.courses.pasleybrothers.com/texts/Report_on_Manufactures.html>.

28. Andrew Carnegie, *Triumphant Democracy* 34–35 (Port Washington, N.Y.: Kennikat, 1886).

29. Quoted by William S. Bernard, *American Immigration Policy* 6 (New York: Harper & Bros., 1950).

30. Dillingham Commission.

31. Kitty Calavita, *U.S. Immigration and Policy Responses: The Limits of Legislation* 57, in Wayne Cornelieus et al., eds., *Controlling Immigration* (Stanford: Stanford University Press, 1994).

32. Carl Schurz, "True Americanism" (1859), in *Speeches of Carl Schurz* (Philadelphia, 1865).

33. Vialet, *Brief History.*

34. Id.

35. Id.

36. Id.

37. Id.

38. Bill Ong Hing, *Making and Remaking Asian America through Immigration Policy 1850–1990* 19–20, 48 (Stanford: Stanford University Press, 1993).

39. Vialet, *Brief History.*

40. Id.

41. Id.

42. Id.

43. Id.

Chapter 2. The Undesirable Asian

1. The San Jose Railroad, connecting San Francisco with San Jose, California, was the first railroad to experiment with Chinese labor in the early to mid-1860s. Ping Chiu, *Chinese Labor in California, 1850–1880: An Economic Survey* 41–42 (Madison: State Historical Society of Wisconsin, 1963).

2. Mary Coolidge, *Chinese Immigration* 21 (New York: Arno, 1909).

3. Rodger Daniels, *The Politics of Prejudice* 19 (Berkeley: University of California Press, 1962).

4. Ping Chiu, *Chinese Labor,* at 100.

5. Richard P. Cole and Gabriel J. Chin, *Emerging from the Margins of Historical Consciousness: Chinese Immigrants and the History of American Law,* 17 LAW & HIST. REV. 325 (1999).

6. Id.

7. Id. at 101.

8. Cole and Chin, *Emerging from the Margins,* at 342.

9. Alexander Saxton, *The Indispensable Enemy: Labor and the Anti-Chinese Movement in California* 72 (Berkeley: University of California Press, 1971).

10. Id.

11. Id.

12. Id.

13. Id. at 73.

14. Chiu, *Chinese Labor,* at 264.

15. Id. at 257.

16. Id. at 252.

17. Id. at 254.

18. Saxton, *Indispensable Enemy,* at 147.

19. Chiu, *Chinese Labor,* at 256.

20. Id. at 261.

21. Id. at 74.

22. Saxton, *Indispensable Enemy*, at 137

23. Id. at 140.

24. Id.

25. Id. at 142.

26. Id.

27. Id. at 145.

28. Id. at 147.

29. Id. at 148.

30. Id. at 149.

31. *Yick Wo v. Hopkins*, 118 U.S. 356, 373–74 (1886).

32. Sexton, *Indispensable Enemy*, at 42.

33. Chiu, *Chinese Labor*, at 265.

34. Saxton, *Indispensable Enemy*, at 42.

35. Id.

36. Id.

37. Id.

38. Id. at 43.

39. Id.

40. Stuart Miller, *The Unwelcome Immigrant: The American Image of Chinese 1785–1882* 131 (Berkeley: University of California Press, 1969).

41. Id. at 132.

42. Edward Hutchinson, *Legislative History of American Immigration Policy 1798–1965* 85–6 (Philadelphia: University of Pennsylvania Press, 1981).

43. See *In re Yup*, 5 Sawyer 155 (1878).

44. Coolidge, *Chinese Immigration*, at 418.

45. HARPER'S WEEKLY, April 1, 1882, 194 (editorial).

46. Peter Irons, *Justice at War* 9 (Berkeley: University of California Press, 1983).

47. Jesse Steiner, *The Japanese Invasion* 57 (Chicago: McClung, 1917).

48. Roy Akagi, *Japan's Foreign Relations, 1524–1936* 437 (Tokyo: Hokaseiko, 1946).

49. James Patterson, *American in the Twentieth Century* 94 (New York: Knopf, 1983).

50. Many Asian Indians who migrated to the Western Hemisphere settled in Canada first, because of the British Commonwealth connection.

51. California Board of Control, *California and the Oriental: Japanese, Chinese, and Hindus* 10–2 (Sacramento: State Printing Office, 1920).

52. Emory Bogardus, *American Attitudes Towards Filipinos*, 14 SOCIOLOGY AND SOCIAL RESEARCH 59, 64 (1929).

53. Id. at 63–64.

54. C. Crow, *What About the Filipinos?* WORLD'S WORK (September 1913), at 519–20.

55. *Roldan v. Los Angeles County*, 129 Cal. App. 267 (1933).

56. 32 Cal.2d 711 (1948).

57. The U.S. Supreme Court eventually struck down antimiscegenation laws in 1967 in *Loving v. Virginia*, 388 U.S. 1, a challenge to Virginia's ban on interracial marriage. The couple had been convicted and "exiled" from Virginia for twenty-five years; they could have received a five-year prison term. The trial judge stated: "Almighty God created the races white, black, yellow, malay and red, and he placed them on separate continents. And but for the interference with

his arrangement there would be no cause for such marriages. The fact that he separated the races show[s] that he did not intend the races to mix." Apparently, Maryland adopted the first anti-miscegenation law. Virginia's was adopted in 1691, forbidding, under penalty of banishment, marriages between whites, on the one hand, and Indians, Negroes and Mulattos.

58. Bill Ong Hing, *Making and Remaking Asian America Through Immigration Policy, 1850–1990* 36–38 (Stanford: Stanford University Press, 1993).

Chapter 3. "Translate This"

1. See *United States ex rel. Friedman v. Tod, Commissioner of Immigration,* 296 F. 888 (2nd Cir. 1924). The court ultimately held that the words used to test Ms. Friedman were not words in ordinary usage, and as such, the test was not contemplated by the statute. The court decided that Ms. Friedman should be reexamined to determine whether she could read ordinary Yiddish.

2. Bill Ong Hing, *Making and Remaking Asian America Through Immigration Policy, 1850–1990* 21 (Stanford: Stanford University Press, 1993).

3. Kitty Calavita, *U.S. Immigration and Policy Responses: The Limits of Legislation* 57, in Wayne Cornelieus et al., eds., *Controlling Immigration* (Stanford: Stanford University Press, 1994).

4. CONGRESSIONAL RECORD, 66th Cong., 3rd sess., 1921: 187.

5. Henry P. Guzda, *Ellis Island a Welcome Site? Only after Years of Reform; History of U.S. Immigrant Receiving Station in New York Harbor,* MONTHLY LABOR REVIEW, Vol. 109, 30, July 1986.

6. "Swat-the-Hyphen Movement," THE LITERARY DIGEST, October 30, 1915, 943–44.

7. Id.

8. "America First," THE WASHINGTON POST, October 13, 1915, at 6.

9. In his book, *Strangers in the Land: Patterns of American Nativism 1860–1925* (New Brunswick, N.J.: Rutgers University Press, 1963), John Higham explains, "Many Americans believed that the influx of aliens threatened their established social structure, endangered the nation's economic welfare, and spelled doom for the existing governmental system." Higham defines nativism as "an intense opposition to an internal minority on the ground of its foreign (i.e., 'un-American') connections."

10. John Higham, *Strangers in the Land,* at 9.

11. This "racial nativism" or "Anglo-Saxon nationalism" gained intellectual and emotional strength following the Civil War. By 1862 the popular national publication, HARPER'S WEEKLY, was featuring the political cartoons of famed Thomas Nast. HARPER'S was not the sole contributor to this media-centered indoctrination of anti-immigrant and anti-Catholic sentiment. In fact, PULITZER'S NEW YORK WORLD, as well as HEARST'S NEW YORK JOURNAL, along with other national publications, began to feature regularly such cartoons. Here one can find a feathered and robed Indian selling "scalper's tickets"; black mammies, uncle toms, and ridiculous dandies; monkey-faced, drunken rowdy Irishmen with shillalahs; and Chinese coolies and laundry workers with queues. To these were added new stereotypes of the recently arrived Jews, Italians, and eastern Europeans, as well as new imagery for those whose reputation had been tarnished by world events, such as Germans, Mexicans, and Latin Americans.

12. *The Murder of Chief Hennessy & the New Orleans "Mafia" Trials,* Tom Smith, fall 2003, unpublished manuscript.

13. Id.

14. In Washington, the organization that became known as the Immigration and Naturalization Service (INS) was moved from the Treasury Department to the Department of Labor in

1913. President Franklin Roosevelt transferred the agency to the Justice Department in 1940. In 2003, immigration and deportation functions were incorporated into the new Department of Homeland Security.

15. See also Higham, *Strangers,* at 101–3 for more details on the politicians (Senator Chadler and Senator Lodge); and also the rise of the Immigration Restriction League.

16. Id.

17. Id.

18. Id. at 130.

19. Higham mentions, first, that William Jennings Bryant's loss to McKinley in 1896 marked the notice by politicians that immigrants were important to their elections, thus "the crest of nativism [had] passed"; and second, that a vociferous immigrant opposition to the literacy test was organizing itself.

20. Id. at 108–9.

21. Id.

22. Id. at 126–27.

23. Id.

24. Id. at 165–66.

25. Id.

26. See also id. at 190–91 for details of politicking and the race between Taft and Wilson.

27. See also id. at 191: "The voting followed the characteristic line-up that had emerged out of twentieth-century nativism: the South and Far West almost unanimous for restriction, the urban areas of the North strongly against it, and considerable opposition lingering in the old immigrant districts of the Midwest."

28. Id. at 202–3.

29. Id.

30. Id.

31. Higham continues with this commentary:

> The 1917 statute was essentially the immigration restriction bill that Wilson had blocked in February 1915; the subsequent German crisis supplied the impetus for reviving and enacting a measure grounded in prewar problems. By the time the law was finally passed, it served no immediately restrictive purpose; the European war had already reduced emigration far more drastically than any legislator could hope to do. Proponents of a literacy test, however, warned that once the war ended a real deluge would begin. Also they made much of the hyphenate issue. In their arguments all of the customary complaints against southern and eastern European immigration mingled somewhat incongruously with the excitement over divided loyalties. Some observers noted that the nationalities that the literacy test was designed to penalize were showing, in contrast to the shocking behavior of German-Americans, "almost incomprehensible" restraint. Nonetheless, the German example suggested that one could never tell when a foreigner might betray the country to an enemy. To the Chicago *Tribune* the problems created by the war in Europe demonstrated the need for a more "intense and inspiring nationality" and made immigration restriction a phase of national defense. (202–3)

32. There were two important exceptions to the literacy requirement imposed upon all new immigrants: (1) an admissible alien might bring in members of his immediate family despite their illiteracy; and (2) in the interest of Russian Jews, the same exemption applied to all aliens who could prove they were fleeing from religious persecution. Significantly, refugees from political persecution received no such exemption.

Chapter 4. The Xenophobic 1920s

1. Charles Gordon and Harry Rosenfield, *Immigration Law and Procedure* 1-11 to 1-12 (New York: Matthew Bender, 1981).

2. Arnold H. Leibowitz, *Immigration Law and Refugee Policy* 1-10 to 1-11 (New York: Matthew Bender, 1983).

3. Interview with Arthur Schlesinger, Jr. accessed at <http://www.courttv.com/greatesttrials/sacco.vanzetti/schlesinger.html on October 18, 2001>.

4. "The Sacco-Vanzetti Project 2002: 75 Years Since the Execution" accessed at <http://www.saccovanzettiproject.org/pages/hstrcl.html> on October 8, 2001.

5. Drawn from *The Case of Sacco and Vanzetti,* an article running in March 1927, in THE ATLANTIC by Feliz Frankfurter. Accessed at <wysiwyg://104/http://www.theatlantic.com/unbound/flashbks/oj/frankff.html> on September 22, 2001.

For more information on this topic see also *Men, Mobs and the Law: Defense Campaigns and United States Radical History* by Rebecca Nell Hill, Ph.D. diss., University of Minnesota, 2000.

6. Another example of the influence the two men played in social culture was the Official Bulletin of the Sacco-Vanzetti Defense Committee of Boston, Massachusetts. The committee was concerned with efforts to obtain a new trial for Sacco and Vanzetti after their conviction for the murder of F. A. Pamenter and A. Bardelli in Massachusetts.

7. David Wieck, *What Need Be Said,* Sacco Vanzetii Project 2002: 75 Years Since The Execution, at <http://www.saccovanzettiproject.org/pages/context/wiecke.html>.

8. Id.

9. Id.

10. Id.

11. There was a nonquota exception of which some southern and eastern Europeans took advantage. The law permitted a person to be admitted to the United States as an immigrant if the individual had resided in the Western Hemisphere for one year (later changed to five years). So by temporarily living in a Western Hemisphere country, the quota could be avoided.

12. David Weissbrodt, *Immigration Law and Procedure* 13 (St. Paul, Minn.: West Group, 1998).

Chapter 5. The 1952 Act

1. 8 U.S.C. § 1182(a)(28) (1952).

1. Veto of Bill to Revise the Laws Relating to Immigration, Naturalization, and Nationality, June 25, 1952.

3. P.L. 414, 82d Cong. (66 Stat. 163).

4. Arnold Leibowitz, *Immigration Law and Refugee Policy* 1-13 (New York: Matthew Bender, 1983).

5. S. Rept. 1515, 81st Cong., 2d sess. 455.

6. 385 U.S. 630 (1967).

7. 279 F.2d 642 (9th Cir. 1960).

8. Immigration and Naturalization Service, 1967 Annual Report.

9. Immigration and Naturalization Service, 1977 Annual Report.

10. Ch. 29 § 3, 39 Stat. 874 (1917) (repealed 1952).

11. S. Rep. No. 1515, 81st Cong, 2d sess., 345.

12. 8 U.S.C. § 1182(a)(4) (1952).

13. 302 F. 2d 652 (9th Cir. 1962), *vacated on other grounds,* 374 U.S. 449, 83 S. Ct. 1804, 10 L. Ed. 2d 1000 (1963).

14. S. Rep. No. 748, 89th Cong., 1st sess. 19, reprinted in 1965 U.S. Code Cong. & Ad. News 3328, 3337; H.R. Rep. No. 745, 89th Cong., 1st sess. 16 (1965).

15. 8 U.S.C. § 1182(a)(4) (1976).

16. 387 U.S. 118 (1967).

17. 673 F. 2d 1036 (9th Cir. 1981).

18. See, e.g., *Matter of Longstaff,* 716 F. 2d 1439, 1441 (5th Cir. 1983).

19. See, for example, the following cases in which the INS required a medical examination and certification prior to exclusion. *In re Beaton,* No. A-11–065-813 (June 6, 1964); *In re Lionel Colin Roberts,* No. A-12-463-838 (May 20, 1964); *In re Anonymous,* No. A-11-065-813 (June 6, 1964); *In re Jose Luis Hernandez-Gutierrez,* No. A-12-633-815 (July 29, 1964); *In re Norman David Flight,* No. A-12-944-125 (September 1965); *In re Caydem,* 12 I & N Dec. 528 (1967); *In re Johan Baptist Berger,* No. A-10379108-New York (July 12, 1967); *In re Antony Denis Hayes,* No. A-12402065-Boston (March 14, 1968).

20. Report on the Public Health Service on the Medical Aspects of H.R. 2379, A Bill to Revise the Laws Relating to Immigration, Naturalization, and Nationality, and for Other Purposes, reprinted in 1952 U.S. Code Cong. & Ad. News 1653, 1700.

In its report on the House bill that became the 1952 Act, the Public Health Service stated:

> In some instances considerable difficulty may be encountered in substantiating a diagnosis of homosexuality. . . . Ordinarily, a history of homosexuality must be obtained from the individual, which he may successfully cover up. Some psychological tests may be helpful in uncovering homosexuality of which the individual, himself, may be unaware. At the present time there are no reliable laboratory tests which would be helpful in making a diagnosis.

Report of the Public Health Service on the Medical Aspects of H.R. 2379, A Bill to Revise the Laws Relating to Immigration, Naturalization, and Nationality, and for Other Purposes, reprinted in 1952 U.S. Code Cong. & Ad. News 1653, 1701.

21. Interview with Jeffrey Appleman, the attorney who represented Carl Hill, San Francisco, Calif., July 17, 2002.

22. Press Release of American Psychiatric Association (December 15, 1973).

23. Memorandum from Julius Richmond, assistant secretary for health, U.S. Department of Health, Education and Welfare, and surgeon general, to William Foege and George Lythcott (August 2, 1979).

24. Report of the surgeon general.

25. Id.

26. Memorandum of John M. Harmon, assistant attorney general, to David L. Crossland, acting commissioner, INS (December 10, 1979), at 8. Further detail of the background of the homosexual exclusion can be found in Note, *The Immigration and Nationality Act and the Exclusion of Homosexuals: Boutilier v. INS Revisited,* 2 CARDOZO L. REV. 359 (1981).

27. Press Release of the Department of Justice (September 9, 1980).

28. Id.

29. Interview with Appleman.

30. November 7, 1980, ALJ decision, at 6.

31. *Lesbian/Gay Freedom Day Committee, Inc. v Immigration & Naturalization Service*, 541 F. Supp. 569, 577–80 (N.D. Cal. 1982), *affirmed*, 714 F. 2d 1470 (9th Cr. 1983).

32. 8 U.S.C. § 1182(a) (1980)

(1) Aliens who are mentally retarded;

(2) Aliens who are insane;

(3) Aliens who have had one or more attacks of insanity;

(4) Aliens afflicted with psychopathic personality, or sexual deviations or a mental defect;

(5) Aliens who are narcotic drug addicts or chronic alcoholics;

(6) Aliens who are afflicted with any dangerous contagious disease;

(7) Aliens not comprehended within any of the foregoing classes who are certified by the examining surgeon as having a physical defect, disease, or disability . . . of such a nature that it may affect the ability of the alien to earn a living.

Section 1182(a) then proceeds to enumerate twenty-six other classes of excludable aliens, none of which constitute medical grounds for exclusion, for example, paupers (1182(a)(8)), anarchists (1182(a)(28)(A)), etc.

33. 8 U.S.C. § 1222 (1980).

34. 8 U.S.C. § 1224 (1980).

35. 8 U.S.C. § 1226(d) (1976).

36. 8 U.S.C. § 1225(a) (1976).

37. H.R. Rep. No. 1365, 82d Cong., 2d sess., reprinted in 1952 U.S. Code Cong. & Ad. News 1653, 1698.

38. Report of the Public Health Service on the Medical Aspects of H.R. 2379, A Bill to Revise the Laws Relating to Immigration, Naturalization, and Nationality, and for Other Purposes, reprinted in H.R. Rep. No. 1365, 82nd Cong., 2d sess., reprinted in 1952 U.S. Code Cong. & Ad. News 1653, 1699 (emphasis added).

39. In the bill as adopted, the exclusion for "paupers, professional beggars, or vagrants" was made the eighth category of exclusions, 8 U.S.C. § 1182(a)(8) (1976), falling after the medical, 8 U.S.C. § 1182(a)(1)–(6) (1976), and joint medical-nonmedical, 8 U.S.C. § 1182(a)(7) (1976), categories.

40. H.R. Rep. No. 1365, 82d Cong., 2d sess., reprinted in 1952 U.S. Code Cong. & Ad. News 1653, 1709.

41. S. Rep. No. 1137, 82d Cong., 2d sess. 45 (1952).

42. 8 U.S.C. § 1226(d) of the U.S. Code.

43. 61 *Interpreter Releases* 377 (1984).

44. *B-2 Visa Available for Non-Spouse Same-Sex Partner of L-1, INS Says*, 70 *Interpreter Releases* 421 (1993).

Chapter 6. 1965 to 1990

1. Edward Hutchinson, *Legislative History of American Immigration Policy, 1798–1965* 376 (Philadelphia: University of Pennsylvania Press, 1981).

2. Comments of Senator Sam J. Ervin Jr. (D.-N.C.), S. Rept. 748, 89th Cong., 1st sess., 52–53 (1965).

3. Hearings before the Subcommittee on Immigration and Naturalization, Committee of the Judiciary, United States Senate, 89th Cong., 1st sess., on S.500 To Amend the Immigration and Naturalization Act, And For Other Purposes. Part 2: March/June/July/August 1965 Congressional Information Service, Inc., 216–18, 226, 242.

4. Hearings before the Subcommittee on Immigration and Naturalization, Committee of the Judiciary, United States Senate, 89th Cong., 1st sess., on S.500 To Amend the Immigration and Naturalization Act, And For Other Purposes. Part 1: February/March; 1965 Congressional Information Service, Inc., 1–3.

5. October 3, 1965, at foot of the Statue of Liberty, signing H.R. 2580 into law (P.L. 89-236), CONGRESSIONAL QUARTERLY ALMANAC, 89th Cong., 1st sess. . . .1965, Vol. XXI, 479, Congressional Quarterly Service).

6. Arnold Leibowitz, *Immigration Law and Refugee Policy* § 1.01 (New York: Matthew Bender, 1983).

7. David Weissbrodt, *Immigration Law and Procedure* 14–16 (St. Paul, Minn.: West Group, 1998).

8. *Health Manpower Programs Hearings Before the Subcommittee on Health and the Environment of the Committee on Interstate and Foreign Commerce*, 94th Cong. 481 (1975) (statement of Hon. Paul G. Rogers, chairman of the Subcommittee on Health and the Environment).

9. Id. at 490 (statement of Leo J. Gehrig, M.D., vice president of the American Hospital Association).

10. Id. at 483 (statement of William D. Holden, M.D., chairman of the Committee on Physician Distribution).

11. Id. at 490.

12. *Health Manpower Legislation, 1975, Part 2, Joint Hearing Before the Subcommittee on Health of the Committee on Labor and Public Welfare on S. 989*, 94th Cong. 689 (1975) (statement of Jack Walsh, supervisor of San Diego County).

13. Id. at 692.

14. *Health Manpower Legislation, 1975, Part 3, Hearings Before the Subcommittee on Health and Public Welfare on S. 989*, 94th Cong. 1527 (statement of Bert Seidman, director of the Department of Social Security).

15. 121 Cong. Rec. H5546, 22333 (daily ed., July 11, 1975).

16. See Charles Gordon and Stanley Mailman, *Immigration Law and Procedure* § 1.4c (1993); Memorandum for the Associate Attorney General, Re: Allocation of Visas under *Silva v. Levi*, Deputy Assistant Attorney General, Office of Legal Counsel, Department of Justice, 3 (May 15, 1978).

17. See U.S. Commission on Civil Rights, *The Tarnished Golden Door* 12 (U.S. Government Printing Office, 1980), *Silva v. Bell*, 605 F.2d 978, 980–982 (7th Cir. 1979); Gordon and Mailman, IMMIGRATION LAW, at § 7.9e.

18. Act of October 20, 1976, P.L. 94-571, 90 Stat. 2703 (1976); *Silva v. Bell*, 605 F.2d at 980–82.

19. *Silva v. Bell*, No. 76C 4268 (N.D. Ill. October 10, 1978) (order granting permanent injunction); see also, No. 76C 1456 (N.D. Ill. June 21, 1977) (final judgment order—visas recaptured).

20. Telegraphic message of Hugh J. Brian, assistant commissioner of detention and deportation, Central Office Immigration and Naturalization Service, CO 242.4-P (August 20, 1982);

memorandum from E. B. Duarte Jr., director, Outreach Program, Central Office Immigration and Naturalization Service, to Outreach Centers, Subject: Silva Update (February 3, 1983).

21. 643 F.2d 471, 476 (7th Cir. 1981).

22. See Visa Bulletin, Visa Office, Bureau of Consular Affairs, U.S. Department of State, Vol. VII, No. 52 (July 1995).

23. See Castro, *Dragnet for Illegal Workers*, TIME, May 10, 1982, at 16; *International Molders and Allied Workers' Local Union v. Nelson*, 799 F.2d 547 (9th Cir. 1986).

24. See *Illegal Alien Raids Trigger Local Lawsuits*, ARGUS-COURIER, August 16, 1982, at 2.

25. See, e.g., *ILGWU v. Sureck*, 681 F.2d (9th Cir. 1982); *Illinois Council v. Pilliod*, 531 F.Supp. 1011 (N.D. Ill. 1982).

26. Immigration and Naturalization Service, 1977 Annual Report 14 (1978).

27. 422 U.S. 873 (1975).

28. 428 U.S. 543 (1976).

29. 468 U.S. 1032 (1984).

30. See earlier chapter quotations from Senators Ted Kennedy and Robert Kennedy, and President Johnson.

31. Karen DeYoung, *Irish Again Look Abroad for Economic Opportunities; Emigration Rates Have Risen Sharply*, THE WASHINGTON POST, December 6, 1986, at A1.

32. Ray Moseley, *In Ireland, An Election, A Dilemma*, CHICAGO TRIBUNE, February 8, 1987, at C12; *Poorest of the Rich*, THE ECONOMIST, January 16, 1988, at 10.

33. Mary Jordy, *West From County Mayo*, THE WASHINGTON POST, March 17, 1987, at A17.

34. *Poorest of the Rich.*

35. DeYoung, *Irish Again Look Abroad.*

36. Howard Kurtz, *Irish Immigrants Struggle in Urban Underground*, THE WASHINGTON POST, March 12, 1989, at A1; Celestine Bohlem, *For Illegal Immigrants, A Time to Test That Luck*, NEW YORK TIMES, March 17, 1989, at B1.

37. Final Report of Select Commission, at 112.

38. Id. at 103.

39. Testimony of Barry R. Chiswick before the Joint Economic Committee, Congress of the United States, S. Hrg. 99–1070, May 22, 1986, 236. Of course this statement was factually incorrect; even under the system at the time, prospective immigrants with skills needed by an employer could qualify for a labor employment category under third or sixth preference.

40. Philip Martin, *Illegal Immigration and the Colonization of the American Labor Market*, Center for Immigration Studies, 1986, at 45 (emphasis added).

41. Annelise Anderson, *Immigration Policy* 21 (Stanford: Hoover Institution, 1988).

42. 67 *Interpreter Releases* 1153–55 (1990).

43. The compromise included portions of S. 3055 sponsored by Simpson, which would speed deportations of criminal aliens. Section 501 expanded the definition of "aggravated felony" to include illicit trafficking in any controlled substance, money laundering, and any crime of violence with a five-year imprisonment imposed. The bill also included both federal and state crimes. Aliens convicted of aggravated felonies would have expedited deportation hearings and would not be released from custody while in deportation proceedings. 67 *Interpreter Releases* 1229–31 (1990).

44. 136 Cong. Rec. S17,109 (daily ed. October 26, 1990) (statement of Sen. Simpson).

45. 8 C.F.R. 214.2(h) (1989).

46. *Matter of Shin*, 11 I.&N. Dec. 686 (Dist. Dir. 1966).

47. 8 U.S.C. 1101(a)(15)(H)(i)(b) (1992).

Chapter 7. Politicizing the Southwest Border

1. Greg Vojtko, *Clinton Joins Opponents of Plan to Punish Immigrants; Feinstein Takes Risky Stand*, CHICAGO SUN-TIMES, October 23, 1994, at 32.

2. John A. Garraty, *The American Nation: A History of the United States* 286 (3d ed., Old Tappan, N.J.: Longman, 1975).

3. Treaty of Peace, Friendship, Limits, and Settlement, February 2, 1848, U.S.-Mex., 9 Stat. 922.

4. John Commons, *Races and Immigrants in America* 107–8 (2d ed., New York: Augustus M. Kelley, 1967).

5. Gerald P. López, *Undocumented Mexican Migration: In Search of a Just Immigration Law and Policy*, 28 UCLA L. REV. 615, 657 (1981).

6. Id.

7. Mark Reisler, *By the Sweat of Their Brow: Mexican Immigrant Labor in the United States 1900–1940* 138 (Westport, Conn.: Greenwood, 1976) (quoting Rep. Edward T. Taylor).

8. California Commission of Immigration and Housing, 1927 Annual Report, at 18.

9. Quoted in Carey McWilliams, *The Great Exception* 156–57 (Berkeley: University of California Press, 1949).

10. U.S. Immigration Commission, Annual Report of the Commissioner General 28 (1923).

11. Fred Bixby, a prominent southwest rancher objected to quotas on Mexican laborers. "We have no Chinamen, we have no Japs. The Hindu is worthless, the Filipino is nothing, and the white man will not do the work." Francisco Balderrama and Raymond Rodriguez, *Decade of Betrayal: Mexican Repatriation in the 1930s* 17 (Albuquerque: University of New Mexico Press, 1995).

12. Balderrama and Rodriguez, *Decade of Betrayal,* at 98.

13. Id. at 98–99.

14. Id. at 99–121.

15. Fred Schmidt, *After the Bracero, An Inquiry Into the Problem of Farm Labor Recruitment,* report submitted to the Department of Employment of the State of California by the Institute of Industrial Relations, University of California, Los Angeles, 1964, at 15.

16. Eleanor Hadley, *A Critical Analysis of the Wetback Problem*, 21 LT. CONTEMP. PROB. 334, 344 (1956).

17. Act of March 20, 1952, P.L. No. 283, 66 Stat. 26.

18. N.Y. TIMES, November 28, 1952, at 24, col. 3.

19. Dan Herbeck, *Family Changed with Keeping Workers in Illegal Conditions,* THE BUFFALO NEWS, June 19, 2002, at B1.

Chapter 8. Patrolling the Border and Sweeping for Mexicans

1. Though these funds created the present-day Border Patrol, the Immigration Service continued as a part of the Department of Labor until 1940.

2. Immigration and Naturalization Service, 1963 Annual Report.

3. Immigration and Naturalization Service, 1964 Annual Report.

4. Immigration and Naturalization Service, 1963 Annual Report.

5. Immigration and Naturalization Service, 1964 Annual Report.

6. Immigration and Naturalization Service, 1966 Annual Report.

7. Immigration and Naturalization Service, 1967 Annual Report.

8. Immigration and Naturalization Service, 1977 Annual Report.

9. Id.

10. Immigration and Naturalization Service, 1966 Annual Report.

11. Immigration and Naturalization Service, 1977 Annual Report.

12. Immigration and Naturalization Service, 1966 Annual Report.

13. *Almeida-Sanchez v. United States*, 413 U.S. 266 (1973).

14. 422 U.S. 873 (1975).

15. *United States v. Brignoni-Ponce*, 422 U.S. 873, 879 (1975).

16. 428 U.S. 543 (1976).

17. 468 U.S. 1032 (1984).

18. 643 F.Supp. 884 (N.D. Cal. 1986).

19. 540 F.2d 1062 (7th Cir. 1976).

20. Julie Charlip, *Sanger Sweep Stirs Questions on Civil Right Violations*, THE FRESNO BEE, October 14, 1984, at A1 (emphasis added).

21. H. G. Reza, *Immigrants Deported in INS Sting Operation*, L.A. TIMES, July 31, 1993, at A1.

22. Id. J. Michael Kennedy, *Aliens Fear Massive Deportations; at El Paso Border, Rumor Mill is the Biggest Worry*, L.A. TIMES, March 14, 1987, at 1–1.

23. 466 U.S. 210 (1984).

Chapter 9. IRCA

1. Act of March 20, 1952, P.L. No. 283, 66 Stat. 26.

2. 424 U.S. 351 (1976).

3. *Amnesty: Do It Right*, L.A. TIMES, May 3, 1987, pt. 5, at 4.

4. HOUSE COMMITTEE ON THE JUDICIARY, THE IMMIGRATION REFORM AND CONTROL ACT OF 1986. A SUMMARY AND EXPLANATION. H.R. Doc. No. 603, 99th Cong., 2d sess. 6 (1986).

5. 132 CONG. REC. 30,005 (1986) (statement of Rep. William E. Dannemeyer).

6. Id. at 31,644 (statement of Rep. Silvio O. Conte).

7. Id. at 29,985 (statement of Rep. Peter Rodino).

8. See, e.g., id. at 33,209 (statement of Sen. Alan K. Simpson).

9. Id. at 31,633 (statement of Rep. Romano Mazzoli).

10. Id. at 31,634.

11. Id. at 31,639.

12. Id. at 31,645 (statement of Rep. Bill Frenzel).

13. Id. at 31,637.

14. Select Commission, at 74.

15. Id.

16. 132 Cong. Rec. 132 (1986).

17. Id. at 31,636 (statement of Rep. James M. Jeffords).

18. Id. at 30,063 (statement of Rep. B. McCollum).

19. 132 Cong. Rec. 32,415 (1986).

20. Id. at 31,639.

21. Senate Hearing 221, at 85.

22. H.R. Rep. No. 682-1, at 49.

23. 132 Cong. Rec. 32,410 (1986).

24. Id. at 30,063.

25. See, e.g., 132 Cong. Rec. 30,064 (1986) (statement of Rep. Bill Richardson).

26. Senate Report No 132, 99th Cong., 1st sess. (1985), at 16.

27. Statement on Signing the Immigration Reform and Control Act of 1986, 1986 PUB. PAPERS 1522.

28. Housing Hearing 28 at 128 (statement of Richard Fajardo, MALDEF).

29. H.R. Rep. No. 682-1, at 71; Statement on Signing of IRCA, at 1522.

30. Statements of Representative H. Fish and Senator D. Moynihan).

31. House Hearing 28, at 203.

32. H.R. Rep. No. 682-1, at 219.

33. 132 Cong. Rec. 31,575 (1986).

34. H.R. Rep. No. 682-1, at 48 (Minority Report).

35. 132 Cong. Rec. 33,214 (statement of Sen. Gramm).

36. Id. at 33,208 (statement of Sen. Chiles).

37. Preparing for Immigration Reform, at 10.

38. 132 Cong. Rec. 33,235 (1986).

39. Id. at 33,221.

40. *Edward J. DeBartolo Corp. v. Florida Gulf Coast Trade Council,* 485 U.S. 568, 585 (1988) (quoting *NLRB v. Fruit & Vegetable Packers and Warehousemen,* 377 U.S. 58, 66 (1964)) (quoting *Schwegmann Bros. v. Calvert Corp.,* 341 U.S. 384, 394-95 (1951) (Jackson, J., concurring)); see also *Selective Serv. Sys. v. Minnesota Pub. Interest Research Group,* 468 U.S. 841, 856 (1984) ("These statements [of opposition congressmen) are entitled to little, if any, weight, since they were made by opponents of the legislation"); *Sedina v. Imrex,* 741 F.2d 482, 490 n.22 (2d Cir. 1984), rev'd 473 U.S. 479 (1985) ("We decline to infer from Rep. Mikva's comments that Congress intended to promulgate a statute as broad as the one he feared it was passing. Deriving legislative intent from a dissenting congressman's 'parade of horrors' speeches in opposition is a notoriously dubious practice").

41. 132 Cong. Rec. at 30,003 (1986).

42. Id. at 30,065 (statement of Rep. H. Daub).

43. Id. at 31,644 (1986) (statement of Rep. Albert G. Bustamante).

44. Immigration and Naturalization Service, *U.S. Dept of Justice. Legalization Training Manual* 17 (1987).

45. Interview with Shari Cruhlac, staff attorney, San Francisco International Institute, San Francisco, Calif., December 11, 1990.

46. Interview with John Davis, deputy district director for legalization of the INS, San Francisco, Calif., November 19, 1990.

47. *Elisabeth Rolph and Abby Robyn, A Window on Immigration Reform: Implementing the Immigration Reform and Control Act in Los Angeles* 67 (Rand Corporation and Urban Institute, 1990).

48. Joseph Cosco, *Bringing Illegal Aliens Out of the Shadows,* 10 PUB. REL. J., October 1988, at 16, 18 (quoting Sam Sinclair, who was hired by the INS to coordinate the public information campaign).

49. Interview with Bill King, director for legalization of the western region of the Immigration and Naturalization Service, Los Angeles, Calif., January 3, 1991.

50. Interview with Fernando Oaxaca, president of the Justice Group, Los Angeles, Calif., December 21, 1990.

51. M. Heiberger, *Massachusetts Immigrant & Refugee Advocacy Coalition, Keeping the Promise? A Report on the Legalization Program of the Immigration Control Act of 1986: Massachusetts at the Halfway Mark* 12 (November 5, 1987).

52. Doris M. Meissner and Demetridus G. Papademetriou, *The Legalization Countdown: A Third Quarter Assessment* (Carnegie Endowment for International Peace, 1988), at 20.

53. Cosco, *Bringing Illegal Aliens,* at 47.

54. Lina M. Avidan, *Employment and Hiring Practices Under the Immigration Reform and Control Act of 1986: A Survey of San Francisco Businesses* (Coalition for Immigrant and Refugee Rights and Services, 1989).

55. Lina M. Avidan, *Employment and Hiring Practices Under the Immigration Reform and Control Act of 1986; A Survey of Businesses in Los Angeles, New York, Chicago and San Francisco* (Master's Thesis, Public Administration Department, 1992).

Chapter 10. The Dark Side of Modern-day Enforcement

1. John Dillin, *Sure in Immigration to U.S. Raises Public Anxiety, Spans a Showdown in Congress,* CHRISTIAN SCIENCE MONITOR, December 17, 1993, at 1.

2. Wayne A. Cornelius, *Death at the Border: The Efficacy and "Unintended" Consequences of U.S. Immigration Control Policy, 1993–2000,* Center for Comparative Immigration Studies, Working Paper No. 27, November 2000, University of California, San Diego, at 3.

3. See Frank Trejo, *Putting Up Barriers: Proposed Border Wall near El Paso Divides Community,* DALLAS MORNING NEWS, July 30, 1995, at A43.

4. Gustavo De La Vina, U.S. Border Patrol San Diego Sector Strategic Planning Document, April 29, 1994, at 1.

5. Id. at 3.

6. Id.

7. Id.

8. Border Patrol, *Operation Gatekeeper: 3 Years of Results in a Glance* (1997).

9. Id.

10. INS Fact Sheet, *Frustrating Illegal Crossers at Imperial Beach and Moving the Traffic Eastward,* October 17, 1997.

11. 72 *Interpreter Releases* 169, January 30, 1995.

12. *Clinton Will Seek Spending to Curb Aliens, Aides Say: Political Balancing Act,* NY TIMES, January 22, 1995, at A1; Matthew Jardine, *"Operation Gatekeeper,"* 10 PEACE REVIEW 329, 333 (1998).

13. U.S. Border Patrol, *Border Patrol Strategic Plan: 1994 and Beyond—National Strategy,* July 1994.

14. Id. at 6.

15. Petition to the Inter-American Commission on Human Rights of the Organization of American States (Feb. 9, 1999), at 16, n. 4.

16. *National Strategy,* at 6–9.

17. Id. at 7; U.S. General Accounting Office, *Illegal Immigration: Status of Southwest Border Strategy Implementation* 3 (May 1999).

18. Id.

19. Id. at 1, 4, 8.

20. Id.

21. Id. at 8.

22. *Operation Gatekeeper: New Resources, Enhanced Results*, INS Fact Sheet, July 14, 1998.

23. 1999 GAO report, at 7.

24. INS Fact Sheet, February 2, 1998.

25. November 19, 1999 letter to Mary Robinson.

26. Id., 1999 GAO report, at 12.

27. November 19, 1999 letter to Mary Robinson.

28. October 6, 2000 letter to Gabriela Rodriquez Pizarro.

29. *National Strategy*, at 4.

30. September 30, 2000 letter to Mary Robinson.

31. *National Strategy*, at 23.

32. 1999 GAO report, at 17–18, 20.

33. Id. at 18–20.

34. November 19, 1999 letter to Mary Robinson.

35. March 1, 2000 letter to Mary Robinson.

36. *Apprehension Statistics for the Southwest Border*, October 7, 1999 (chart prepared by California Rural Legal Assistance Foundation).

37. October 6, 2000 letter to Gabriela Rodriguez Pizarro. Stats cited by Kirke Wilson, *Changing Environment*, Report to the Rosenberg Foundation Board, November 22, 2000 at 11.

38. Ken Ellingwood, *Arrests of Illegal Migrants Plunge*, L.A. TIMES, April 4, 2001, at A1. The record-setting arrest figure for 2000 was 1,643,679, compared to the old 1986 record of 1,615,844. CRLAF Fact Sheet.

39. Cornelius, *Death at the Border.*

40. Binational Study on Migration (1997), at 7.

41. Id. at 28.

42. Ken Ellingwood, *INS Chief Targets Risky Rural Crossings*, L.A. TIMES, September 7, 2000.

43. U.S. Commission on Immigration Reform, *Border Law Enforcement and Removal Initiatives in San Diego, California* (1995), at 3.

44. *The Cost of a Tighter Border: People Smuggling Networks*, L.A. TIMES, May 3, 1998 (citing Brookings Institution).

45. 1999 GAO Report, at 16.

46. Claudia E. Smith, *Operation Gatekeeper Report*, May 10, 2000 (unpublished paper on file with author) at 23; 1999 GAO Report, at 2 and 16.

47. Cornelius, *Death at the Border.*

48. Id.

49. Id.

50. 1999 GAO Report, at 2, 16.

51. Id. at 22. The fraudulent entry documents principally are fake passports and visas.

52. Kevin R. Johnson, *Race Matters: Immigration Law and Policy Scholarship, Law in the Ivory Tower, and the Legal Indifference of the Race Critique*, U. ILL. L. REV. (2000) 525.

53. Immigration and Naturalization Service, *Border Management Overview*, September 20, 1999, at 6–7 (unpublished).

54. INS Fact Sheet, *Frustrating Illegal Crossers at Imperial Beach and Moving the Traffic Eastward*, October 17, 1997.

55. INS Fact Sheet, *Frustrating Illegal Crossers at Imperial Beach and Moving the Traffic Eastward*, October 17, 1997.

56. 1997 Houston study: Death at the Border, at 29.

57. Rosenberg Foundation, *Changing Environment*, November 22, 2000, at 2.

58. November 19, 1999 letter to Mary Robinson.

59. Border Patrol, *Operation Gatekeeper: 3 Years of Results*, cited in CRLA draft, at 23.

60. Id. at 23.

61. Id.

62. Smith, *Operation Gatekeeper Report.*

63. Id. at 25. One migrant had to have his foot amputated because an injury became infected after he crossed the river.

64. December 14, 1999 letter from Claudia E. Smith, Border Project director, to Gabriela Rodriguez Pizarro, special rapporteur, U.N. High Commissioner for Human Rights.

65. *Powell, Mexican Envoy Discuss Migrant Safety at Boarder*, Dow Jones Int'l News, January 30, 2001. Forty-three deaths were reported along the Arizona–Mexico border death in 1999. Id.

66. Jacques Billeaud, *Border Deaths Double in Arizona*, Associated Press, October 6, 2000.

67. *Illegal Entrant Dies*, Arizona Daily Star, April 28, 2001.

68. *Illegals Seek Help From Border Patrol*, San Francisco Chronicle, April 7, 2001, at A9.

69. July 22, 1999 letter to Jorge Taiana; October 6, 2000 letter to Gabriela Rodriguez Pizarro.

70. INS Fact Sheet, *Operation Gatekeeper: Three Years of Results at a Glance*, October 7, 1997. A May 20, 1998 INS Fact Sheet says that sixty agents had received EMT training and that ten vehicles had been retrofitted for emergency medical emergencies. Smith, *Operation Gatekeeper Report*, at 34.

71. Id. at 34–35.

72. INS Fact Sheet, *Helping Hand of the Border Patrol*, April 30, 1998.

73. Ken Ellingwood, *INS Chief Targets Risky Rural Crossings*, L.A. Times, September 7, 2000.

74. Immigration and Naturalization Service, *Fact Sheet: INS Border Safety Initiative*, August 24, 1998; see also Immigration and Naturalization Service, *Overview: Border Management Pages Border Management Overview*, September 20, 1999.

75. *Border Crossing Fatalities Targeted: Joint U.S.-Mexico Venture Aims to Cut Migrant Deaths*, North County Times, June 17, 1998.

76. Smith, *Operation Gatekeeper Report*, at 36.

77. Id. at 35.

78. Id. at 36.

79. *U.S. Stretches the Boundaries of Its Patrol*, El Universal, August 12, 1998.

80. *Border Patrol Fields New Helicopter*, San Diego Union-Tribune, January 2, 1999.

81. July 22, 1999 letter from Claudia E. Smith to Jorge Taiana.

82. CRLAF Fact Sheet.

83. Id.

84. Tim Vanderpool, *Border "Samaritans" Risk the Law to Offer Aid*, Christian Science Monitor, August 4, 2000.

85. Smith, *Operation Gatekeeper Report*, at 35.

86. See generally Gerald P. López, *Undocumented Mexican Migration: In Search of a Just Immigration Law and Policy*, 28 UCLA L. REV. 615 (1981).

87. Susan Ferriss, *Mexico's Troubles Are Felt up North*, SAN FRANCISCO EXAMINER, January 1, 1995, at C1.

88. Brendan M. Case, *A Sale Gone Sour; Much of Mexico's Economic Crisis Traced to the Privatization of 18 Banks*, DALLAS MORNING NEWS, December 18, 1998, at F1.

89. Tracey Eaton, *Zedillo Predicts Strong Grown by 2000; Mexican President Details 5-Year Plan*, DALLAS MORNING NEWS, June 1, 1995.

90. *U.S. Says Mexico Recovering*, UNITED PRESS INT'L, May 31, 1995.

91. James Pinkerton, *Lackluster Peso Stifles Border Merchants' Sales*, HOUSTON CHRONICLE, November 25, 1995, at A1.

92. Jacques Billeaud, *Border Deaths Double in Arizona*, The Associated Press, October 9, 2000 (citing Miguel Escobar, Mexican consul in Douglas, Ariz.).

93. Smith, *Operation Gatekeeper Report*, at 13.

94. Id. at 12.

95. Id. at 15

96. Ignacio Ibarra, *Migrants Will Die in Arizona Desert until U.S. Strategy Shifts, Expert Says*, ARIZONA DAILY STAR, June 9, 2000.

97. Smith, *Operation Gatekeeper Report*, at 18–19 (citing Philip Martin).

98. Given that the expected economics benefits of staying home is zero, in economics terms as long as the expected benefits of crossing is greater than zero (EB > 0), an individual will attempt to cross. The expected benefit is equal to the probability of surviving the trip times the salary to be had: EB = (P)($), or the expected return upon entering the United States. Operation Gatekeeper is changing the probability of entering (P), but as long as the probability is greater than zero (P > 0), there is an expected benefit and a person will take a chance to cross.

99. See notes 87–98, *supra*, and accompanying text.

100. December 14, 1999 letter to Gabriela Rodriguez Pizarro.

101. Gregory Alan Gross, *U.S. Mexican Border Agents Train for Immigrant Rescues*, SAN DIEGO UNION-TRIBUNE, November 17, 2000, at B1.

102. Smith, *Operation Gatekeeper Report*, at 3.

103. December 19, 1999 letter to Gabriela Rodriguez Pizarro; see also notes 43–49, *supra*, and accompanying text.

104. E-mail from Claudia Smith, *Gatekeeper*, January 16, 2001 (on file with author).

105. See notes 43–49, *supra*, and accompanying text.

106. Smith, *Operation Gatekeeper Report*, at 41.

107. Id. at 43.

108. Id. at 40.

109. Id. at 42.

110. U.S. Commission on Immigration Reform, U.S. IMMIGRATION POLICY: RESTORING CREDIBILITY 50–53 (1994). The commission criticized the current verification process as "time-consuming and confusing," and urged a more efficient use of resources. Id. at 53.

111. Smith, *Operation Gatekeeper Report*, at 14 (citing Susan Martin)

112. Brae Canlen, *The Border Honcho*, 17 CALIFORNIA LAWYER 34, 37 (1997).

113. *A Losing Battle: Border Patrol Scores Tactical Gains, Strategic Losses*, SAN DIEGO UNION-TRIBUNE, November 5, 1999, B8. The editors noted: "Gatekeeper's physical measures have slowed the flow in San Diego County, replacing the chaos that once defined the border here [illegals dashing across freeways or stampeding checkpoints." Id.

114. Smith, *Operation Gatekeeper Report,* at 41.

115. Id. at 22.

116. Binational Study, at 66.

117. December 14, 1999. Letter to Gabriela Rodriguez Pizarro.

118. CRLAF Fact Sheet.

119. Ann O'Hanlon, *Hiring Bias Attributed to '86 Immigration Act; Fear May Push Employers to Shun Foreign-Born,* THE WASHINGTON POST, August 6, 1994, at B1.

120. *National Strategy,* at 2.

121. Id. at 7.

122. Id. at 2.

123. Id. at 3.

124. Id.

125. Smith, *Operation Gatekeeper Report,* at 28 (citing De La Vina).

126. U.S. Commission on Immigration Reform, at 9.

127. Smith, *Operation Gatekeeper Report,* at 28 (citing de la Vina of INS in 1997).

128. See notes 87–98, *supra,* and accompanying text, Tables 10-1, 10-2.

129. Alan D. Bersin, statement of Alan D. Bersin, Attorney General's Special Representative for Southwest Border Issues, April 23, 1997 (unpublished), at 8–9.

130. U.S. Border Patrol, at 6–7.

131. Doris Meissner Commissioner, Immigration and Naturalization Service, SAN DIEGO UNION-TRIBUNE, July 21, 1996, at G5.

132. December 14, 1999 letter to Gabriela Rodriguez Pizarro.

133. *Operation Gatekeeper,* at 7.

134. *Illegal Immigrant Deaths from Weather Reach 12,* SAN DIEGO UNION-TRIBUNE, January 17, 1997.

135. Smith, *Operation Gatekeeper Report,* at 25.

136. U.S. General Accounting Office, *Illegal Immigration: Status of Southwest Border Strategy Implementation* 3 (1999).

137. Id. at 16.

138. For example, W. R. Grace & Co. pleaded guilty to lying to the Environmental Protection Agency in a 1982 probe of two contaminated water wells that were blamed for eight leukemia deaths in the Boston area. See *W. R. Grace & Co. Changes Plea in Pollution Case,* UPI Newswire, May 31, 1988. FDA investigators determined that Bodine's Orange Juice had sold 28 million more pounds of orange juice concentrate than it had purchased and that the firm had bought 35 million pounds of beet sugar more than was needed for the drink products sold during the same period. Faced with the evidence, Bodine's CEO pleaded guilty to felony violations and was sentenced to two years' imprisonment, a $250,000 fine, 1,000 hours of community service, and five years' probation. In a different case involving Beech-Nut Nutrition Corp., the company pleaded guilty to 215 felony violations and the vice president was tried, convicted and sentenced to a year in jail.

139. Vanderpool, *Border "Samaritans."*

140. See generally Bill Ong Hing, *The Immigrant as Criminal: Punishing Dreamers,* 9 Hastings Women's L. J. 79 (1998).

141. CRLAF Fact Sheet.

142. Karen Hastings, *Crossing the Line,* 5 Civil Rights J. 12, 13 (fall 2000).

143. See, e.g., Joseph Nevins, *The Nation; Immigration; How High Must Operation Gatekeeper's Death Count Go?* L.A. TIMES, November 19, 2000, at M2.

144. For example, in *Caro v. Calderon*, 165 F.3d 1223 (9th Cir. 1998), Caro won the right to have his penalty phase at his death trial reheard based on the fact that the jury never heard the evidence of his lifelong exposure to extremely toxic chemicals, or learned of the effect these probably had on him. Reading about his home life and labor conditions as a field worker is quite overwhelming; the conditions to which he was subjected suggested that he was disposable in the eyes of employers.

145. Professor Charles Lawrence points out that

Americans share a common historical and cultural heritage in which racism has played and still plays a dominant role. Because of this shared experience, we also inevitably share many ideas, attitudes, and beliefs that attach significance to an individual's race and induce negative feelings and opinions about nonwhites. To the extent that this cultural belief system has influenced all of us, we are all racists. At the same time, most of us are unaware of our racism.

Charles R. Lawrence III, *The Id, The Ego, and Equal Protection: Reckoning With Unconscious Racism*, 39 STAN. L. REV. 317, 322 (1987).

146. Eric Schmitt, *Ambivalence Prevails in Immigration Policy*, NY TIMES, May 27, 2001.

147. Statement of Alex Aleinikoff, former INS general counsel, American Association of Law Schools Immigration Law Section, San Francisco, Calif., January 6, 2001. Unfortunately, the Bush administration continued the spend-more philosophy even before September 11, 2001, in the belief that "a massive buildup of personnel and technology along the border is working," and proposed another $75 million to add more than a thousand Border Patrol agents over a two-year period. Daniel Gonzalez, Arizona Republic, May 8, 2001. Even after the highly publicized deaths of fourteen Mexican migrants in the Arizona desert on May 19, 2001, President Bush remained committed to increasing enforcement with more guards and patrols. Christopher Marquis, *At Border, Fortification Conflicts with Compassion*, NY TIMES, May 25, 2001.

148. As pointed out in n. 149, there is direct evidence that undocumented immigrants contribute to the U.S. economy. But we should also keep in mind the unquantifiable psychic value of family reunification. Simply begin by thinking of our own families and what each one of our loved ones means to us. We would be much less productive without one or more of them, if we had to be constantly concerned about their sustenance, safety, or general well-being. We are much more productive when we know that we can come home at the end of the day and enjoy their company or share in our day's events with them. Family promotes productivity after resettlement through the promotion of labor force activity and job mobility that is as important—perhaps more important—than the particular skills with which individuals arrive.

149. The bulk of empirical research on the economic impact of undocumented immigrants demonstrates that undocumented workers actually help the economy as they fill important job needs, add to public coffers, and contribute as consumers. See Bill Ong Hing, *To Be An American—Cultural Pluralism and the Rhetoric of Assimilation* 101–2 (New York: New York University Press, 1997); Julian L. Simon, *The Economic Consequences of Immigration* 277–305 (Ann Arbor: University of Michigan Press, 1989).

150. Tolerating one evil to avoid a greater evil is sometimes referred to as the "harm principle." See Jeremy Ofseyer, *First Amendment Law: Taking Liberties with John Stuart Mill*, 1999 ANN. SURV. AM. L. 395 (1999), 403–5.

151. David Vlahov and Benjamin Junge, *The Role of Needle Exchange Programs in HIV Prevention*, 113 PUBLIC HEALTH REP. 75–80 (June 1998).

152. James Ostrowski, *Thinking About Drug Legalization*, CATO POLICY ANALYSIS No. 121, May 25, 1989 (Internet cite: <http://www.cato.org/pubs/pas/pa121.html>).

153. See notes 84–98, *supra*, and accompanying text.

154. In criticizing Operation Safeguard (the Arizona border version of Gatekeeper) and the INS desert rescue plans, Douglas, Arizona mayor Ray Borane chastises the efforts as "sinister." "To me, it's like throwing a young child in the swimming pool, exposing him to the danger, and then saying that we have a method for rescuing the child," he said. "We're saying we have a method of rescuing these people after we've forced them out there." Tessie Borden, *INS: Border Policy Failed*, ARIZONA REPUBLIC, August 10, 2000.

155. Consider an analogy to the war on drugs. As a nation we have not yet figured out that the drug war is futile and immoral—a point of enlightenment (although we have accepted the notion of needle exchange to minimize the suffering of those whom we would stop). New Mexico governor Gary Johnson raises an interesting argument in favor of legalizing drugs that seems relevant to Operation Gatekeeper. For the amount of money spent on the war on drugs, he believes it is an absolute failure, arguing "under a legalized scenario, we would see the level of drug use remain the same or decline. And the same would happen with respect to drug abuse." See Debra J. Saunders, *A Sensible Salvo in the "War on Drugs,"* SAN FRANCISCO CHRONICLE, December 6, 2000, at A27.

156. See generally Douglas S. Massey, *March of Folly: U.S. Immigration Policy After NAFTA*, 9 AMERICAN PROSPECT 22 (1998).

157. Smith, *Operation Gatekeeper Report*, at 4, n. 10.

158. See generally Hing, *The Immigrant as Criminal*.

Chapter 11. Removal

1. See Chapter 1.

2. Jack Wasserman, *The Immigration and Nationality Act of 1952—Our New Alien and Sedition Law*, 27 TEMPLE LAW QUARTERLY 62 (1953–54).

3. 12 Stat. 340 (1862).

4. Wasserman, *Immigration and Nationality Act of 1952*.

5. *Ng Fung Ho v. White*, 259 U.S. 276, 284 (1922).

6. *The Chinese Exclusion Case, Chae Chan Ping v. United States*, 130 U.S. 581 (1889).

7. 25 F.2d 574 (9th Cir. 1928).

8. 1962 INS Annual Report.

9. Hysterical fears of red Russia continued to color American thinking for several years after the Bolshevik revolution of 1917, which spawned a tiny Communist Party in America. Tensions were heightened by an epidemic of strikes that convulsed the Republic at war's end, many of them the result of high prices and frustrated union-organizing drives. Upstanding Americans jumped to the conclusion that labor troubles were fomented by bomb-and-whisker Bolsheviks. A general strike in Seattle in 1919, though modest in its demands and orderly in its methods, prompted a call from the mayor for federal troops, to head off "the anarchy of Russia."

10. From THE NATION, Edward de Grazia, *Free Speech in Its Forgotten Years; Book Reviews*, September 7, 1998, No. 7, Vol. 267, 35.

11. *Goldman v. United States*, 245 U.S. 474 (1918).

12. *Toronto's Anarchist Guest*, TORONTO STAR WEEKLY, December 31, 1926.

13. *Goldman in Red Russia*, L.A. TIMES, January 20, 1920.

14. *Emma Goldman Says There is No Freedom in Bolshevik Russia*, MONTREAL HERALD, October 20, 1926.

15. NY TIMES, May 2, 1919.

16. NY TIMES, November 7, 1919. This article also noted that the second anniversary of the Bolshevist revolution in Russia was chosen as "the psychological moment to strike."

17. NY TIMES, November 9, 1919.

18. *Attorney-General A. Mitchell Palmer on Charges Made Against the Dept. of Justice by Louis F. Post and Others*, 66th Cong., 2d sess., 156–57 (1920) (statement of Attorney General A. Mitchell Palmer regarding action by the Radical Division in the Naugatuck valley in Connecticut).

19. NY TIMES, January 3, 1920; see also *2,000 Reds Arrested in 56 Cities Throughout Nation in Greatest Simultaneous Federal Raids of History; Vast Working Plot to Overthrow Government Feared*, NEW YORK WORLD, January 3, 1920; *Reds Plotted Country-Wide Strike; Arrests Exceed 5,000, 2635 Held; Three Transports Ready for Them*, NY TIMES, January 4, 1920.

20. NY TIMES, January 3, 1920 (noting that 700 people were seized in New York City the night before).

21. U.S. Department of Justice, Report of the Attorney General 173–78 (1920) (statement by Attorney General Palmer explaining the "Radical Division" in the Department of Justice's Bureau of Investigation, created to detect and prosecute persons committing crimes against the United States).

22. 265 F. 17 (Ma. 1920).

23. *Colyer v. Skeffington*, 265 F. 17, 43–44 (Ma. 1920).

24. Henry P. Guzda, *Ellis Island a Welcome Site? Only After Years of Reform; History of U.S. Immigrant Receiving Station in New York Harbor*, MONTHLY LABOR REVIEW, Vol. 109, 30, July 1986.

25. 79 F.Supp. 468 (Pa. 1947).

26. See, e.g., *McGrath v. Takayasu Abo*, 186 F.2d 766 (9th Cir. 1951).

27. Id.; *Acheson v. Murakami, et al.*, 176 F.2d 953 (9th Cir. 1949).

28. The Supreme Court upheld his denaturalization in *Fedorenko v. United States*, 449 U.S. 490 (1981).

29. Eric Slater, *Nazi Saga Takes a New Turn; Once Accused of Being "Ivan the Terrible," John Demjanjuk, 81, Is Now the Target of Renewed U.S. Efforts to Deport and Denaturalize Him*, L.A. TIMES, July 14, 2001, A1.

30. John Caniglia, *Poles Examining Demjanjuk Case*, PLAIN DEALER, July 8, 2002, A1 Elli Wohlgelernter, *Costa Rica Praised for Expelling ex-Nazi*, THE JERUSALEM POST, February 13, 2003, 4.

31. 8 C.F.R. § 214.5 (1980).

32. *Narenji v. Civiletti*, 617 F.2d 745, 748 (C.A.D.C. 1979).

33. Id. at 749 (concurrence by Circuit Judge MacKinnon).

34. 618 F.2d 1356 (9th Cir. 1980).

35. Leon Wildes, *The Nonpriority Program of the Immigration and Naturalization Service Goes Public: The Litigative Use of the Freedom of Information Act*, 14 SAN DIEGO L. REV. 42 (1976).

36. 527 F.2d 187 (2d Cir. 1975).

37. Joe A. Tucker, *Assimilation to the United States: A Study of the Adjustment of Status and the Immigration Marriage Fraud Statutes*, 7 YALE L. & POL'Y REV. 20 (1989).

38. Id.

39. 66 *Interpreter Releases* 1011–12 (1989).

40. Lisa C. Ikemoto, *Male Fraud*, 3 J. GENDER RACE & JUST. 511 (2000).

41. Id.

42. Id.

43. 67 *Interpreter Releases* 1229–31 (1990).

44. 68 *Interpreter Releases* 197 (1991).

45. 533 U.S. 678 (2001).

46. 345 U.S. 206 (1953).

Chapter 12. The Politics of Asylum

1. J. T. Flexner, *Washington: The Indispensable Man* 80 (New York: Little, Brown, 1974).

2. P.L. 80-774, 64 U.S. Statutes at Large 1009, amended by Act of June 16, 1950, P.L. 81-555, ch. 262, 64 Statutes at Large 219.

3. Select Commission on Immigration and Refugee Policy, *U.S. Immigration Policy and the National Interest* (1981), at 154.

4. P.L. 82-203, 76 Statutes at Large 400 (1953), amended by the Act of August 31, 1954, P.L. 83-751, 68 Statutes at Large 1044.

5. Victor Nee and B. Nee, *Longtime Californ': A Documentary Study of an American Chinatown* 410 (New York: Pantheon, 1973).

6. Immigration and Naturalization Service, 1959 Annual Report.

7. Immigration and Naturalization Service, 1962 Annual Report.

8. See *Immigration and Naturalization Service v. Stevic*, 467 U.S. 407, 415 (1984); *Rosenberg v. Yee Chien Woo*, 402 U.S. 49, 52 (1971).

9. Select Commission on Immigration and Refugee Policy, U.S. Immigration Policy and the National Interest (U.S. Government Printing Office, 1981) 1981: 155.

10. Id. at 154; Harry Kitano and Roger Daniels, Asian Americans: Emerging Minorities 13–14 (Eaglewood Cliffs, N.J.: Prentice Hall, 1988).

11. James A. Haught, *The Horror and Guilt of the Holocaust*, THE CHARLESTON GAZETTE, April 22, 1994, at P8A; William J. vandem Heuvel, *America, FDR, and the Holocaust*, 34 SOCIETY 54, September 1, 1997.

12. Id.

13. Id.

14. Id.

15. 66 Statutes at Large 163; 8 U.S.C. § 1182(d)(5) (1956).

16. Deborah E. Anker and Michael H. Posner, *The Forty Year Crisis: A Legislative History of the Refugee Act of 1980*, 19 SAN DIEGO L. REV. 9 (1981), at 15.

17. See Fair Share Law of 1960, Pub. L. 86–648, 74 Statutes at Large 504 (1960).

18. A. Schwartz, *The Open Society* 139–40 (New York: William Morrow, 1968); T. Chinn, et al., *A History of the Chinese in California: A Syllabus* (1969), at 29.

19. By the mid-1960s more than 3,000 Cubans were admitted each month. 1966 INS Annual Report, at 6. By 1976, 145,000 Cubans were paroled into the United States. See *Silva v. Bell*, 605 F.2d 978 (7th Cir. 1979).

20. L. Gordon, *Southeast Asian Refugee Migration to the United States*, in J. T. Fawcett and B. V. Carino, eds., *Pacific Bridges* 156 (Staten Island, N.Y.: Center for Migration Studies, 1987).

21. D. H. Laufman, *Political Bias in United States Refugee Policy Since the Refugee Act of 1980*, GEORGETOWN IMMIG. L. J. 495 (1986), at 504.

22. 19 United States Treaties 6223.

23. 189 United States Treaty Series 150 (July 28, 1951); see *Immigration and Naturalization Service v. Cardoza-Fonseca*, 480 U.S. 241 (1987).

24. H.R. Rept. 608, 96th Cong., 1st sess., 2 (1979).

25. P. J. Strand and W. Jones Jr., *Indochinese Refugees in America: Problems of Adaptation and Assimilation* 32 (Durham, N.C.: Duke University Press, 1985).

26. Id.

27. R. Gardner, et al., *Asian Americans: Growth, Change, and Diversity*, 40 POPULATION BULLETIN, no. 4 (1985), at 9.

28. In early 1979, the United States had committed itself to accept 7,000 refugees monthly, but the figure doubled by summer in response to the desperate conditions in the refugee camps. Gordon, *Southeast Asian Refugee Migration*, at 155.

29. Id.

30. Id.

31. Anker and Posner, *Forty Year Crisis*, at 30–33.

32. Some felt that the parole authority had been misused and were dissatisfied with the inconsistent treatment for refugees that resulted in some being granted parole while others received "indefinite voluntary departure." S. Rept. 256, 96th Cong., 1st sess. 9 (1979). Indefinite or extended voluntary departure was a type of group temporary safe haven that the attorney general used for certain nationals of particular countries. See *Hotel & Restaurant Employees Union Local 25 v. Attorney Gen.*, 804 F.2d 1256 (D.C. Cir. 1986).

33. P.L. 96-212; 94 Statutes at Large 107 (1980).

34. Statements of Senator Alan Simpson and Senator Strom Thurman during floor debates on the Refugee Act of 1980.

35. The position was eliminated in 1994.

36. Warren Brown, *Administration Officials Urge Law Change to Widen Diversity of Refugees Admitted*, THE WASHINGTON POST, March 15, 1979, at A21.

37. *Two Reports Recommend Changes in U.S. Asylum Process*, 70 Interpreter Releases 1364 (1993).

38. 480 U.S. 421 (1987).

39. 467 U.S. 407 (1984).

40. 480 U.S. at 424.

41. Id. at 431.

42. Id. at 440.

43. 19 I&N Dec. 439 (BIA 1987).

44. 8 C.F.R. § 208.13(a).

45. Harvey Kaplan and Maureen O'Sullivan, *The Role of the BIA in Reviewing Negative Credibility Findings: Circumventing the Well-Founded Fear Standard*, 75 Interpreter Releases 1181 (1998).

46. Int. Dec. 3337 (BIA 1998).

47. Int. Dec. 3336 (BIA 1998).

48. *Haitian Refugee Center v. Smith*, 676 F.2d 1023 (5th Cir. 1982).

49. 600 F.Supp.(D.C. 1985).

50. 919 F.2d 549 (9th Cir. 1990).

51. 760 F.Supp. 796 (N.D. Cal. 1991).

52. Katherine Bishop, *U.S. Adopts New Policy for Hearings on Political Asylum for Some Aliens*, NY TIMES, December 20, 1990, at B18.

53. 682 F.Supp. 1055 (N.D. Cal. 1988).

54. 530 F.Supp. 924 (S.D. Fla. 1981).

55. *Roshan v. Smith*, 615 F.Supp. 901 (D.C. 1985).

56. The father of making things inconvenient at INS may have been former INS Commissioner Joseph Swing. In the 1950s, he "gleefully volunteered that he decentralized the INS and deliberately placed regional offices in out-of-the-way places in order to make it difficult for immigration lawyers to access them." Kitty Calavita, *Inside the State: The Bracero Program, Immigration, and the INS* (New York: Routledge, 1992).

57. Soon after the enactment of IIRAIRA on September 30, 1996, the INS began to implement its provisions, and in January 1997 published proposed regulations. In its rules, the INS had the opportunity to ameliorate the unfairness of the new statute. INS significantly improved the one-year deadline rule, but the rule with respect to the expedited removal process offered modest improvement. Many times, governments that violate human rights are able to cover up their abuses for months or years. Refugees in the United States might not know that conditions in the home country have worsened. 8 C.F.R. § 208.4(a)(4)(ii)(2001) provides that "if the applicant can establish that he or she did not become aware of the changed circumstances until after they occurred, such delayed awareness shall be taken into account in determining what constitutes a 'reasonable period'" for submitting an otherwise late application.

58. John Moreno Gonzales, *McKnight Comes Home; INS Officials Apologize for Blunder*, Newsday, June 19, 2000, at A7.

59. The term *credible fear* is statutorily defined to mean "that there is a significant possibility, taking into account the credibility of the statements made by the alien in support of the alien's claim and such other facts as are known to the officer, that the alien could establish eligibility for asylum." The INS has interpreted this test to require a showing that there is a "significant possibility that the assertions underlying his or her claim could be found credible in a full asylum or withholding of removal hearing."

60. After 1996, the definition of "refugee" now provides, in pertinent part,

for purposes of determinations under this Act, a person who has been forced to abort a pregnancy or to undergo involuntary sterilization, or who has been persecuted for failure or refusal to undergo such a procedure or for other resistance to a coercive population control program, shall be deemed to have been persecuted on account of political opinion, and a person who has a well founded fear that he or she will be forced to undergo such a procedure or subject to persecution for such failure, refusal, or resistance shall be deemed to have a well founded fear of persecution on account of political opinion. (8 U.S.C. § 1101(a)(42))

Epilogue

1. *Muslims Living in America Come under Fire; Terror War on US: Backlash—Terrorism USA*, THE EVENING STANDARD, September 13, 2001, at 10.

2. Eileen E. Flynn, *Gas Station is Target of Arsonist, Authorities are Investigating Late Night Attempt to Set Fire at Muslim-Owned Business*. THE AUSTIN AMERICAN STATESMAN, September 16, 2001, at B1.

3. Jenifer Hanrahan, *Sikh Woman Stabbed in Suspected Hate Crime Linked to Terror Attack*, SAN DIEGO UNION-TRIBUNE, October 5, 2001, at B2.

4. <www.sikhcoalition.org/hatecrime.asp?mainaction=viewreport&reportid=97> September 22, 2001.

5. *The Heinous Crime of Racial Profiling Lives On*, THE GULF NEWS, November 7, 2001 [at A1]; John Donnelly and Wayne Washington, *Fighting Terror Global Impact*, THE BOSTON GLOBE, November 1, 2001, at A1.

6. Deborah Berry, *FBI was at the Door*, NEWSDAY, September 19, 2002, at A6.

7. William Glaberson, *A Nation Challenged: The Interviews; Legal Experts Question Legality of Questioning*, NY TIMES, November 30, 2001, at B6.

8. Kareem Shora and Carol Khawly, *US Citizens Part of Voluntary Interview Program*, e-mail of November 30, 2001.

9. Susan Akram and Kevin R. Johnson, *The Civil Rights and Immigration Aftermath of September 11, 2001: The Targeting of Arab Americans*, 58 NYU ANNUAL SURVEY OF AMERICAN LAW 295 (2002).

10. Marsha Ginsberg, *Shattered Dream; Brick Hurled at Muslim-Owned Store Drives out S.F. Man*, SAN FRANCISCO CHRONICLE, December 29, 2001, at A1.

11. For example, consider the presumed disloyalty of Wen Ho Lee, the Chinese American engineer suspected of selling government secrets, because of long-held stereotypes about Asian Americans. See Leti Volpp, *"Obnoxious to Their Very Nature": Asian Americans and Constitutional Citizenship*, 8 ASIAN L.J. 71, 79–82 (2001).

12. The actions of these private actors is reminiscent of vigilance committees who take the law into their own hands, passionately believing that they are enforcing laws that law enforcement officials are unable or unwilling to enforce. In some countries these groups are called death squads. Scott Anderson and Jon Lee Anderson, *Inside the League: The Shocking Expose of How Terrorists, Nazis, and Latin American Death Squads Have Infiltrated The World Anti-Communist League* (New York: Dodd Mead, 1986); Richard Maxwell Brown, *Strain of Violence: Historical Studies of American Violence and Vigilantism* (London: Oxford University Press, 1975).

13. Mary Rourke, *Values: Our Culture, Our Beliefs, Our Responsibilities*, L.A. TIMES, November 24, 1999, at E1.

14. Gregory Kane, *Islam's Good Deeds Should Be Remembered.* NEWSDAY, October 10, 2001, at A43.

15. Mary Paik Lee, *Quiet Odyssey*, 12 (Seattle: University of Washington Press, 1990). This kind of story shows that for some immigrants, there are barriers to getting any type of immigration status at all, much less getting American status, then being de-Americanized.

16. Id. at 48–49.

17. Sucheng Chan, *Asian Americans—An Interpretative History* 46 (New York: Twayne, 1991).

18. R. Clinton Taplin, *4 Teens to be Tried as Adults in Death of Indian*, THE RECORD, February 28, 1988, at A3; Iver Peterson, *County by County, a Fight Against Bias*, NY TIMES, January 5, 1993, at B1.

19. Chan, *Asian Americans*, at 48.

20. See id. at 49.

21. Id.

22. Id. at 52.

23. Id.

24. Id. at 53.

25. *United States v. Ebens*, 800 F. 2d 1422, 1427 (6th Cir. 1986).

26. Id.

27. Id.

28. Id. at 1428.

29. Id. at 1427.

30. See Steven Lee Myers, *Collision with China, The Pentagon: U.S. Tape is Said to Show Reckless Flying by Chinese*, NY TIMES, April 14, 2001, at A6.

31. Richard Roeper, *China Standoff Reveals Racism's Tenacious Grip*, CHICAGO SUN-TIMES, April 18, 2001, at 11.

32. Id.

33. Marsha Ginsberg, *Crisis Inflames Bias Against Asians*, SAN FRANCISCO CHRONICLE, April 14, 2001, at A1.

34. Id.

35. Thomas B. Edsall, *25% of U.S. View Chinese Americans Negatively, Poll Says*, THE WASHINGTON POST, April 26, 2001, at A4.

36. Bill Ong Hing, *Making and Remaking Asian America Through Immigration Policy, 1850–1990*, 49–50 (Stanford: Stanford University Press, 1993)

37. *Yick Wo v. Hopkins*, 118 U.S. 356 (1886) (San Francisco's ordinance barring laundries of wooden construction struck down by the Supreme Court on the grounds that it was applied in a racially discriminatory manner).

38. *People v. Hall*, 4 Cal. 399 (1854) (murder conviction of a "free white citizen" reversed, on the grounds that Chinese witnesses were permitted to testify against the defendant).

39. Hing, *Making and Remaking*, at 30, 45.

40. *In Re Ah Yup*, 5 Sawyer 155, 156 (1878).

41. Id. (district court finding that the clear intent of the naturalization law was to exclude Chinese immigrants from eligibility).

42. *The Chinese Exclusion Case, Chae Chan Ping v. United States*, 130 U.S. 581, 595 (1889). This was not the first time that the perceived inability of a group to assimilate was used to defend the legal regime. In 1823, the Supreme Court justified the taking of Native American lands on the theory that Native Americans were incapable of assimilation. See *Johnson v. M'Intosh*, 21 U.S. 543, 589–91 (1823).

43. Hing, *Making and Remaking*, at 57.

44. Id. at 57.

45. *Richardson Denies Leaking Wen Ho Lee's Name to Media*, THE SANTA FE NEW MEXICAN, October 5, 2000, at A1; Howard Kurtz, *New York Times Chastises Itself for Flaws in "Wen Ho Lee" Story*, THE WASHINGTON POST, September 27, 2000, at C1. For a discussion of the facts and troubling consequences of the Wen Ho Lee case, see Frank Wu, *The Profiling of Threat Versus the Threat of Profiling*, 7 MICH. J. RACE & L., 135 (2001).

46. *Richardson Denies Leaking Wen Ho Lee's Name*, at A1.

47. Kurtz, *New York Times Chastises Itself*, at C1.

48. James Glanz, *Fallout in Arms Research: A Special Report; Amid Race Profiling Claims, Asian-Americans Avoid Labs*, NY TIMES, July 16, 2000, § 1, at 1: Vernon Loeb, *At U.S. Labs, a Residue of Anger; Asian American Scientists Feel Spy Case Stereotyping Affects Their Futures Too*, THE WASHINGTON POST, December 24, 1999, at A13.

49. Hing, *Making and Remaking*, at 26–36.

50. Bill Ong Hing, *To Be an American—Cultural Pluralism and the Rhetoric of Assimilation*, 23–26 (New York: New York University Press, 1997).

51. Id. at 19.

52. Id. at 19–20.

53. Id. at 28–29; see also *Haitian Refugee Center v. Smith,* 676 F. 2d 1023 (5th Cir. 1982); *American Baptist Churches v. Thornburgh,* 760 F. Supp. 796 (N.D. Cal. 1991).

54. And as we have seen, even recent enforcement schemes often have disparate impact. Consider the asylum barriers faced by Haitians, Guatemalans, and El Salvadorans, and interior enforcement strategies that focus on Mexicans. See, e.g., *Orantes-Hernandez v. Thornburgh.* 919 F. 2d 549 (9th Cir. 1990) (court of appeals critical of immigration officials encouraging El Salvadorans to sign voluntary departure agreements without being fully informed of the right to apply for asylum); *Haitian Refugee Center v. Smith,* 676 F. 2d 1023 (5th Cir. 1982) (court of appeals critical of the lack of fairness and procedural due process afforded to Haitian asylum applicants in Miami); *American Baptist Churches v. Thornburgh,* 760 F. Supp. 796 (N.D. Cal. 1991) (finding that immigration officials were biased against El Salvadoran and Guatemalan asylum applicants); *United States v. Brignoni-Ponce,* 422 U.S. 873 (1975) (roving Border Patrol officers in the vicinity of the Mexican border could stop motorists to question about residence status); *United States v. Martinez-Fuerte,* 428 U.S. 543 (1976) (fixed checkpoints away from the Mexican border could be set up by the Border Patrol in locations where undocumented aliens might travel); *INS v. Lopez-Mendoz,* 468 U.S. 1032 (1984) (the Fourth Amendment exclusionary rule does not apply in deportation proceedings involving undocumented Mexicans apprehended in factory settings).

55. See generally, Hing, *Making and Remaking.*

56. 261 U.S. 204 (1923).

57. Id. at 214–215 (emphasis added).

58. While it is true that many immigrants of European origin were originally discriminated against upon arrival to the United States—for example, Irish Americans—their physical appearance enabled them to be easily integrated into the American mainstream. Unfortunately, for most immigrants of color, such integration has proven impossible because they are not white.

59. Kevin R. Johnson, *An Essay on Immigration Politics, Popular Democracy, and California's Proposition 187: The Political Relevance and Legal Irrelevance of Race,* 70 WASH. L. REV. 629 (1995).

60. *7 Teens Face Trial as Adults in Migrant-Camp Beatings,* SAN DIEGO UNION TRIBUNE, July 19, 2000, at B1.

61. Karima A. Haynes, *Tests Ordered for Hate-Crime Suspect,* L.A. TIMES, September 23, 2000, at B4.

62. *National ID Cards Let Uncle Sam Spy on You,* USA TODAY, July 15, 1994, at 14A.

63. Carlos Guerra, *Growing Anti-Immigrant Sentiment Victimizing Citizens,* AUSTIN AMERICAN-STATESMAN, June 11, 1994. The incident is also discussed in Michelle A. Heller, *U.S. Citizens Mistaken for Illegals,* THE PLAIN DEALER, September 25, 1994, at 1C. A case can be made for immigration overtones, albeit distorted, in certain hate situations directed at African Americans. It is quite common for African Americans to be subjected to situations like that faced by James Lawrence, an African American who was the chief electrical inspector of Huntington Beach, California. One Fourth of July, he and his nephew were confronted by a band of skinheads who called them "niggers" and told them to "go back to Africa." Aurelia Rojas, *Turning a Bland Eye to Hate Crimes,* SAN FRANCISCO CHRONICLE, October 22, 1996, at A1. Such statements confirm and enforce the idea that those perceived to be immigrants are foreign and without rights or claims to being true Americans. The connection between the de-Americanization of *immigrant* America and hate directed at African Americans and gays should not be surprising.

After all, from the perpetrator's perspective, this is about excluding certain groups from membership into the *real* American community. Jewish Americans, unfortunate victims of many incidents of hate, also faced immigration policy hostilities in the past, Jews were targeted by the 1917 Act and the *SS St. Louis* incident.

64. For an excellent discussion of unconscious racism and institutions, see Charles R. Lawrence III, *The Id, the Ego, and Equal Protection: Reckoning with Unconscious Racism,* 39 STAN. L. REV. 317 (1987).

65. The union realized that companies commonly use employer sanctions as a weapon to resist organizing drives. So the AFL-CIO coupled its call for the repeal of sanctions with a resolution supporting legalization for undocumented immigrants. David Bacon, *Labor Fights for Immigrants,* THE NATION, May 21, 2001, at 15. The pool of undocumented workers in the United States varies from between 5 million and 8 million. The unions are recognizing the value and import of immigrant workers to the workforce, but more important, their own membership. Additionally, the union organizing by immigrant workers even without the protection of labor law or support from other local unions establishes a foundation from which to draw this wide range of new support. Congressional Republicans have called for reinstitution of the Bracero program, in which immigrant workers are contracted for seasonal or long-term work and remain in the United States as guest workers. Under this program, immigrant workers may not be unionized.

In 2000, 10 percent of all union members were foreign-born. The president of the AFL-CIO, John Sweeney, uses this number to support the development of a new immigration policy that protects the labor rights of all workers living in the United States. The access to union membership will help guarantee better wages and health care for immigrant workers within the United States. The early labor movement was full of examples of union resistance to immigrant and minority membership. However, the AFL-CIO now calls for full "inclusion and opportunity" to all immigrant workers. The AFL-CIO is calling for the legalization of undocumented workers in order to grant them full protection of the law as well as the benefits of their tax dollars. Employer sanctions should be repealed because the system not only fails to deter migration, but also harms workers who may suffer immediate job threat upon requesting wage increase or time off. The AFL-CIO also notes the adverse effect the law has had on employers who unfairly assume that workers who may appear foreign will not have the requisite verification to gain employment. Testimony of AFL-CIO President John J. Sweeney on "U.S.–Mexico Migration Discussions: An Historic Opportunity." September 7, 2001, available at http://www.aflcio.org/publ/test2001/tm0907.htm.

In September 2003, after five years of negotiations, bipartisan members of Congress, farm worker representatives, and growers reached a compromise on an agricultural-worker reform bill that would legalize up to half a million undocumented farm workers. The proposal would allow farm workers to earn legal *immigration* status through work. To be eligible for temporary legal status, workers must have worked in agriculture for at least 100 days within one year since March 2002. To get permanent residency, workers would have to work at least 240 days in the next three years and a total of at least 360 days over the next six years. Spouses and minor children of workers would be eligible for limited benefits.

66. This was the second time in less than a decade that antiterrorism legislation was enacted. One year after the bombing of the federal building in Oklahoma City, Congress approved and sent President Clinton a bill designed to combat domestic and international terrorism. The Antiterrorism and Effective Death Penalty Act (AEDPA) of 1996 included very significant changes to the immigration laws relating to exclusion, criminal aliens, and special removal proceedings for alien terrorists. 73 IR 521. Special removal procedures for alien terrorists set forth

the establishment of a new removal court composed of five district court judges appointed by the chief justice of the United States Supreme Court. The court could hear a case whenever the attorney general certified that an alien terrorist physically present in the United States would pose a risk to national security if removed by normal deportation procedures. A judge could then grant the application for removal, ordering the alien detained pending removal. If an alien removed attempted to reenter without authorization, he or she would be subject to imprisonment for ten years. The bill denied other forms of relief for terrorists, including asylum and voluntary departure. Habeas corpus is also unavailable.

67. Greg Miller and Nick Anderson, *Borders: Legislators and White House to Seek Tighter Restrictions; Policies with Mexico Will Face New Scrutiny, in Sharp Contrast to Recent Pledges Made to President Fox*, NY TIMES, September 18, 2001.

68. One person, Osama Awadallah, a Jordanian student, sued the FBI and federal prosecutors for violating his civil rights. He was imprisoned after FBI agents confronted him outside his San Diego home on September 20, 2001. He was detained as a high-security prisoner, but was finally released in December; all along no charges were filed against him. *Jordanian Student Sues FBI Over Civil Rights*, SAN FRANCISCO CHRONICLE, September 13, 2002, at A4.

69. *Detroit Free Press v. Ashcroft*, 303 F.3d 681 (6th Cir. 2002).

70. Dan Eggen, *Deportee Sweep Will Start With Mideast Focus*, THE WASHINGTON POST, February 8, 2002.

71. Jennifer Mena, *Anger Over INS Arrests*, L.A. TIMES, December 18, 2002, at part 2–1.

72. David Cole, *Enemy Aliens and American Freedoms*, THE NATION, September 23, 2002, at 20.

73. The only executive of any of the Muslim charities to be charged criminally is Enaam Arnaout, head of the Illinois-based Benevolence International Foundation, who authorities said was a longtime close associate of al Qaeda. On February 10, 2003, he reached a plea agreement with prosecutors, admitting to no terrorism charges, but acknowledging that he illegally diverted contributions intended for the needy to armed fighters in Bosnia and Chechnya.

74. Dave Boyer, *Troops for Border Sought*, THE WASHINGTON TIMES, June 20, 2002.

75. *Ashcroft Alters BIA Structure, Procedures*, 79 *Interpreter Releases* 1273 (August 26, 2002)

76. Nathan Glazer, ed., *Clamor at the Gates: The New American Immigration* 3 (Oakland, Calif.: Institute for Contemporary Studies, 1985).

77. Mercedes Tira Andrei, *Asians Soar in Number in Big American Cities*, BUSINESS WORLD, April 6, 2001, at 27.

78. Laurent Belsie, *Hispanics Spread to Hinterlands*, CHRISTIAN SCIENCE MONITOR, March 26, 2001, at 1.

79. Genaro C. Armas, *Hispanic Population Surges in Small Towns, Rural Communities*, SOUTH BEND TRIBUNE, April 1, 2001, at A7.

80. Tony Pugh, *U.S. Hispanic Population Surges to 20.6 Million*, KNIGHT RIDDER WASHINGTON BUREAU, May 10, 2001.

81. Id.

82. Andrei, *Asians Soar* at 27.

83. Butch John, *Asian Populations Surge in Kentucky and Indiana*, THE COURIER-JOURNAL, May 20, 2001, at 4a.

84. Id.

85. Ray Waddle, *Bible Belt Getting Stretched; City Known as "Protestant Vatican" Now Includes Variety of Religions, Study Shows*, THE TENNESSEAN, April 1, 2001, at 1B.

86. Id.

87. *Growth of California's Foreign-born Population Slows as Immigrants Move to Other States*, News Release, the Urban Institute, January 11, 2001.

88. Id. The South also gained a record number of African Americans during the 1990s, an increase that made it the only region in the country where more blacks arrived than left. The departure of blacks from the rest of the country and migration to the South represents a historic pattern that has come full circle: African Americans spent most of the past century fleeing the South's racial oppression and lack of economic opportunity. The pattern of flight slowly began to change three decades ago and accelerated dramatically in the 1990s, when the South's black population grew by nearly 3.6 million through births, immigration, and migration. That was twice the increase of the 1980s and the result of a combination of attractions: family ties, the region's improving fortunes, and easing racial prejudice. D'Vera Cohn, *Reversing a Long Pattern, Blacks are Heading South*, THE WASHINGTON POST, May 5, 2001, at A1.

89. *New Census Data Gives a More Detailed Portrait of Asian Americans in New York City*, June 27, 2001 (News Release) (on file with author).

90. *Immigrants Frustrated by Laws That Take Kids from Home*, 37 NATIONAL CATHOLIC RPTR 6 (June 29, 2001).

91. Tina Griego, *Hispanics a Multicultural Nation of our Own*, THE DENVER POST, March 21, 2001, at B1.

92. Jorge Amaya, *Mexican Immigrants Need to Get Involved*, THE DENVER POST, February 21, 2001, at B11.ThTTh

93. Louis Aguilar, *Language of Business Binds Cultures; Latino, Asian Markets Thrive*, THE DENVER POST, May 29, 2001, at C1.

94. Id.

95. Id.

96. Thomas Beaumont, *What is Abuse? Cultures Vary*, THE DES MOINES REGISTER, January 2, 2001, at 1.

97. Laurent Belsie, *Hispanics Spread to Hinterlands*, CHRISTIAN SCIENCE MONITOR, March 26, 2001, at 1.

98. Genaro C. Armas, *Hispanic Population Surges in Small Towns, Rural Communities*, SOUTH BEND TRIBUNE, April 1, 2001, at A7.

99. Ginnie Graham, *Jump in Hispanics Has Advocates Busy; Recent Arrivals Need More Assistance*, TULSA WORLD, May 18, 2001.

100. Charisse Jones, *New-Timers' Lives Revive Old Cities; Immigrants Feed a Population Boom, and Help Communities That Need to Fill New Jobs and Positions Left Vacant by Retirees*, USA TODAY, April 20, 2001, at 3A.

101. *Population Shifts During the 1990s State-by-State Breakdown of Ups and Downs*, THE SEATTLE TIMES, April 1, 2001, at A20.

102. Within the Asian American population, Vietnamese grew at the highest rate. John, *Asian Populations Surge*, at 4a: Joseph Gerth, Bridging a Language Gap; Need for Court Interpreters Grows Quickly, THE COURIER-JOURNAL, July 31, 2001, at A1.

103. John, *Asian Populations Surge*.

104. *Population Shifts During the 1990s State-By-State Breakdown of Ups and Downs*, THE SEATTLE TIMES, April 1, 2001, at A20. See the Appendix for an immigrant-impact summary for most states from the 2000 census.

105. Anastasia Hendrix, *Fear Keeps Immigrants in Hiding*, SAN FRANCISCO CHRONICLE, August 3, 2003, at A25.

106. Unfortunately, the broad answer by President Bush and Attorney General Ashcroft seemed to be retracted when the war on terrorism was implemented based on racial profiling.

107. Beverley J. Armento et al., *America Will Be* (Boston: Houghton Mifflin, 1991), at 6.

108. From the Asian American Legal Defense and Education Fund's partial list of reported incidents of Anti-Asian, bias-related incidents, ASIANWEEK, September 20–26, 2001, at 9.

109. John M. Hubbell, *Trucker Chatter Betrays Attitude of Intolerance*, SAN FRANCISCO CHRONICLE, October 7, 2001, at A19.

110. Maia Davis, *A Painful Reminder for Japanese Americans; Anti-Muslim Incidents Recall WWII Bias; the Backlash*, THE RECORD, October 20, 2001, A15.

111. Carlos Bulosan endured a life of hardship, constantly victimized by bigots, and being forced to feel as though being Filipino in California was a crime. Yet others showed kindness to him and that gave him hope. Carlos Bulosan, *America is in the Heart* 314 (Seattle: University of Washington Press, 1946).

Index